JOHN ADAMS, LL.D.

THE BEGINNINGS OF THE
AMERICAN REVOLUTION

BASED ON CONTEMPORARY LETTERS DIARIES AND OTHER DOCUMENTS

By

ELLEN CHASE

Volume III

THE BAKER AND TAYLOR COMPANY
NEW YORK

973.3
C387b
101057 v.3

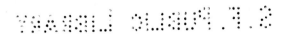

CONTENTS

ILLUSTRATIONS

THE BEGINNINGS OF THE AMERICAN REVOLUTION

CHAPTER I

THE CONCORD BRIDGE ENCOUNTER

THE pause at Lexington was invaluable to Concord, giving its people just so much more time in which to remove and conceal the stores entrusted to their keeping. "Many thousands were saved to the Colony, and (the British) were in a great manner frustrated in their design," writes old Parson Clark.[1]

From Lieutenant Barker[2] we find that his first knowledge of the object of the march was at this moment, when they set forth from Lexington Green on the Concord road. As the troops moved along, with the alarm signals sounding from the outlying villages, they kept a sharp outlook, but were not interfered with. Some were seen in the woods by Colonel Smith's[3] report, but nothing further happened on their way. It was now getting toward six or perhaps a little after, and the usual peaceful travel along the highway had begun; so soon to be abruptly interrupted. Captain Samuel Farrar,[4] of the Lincoln Militia, on his way early to mill, we are told, when he heard of the trouble tossed his saddle-bags filled with grist over a wall, and rallied his men. Abel Hosmer[5] was on his way from Concord to Charlestown

---

[1] *Narrative Appended to Parson Clark's Sermon, April 19, 1776.*
[2] *Atlantic Monthly*, April, 1877.
[3] *Mass. His. Soc. Pro.*, May, 1876.
[4] *Beneath Old Roof Trees*, 221–2. Brown.
[5] *Concord Historic, Literary and Picturesque.* Third edition, 42. George B. Bartlett. Boston, 1894: Lothrop Publishing Company.

1

for a load of brick when he met the British coming on from Lexington, and quickly turned himself to a different day's work. It is said that a Bedford [1] man with a load of wood drawn by a yoke of oxen and a horse came upon the soldiers at Lexington, perhaps during the halt. He passed them quietly, unyoked his team as if one of the village, and then getting on his horse, again went quietly through their midst; once past, he broke into a run and warned Concord.

When Revere was taken prisoner by Folly Pond, about a mile west from the Old Bull Tavern, on the borders of Lexington and Lincoln, Dr. Prescott, knowing the country, made a long détour northward through swamp, wood, and field and regained the road at Hartwell's tavern.[2] Rousing the old men who kept it, he put his horse at its best speed for Concord. The brothers, John and Ephraim, were too aged and feeble to play an active part in the coming fray, but they immediately sent a black woman, a former slave, to rouse Captain William Smith of the Lincoln Minute Company, who lived nearly half a mile back toward Lexington. The road just beyond her was overhung with trees, and, panic-stricken, the old soul flew panting to Samuel Hartwell's door (a son of one of the tavern keepers), waking all within by her frantic cries that the British were after her. Seeing she was too unstrung to go further, Mrs. Hartwell put the three months old baby in her arms, saying, "If you will take care of my baby, I will go and rouse the Captain," adding, "Sam, make yourself ready, and saddle your horse. I'll be back in time to get you some breakfast." Soon after she had returned, the sergeant rode off with musket and powder-horn to Concord to join the Militia; and Captain Smith, having first sent messengers some two miles south to ring the Lincoln Meeting-house bell as an alarm, also rode off to Concord.

When her husband had gone Mrs. Hartwell did up his morning chores about the barn, turned the cattle loose, and

[1] *History of Middlesex County*, I, 245. Drake. "Bedford," by Josiah A. Stearns.
[2] *Boston Evening Transcript*, April 18, 1900.

had just collected a few cherished articles — a mirror and some silverware — and laid them beside the baby, when the tramp of the British could be heard marching nearer and nearer. Going to the door she shaded her eyes and saw the winding line of red and flashing bayonets coming on and on between the pasture lands. As they passed, the scarlet coats, white gaiters, powdered wigs, and bosom pins made a rare show and she used to say [1] years after: "If it hadn't been for the purpose they came for, I should say it was the handsomest sight I ever saw in my life!" When they were all gone by, she and her flock of little ones went two miles off the road to her father Flint's in Lincoln. Susanna Parker,[2] whose parents also lived on the main road, used to recall running with her sister over the hill back of the house and watching from a distance the Regulars marching by. She could even catch the clear English voices as they went along the road.

To return to Dr. Samuel Prescott, whom we left riding post haste to Concord. Since the attempt [3] in February to seize the Salem cannon a guard of men had been patrolling the Concord streets at night, some stationed at the north, others at the south bridges, some in the centre of the town, and again below Mrs. Jonathan Heywood's on the Lincoln road, under the command of Jonathan Farrar. In case of alarm they were to rally at Wright's tavern. On reaching the town therefore, between one and two in the morning, Prescott found Amos Melven on guard at the Court-house and told him to ring an alarm. The first to respond was the Rev. William Emerson, carrying his gun. This so impressed the sentinel that he named two boys the one, William, the other Emerson Melven. Major John Buttrick [4] lived

---

[1] *Boston Evening Transcript*, April 18, 1900.

[2] *Life of Amos A. Lawrence*, 1. William Lawrence. Boston, 1888: Houghton, Mifflin and Company.

[3] Thaddeus Blood's Narrative, *Boston Daily Advertiser*, April 20, 1886. Also in *The Story of Patriots' Day, Lexington and Concord, April 19, 1775*. Geo. J. Varney. Boston, 1895: Lee and Shepard.

[4] "The Concord Fight." Frederick Hudson. *Harper's Monthly*, May, 1875.

half a mile across the river, west of Flint's bridge. As the warning notes of the bell reached him, he sprang up calling to his sixteen year old son, "John, the bell's a-ringing; jump up, load your pistols, take your fife; we'll start immediately for the village." The Easter moonlight helped all to move swiftly. Dr. Prescott did not draw rein, but kept on as far as Acton, where he called up the Colonel of the Minute Company, Francis Faulkner. Francis Faulkner, Jr., was in his sixteenth year; waking to listen to hoof-beats sounding nearer, he ran to his father's door, saying,[1] "Father, there's a horse coming, on the full run; and he's bringing news!" The Colonel had already pulled on his trowsers and caught up his gun. Receiving the message to "rouse his men," he immediately fired three times and faint echoes were repeated from the scattered farmhouses. Signal fires blazed up, and the men poured in with pouches of bullets, and hastily prepared breakfasts of bread and cheese in their pockets. The wives and children of some of the older Minute-men had come along with them and huddled together in suspense; a few of the younger children presently started to cry, fearing that the British would come and kill them! The women, meanwhile, hung kettles, gypsy fashion, outside in the yard and began cooking beef and pork, potatoes and cabbage, for the men's dinner. The lad Francis and the other boys were told, much to their satisfaction, to get saddle-bags in readiness for carrying the food as soon as it was done a-horseback after the men, as it was supposed that it would travel safer among many bearers. When they came to the packing, however, the women were forced to give up their plan of sending each man's meal separately, as they found it could be handled to much better advantage by keeping the various supplies together, each sort by itself. The press of business was even greater in Concord than at Acton. Not only was the

[1] *My Grandfather Colonel Francis Faulkner and my Uncle Francis Faulkner, Jr., in the Battle of Lexington.* Rev. Cyrus Hamlin, D.D., LL.D. Read before the Lexington Historical Society, 1886. Boston, 1887.

local company gathering, but messengers were being sent to inform the neighboring towns of their danger, while every nerve was strained to get the Colony stores out of the way before the enemy should come.

Already on the 18th, in deference to the suspicions expressed by Revere the previous Sunday, the removal had begun. A portion of the stores had been carried to Sudbury [1] and placed in a house near the gravel-pit, west of the river. Four cannon and quantities of ammunition were carried to Stow,[2] covered with hay and litter from curious eyes. These were concealed in the woods near Henry Gardner's [3] residence, in the northerly part of the lower village. He was at this time treasurer of the Provincial government, and known to his contemporaries as a "courageous, uniform, industrious patriot, and a discreet, humane and upright judge." Loads of supplies were also forwarded to Acton.

The despatch with which the stores were scattered was of the utmost service in every respect. Captain Nathan Cory's [4] grandson, Mr. Wright, for instance, says that while ploughing on the afternoon of the 18th at Groton, Cory received word the Minute-men were to meet, and at once unhitched, drove his oxen home, took down his gun and belt, telling his wife Molly to care for the stock as it was uncertain when he would be back, and then went on to join his comrades. The meeting, it appeared, was held because some brass cannon had been sent over from Concord and they hardly knew what was expected. Some thought that possibly they might be needed at Concord. Upon putting it to vote, the majority decided to wait for a definite call; he, however, and eight more, marched off that very night, carrying pine torches part of the way. They probably came in through Acton, as they are said to

[1] *History of Middlesex County*, II, 370. Drake.
[2] *History of Concord*, 104. Shattuck.
[3] *History of Middlesex County*, I, 652, 661. Hurd.
[4] *Beneath Old Roof Trees*, 295, and *Beside Old Hearth-Stones*, 4. Brown.

have breakfasted at Colonel Barrett's before the British arrived. There was much to do there, and nine men dropping in would be a decided help.

Colonel James Barrett [1] had seen service as a captain in the French and Indian War, having been at Oswego with Shirley, at Ticonderoga with Abercrombie, and at Crown Point with Amherst. More recently he had been a member of the General Court and of the Provincial Congress. He was now sixty-five years of age, and would have preferred to have been relieved of militia duties, but had been persuaded by his command to continue in office. He had five sons and four daughters — James, Nathan, Ephraim, Stephen, Peter, Lydia, Rebecca, Persis, and Lucy. One or more of them were now married and settled near. His wife was Rebecca Hubbard,[2] descended in the fourth generation from the Rev. Peter Bulkeley, a graduate of St. John's, Cambridge University. She had been married in her early teens and at first, the story runs, her mother had to help her a great deal; she was now a woman of fifty-eight, exceptionally capable, and her ready wit prevented much loss this April day. Foreseeing that the house would probably be searched, the family wanted her to go to a safer place, but she answered,[3] "No, I can't live very long anyway, and I'd rather stay and see that they don't burn down the house and barn."

In preparing for the redcoats' coming, little James Barrett,[4] a fourteen year old grandson, had first helped to run bullets and then, when a team had been loaded with stores, he with other boys ran beside the oxen, using goads to hurry their lumbering steps to a trot as they made for a swamp in the rear of the house, called Spruce Gutter,[3] where the stores were hidden under pine boughs. He also drove

[1] *The Spirit of '76*, April, 1895.

[2] *Under Colonial Roofs*, 171–4. Alvin Lincoln Jones. Boston, 1891: C. B. Webster.

[3] *Old Concord, Her Highways and Byways*, 18, 24, 20. Margaret Sidney. Boston, 1888: Lothrop Publishing Company.

[4] *Field Book of the Revolution*, I, 551. Lossing.

an ox-team of flour [1] to a neighboring town. South of the barn, in the present kitchen garden, about thirty square feet were ploughed up and sown with muskets, a man dropping them behind the oxen as the trench was opened, after which the ground was carefully raked smooth. Elsewhere a man ploughed long, deep furrows and filled them with kegs of powder, turning the next furrow over on top. It is even said [2] that a bed of sage was lifted and a cannon, wheels and all, buried below and the bed replanted! Others are said to have been ploughed under as the redcoats came into sight.[3] Some too were buried in manure.[4]

On the first alarm, the Colonel's son Stephen was sent to Price Place (now called Prison Station) to tell the Minutemen of Harvard and Stow not to take the road which would bring them by their house, but to take the great road, leading to the North bridge. Close by the cross-roads here lived Milicent Barrett, a daughter of James Barrett, Jr. From a British officer she had learned how to fashion cartridges, and now led busily in practising and teaching the art.[5] The scissors used by her at this time may be seen in the Town Library.

Thaddeus Blood's [6] narrative shows us, meanwhile, what was happening down in the village. He tells us: "About 2 o'clock in the morning I was called out of bed by John Barrett, a sergeant of the militia company to which I belonged. I was twenty years of age the 28th of May next following. I joined the company under Captain Nathan Barrett, at the old Court House, about three o'clock, and was ordered to go into the Court House to draw ammunition. After the company had all drawn their ammunition we were paraded near the Meeting House."

---

[1] *The Spirit of '76*, April, 1895. Hon. Edwin S. Barrett.
[2] "The Concord Fight," Rev. Grindall Reynolds. *Unitarian Review*, April, 1875.
[3] "Events of April 19." George Tolman. Concord Antiquarian Society.
[4] *A History of the Fight at Concord*, 14. Rev. Dr. Ezra Ripley, 1827.
[5] *Old Concord*, 23, 25–6. Sidney.
[6] *Boston Daily Advertiser*, April 20, 1886.

Blood supposed that there were about sixty or seventy men lined up, for they numbered one hundred ordinarily, and something like thirty had been detached to guard the cannon carried into the woods, while others had joined the Minute Company, under Captain David Brown; about two hundred men in all being under arms in the town that day. A story [1] has come down to us of a man temporarily working in Concord, who was enrolled with the Minute-men. Called from bed and standing in suspense, his first sensation was that he could never face the Regulars, until feeling Mr. Emerson's hand on his shoulder, he was quieted by his courage. One good lady,[2] hearing the alarm, hurried to the meeting-house and brought away the church silver, dumping it for safety into the family soft-soap barrel, and thrusting it into the shadow of the great chimney-arch in the cellar at Wright's tavern. When taken out next day it was so blackened as to call for reburnishing by a silversmith. One of these pieces, a tankard dated 1700, was loaned to the Beacon Street Exhibit by Dr. Edward W. Emerson during the Centennial year. Another woman,[2] making ready to carry her children for safety to the woods, went to her drawer and took out a checkered apron appropriate to the occasion. Mechanically she repeated the act, until when the flurry was over she was found to have on seven!

In the meantime, on the road to Sudbury [3] galloped William Parkman at his best speed bearing the alarm brought by Dr. Prescott. Hawthorne [4] has pictured one of these riders for us. "Along the road, a considerable stretch of which was visible, they heard the clatter of hoofs and saw a little cloud of dust approaching at the rate of a gallop, and disclosing, as it drew near, a hatless countryman in his shirtsleeves, who, bending over his horse's neck, applied

[1] *Beside Old Hearth-Stones*, 360. Brown.
[2] "Wright's Tavern," 18. George Tolman. Concord Antiquarian Society. Concord. Published by the Society. Patriot Press.
[3] *History of Middlesex County*, II, 585. Hurd.
[4] *Septimius Felton*. Nathaniel Hawthorne. Boston, 1872: James R. Osgood.

a cart whip lustily to the animal's flanks, so as to incite him to most unwonted speed. At the same time, he lifted up his voice and shouted in a strange, high tone, that communicated the tremor and excitement of the shouter 'Alarum! Alarum! The Redcoats! the Redcoats! To arms! To arms! Alarum!' and trailing this sound far wavering behind him like a pennon, the eager horseman dashed onward to the village."

Another messenger was sent to Watertown; Major Buttrick meanwhile asking Reuben Brown [1] to ride toward Lexington and learn what news he could and bring back word. Brown seems to have hastened back at the first firing with his report, for he could not be sure if bullets or blank cartridges had been used, though he thought probably bullets. He seems next to have ridden to Hopkinton.[2] Doubtless with this increased information of what was at hand, the exertions to conceal the stores were redoubled.

Bedford men were already in town, summoned the night previous by Nathan Munroe and Benjamin Tidd, who had been sent by Captain Parker and ordered to return by way of Merriam's Corner, alarming the country as they rode.[3] They probably first called Captain Wilson and Captain Moore and afterward roused Ensign Page[3] from his bride. Captain Wilson was somewhat prepared for the tidings, for his brother-in-law, Thompson Maxwell,[4] was spending the night with him, and being familiar with camps, had noticed little matters in Boston leading him to suspect some action afoot, and they were talking it over excitedly when Captain Parker's messenger arrived about one in the morning. Another Bedford man, Lieutenant Edward Stearns, had married a half sister of Captain Wilson's, and is said to have taken command later in the day, when

[1] Frederick Hudson. *Harper's Monthly*, May, 1875.

[2] *History of Concord*, 104. Shattuck.

[3] *Bedford Sesqui-Centennial Celebration, 1879*, 22. Jonathan F. Stearns, D.D. Boston, 1879.

[4] *Beneath Old Roof Trees*, 176, 185. Brown.

Wilson fell.   His son Solomon,[1] nineteen years of age, and a nine year old brother Abner were sleeping side by side when the call came.   Sol marched away never to come home alive, sickening in Cambridge camp, where he died May 18th following.   There were three girls,[2] Rachel sixteen, Susanna thirteen, and Alice eleven, who melted pewter spoons and made cartridges, besides preparing breakfast supplies for the men.   Their home[3] being near the river, the sound of the firing was carried there by water when the affair took place at the North bridge.   Rachel Stearns had much to try her.   The twins,[4] John and Matthew Fitch, had reported early at Fitch's tavern, the Bedford rendezvous, their mother having called after them, "Be sure and get something warm at Jeremiah's."   An elder brother, Moses, a lad of nineteen, followed on after them, stopping on his way for a last word with Rachel, to whom he was engaged.   Goodies from home and goodies from Rachel followed him to Cambridge, and at length, 1782, on Thanksgiving Day, the two were united. The wedding ring then used has, so the story runs, been worn by three Rachels since, in 1819, 1868, and 1893.

As we have seen, the Bedford men rallied at the tavern. Sol Lane used to say[5] Captain Wilson drew his men up at Sergeant Jeremiah Fitch's door and said, "Come, boys, we'll take a little something, and we'll have every dog of them before night."   And as they ate[3] their rye bread and cheese he said, "We give you a cold breakfast, boys, but we will give the British a hot supper."   "Ah," ended Lane's story, "he was as lively as a bird, but he never came home 'till they brought him home."

The flag[4] carried by Ensign Page still exists in the Bedford Public Library and has an exceptionally interesting history, being no less, so it is claimed, than the flag designed

[1] *History of Bedford,* "Genealogical and Biographical," 34.   Abram English Brown.   Bedford, 1891.   Published by the author.

[2] *American Monthly Magazine,* October, 1895.

[3] *Story of Patriots' Day,* 97, 94.   Varney.

[4] *Beneath Old Roof Trees,* 204–12, 198–203.   Brown.

[5] *Bedford Celebration, 1879,* 23.   Stearns.

in England between 1660 and '70 for the "Three Counties" of Middlesex, Suffolk, and Essex. It is of red silk, and bears the device of three silver balls, and a hand holding a dagger, with the motto "*Vince aut morire.*" It or its predecessor had been carried by a previous Ensign Page in the French and Indian War, and even earlier, in King Philip's. It was intended apparently for a cavalry flag, being about two feet square and fixed on a long staff. Originally it was ornamented by a border, but Madam Ruhamah Lane,[1] when past ninety, owned that she had, as a "giddy girl," spoiled the old flag of its silver fringe and gone to a military ball decked grandly in its trimmings.

While toiling over the stores the Ensign laid his beautiful flag against a stone wall for the time being. On his return[2] he is said to have found some boys playing soldier with it, all unconscious that a war had broken out which would not have finished until some of them were men.

About 4 o'clock, while it was still dark, two companies from Lincoln[3] reached Concord — the Militia, under Captain Abijah Pierce, and the Minute-men, led by Captain William Smith, Samuel Hoar being one of his lieutenants. A little before seven the advance guard, stationed a mile and a quarter toward Lexington at the end of the Ridge, in the easterly part of the town, brought word that the British troops were at hand, "and their numbers treble ours."[4] Thaddeus Blood continues:[5] "We were then formed, the minute men on the right, and Captain Barrett on the left, and marched in order to the end of Merriam's Hill, then so called, and saw the British troops a-coming down Brook's Hill. The sun was rising and shined on their arms, and they made a noble appearance in their red coats and glistening arms." The Bedford men were with the rest on the Ridge and saw the Regulars enter, saying

---

[1] *Beneath Old Roof Trees*, 200. Brown.

[2] *History of Middlesex County*, II, 830. Hurd.

[3] *Concord Gazette and Middlesex Yeoman*, April 8, 1826.

[4] Rev. William Emerson. *Concord Guide Book*, 34. Bartlett.

[5] *Boston Daily Advertiser*, April 20, 1886.

grimly,[1] "We must spoil their fine uniforms before night."
Josiah Merriam[2] and his older boys, Josiah, Jr., and
Timothy, had joined the neighbors in the village, leaving
little Joseph, a boy of seven, at home, as he always said,
"to take care of the women." Before long the family
left the house, which still stands at the corner of the Bedford
road, and went into the woods behind the hill. The hungry
British soon after came by and drew unbaked pies from the
oven and took the soft-soap kettle from the crane, scattering
soap and ashes over the hearth, in a hasty search for food.
Daniel Hoar,[3] son of Timothy, was born in 1752; he married
Mary Rogers, who was sixteen at this time. They lived
in the house since made famous as the Wayside by Hawthorne. When the British soldiers came along some of
them stopped at the well for a cool drink, ordering Mary
to draw water for them. But "the Concord people were not
obeying the orders of the redcoats that day, and she refused."
A soldier pointed a musket at her without effect, and they
finally drew what was wanted themselves. A similar story [4]
is told of an aged man who was ordered by one of the officers to fetch him a glass of water; his reply being, "There is
the well; get it yourself." As they stood on the Ridge
looking down, the small body of Patriots, some 150 at that
time, could see the bayonets of 800 Regulars glittering as
they came round the bend by John Beaton's, the long line
wavering and rippling as they kept step. A counsel was
held. The impetuous young minister, feeling the momen-
tousness of the occasion, besought them to "keep their
ground, and if they died, die there." [5]

Colonel Barrett,[6] — suffering from a disease which
made walking almost impossible, but left him the use of

---

[1] *Bedford Celebration, 1879,* 23. Stearns.

[2] *American Antiquarian Soc. Pro.* "Concord," by John McKinstry Merriam.
April, 1894.

[3] *Under Colonial Roofs,* 163–4. Jones.

[4] "Wayside Happenings in 1775." Rev. Edward G. Porter.

[5] *Harper's Magazine,* May, 1875.

[6] "Events of April 19." George Tolman. Concord Antiquarian Society.

the saddle, — on the point of going back to make sure that the stores were concealed and nothing suspicious in sight, warned his men [1] "not to expose themselves without the prospect of doing good service" and rode off. "Let us go and meet them," said one impulsively; then Eleazar Brooks [2] of Lincoln spoke his mind, which was clearly to the effect: It would not do for them to begin the fight while uncertain as to what had befallen at Lexington. More were continually arriving, it would be more prudent to fall back, and let the British distinctly deal the first blow.

Accordingly the Provincials remained on the Ridge until the redcoat flank was within a few rods, when they fell back some eighty rods, [3] retreating "in order," says Blood, [4] "over the top of the hill to the liberty pole erected on the heights opposite the Meeting House and made a halt." Amos Barrett, [5] a member of the Concord Minute Company (whose powder horn was carved with horses, fish, ships, and wheels and the legend "Amos Barrett, His Horn," [6]), in an account written in 1825, adds, "We halted and staid till they got within about 100 rods, then we was ordered to the about face and marched before them with our drums and fifes a-going, and also the British. We had grand musick." "The main body of the British," continues Blood, "marched up in the road, and a detachment of [6 companies [7]] of Light Infantry followed us over the hill and halted in half gun shot of us at the liberty pole. We then marched over the burying ground to the road, and then over the bridge to Hunt's Hill, or Punkatassett, so called at that time." Respecting these movements, we have the

[1] *Concord Gazette and Middlesex Yeoman*, April 8, 1826.
[2] *History of Concord*, 105–6. Shattuck.
[3] *Harper's Magazine*, May, 1875.
[4] *Boston Daily Advertiser*, April 20, 1886.
[5] *Journal and Letters of Rev. Henry True, etc. Also An Account of the Battle of Concord*, etc. Ed. Henry True.
[6] *Boston Morning Journal*, April 20, 1875. Supplement.
[7] *Concord Guide Book*, 29. Bartlett.

British side from Lieutenant John Barker's[1] diary; taking up the narrative after their departure for Concord, it runs, "We met with no interruption 'till within a mile or two of the Town, where the Country People had occupied a hill which commanded the road; the light Infantry were order'd away to the right and ascended the height in one line, upon which the Yankies quitted it without firing, which they did likewise for one or two more successively. They then crossed the River beyond the Town, and we march'd into the Town after taking possession of a Hill with a Liberty Pole on it and a flag flying [said to have been the Pine Tree flag], which was cut down; the Yankies had that Hill but left it to us; we expected they wou'd have made a stand there, but they did not chuse it." Now that the interest centres in Concord[2] it may be well to look at the town as it then appeared. Being a shire town and on the route to No. 4, Crown Point and the New Hampshire Grants, it maintained several publics. Wright's tavern has already been mentioned; this still stands on the left of Main Street as you come from Lexington near the Common. Dr. Minot's house then stood on the opposite corner, where the Middlesex Hotel stands, and by its side, fronting the Common, was the Court-house, a square building with a little belfry and steeple, built in 1719. Next came the meeting-house, dating from 1712, where the Provincial Congress had just been in attendance. Following the Common round to the north, came Colonel Shattuck's house, still standing; then retracing one's way alongside of the Common and across from the church, rose the hilly burying ground; after which came a yellow block,[3] put up in 1750 and used for stores. Then the house of Jonas Lee, a Patriot; next Dr. Joseph Hunt's house; nearly opposite Wright's tavern, Dr. Ezekial Brown's, and below, as you went toward Lexington, Reuben Brown's. At the further end of the square, Monument Street bears away

---

[1] *Atlantic Monthly*, April, 1877.   [2] *Historic Mansions*, 380–5.   Drake.
[3] *Concord Guide Book*, 37–8.   Bartlett.

to the right and leads past the Manse; it was this road Captain George Minot and the others had taken as they fell back on their way to the North bridge. The left-hand turn from Wright's brought one to Ephraim Jones's tavern, just beyond the burying ground; this road (Main Street) continued on and crossed the South bridge near the Hosmer house. The Fitchburg railroad bridge now crosses Main Street on the site of the South bridge; Main Street then being a mere causeway leading to a grist-mill. Next the present bank, opposite Walden Street, stood the Hubbard house and its well-sweep. Beyond lived Captain Timothy Wheeler, a miller, and not far away was Heyward's tavern. At this period [1] a mill-pond lay in the meadow between Heywood Street (then Potter's Lane) and the mill-dam, and Lexington and Walden Streets.

Drawing up on the Common, the troops now halted and were divided into detachments. The Grenadiers and Marines were to remain, under Colonel Smith and Major Pitcairn, to seek out and destroy public stores near the centre of the town. At the same time, Captain Pole of the 10th Regiment was sent with one company to hold the South bridge and to seize any stores he could find, and five companies were sent in the direction taken by the Concord companies, with orders to hold the North bridge.[2] Each party was supposed to have a Tory guide.[3] This accomplished,[4] Smith and Pitcairn mounted Burying Ground Hill and used their field glasses in following the Light Infantry's dispersal. They then repaired to Jones's tavern. This it will be remembered was on the west end of the Main Street burying ground. Ephraim Jones, an old Louisburg [5] veteran, was publican and gaolkeeper both; he had locked up his tavern, and was somewhere about, when set upon by a couple of soldiers. Just as Lieutenant-Colonel Smith

[1] *Old Concord*, 32. Margaret Sidney.

[2] *History of Middlesex County*, II, 585. Hurd.

[3] *American Archives*, II, 438. Force.

[4] *Harper's Magazine*, May, 1875.

[5] *History of Middlesex County*, I, 123. Drake.

tried to enter, Jones, under full headway, came round the house with such force that he fairly threw Smith, who was a man of unwieldy build weighing between two and three hundred pounds, off his feet.[1] They both rolled over, and Pitcairn, enraged, had the door burst in;[2] Jones resisting the while, for Lieutenant-Colonel Smith reported[3] to General Gage that the inhabitants were "sulky, and one [Jones] even struck Pitcairn." But he was overpowered at length and made captive in his own bar under a guard of five men with bayonets fixed and pointing towards him.[4] The next thing was, by bribes or threats, to get Jones to lead the way to the gaol, on the northwest side of the old burying ground. A pistol was held at his breast, and reluctantly he took them to the gaol yard, where three 24-pounders were found.[5] These the redcoats destroyed by knocking the trunnions from the guns, which they spiked. Then setting free[6] a Tory prisoner, Pitcairn returned well satisfied to the tavern and breakfasted, paying his scot to Jones, who had been set at liberty in order that he might fetch the needed liquor. Parson Gordon[7] thought that Pitcairn was too readily elated, that he should "crow over the two four and twenty pounders as a mighty acquisition," and perhaps he would have been less triumphant if he had foreseen that Dr. Preserved Clapp would invent a special carriage for them, so that strictly speaking they were merely disabled.[5]

Henry Gardner, treasurer of the Province, had been boarding with Jones, and a chest of papers was in his keeping which it was important should not fall into unfriendly hands. As the soldiers were about to enter his quarters, Hannah Barns, who lived with the family, prevented them by maintaining it was her own room, and so inducing them to move on.[4]

---

[1] *Story of Patriots' Day*, 48.   Varney.
[2] *Harper's Magazine*, May, 1875.
[3] *Mass. His. Soc. Pro.*, May, 1876.
[4] *History of Concord*, 108.   Shattuck.
[5] *Historic Mansions*, 382, 154.   Drake.
[6] *History of Middlesex County*, 123.   Drake.
[7] *American Archives*, II, 4th ser.   Force.

A mill stood at this time on the north side of the mill-dam, next to the present bank; the miller, Captain Timothy Wheeler, having his barn or store-house on the west side of Walden Street, the present Trinitarian church occupying its site.[1] On the Regulars' approach Wheeler opened the door and received them with bread, cheese, and cider.[2] At the same time he remarked casually to the officer in charge,[3] "I am a miller, Sir, yonder stands my mill. I get my living by it. In the winter I grind a great deal of grain and get it ready for market in spring. This," touching a sack of meal really his own, "is the flour of wheat, this," pointing to another, "is the flour of corn; this is the flour of rye; raised and manufactured on my own farm. This is my store house. I keep my flour here until such time as I can make a market for it." The British officer taking him to be an "honest old chap"[4] and careful to respect private property at once withdrew, little imagining how he had been gulled and that public stores in excess of Wheeler's own were under the one roof. Amos Barrett,[5] already quoted, subsequently became Wheeler's son-in-law. At Ebenezer Hubbard's[6] malt-house they beat off the boards of one end, rolled out, and broke open sixty barrels of flour. Part of the flour from a grist-mill nearby was tossed into the mill-pond, but about half of it was saved after the soldiers had gone on. The appearance of the ground, flaked as if by snow where the flour lay scattered about, was often recalled by those who saw it. Here the soldiers likewise drank from the well and helped themselves to food. While all this was taking place, others were entering houses and shops and unheading barrels,[7] chests, etc., on every side. About

---

[1] *Beneath Old Roof Trees*, 132. Brown.

[2] *History of Massachusetts*, 304. George Lowell Austin. Boston, 1876: Estes and Lauriat.

[3] *History of Concord*, 107-8. Shattuck.

[4] *Historic Mansions*, 384-5. Drake.

[5] *Journal and Letters of Rev. Henry True*, etc., 33.

[6] *Harper's Magazine*, May, 1875, and *History of the Fight*, 19. Ripley.

[7] *American Archives*, II, 4th ser., 438. Force.

five hundred pounds of balls [1] were discovered and thrown into the mill-pond, and some sixteen gun-carriages, some harness, and a few barrels of wooden trenchers and spoons burnt.

Colonel Barrett's brother, Deacon Thomas Barrett,[2] kept a gun factory. Undauntedly protesting against the action of the soldiers and England's attitude to the Colony, he was, according to one account,[3] pulled from the house by the hairs of his head, but on meeting their threats with a quiet, "You will do better to leave me alone, I shall soon die myself, and then do you no harm," they replied, rather shamefacedly, "Well, old Daddy, go in peace."

Old Samuel Buttrick was less fortunate, receiving a blow on his back from the breech of a British musket, which injured him so that he could never after recover an erect posture.[4]

While this was going on in the heart of the town, Captain Mundey Pole was having small success in his efforts near the South bridge. His detachment failed to find the town clerk, Ephraim Wood,[5] at home, and attempting to find stores at Amos Wood's,[5] nothing appeared; one door, indeed, was locked, but instead of forcing it, Captain Pole asked if women were in hiding there, and an evasive reply being made he gallantly withdrew with many apologies; giving each woman present a guinea, in consideration of the annoyance he had occasioned. Mrs. Joseph Hosmer,[1] wife of the adjutant, living.[6] just beyond the line of the present Fitchburg railroad, had skilfully hidden kegs of powder under a mass of feathers below the garret-eaves and some cannon-balls, even, were so well concealed that nothing was discovered, although several mattresses were ripped open. Totally baffled, Captain Pole then retired, wholly

---

[1] *Concord Guide Book*, Rev. William Emerson's Diary, 35, 41.   Bartlett.

[2] *Harper's Magazine*, May, 1875.

[3] *Beneath Old Roof Trees*, 116.   Brown.

[4] *Concord Gazette and Middlesex Yeoman*, April 8, 1826.   Concord.

[5] *History of Concord*, 108, 109.   Shattuck.

[6] *Boston Journal*, April 20, 1875.

unconscious of the many relieved and amused women he had left behind.

The later doings back in the Square are best told by the following petition[1] of Martha Moulton, widow,

On the 19 of April, 1775, in the forenoon, the town of Concord, wherein I dwell, was beset with an army of regulars, who, in a hostile manner, entered the town, and drawed up in form before the door of the house where I live; and there they continued on the Green, feeding their horses within five feet of the door; and about fifty or sixty of them was in and out the house, calling for water and what they wanted, for about three hours. At the same time, all our near neighbors, in the greatest consternation, were drawn off to places far from the thickest part of the town, where I live, and had taken with them their families and what of their best effects they could carry, — some to a neighboring wood, and others to remote houses, — for security. Your petitioner, being left to the mercy of six or seven hundred armed men, and no person near but an old man of eighty-five years, and myself seventy-one years old, and both very infirm. It may easily be imagined what a sad condition your petitioner must be in, under these circumstances, your petitioner committed herself more especially to the Divine Protection, and was very remarkably helpt with so much fortitude of mind, as to wait on them, as they called, with water, or what we had, — chairs for Major Pitcairn and four or five more officers, — who sat at the door viewing their men. At length your petitioner had, by degrees, cultivated so much favor as to talk a little with them. When all on a sudden they had set fire to the great gun carriages just by the house, and while they were in flames your petitioner saw smoke arise out of the Town House higher than the ridge of the house. Then your petitioner did put her life, as it were, in her hand, and ventured to beg of the officers to send some of their men to put out the fire; but they took no

---

[1] *Siege of Boston*, 369. Frothingham.

notice, only sneered. Your petitioner seeing the Town House on fire, and must in a few minutes be past recovery, did yet venture to expostulate with the officers just by her, as she stood with a pail of water in her hand, begging of them to send &c. When they only said, "O, Mother, we wont do you any harm!" "Don't be concerned, Mother," and such like talk. The house still burning, and knowing that all the row of four or five houses, as well as the School house, was in certain danger, your petitioner not knowing but she might provoke them by her insufficient pleading, yet ventured to put as much strength to her arguments as an unfortunate widow could think of; and so your petitioner can safely say that, under Divine Providence, she was an instrument of saving the Court House, and how many more is not certain, from being consumed, with a great deal of valuable furniture, and at the great risk of her life. At last, by one pail of water after another, they sent and did extinguish the fire. And now, may it please this honored Court, as several persons of note in the town have advised your petitioner thus to inform the public of what she had done, and as no notice has been taken of her for the same, she begs leave to lay this her case before your honors, and to let this honored Court also know that the petitioner is not only so old as to be not able to earn wherewith to support herself, is very poor, and shall think her highly honored in the favorable notice of this honored Court. As what the petitioner has done was of a public as well as a private good, and as your honors are in a public capacity, your petitioner begs that it may not be taken ill, in this way, to ask in the most humble manner something, as a fatherly bounty, such as to your great wisdom and compassion shall seem meet; and your petitioner, as in duty bound, for the peace and prosperity of this our American Israel, shall ever pray.

Martha Moulton.

Concord, February 4, 1776.

All will be glad to learn her petition was granted, a vote being passed to pay [1] "out of the Publick Treasury to James Barrett Esq. £3 for the use of Martha Moulton the petitioner for her good services in so boldly and successfully preventing the enemy from burning the Court House." Betty Hartshorn,[2] Dr. Minot's servant, is said to have joined Mrs. Moulton in entreaty. The upper loft held powder, making the fire doubly dangerous. There is a story [3] to the effect that the British were somewhat influenced to act by a person going to them in the garb of a foreigner, and telling them, "By G—d, if you do not put this fire out, you will all be massacred, for there are five hundred men secreted behind the hill ready to fall upon you." Still another tale [2] is that an indignant Patriot originally set the building alight hoping to involve some of the enemy in its ruin, and asserts that the tongs which held the coals are now in Maine! Amos Barrett's [4] account states simply, "We marched into town and over the north bridge a little more than half a mile and then on a hill not far from the bridge, where we could see and hear what was going on. What the British came out after was to destroy our stores that we had got laid up for our Army. There was in the town a number of intrenching tools which they carried out and burnt. At last they said it was best to burn them in the house and set fire to them in the house. But our people begged of them not to burn the house and put it out. It wan't long before it was set on fire again, but finally it was not burnt."

It is time now to see what took place at the North bridge. In spite of the presence of Tory guides and spies the British missed much within their reach, and it has been claimed [5] that a shed, within one hundred feet of the Light Infantry's path, alone held some eight tons of provisions.

[1] *Mass. State Archives*, Vol. 180, p. 306.

[2] *Harper's Magazine*, May, 1875.

[3] *Concord Gazette and Middlesex Yeoman*, April 24, 1824.

[4] *Journal and Letters*, etc. Rev. Henry True.

[5] "The Concord Fight," Rev. Grindall Reynolds. *Unitarian Review*, April, 1875.

On coming to the river one hundred men, under the command of Captain Lawrence Parsons of the 10th Regiment, led by the spy [1] Ensign DeBernière, kept on over the bridge, toward Colonel Barrett's house two miles distant, having left three companies at the bridge and on the heights near it, under the command of Captain Walter Sloan Lawrie of the 43d Regiment. Lieutenant Gould was stationed at the bridge itself; of the two remaining companies, belonging to the 4th and 10th Regiments, one was posted on a hill about a quarter of a mile in his rear, and another on a hill a quarter of a mile from that,[2] and these were allowed to scatter for food; some gathering about the well at the Elisha Jones house.[3]

While sitting at the eastern window, full of suspense, Mrs. James Barrett saw the two companies of redcoats coming up the road. They stopped by the way to refresh themselves at a well [4] still existing (1894) in a corner of a field, near the Acton road which runs a few rods east of the house. This well was close to Samuel Barrett's house, a brother of the Colonel's, and a gunsmith. Here a woman is said to have held a child up so that she could see the men better, crowding about the gray old well in their gay red coats. Lest there should be any slip through the multiplicity of Barrett surnames, Tory Bliss was at the pains to ride up and point significantly toward Colonel James's own dwelling.

The delay at the well was turned to good account up at the homestead. While the men were still busily drinking, one of the Barrett girls ran up to her mother with a quantity of bullets which had been forgotten.[5] The old lady hastily dropped them into an empty barrel up garret, and threw on top some feathers from a neighboring barrel. On coming

---

[1] *History of Concord*, 107. Shattuck.

[2] *Atlantic Monthly*, April, 1877.

[3] "Story of an Old House," 11–12. Hon. John S. Keyes. Concord Antiquarian Society.

[4] *Old Concord*, 27. Margaret Sidney.

[5] *Under Colonial Roofs*, 172–3. Jones.

down she found the soldiers surrounding the house. The commanding officer came up and said, "Madam, I have orders to search this house from top to bottom." Mrs. Barrett replied, "Very well, Sir, I shall expect you to respect private property," to which he readily assented. Immediately the men filed off to ransack the premises within and without. Wherever they went, there in the nick of time was the spirited old lady, quick to act and remind Captain Parsons of his promise. The men spied an old locked trunk full of pewter plates,[1] and being heavy dragged it forth and would have forced it open. But Mrs. Barrett turning to the officer said, "You must not touch it for it contains a maiden lady's belongings," and he called the men off. One soldier, seeing the barrels of feathers, thrust in his bayonet, making the feathers flutter about the attic. The officer[2] nearest cried, "What do you expect to find there, you fool?" bringing on him the jeers of his mates — the musket-balls laughing quietly to themselves, in the dark, as the last bustling footfall died away down the narrow staircase. Out in the barn some gun-carriages were found and set afire on the spot, but since the barn of that day[1] was only forty feet from the house, Mrs. Barrett promptly interposed, "You promised to respect private property; if you burn those carriages there, the barn will be destroyed." The officer, true to his word, had the smouldering straw stamped out and the pile shifted into the road near the corn barn, ten feet square, where they were partially destroyed. While the soldiers were still searching, Stephen Barrett returned from Price Place, an officer arresting him on the threshold, as he cried, "We have you now, Colonel, and you will go with us as our prisoner." But Mrs. Barrett was ready even for this emergency and said, "This is my son, not the master of the house; you may take Colonel Barrett when you can find him." Another son, James, was present, but as he was lame and inactive at the time he attracted

---

[1] *Old Concord*, 20, 24. Sidney.
[2] *Under Colonial Roofs*, 173. Jones.

little attention.   Colonel Barrett, when he had seen to the stores in his keeping, took a by-way [1] back to his command, purposely leaving his family in doubt as to his motions, that they might if questioned answer freely they did not know his whereabouts.

About eight, their rummaging done, the men wanted food. One soldier asked for spirits, but they were refused, and Captain Parsons also forbade them to touch liquor, adding, "We shall have bloody work today, we have killed men in Lexington." [2] Food was a different matter, for as the old lady remarked,[3] "we are commanded to feed our enemy if he hunger;" she then brought out loaves of brown bread from her closet and several pans of new milk from her cellar and set it before them.   They ate [3] in the lower room on the right of the door, called the muster room, from its being used to organize the Minute-men and muster in the Militia.   This has two front windows, and another at the side, with comfortable window-seats.   In the door [4] a clover-shaped hole has been cut for ventilation.   Pieces of the pewter service from which the British ate that day have been scattered throughout the family as heirlooms. One of the searching party, named Thorpe, or Trott, later on deserted and worked for the Barretts as a farm hand.[5] We must now see what was taking place at Acton.   About three A.M. a horseman rode up to Captain Joseph Robbins' door.   The site of the old homestead has recently been marked, half-way from East Acton to the burying ground, on the crest of a small hill; stone walls and fields lying all about it.   Striking[6] the corner of the house a heavy blow which woke the baby in its cradle, the rider shouted his message, "Captain Robbins, Captain Robbins, up! up! The Regulars are coming to Concord.   Rendezvous at

---

[1] *History of the Fight*, 19.   Ripley.
[2] *History of Concord*, 109.   Shattuck.
[3] *Under Colonial Roofs*, 173.   Jones.
[4] *Old Concord*, 18, 24.   Sidney.
[5] *Old Roof Trees*, 117, 116.   Brown.
[6] *History of Middlesex*, I, 255.   Hurd.

the old North bridge as quick as possible. Alarm Acton!"
Then he sprang on his horse's back again, and rode off, it
is supposed to notify the interior towns. Captain Robbins [1]
was a large-built, vigorous man, six and a half feet in his
stockings, weighing 250 pounds, with a voice, it is claimed,
that could reach a mile. The little ten year old Robbins
boy, John, was sleeping up garret, but woke with the commotion and saddled his father's old mare. He was told [2]
not to let the grass grow under him, and started off, 'cross
country half a mile, to call Isaac Davis, Captain of the
Minute-men. After which he kept on to the western part
of the town and called Lieutenant Simon Hunt, in command
of the second Militia company. The population of Acton was
then about five hundred, and there were three companies. [2]

Captain Davis's men had been drilling twice a week
since November. They were a little better provided than
most companies, for Davis was a gunsmith and had fitted
bayonets to all their guns. [3] He carried a beautiful gun
himself of his own make. [2] About twenty men gathered at
his house, some breakfasting there; [4] while making cartridges and adjusting new flints several joked at the idea
of a brush with the Regulars, saying they "would like a
hit at Old Gage," [3] but Captain Davis seemed "heavy-
hearted" and reproved them. It would be a "most event-
ful day," he said, "and no one knew who would be the first
to fall." He "had great hopes [2] the country would be free,
though he might not live to see it." Thomas Thorp, one
of the company, on his way to the house passed the parsonage, and Dr. John Swift, the minister's son, seeing that
he was without a cartridge-box, made him a present of one
decorated with a heart on the cover. Doubtless this
went from hand to hand and was duly admired in the
interval before marching.

[1] *Boston Journal*, April 20, 1895.

[2] *Lexington Centennial Celebration*, 86.

[3] *History of Middlesex County*, II, 585; I, 259. Hurd.

[4] *An Address delivered at Acton, July 21, 1835, being the First Centennial Anniversary of the Organization of that Town*, 22. Josiah Adams. Boston, 1835.

While the men gathered, Mrs. Davis may have helped them as they powdered their hair that they might go neat and trim to meet the British.[1] Her portrait now hangs in the Acton Public Library,[2] — she was a large woman of marked features.[3] Her brother, Lieutenant Samuel Brown,[2] was in her husband's company. Captain Davis at length issued orders for his men to parade, ate a hasty breakfast, and took his accoutrements down from the kitchen wall.[4] He was but thirty years of age and had four children, the eldest [1] about ten, the baby about fifteen months. They were all unwell that day, several having canker rash. Mrs. Davis in her deposition [1] tells us: "My husband said little that morning. He seemed anxious and thoughtful, but never seemed to hesitate as to the course of his duty. As he led the company from the house he turned himself around and seemed to have something to communicate. He only said 'Take good care of the children,' and was soon out of sight." The sun was then one to two hours high and the time about seven A.M. Turning from the lane into the highway, the road stretched on six miles to the North bridge in Concord. Declaring,[5] "I have a right to go to Concord on the King's highway, and I intend to go, if I have to meet all the British troops in Boston," he set forward. Their route [3] was past Parson Swift's and the meeting-house, a mile to the eastward; at Brook's tavern, handkerchiefs were waving from doors and windows and here they went down the hills and up the high ascent to the right, crossing an old bridge since removed, and up another hill with another right-hand turn by the old Brabrook house. Not far from here they took a short cut two miles through the woods, and came out within about twenty rods of the Barrett house. As they went along, their number had been continually reinforced by the remainder

[1] *Acton Centennial, 1835,* 15, 22, 47. Josiah Adams.

[2] *Boston Evening Transcript,* October 8, 1898.

[3] *History of Middlesex County,* I, 262, 255–6. Hurd.

[4] *Account of the Union Celebration at Concord, April 19, 1850,* 93.

[5] *Harper's Magazine,* May, 1875.

of the company falling in line, until thirty-eight, or about the entire number, had turned out.[1] The rest came up during the forenoon. At Hildreth's Corner Lieutenant John Heald and some sixteen men from Carlisle [2] probably joined them. These last had been summoned by Timothy Wilkins beating his drum and James Kent blowing his horn. In their ranks was an Indian fighter, James Russell.[3] They are said to have come down the "two-rod way," and turned in toward Concord at a run; Stephen Barrett being on hand to send them direct to the bridge.[4] During the little pause they watched Captain Parsons' soldiers at their work. Sol Smith,[5] an Acton Minute-man, in his deposition says: "When we arrived near Col. Barrett's, we left the Strawberry-hill road, and went, partly in a cross road, and partly across the fields, in nearly a straight course, to the Widow Brown's tavern. We there took the back, or east road, to the high ground." The Brown tavern stood about one mile northwest of the bridge. Charles Handley,[5] a thirteen year old lad, lived at the tavern at the time, and tells us that he saw Captain Davis's company as they came up. He says: "I first saw them coming through the fields north of Barrett's mill, and they kept the fields till they came to the road at Mrs. Brown's tavern. They there took the back road, leading to the bridge. They marched quite fast, to the music of a fife and drum. I remember the tune, but I am not sure of its name; think it was called *The White Cockade.*" The weather was mild for the season. Dr. Belknap [6] of Dover, New Hampshire, tells us he had set posts for his garden and had his garden made and sown by this date. Cherry trees

[1] *History of Middlesex County*, I, 263. Hurd.

[2] "Events of April 19," p. 27. George Tolman. Concord Antiquarian Society.

[3] *History of Middlesex County*, I, 388. Drake. "Concord," by Rev. Grindall Reynolds.

[4] *Under Colonial Roofs*, 172. Jones.

[5] *Acton Celebration, 1835*, 16, 18. Josiah Adams.

[6] *Mass. His. Soc. Pro.*, September, 1882, 377.

were a-bloom, the door-yards bright with dandelions, and
fifty years later eye-witnesses recalled the peculiar "swish,
swish" made by the grass as the Regulars brushed through
it. It was a day when you "felt the first heat," not unlike
the April 19th of 1891, when the thermometer fell back to
23° by night, but marked 84° at noon in Hartford.[1] So it
is not surprising that when Captain Davis arrived, about
nine A.M., big drops of perspiration were rolling down his
face as he reported, after his hurried march, to Adjutant
Hosmer for duty.[2]

   We must now go back again and trace what happened
to the Patriots from the time they first crossed the bridge
until now. Thaddeus Blood tells us, they "were followed
by two companies of the British over the bridge. One company went up to destroy some stores at Col. James Barrett's
before mentioned, and the other tarried near the bridge.
Some of them went to Capt. David Brown's, some [to]
Mr Ephraim Buttrick's, where Col. Jonas Buttrick now
lives." By road and 'cross lots Minute-men and Militia,
besides undrilled citizens, were constantly arriving and
forming in groups on Ponkawtasset Hill, until by half
past nine, as many as 350 were collected. Among them [3]
were companies and individuals from the following towns:
Bedford, Chelmsford, Carlisle, Littleton, and Westford.
Despite the bustle incident to the day an account [4] was kept
with business-like precision at Littleton of "Articles Dd.
out of the Town Stock," showing that John Green received
$\frac{1}{2}$ lb. Powder, 14 Bullets; Daniel Whitcombe, 14 bullets;
Thomas Wood, 1 Flint; Nathaniel Whitcombe, $\frac{1}{4}$ lb. Powder;
Jonathan Warren, $\frac{1}{2}$ lb. Powder, 1 lb. Bullets. Sudbury
too had representatives present from the West side. A
return of all the companies in this town made on the 27th
of March mentions the troop as in good condition. Of

[1] *Boston Evening Transcript*, April 20, 1891.
[2] *Harper's Magazine*, May, 1875.
[3] *Siege of Boston*, 67–8. Frothingham.
[4] *Lowell Daily Courier*, April 1, 1875.

Captain Stone's company, eighteen had no guns and "at Least one third part of ye firelocks unfit for Sarvis other wais un a quipt." Captain Haynes' men were on the other hand "weel provided with Bayonets or hatchets, a boute one quarter Part with catridge Boxes." Captain Smith reported "near forty well a quipt twenty Promis to find and a quip themselves Emedetly fifteen no guns and other wais un a quipt." One fifth of the entire population was on the muster rolls, and there was not a Tory in town. Captain John Nixon's roll call, between the 13th March and 17th April, 1775, from out a total of sixty names, including Caleb Brown and his "Phiffe," records but six absences.[1] Sudbury lay off the highway, eight miles southwest of Concord. Word of the British advance reached Thomas Plympton,[2] member of the Provincial Congress here, about four A.M. He fired a signal gun and had the Sudbury town bell rung. The alarm at Captain Nixon's door was, "Up, up! The redcoats are up as far as Concord." He at once started on horseback. One of the Sudbury men engaging tells us: With a full belief that the Father of Mercies would "Make his arm beare For us as he did for our Ancesters . . . Husbands left their wives and Fathers their daughters. Sones their Mothers Brothers their Sisters to Meet a Haughty Foe. . . . By Sunrise the greatest part of the inhabitants were Notified. The morning was Remarkably fine and the Inhabitants of Sudbury Never can make such an important appearance Probably again. Every Countenance appeared to Discover the importance of the event."[1] The two West side companies and North Militia and Minutemen would naturally go by the north Sudbury road, and the East companies would take the Lincoln road. Nixon's men rallied at the West side meeting-house, aiming to enter the town by the South bridge or Wood's bridge, on the site of the county bridge by the Fitchburg railroad;

---

[1] *History of Sudbury*, 370–1, 364. Alfred Sereno Hudson. Published by the Town, 1889.

[2] *History of Middlesex County*, II, 401. Hurd.

this being on the westerly side of Concord. Captain Aaron Haynes, with sixty men, and Colonel Ezekiel Howe of the Wayside Inn [1] were with Nixon when, near Dugan's Corner, they were met by Stephen Barrett with a message from his father, the Colonel, to the effect that a file of Regulars held the South bridge, the Sudbury companies were therefore to halt for the present and on no account begin an attack. This was about nine A.M. Old Deacon Josiah Haynes, eighty years of age, a volunteer-exempt, reproached Nixon for not stirring, with the words,[2] "If you don't go and drive them British from that bridge, I shall call you a coward!" Nixon goodnaturedly replied that he must follow orders. Removing the lace from his hat and hiding his sword to conceal his rank, Colonel Howe cried,[3] "If any blood has been shed, not a rascal shall escape," and then rode forward, as if he would cross the South bridge. He was at once halted by the Regulars, who asked his business and where he was going. "Down along," he answered, "and I should not like to be hindered." They then let him pass and he appears to have ridden to the neighborhood of the Barrett house, when, warned by the firing at the North bridge, he wheeled about, observing as he repassed Captain Pole's soldiers, "I find there's trouble ahead; and I believe on the whole, I had better get back to my family."[2] Word now came to the Sudbury companies to march directly to Colonel Barrett's house; on their way they saw a squad of Parsons' men and could have cut them off, but for their orders not to begin an attack. Many of the men had hurried eight, ten, and twelve miles, — they had drilled, mittens on, in a barn all winter in preparation for this very event, — hastening across the hills and fields without stopping [4] to put up fence bars. Anxious hearts were left behind, and during the day

[1] *Under Colonial Roofs*, 180. Jones.

[2] *History of Framingham*, 276. Temple.

[3] *Harper's Magazine*, May, 1875.

[4] "The Concord Fight," Alfred S. Hudson. *Boston Evening Transcript*, April 18, 1895.

Mrs. Nixon,[1] whose home was on Nobscot hillside, went out and laid her ear to the ground, when she could plainly hear the firing.

At the Hunt house,[2] still standing, next to that of Colonel Nathan Barrett's, needed refreshments were willingly given to the rallying men, many of whom had started off without waiting for their breakfasts. The Minute-men came in so fast Major Buttrick called Lieutenant Joseph Hosmer[3] from his company and asked him to be Adjutant, even if his own men were left alone by it. When marshalled, these men marched from the hill to Major John Buttrick's field, about fifty rods from Concord River. Here they were joined by Captain Isaac Davis, who took his stand on the left of the Concord companies, being the position he had held at a recent muster, as the Concord Minute Company was the oldest.[4] James Nichols,[3] an Englishman, one of the Lincoln Minute-men, "a droll fellow and a fine singer," said, "If any of you will hold my gun, I will go down and talk to them." He then went on alone and talked to the British; on his return he said that he was going home. Later he enlisted in our army, but deserted at Dorchester Heights to the British. John Buttrick,[3] the boy fifer, counted the Patriots' front line as 250. There were probably then as many as 450 all told.[3] Colonel John Robinson of Westford, forty years of age, was also there, having started at the first summons, leaving directions for his hired man to follow after them with provisions.[5] The Rev. Mr. Joseph Thaxter, thirty-one years of age, later of Edgartown, had likewise ridden over, with a brace of pistols, and there too was Major Abijah Pierce of Lincoln, just elected Colonel of the Minute-men, who came with a walking-cane only.[3]

Lieutenant John Barker's[6] diary again best fills out

[1] *History of Sudbury*, 375. A. S. Hudson.
[2] *Concord Guide Book*, 44. Bartlett.
[3] *Harper's Magazine*, May, 1875.
[4] *Acton Celebration, 1835*, 15. Josiah Adams.
[5] *History of Middlesex County*, II, 695. Hurd.
[6] *Atlantic Monthly*, April, 1877.

the story from the British side. Referring to the Patriots
he says, "During this time the People were gathering
together in great numbers, and, taking advantage of our
scatter'd disposition, seemed as if they were going to cut
off the communication with the Bridge, upon which the
two companies joined and went to the Bridge to support
that Company. The three Compys. drew up in the road
the far side the Bridge, and the Rebels on the Hill above,
cover'd by a Wall; in that situation they remained a long
time, very near an hour, the three Companies expecting to
be attacked by the Rebels, who were about 1000 strong.
Captn. Lawrie, who commanded these three Companies,
sent to Coll. Smith begging he would send more Troops to
his Assistance and informing him of his situation; the
Coll. order'd 2 or 3 Compys. but put himself at their head,
by which means stopt 'em from being time enough, for
being a very fat heavy Man he wou'd not have reached the
Bridge in half an hour, though it was not half a mile to it."
As they waited, west of the place later known as Jonas
Buttrick's,[1] facing the King's troops, the Patriots saw smoke
rising from the Court-house, occasioned by the burning
Liberty pole and some of the cannon wheels. Supposing
the building in danger, Adjutant Hosmer[2] cried: "Will
you let them burn it down?" An immediate consultation
was held. Major Buttrick[3] is quoted as saying, "Men, if
you will follow me, we will go and see what they are about,
and if occasion occurs be sure not to give the first fire."
They then "resolved to march into the village and defend
their homes or die in the attempt."[2]

Captain William Smith, of the Lincoln Minute Company,
had left his horse at Wright's tavern and gone afoot to the
hill. He now volunteered to dislodge the troops with his
single company. Captain Davis[4] is likewise said to have

[1] *History of Concord*, 111. Shattuck.
[2] *Harper's Magazine*, May, 1875.
[3] *Concord Gazette and Middlesex Yeoman*, April 24, 1824.
[4] *Union Celebration at Concord, 1850*, 94.

asked for the privilege of leading the charge since his company alone was fully armed with bayonets. Thomas Thorp [1] of Acton deposed in reference to their arrival at the bridge: "We found a great collection of armed men, from Concord, and other towns; there were several hundreds, cannot say how many. The officers seemed to be talking by themselves, and the British were then at the bridge. Our officers joined the others; and, in a few minutes, not exceeding five, Captain Davis returned to his company ["To the head of his company," as Sol Smith, another Acton man, testifies] and drew his sword, and said to the company, 'I haven't a man that is afraid to go,' and gave the word 'March!'" This they did by wheeling [2] from the right, being first charged by Colonel Barrett, who rode along the line (as we hear from Thaddeus Blood), on no account to fire first. The schoolmaster of Concord, who was present, could never find words strong enough to express how deeply Davis's face reddened at the word of command. [3]

The companies then proceeded toward the bridge in double file. Major Buttrick went first, Colonel Robinson, [4] who declined the command, on Buttrick's right as a volunteer, marching with Captain Davis. When they came to the road from Captain Brown's, Captain Davis's company [2] passed by, in advance of Captain Brown's Concord Minutemen, who had been leading. Captain Charles Miles [5] and Captain Nathan Barrett followed next, and behind came other companies. As they marched the Acton men in the left hand held their fusees, trailed; they kept step to Captain Davis's favorite tune, [6] "The White Cockade," a peculiarly quick march played by Luther Blanchard, fifer, and Francis Barker, drummer; the latter being

---

[1] *Acton Celebration, 1835,* 15, 17.
[2] *History of Concord,* 111. Shattuck.
[3] *History of the United States,* VII, 302. George Bancroft. Boston, 1858.
[4] *History of Middlesex County,* II, 694–5. Hurd.
[5] *Harper's Magazine,* May, 1875.
[6] *Lexington Centennial Celebration,* 87.

described on the State House Records[1] as: nineteen years of age, five feet seven in height, of a ruddy countenance. As our men moved off to meet the Regulars, Jonas Buttrick,[2] then a young lad, watched his father and brother with a beating heart, we may well suppose, from behind a button-wood tree. Another looker-on was Timothy Minot, Jr.,[3] of Concord, who deposed later, he thought it his "incumbent duty to secure his family," which he did, but succeeded in getting back in time to see the action. Lieutenant Hunt [4] had made good time with the Acton Militia, as they had begun to turn the corner and pass into the main road, leading to the bridge, when the firing took place.

The road [5] leading to the bridge was low and subject to flooding. Its upper end had a wall of large stones, capped by posts and a hand-rail to use when crossing in bad seasons. Seeing that the Patriots were shifting their position nearer, a few redcoats,[6] lingering on the west side of the stream, started back to rejoin their comrades, hurriedly pulling up some of the planks as they crossed the bridge. When this was noticed, Thorp says, "we quickened our pace and ran toward them." He adds elsewhere, "according to the best of my recollection and judgement, the number of the British at and near the North bridge, before the fight was about eighty; but they were scattered about, so that I cannot be certain, there might be more." Seeing that the Regulars were tampering with the bridge — to continue the story from Solomon Smith's[4] narrative — "some one, (I believe it was Major Buttrick) remonstrated in a loud voice; and, about the same time, they desisted, and formed for action." "Upon our beginning to march," says Thaddeus Blood,[7]

---

[1] "Tune that helped to make history." Alexander Corbett, Jr. *Boston Daily Globe*, April 19, 1901.

[2] *Beneath Old Roof Trees*, 20. Brown.

[3] *History of Concord*, 348. Shattuck.

[4] *Acton Celebration, 1835*, 21, 15, 16, 17.

[5] *Harper's Magazine*, May, 1875.

[6] *Concord Gazette and Middlesex Yeoman*, April 8, 1826.

[7] *Boston Daily Advertiser*, April 20, 1886.

"the British formed first on the Causeway in platoons. They then retreated over the bridge, and in retreating took up three planks and formed part in the road and part on each side."

The British reinforcements were nowhere in sight or hearing, and young Lieutenant Barker [1] tells us, while still looking for aid, "the Rebels marched into the Road and were coming down upon us, when Captain L—e made his Men retire to this side the Bridge (which by the bye he ought to have done at first), and then he wou'd have had time to make a good disposition, but at this time he had not, for the Rebels were got so near him [within about fifteen rods, says Amos Barrett [2]] that his people were obliged to form the best way they could; as soon as they were got over the Bridge the three Companies got one behind the other so that only the front one could fire; the Rebels when they got near the Bridge halted and fronted, filling the Road from the top to the bottom. The fire soon began from a dropping shot on our side." From Thaddeus Blood's [3] narrative we learn that, "our men at the same time [as the British formed, were] marching in very good order along the road in double file. At that time an officer rode up and a gun was fired. I saw where the ball threw up the water about the middle of the river, and then a second and third shot, and the cry of 'Fire,' 'fire,' was made from front to rear." The troops probably first fired with the well-meant design of intimidating our men and preventing further action, for they aimed to the left,[4] and several of the Provincials mention that they saw the bullets splash into the quiet, flowing river on their right. The report of two other guns fired over their heads followed almost immediately, and then came a volley from the redcoats. Amos Barrett,[5] marching with Captain Allen's Minute Company, behind Davis, says, "I see the

[1] *Atlantic Monthly*, April, 1877.

[2] *Journal and Letters*, etc. Rev. Henry True.

[3] *Boston Daily Advertiser*, April 20, 1886.

[4] *Concord Gazette and Middlesex Yeoman*, April 8, 1826.

[5] *Journal and Letters*, etc. Rev. Henry True. Facsimile, p. 33.

Ball strike in the River on the Right of me. . . . Their
balls whistled well. We then was all ordered to fire that
could fire and not kill our own men." The bridge which
divided the men was only about one hundred feet long, and
our men, tightly massed, made an easy mark. It is surprising that more were not killed. As it was, one of the
single gunshots intended for Buttrick passed under Colonel Robinson's [1] arm slightly wounding the Acton fifer
Luther Blanchard in his side, and also hitting Jonas Brown,
a Concord Minute-man. Sol Smith says, "Hearing our fifer
cry out, Major Buttrick [1] exclaimed, 'Fire, for God's sake,
fellow soldiers, fire!'" at the same moment leaping from the
ground and discharging his own gun. [Preserved in the
State House since 1902.] Tilly Buttrick [2] being in the front
row of the first Concord company heard him plainly.

Davis had asked [3] if the British were using balls and at
the reply, "Yes, for Luther Blanchard is wounded" he
impulsively stepped to the wall beside the road and sighted
his gun. Directly a second volley from the British was
discharged, and Davis [1] was seen to spring two or three feet
in the air and then drop motionless on the north side of the
lane, still grasping in death his gun. The stone against
which he fell was long stained with his blood. He was
shot in the heart, the ball passing through his body, and
perhaps driving a button in before it, as his blood spirted
out more than ten feet, sprinkling Orderly Sergeant David
Forbush and Thomas Thorp, who was file leader.[3] Thorp
used to say that wherever he went in the long war that
followed, he seemed to see Davis's blood which had spattered
him, urging him on to do his duty.[4]

According to family tradition Saml. Whitney [5] of Sudbury, when the volley came, dodged, and a ball passed, mortally wounding the man behind him. Possibly this would

[1] *Harper's Magazine*, May, 1875.
[2] *Concord Gazette and Middlesex Yeoman*, April 8, 1826.
[3] *History of Middlesex County*, I, 256, 260-1. Hurd.
[4] *History of Middlesex County*, I, 206. Drake.
[5] Statement of Mrs. Elizabeth Goodnough Whitney, a granddaughter, 1895.

THE ENGAGEMENT AT THE NORTH BRIDGE IN CONCORD

be Abner Hosmer, another of the Acton company, who was instantly killed by a bullet in the head. Ezekiel Davis, a brother of the Captain, had a ball pass through his hat grazing his head, and Joshua Brooks of Lincoln was struck by a ball which cut his hat and drew blood on his forehead. "I concluded," said private Baker, "that the British were firing jack knives." Noah Parkhurst, also of Lincoln, turned to Amos Baker saying,[1] "Now the War has begun, and no one knows when it will end."

Joseph Barker had left his wife in tears when he set forth that morning, as his daughter, Mrs. Mehitable Piper, used to recall. He stood near Davis and now exclaimed to the rest, "Boys, don't give up." [2] Captain David Brown, who never before or after used a profane word, cried in the heat of the moment, "G—d d—d them, they are firing balls! Fire men, fire!" and himself took aim. It is believed that he hit one [1] of the redcoats that lie buried near the Monument. After returning the volley some of the Americans jumped over a wall on their left and fired from behind it.[3] The men had been blocked in the lane and forced to fire "over one another's heads, being in a long column, two and two," says the Rev. Mr. Thaxter.[4] As for the British, as soon as the first platoon of the enemy fired, they wheeled by sections to make room for others to do likewise.[3] But the American aim was true and the British were receiving such injury it took but a forward movement to break their line. Some of the foremost Yankees ran over the bridge and fired again, kneeling down in order that those behind them might fire with safety overhead.[4] Hawthorne, referring to the Manse, writes:[5] "The Study had three windows, set with little, old-fashioned panes of glass, each with a crack across it. . . . The third, facing northward, commanded a broader view of the river, at a spot where its

[1] *Harper's Magazine*, May, 1875.
[2] *History of Middlesex County*, I, 257. Hurd.
[3] *Concord Gazette and Middlesex Yeoman*, April 8, 1826, April 24, 1824.
[4] *Historical Magazine*, March, 1869, February, 1863.
[5] *Mosses from an Old Manse*. Nathaniel Hawthorne. Published 1846.

hitherto obscure waters gleam forth into the light of history.
It was at this window that the clergyman who then dwelt
in the Manse [the Rev. William Emerson] stood watching
the outbreak of a long and deadly struggle between two
nations.   He saw the irregular array of his parishioners on
the farther side of the river and the glittering line on the
hither bank.   He awaited in an agony of suspense the rattle
of the musketry.   It came; and it needed but a gentle wind
to sweep the battle smoke around his quiet home." [1]   Many
women and children took refuge at the Manse when their
husbands left home, and Mr. Emerson stayed to protect
them and his own little family, there being only an excited
negro servant and himself at hand by way of menfolks.
There were four Emerson children:[2] three girls, and an
only son, William, then six years old, the future father
of Ralph Waldo Emerson.   We have Parson Gordon's [3]
word for it that Mr. Emerson was "very uneasy until he
found that the fire was returned."   He was only thirty-
two at the time, and going with the army to Ticonderoga,
as chaplain, he died of camp fever the following year
in Rutland, Vermont.[2]   To Thaddeus Blood [4] it seemed
barely two minutes before the British were on the "run."
Their losses were heavy and justified Captain Lawrie in
withdrawing.   Three Regulars lay where they had fallen,[5]
two close together, one a little aside; nine or ten wounded
retreated with their fellows toward the town.   Half the
officers present, Lieutenant Barker [6] tells us, were injured.
Their names are Lieutenants William Sutherland of the
38th, a slight wound in the breast; Waldron Kelly of
the 10th, in the arm; Edward Thoroton Gould, of the
King's Own, in the foot, and Edward Hull of the 43d in
the arm.   A sergeant and four or five privates probably

---

[1] *Beside Old Hearth-Stones*, 361.   Quoted by Brown.
[2] *Beneath Old Roof Trees*, 83, 82.   Brown.
[3] *American Archives*, II, 4th ser.   Force.
[4] *Boston Daily Advertiser*, April 20, 1886.
[5] *Journal and Letters of Rev. Henry True*, 33.
[6] *Atlantic Monthly*, May, 1875.

completed the number, since two of the British were killed and eleven wounded, according to the Rev. Mr. Thaxter,[1] an eye-witness. The officers at first are said to have told their men that the Yankees were only firing blank cartridges, upon which one who had been struck by a bullet, asked his Captain feelingly, how *he'd* like some of that powder![2] Parson Stiles [3] heard through the Rev. Mr. Wheeler, who had brothers living in Concord, that one of the wounded officers "walked a little ways and gave out; upon which they carried him into Town; he asked his Surgeon whether his wound was mortal? Yes: is there a Clergyman near? No." This probably has reference to Lieutenant Hull, since he was carried along later in a chaise.[3] When Amos Barrett[4] got over the bridge, he says, "there was 8 or 10 that was wounded and a running and a Hobbling about, looking back to see if we was after them. We then saw the whole body acoming out of town." Lieutenant Gould[5] was wounded in his ankle and soon lagged by the way; the Provincials were pressing on, excited and sore over the loss of Davis and Hosmer, and it might have gone hard with him, as we learn from Parson Gordon,[6] but for the intervention of a minister present (possibly meaning Thaxter), who took the young officer into his protection.

From now onward, as Thorp remarks,[7] "Everyone appeared to be his own Commander." Lieutenant Barker,[8] speaking of the British as being "forced to quit the bridge" says, "some of the Grenadiers met 'em in the road" two companies, as we find from another account,[9] half-way to the meeting-house, and they "then advanced to meet the

[1] *Historical Magazine*, March, 1869.
[2] *History of Middlesex County*, I, 125. Drake.
[3] *Diary*, I, 551–2.
[4] *Journal and Letters*, etc. Rev. Henry True.
[5] *History of Middlesex*, III, 178. Hurd.
[6] *History of the American Revolution*, I, 480. Gordon.
[7] *Acton Celebration, 1835.*
[8] *Atlantic Monthly*, April, 1877.
[9] Parson Emerson.

Rebels, who had got this side the Bridge and on a good height, but seeing the manœuvre they thought proper to retire again over the Bridge; the whole then went into Concord." Respecting this movement, Amos Barrett [1] says: upon the approach of the reinforcements "We were ordered to lay behind a wall that run over a hill, and when they got nigh enough, Major Buttrick said he would give the word fire. But they did not come quite so near as he expected, before they halted. The commanding officer ordered the whole batallion to halt and officers to the front, the officers then marched to the front, then we lay behind the wall, about 200 of us, with our guns cocked, expecting every minute to have the word, fire. Our orders was if we fired, to fire 2 or three times and then retreat. If we had fired, I believe we could have killed almost every officer there was in the front; but we had no orders to fire and they wan't again fired [on]. They staid about 10 minutes and then marched back and we after them."

As for the British, Parson Emerson [2] writes: "The 3 Royal troops soon quitted their Post at ye Bridge, & retreat^d. in grt^est. Disord^r. & Confu to ye main Body, who were soon upon ye March to meet them. For half an hour ye Enemy by yr Marches & counter Marches discov^d. gt Feeklness & Inconstancy of Mind, sometimes advancing, sometimes returning to yr former Posts." In the rush over the bridge, Major Abijah Pierce [3] of Lincoln caught up a gun from one of the fallen redcoats and was well armed for the afternoon's pursuit; this was long treasured as an heirloom. A sword taken at the bridge may be seen at the Antiquarian Rooms here; it is lettered "X Rgt, Co. VI, No. 10." Of the British killed, one died immediately from a shot in the head. He lay where he fell, and William Fletcher [4] of Chelmsford had to step over his body, as he

---

[1] *Journal and Letters,* etc.   Rev. Henry True.
[2] *Concord Centennial Celebration.*   From the heliotype facsimile.
[3] *Acton Celebration, 1835,* 21.
[4] *Beside Old Hearth-Stones,* 294.   Brown.

followed on with his mates. Another Regular, mortally wounded at the bridge, expired before his comrades reached the village; he was buried [1] in the old graveyard at the point of the hill where the road turns and comes into the Square. A third lay as though dead beside the first to fall, and these two men were much noted by the Provincials passing over the bridge. Though in a swound at first, this last redcoat recovered consciousness amidst the hurrying feet, passing over and all about him. Still dazed by what had taken place he was sitting up when Thorp crossed the bridge. It would have been well for him if the pitiful minister had been near. He is thought by some to have attempted to get on his feet and rejoin the rapidly vanishing scarlet line of his comrades. At all events, according to tradition, the minister's chore boy, a youth of twenty-one, after the pursuit had passed ran over toward the river "to join the country people,"[2] as he went, picking up at the back door a small hatchet lying beside the woodpile. Confronted by this poor man on his hands and knees who gave him a ghastly stare, the lad, Ammi White, went to the riverside to fetch water, but the Regular, mistaking his kindly intention, made a bayonet [3] thrust at him, upon which young White, unnerved by all that had taken place, without stopping to realize the redcoat's helplessness, in supposed self-defence, struck out impulsively with the axe and clove his skull. "The poor object," says the Rev. William Gordon,[2] "languished for an hour or two before he died." "This act," says Thorp, "was a matter of horror to us all." "This act," writes Sol Smith,[4] "met with universal disapprobation, and was excused only by the excitement and inexperience of the perpetrator." The story had a peculiar fascination for Hawthorne, who[5] "often-

[1] *Unitarian Review*, April, 1875.

[2] *American Archives*, II, 4th ser., 630. Force.

[3] *History of Middlesex County*, I, 389. Drake. And as currently told winter of 1895.

[4] *Acton Celebration, 1835.* Depositions.

[5] *Mosses from an Old Manse.*

times as an intellectual and moral exercise sought to follow
the poor youth through his subsequent career, and observe
how his soul was tortured by the blood stain, contracted,
as it had been, before the long custom of war had robbed
human life of its sanctity, and while it still seemed murder-
ous to slay a brother man. This one circumstance," he
writes, "has borne more fruit for me than all that history
tells of the fight." We are not surprised to read that the
boy bitterly regretted the act. In 1807 he told Charles
Handley,[1] himself, who mentions it in his deposition, that
it had "worried him very much; but that he thought he was
doing right at the time." Years ago a phrenologist prevailed on the townsfolk to sell him the skulls of both the
British soldiers buried at the bridge, for scientific purposes,
at least so he said, but presently it was learned that they had
come into the possession of the Worcester Historical Society.
Subsequently they were recovered and reburied through
the efforts of the late Mr. George Tolman of Concord. It
was remarked on this occasion by several that one skull
had a bullet hole, and that the other was broken by a blow,
thus confirming the tradition. A button belonging to one
of the soldiers was kept out, and may be seen in the Antiquarian Rooms.

[1] *Acton Celebration, 1835.*

CHAPTER II

AFTER the British had retreated from the bridge, Major Buttrick paraded fifty men near Humphrey Barrett's; other Provincials went behind a hill east of the road, above Elisha Jones's. Among these last were the Acton men, the Concord Minute-men, and many others.[1] Lieutenant John Hayward[2] of Acton, who succeeded Captain Davis in command of his company, is said to have died at Bridgton, Maine, in 1825. Sol Smith[1] writes of him, "Captain Davis was a man of great firmness, and energy of character, an excellent officer, and had the respect and esteem of all who knew him. Lt. Hayward did all that could be done; but it was felt, at the time, that the loss of our Captain was the cause of much of the confusion that followed." When Smith's reinforcements came up our men divided; some, keeping on along the Ridge and by a bridle-path through the woods, skirted the centre of the town, purposing to intercept the British retreat, and others went back to help with the killed and wounded. Luther Blanchard,[3] eighteen years of age, the first to be hit, went after the action to Mrs. Humphrey Barrett's. He did not make much of the wound, and when Mrs. Barrett, examining it, said with concern, "a little more and you'd been killed," he replied stoutly, "Yes, and a little more and it wouldn't have touched me at all." But although he took it so lightly and lost no time in rejoining his company, besides engaging

---

[1] *Acton Celebration, 1835,* 17.

[2] "The Leader of the Charge across Concord Bridge." Charles O. Stickney. April 18, 1891, *Boston Evening Transcript.*

[3] *History of Concord,* 112. Shattuck.

in the battle of Bunker Hill the following June, his nephew [1] always believed that his death in the College Hospital at Cambridge during September was due to this early wound. He and his brother Calvin, who served in the same company as orderly sergeant, were born in Boxborough and were learning the mason's trade, making their home with Deacon Jonathan Hosmer, the father of Abner. Their own father, Simon Blanchard, had been killed in 1759, before Quebec. The farm from which they marched lies about midway between South and West Acton and is suitably marked by a memorial stone. Luther lies buried at Littleton. One of the Acton men present, Aaron Jones,[2] named a son for him. This same Jones could never speak of Isaac Davis unmoved.

Sol Smith [3] says, "The bodies of Davis and Hosmer were carried, as I was told, to the house of Major Buttrick, very soon after they were killed, and before the detachment returned from Colonel Barrett's." Amos Baker of Lincoln was one of many who went into the house and saw them as they lay there, before their removal that afternoon to the Davis house in Acton. The Captain's widow says of her husband, "His countenance was pleasant and seemed but little altered."[3] Abner Hosmer had an older brother Jonathan and two younger, Stephen and Jonas. Mrs. Sarah Hosmer, a child at the time, used to tell in her old age of how her grandfather, the lad's father, who had been into the village seeking news, returned 'round the corner of the house and groaned as he passed the window, to go in at the front door.[2]

In 1851, at the dedication of the Acton Monument, Hosmer's body was removed, his cheek-bone still showing traces of the ball which caused his death. It had entered just below the left eye and come out at the back of his neck.[2]

[1] *Memorial to Luther Blanchard, Fifer of the Acton Minute-men, April 19, 1775,* 14–15, 22–3, 24, 95, 51. Alfred Sereno Hudson. West Acton, 1899. Published by Luke Blanchard.

[2] *History of Middlesex County,* I, 256, 270, 276. Hurd.

[3] *Acton Celebration, 1835,* 18, 21, 19.

At the same time a silver bosom pin in the form of an eagle was recovered which he had worn into the battle.[1] In 1894 this brooch was owned by Nelson Tinny [2] of Acton; it bears the monogram "S. H.," and is supposed to have come to him on his twenty-first birthday, just before his death. Later the body of Hayward, whose death occurred during the pursuit, was brought home and laid beside that of Hosmer at the Davis house.[3] The whole town attended a few days later when the Rev. Mr. Swift,[4] parson of the town for thirty-seven years, held the funeral services. Captain Davis's father was Deacon Ezekiel Davis,[5] and as we learn from the inscription on Hosmer's grave, his father also was a deacon.

HERE LIES THE BODY OF MR. ABNER HOSMER,
SON OF DEA. JONA. HOSMER, AND MRS. MARTHA HIS WIFE,
WHO WAS KILLED IN CONCORD FIGHT
APRIL 19TH 1775,
IN YE DEFENCE OF YE JUST RIGHTS OF HIS COUNTRY,
BEING IN THE 21ST YEAR OF HIS AGE.

Captain Davis's epitaph [1] reads:

I SAY UNTO ALL WATCH.
IN MEMORY OF CAPT. ISAAC DAVIS
WHO WAS SLAIN IN BATTLE AT
CONCORD APRIL YE 19TH 1775 IN
THE DEFENCE OF YE JUST RIGHTS
AND LIBERTRIES OF HIS COUNTRY
CIVIL & RELIGIOUS. HE WAS A LOVNG
HUSBAND A TENDER FATHER & A
KIND NEIGHBOUR AN INGENEOUS
CRAFTSMAN & SERVICEABLE TO
MANKIND DIED IN YE PRIME OF
LIFE AGED 30 YEARS I M., & 25 DAYS.

Is there not an appointed time to man upon ye earth? are not his days also like the days of an hireling? As the cloud is consumed and vanisheth away, so he that goeth down to the grave shall come up no more. He shall return no more to his house, neither shall his place know him any more. — JOB vii. 1, 9, 10.

[1] *Beneath Old Roof Trees*, 168–170, 166. Brown.
[2] *Boston Herald*, April 18, 1894.
[3] *Acton Celebration, 1835*, 19.
[4] *History of Middlesex County*, I, 261, 244. Hurd.
[5] *Account of the Union Celebration at Concord, 1850*, 93.

Captain Davis is said to have had a presentiment of trouble, because shortly before, on returning home, he and his wife found a large owl indoors, sitting on his gun, which stayed 'round several days.[1] Mrs. Isaac Davis continued to live in Acton to a great age. She was subsequently married in 1782 to Samuel Jones, and in 1802 to Francis Leighton.[1] In her 89th year she made a deposition respecting Captain Davis's death, and through the efforts of the Rev. Mr. Woodbury received an annuity of fifty dollars from the Commonwealth, and $200 from the National Government. In her gratitude she hobbled to a chest and begged Mr. Woodbury[1] "to take his pay" by accepting as a keepsake the buckles that Captain Davis wore when he fell. It is now high time to go back to Captain Parsons' command, left all this while at the Barrett homestead. When they had finished eating, one of the soldiers offered Mrs. Barrett payment, which she refused with the words, "It is the price of blood," but the soldier was not satisfied until he had flung the coin in her lap. The commanding officer then started to his feet crying, "We shall have hot work before night, let us go," and the companies filed off as they had come. After they were gone it was discovered that fifty dollars had been pilfered from the Colonel's desk.[2]

As they went along back, the soldiers came to Mrs. Brown's tavern, and three or four of the officers went into the house to take some drink. The boy, Charles Handley,[3] was there and says: "The soldiers were sitting by the roadside, and some drink was carried out to them. The officers offered to pay, and Mrs. Brown declined; they told her not to be afraid, for they should do her no harm, and paid for their drink. I heard the guns at the bridge [a mile to the southeast] but the British did not appear to hear them. They marched on very soon, but were in no haste. It was

---

[1] *History of Middlesex County*, I, 260, 262. Hurd.
[2] *Under Colonial Roofs*, 173. Jones.
[3] *Acton Celebration, 1835.*

always said that they had no knowledge of the fight, 'till they passed the bridge, and saw the men that had been killed." Colonel Barrett's oldest son lived in the house next west of his father's, still standing in 1894. After the firing was heard, his wife gathered her children together, put some clothing and food into a bushel basket, and started for the woods. The family still relate the pleasant story [1] of the mother and eldest boy carrying the basket between them, the baby laughingly enjoying a ride on the top. The children seemed to scent danger in the air, and each carried their favorite playthings, one of the little girls timorously choosing her catechism as the one thing most dear! Happily the fortune of war left their home untouched, and when James Barrett, Jr., came back, he was undismayed by the vacant rooms, and soon recovered his wanderers.

Sol Smith of Acton says in reference to their following Captain Parsons: "After a short time, we dispersed, and without any regularity, went back over the bridge, while we were there the detachment which had been to destroy stores at Col. Barrett's, returned, and passed us without molestation. It was owing to our want of order, and our confused state, that they were not taken prisoners." "I do not remember," says Thorp,[2] "that any one was there, who assumed any command." Smith continues, "They passed the two of their number, who had been killed, and saw that the head of one had been split open. It was said this circumstance gave them the impression that the Americans would give no quarter." The Circumstantial [3] Account gives the British version of this. "When Captain Parsons returned with the three companies over the Bridge, they observed three soldiers on the Ground, one of them Scalped, his head much mangled, and his ears cut off, though not quite dead: a sight which struck the soldiers with horror." In order to set right this erroneous impression, on May 11th

---

[1] *Under Colonial Roofs*, 172. Jones.
[2] *Acton Celebration, 1835.* Depositions.
[3] *Mass. His. Soc. Coll.*, II, 2d ser., 226.

Zaccheus Brown [1] and Thomas Davis, Jr., who had buried the dead were required to give testimony and solemnly deposed that: The man was not scalped, neither had his ears been cut off, as currently rumored in Boston. The companies under Parsons supposed that the Americans and not their own men had taken up the planks. Says DeBernière [2] "They had taken up some of the planks of the bridge but we got over, had they destroyed it we were most certainly all lost." On coming thus suddenly on their dead comrades the Regulars were seized in a panic and "ran with great speed" to the far end of the Common; their flight being observed by Mr. Emerson at the Manse. [3]

Now again we must go back and follow Captain Lawrie's companies. The Elisha Jones house, now known as the Keyes, still stands not far from the Manse and about opposite where the lane leaves the main road to meet the bridge. There are said to have been concealed here in the cellar and shed fifty-five barrels of beef and 1,700 pounds of salt fish. To protect the stores Jones had taken post in the cellar [4] where his young wife and two little children also found shelter. After the firing took place and the soldiers were in retreat they ran upstairs again. Maddened by what had taken place, Jones [5] would have fired from the window upon the Regulars but his wife thought it imprudent, so that he stood indignantly regarding them from the open shed door, when a bullet suddenly sped back as a parting souvenir from the British ranks. A diamond-shaped bit of marble in the L marks to this day where it struck. Within doors a little four year old girl [6] stood on a pile of salt fish — a portion of the undiscovered stores — watching the soldiers pass. With them was passing

[1] *History of Concord*, 350. Shattuck.

[2] *Mass. His. Soc. Coll.*, IV., 2d ser., 216.

[3] *Harper's Magazine*, May, 1875.

[4] *History of Concord*, 301–3. Alfred Sereno Hudson. Concord, 1904: The Erudite Press.

[5] *Historic Mansions*, 392. Drake.

[6] *Concord Guide*, 43. Bartlett.

England's hold on the Colony, but the child knew nothing of that, and only remembered [1] when "grown-up," that they went by gay and bright toward the bridge, with scarlet coats and white smallclothes, and now were hurrying back, muddy, bound up, and bleeding.

In 1897 a handbag was exhibited at Copley Hall by Mrs. Ellen E. Lane, embroidered by Lucy Jones of Concord. Her home was near the battlefield and she is said to have been taken by her mother with the other children to a hill from which they overlooked the fight. [2] She afterwards married Nathan Warren. On reaching the town Captain Lawrie drew up his command and waited for the companies under Captain Parsons, who arrived in about an hour. [3] Recalled by the sound of firing carried by the river, Captain Pole's company had already joined the main body. In the interval, attention was given to the wounded.

The result of the affair at the North bridge had been: [4]

	Killed	Wounded	Total
Americans	2	4	6
British	4	13	17

More than a dozen British had their wounds dressed by Drs. Minot and Cummings. The latter, it is said, cared at least for eight, none of whom were known to return to the King's army. [5] One of the men, Sam Lee of the 18th Regiment as the story goes, [6] was a Londoner, thirty years of age. He had liked a young Boston girl, and been cast down to find her home deserted one day, until a passer had told him that "Mary" had "gone to Concord." So the march out had been welcomed, but he had no heart for the clash at the bridge, and when wounded made no effort to rise. "There's no life in you, Sam," the men had said before; now, they said, that he was "too far gone to take

[1] *History of Middlesex County*, I, 389. Drake.
[2] *Catalogue.*
[3] *Atlantic Monthly*, April, 1877.
[4] *Harper's Magazine*, May, 1875.
[5] *History of Concord*, 113, 117. Shattuck.
[6] *Beneath Old Roof Trees*, 93–101. Brown.

back," and left him at Dr. Minot's, where he had been carried.[1] Strangely enough, the tale goes on, who should be helping with the wounded but his long-lost Mary Piper, and declaring that he never would go back to the army to fight against such friends, Lee declined to be exchanged, and was married before the evacuation of Boston. Another Britisher, Sergeant Cooper,[1] who helped search at Colonel Barrett's, married a woman living at Dr. Cummings'.

It would seem from the British Spy's journal, already referred to, that this march had been some time under contemplation. By appointment, the day following his return to town, i.e., April 13th, Howe [2] tells us "at nine o'clock I called at the General's headquarters. He said he should want me to put on my Yankee dress and go on horseback through Malden, Lynn, and Marblehead to Salem, on the 18th, at night to carry letters to the Tories in those places, to have them use their influence to restrain the Militia and secure the arms and ammunition, if they should attempt to take up arms against his majesty's regulars, as I shall detach Major Pitcairn to march on the 19th, at 1 o'clock in the morning with 800 grenadiers; to have me on my return from Salem, if I heard of any alarm from the Americans to ride through the adjacent towns east of Concord to see what preparations were making, if any, to let Major Pitcairn know without delay. This I told the general I would undertake; he might rely on my faithfulness in this dangerous undertaking.

Accordingly, on the 18th, the troops were put in readiness; about two o'clock we embarked and crossed over to Charlestown. Here I left the troops, mounted on a country horse prepared for the purpose, with my Yankee dress. I called at Malden on one Mr. Goodridge, delivered him a letter from the British general. I rode from this place to Lynn. Here I called on another tory; delivered my letter.

---

[1] *History of Concord*, 117. Shattuck. Here, however, he is said to have been taken prisoner between Lexington and Concord, in the early morning.

[2] *History of Middlesex County*, II, 583–4. Hurd.

I now proceeded to Marblehead; there I delivered another message. Then I proceeded to Salem, where I arrived about daybreak, making the distance about fifteen miles. Here I refreshed myself and my horse. About sunrise I mounted, returned back to Lynn, where I called for a breakfast. While at breakfast, the thundering news came that the regulars had gone to Concord, and had killed 8 men at Lexington. Such a confusion as the people were in I never heard or saw. They asked me where I had been and where I was going. I told them I was a Bostonian and had been to Salem to notify the people that the regulars we were afraid were going out of there to Concord. They said I had better make my way through Reading and Woburn, also through Billerica to Bedford and Concord, and notify the people that the regulars had gone on, and have themselves in readiness to march to Concord. Now I set out full speed; wherever I saw the people were alarmed, I informed them that the British had come out and gone to Concord, and for their lives and country to fly to arms. Where there was no alarm I made none. When I arrived at Woburn, ten miles from Boston, I found the Militia about on their march for Concord. Here I omitted going to Billerica, it being ten miles further into the country.

I made the best of my way through Bedford to Concord. Here my horse failed me in some measure. Here I overtook crowds of Militia; I told them to drive on. I also told them there had been eight men killed at Lexington by the British. I told them I was afraid the regulars would leave the town of Concord. This kind of alarm I gave the people all the way. I soon arrived at Concord, where I found confusion, sure enough. Here I found the militia pouring in from every quarter. I rode up to Major Pitcairn and informed him that the militia were turning out all the way from Concord to Salem. Major Pitcairn informed me that he must have a reinforcement from Boston, or else he could not get a man back to Charlestown, for they were very sore and fatigued. I was furnished with a fresh horse and set off for Boston and alarmed the people on the road to fly to arms and waylay the regulars from behind fences and walls and anything that would cover them from their fire. No person mistrusted but what I was a faithful American through the whole route."

.. For half an hour Colonel Smith [1] delayed ordering a retreat, in expectation, it is supposed, of relief from Boston in response to his first express; but at length, when well-nigh so late as to be desperate, he began preparations for return. The most pressing need was a sufficiency of horses and other comforts for the wounded. In the attempt to bring off the officers both Reuben Brown and John Beaton had a chaise confiscated. Later while driving Brown's horse in Arlington, Lieutenant Potter was captured, Lieutenant Hull at the same time receiving a second and mortal wound. Potter was afterward brought back to Concord and placed in Brown's charge, being allowed the freedom of the house, with three men continually on guard.[2] Another wounded man was set on Captain Smith's [1] horse, brought forth from Wright's tavern. Captain Smith says it was a large bay horse valued at £13 6s. 8d. The saddle he valued at £3 12s. 0d., and the bridle at 7s. 4d., the surcingle at 6s. 8d., and a pair of plated spurs at 8s. 8d., making a total loss of £18 1s. 4d., the value of aforesaid horse and "Tackle," as several neighbors testify, being "sett at a Low price To the best of their judgement." [3]

Just before leaving town a British guard[4] stationed near Reuben Brown's spied Abel Prescott riding briskly back from giving the alarm to Sudbury. They eyed him suspiciously, causing him to wheel his horse, when they fired and made toward him; but he contrived to reach Mrs. Jonathan Heywood's, where he darted upstairs, and crept into the shade of a cask up garret behind her enormous chimney. As he lay concealed,[1] Prescott heard the redcoats

[1] *Harper's Magazine*, May, 1875.
[2] *History of Concord*, 114, 117. Shattuck.
[3] *Mass. State Archives*, Vol. 182, pp. 299, 300.
[4] *A History of the Fight*, 29. Edition of 1827. Ripley.

grumble, but they failed to find him, smashing the windows in spite as they left. He had been slightly wounded in the arm at the outset, but Mrs. Heywood and her son Abiel, later a famous doctor, dressed it for him after the soldiers had gone on. These same soldiers, Dr. Ripley tells us, saw a party of men running 'cross lots towards a barn and fired on them, but without effect. Luckily for Mrs. Heywood, she had taken the precaution to throw her silver in the well before the British paid their visit.

At Wright's tavern an officer whose finger had been cut used it to stir a glass of brandy, and gave for a parting toast, "So might they stir the cussed Yankee blood before night!" Just as they were off an honest old black woman at Dr. Minot's called after a hurried officer, "Hallo, Sir, You have left your watch." [1] Then they were gone and the people of the town could breathe a little. At some stage of the day Brown's shop [2] had been slightly burned, but compared to what they might have been, the losses were trifling. We have an amusing bill [3] as a token of how some of the damaged property was put to rights.

Richard Devens Esq. and others, Commity of Safety for ye Province of the Massachusetts Bay, N. E.
Dr. to Aaron Hobart, June 20, 1775.
Repairs of two Large Cannon at Conkerd

by agreement for 3.0.0. of Refuc.d Iron 26–8	£4.00
To 20 day Labor 6.	6.00
to Use of forge 1 day & Cole	1.00
to Expencis & Cost at Concerd	2.6.8
to my going 40 miles two times & Expencis to accomodate the affair	2.13.4
A true Account.	£16.0.0.

Colonel Smith in reporting to General Gage expressed his surprise at the general tone of the people of the town.

[1] *History of Concord*, 113. Shattuck.

[2] "Events of April 19th," 27. George Tolman. Concord Antiquarian Society.

[3] *Mass. State Archives*, Vol. 182, p. 122.

He says [1] that they saw "very few inhabitants; those we met with both Major Pitcairn and myself took all possible pains to convince that we meant them no injury, and that if they opened their doors when required to search for Military stores, not the slightest mischief would be done. We had opportunities of convincing them of our good intentions, but they were sulky." Some will think they could scarcely be expected to look gracious! After the British had left the town, it being noon, some of the Militia took refreshment; Rev. Joseph Thaxter [2] for his part taking what might be considered as either breakfast or lunch at the Manse.

And now it is time before the tide of pursuit sets in to take a moment to consider what had just taken place. The Rev. Grindall Reynolds points out that, "The invader was turned back, once for all, never to make another hostile advance on Massachusetts soil, unless the few acres enlargement of his prison house, won by the awful slaughter at Bunker Hill [June 17th], be called an advance. Had the 400 Militia gathered on Ponkawtasset Hill, held aloof, and left the Provincial stores to the mercy of the British troops twenty-four hours, Gage had struck a deadlier blow than if he had slain 500 on the battlefield." Again he says,[3] "Was there not real courage in Col. Barrett, man of mark and position, foremost person of his town and neighborhood, with little to gain and much to lose, who, with his hair already whitening with age, sat there on his horse, and issued a command which was nothing less than flat rebellion, which could never be forgiven, except at the end of a successful civil war." And of Davis the Rev. Mr. Woodbury says,[4] "There never can be but one man who headed the first column of attack on the King's troops in the Revo-

[1] *Mass. His. Soc. Pro.*, May, 1876.

[2] *A History of the Fight at Concord.* Rev. Dr. Ripley.

[3] "The Concord Fight," Rev. Grindall Reynolds. *Unitarian Review.* April, 1875.

[4] *History of Middlesex County*, I, 261. Hurd.

lutionary War." Reynolds [1] has likewise said in Major
Buttrick's honor, that, "within sight and sound of his own
home, he led the advance, and at the right moment gave
the word of command." The Major had three brothers,[2]
Samuel, Joseph, and Daniel, fighting with him at the
bridge. He died 1791, aged sixty; part of his epitaph reads,[3]
"Having laid down the sword with honor, he resumed the
plow with industry; by the latter to maintain what the
former had won." On Colonel Barrett's [4] gravestone it
is said, "he early stepped forward in the Contest with
Britain, and distinguished himself in the cause of America."
Two brass pieces [3] in Doric Hall, at Boston State House,
and two cannon belonging to the Concord Artillery, are
inscribed, "Consecrated to the names of Major Buttrick
and Captain Davis by the Legislature." To the foresight
of a Concord farmer, Ebenezer Hubbard,[5] who started
the fund, we owe the marking of the North bridge by
Daniel French's famous statue of the Minute-man. Completed by the sculptor at the early age of twenty-five, it
was set up on the western bank of the stream on land
presented by Stedman Buttrick,[6] the Major's grandson,
the Centennial year; Emerson's well known lines being
engraved on its base.

> By the rude bridge that arched the flood,
> Their flag to April's breeze unfurled,
> Here once the embattled farmers stood
> And fired the shot heard round the world.

Well has it been said that[2] "few towns can furnish an
Occasion, a Sculptor and a Poet."

It has been proposed by a recent English visitor that
an inscription from James Russell Lowell's "Lines suggested

---

[1] *Unitarian Review*, May, 1875.

[2] *Concord Guide*, 44, 112. Bartlett.

[3] *Harper's Monthly*, May, 1875.

[4] "Graves and Worms and Epitaphs," 21. George Tolman. Published by
the Concord Antiquarian Society.

[5] *Beneath Old Roof Trees*, 133, 137. Brown.

[6] *Proceedings at the Centennial Celebration of Concord Fight*, 17, 12. Concord,
1876. Published by the Town.

by the graves of the two English soldiers on Concord Battleground" might well mark [1] their resting place under the pines by the river's brink.   Such a memorial has much to recommend it, the third verse having especial fitness.[2]

> These men were brave enough and true
>   To the hired soldiers' bull-dog creed;
> What brought them here they never knew,
>   They fought as suits the English breed:
> They came three thousand miles and died
>   To keep the past upon its throne —
> Unheard, beyond the ocean tide,
>   Their English mother made her moan.

A tablet has been set up near the bridge to Jonas Brown,[3] a Concord man, twenty-three years of age, who, notwithstanding a wound in the fleshy part of his shoulder, near the neck, chased the British nine miles.   It seems, his gun having flashed in the pan, he had dropped on his knee to reprime when he was hit at the North bridge.   He tells us however that he kept with his company to Menotomy — West Cambridge — and returned home.   "Captain Buttrick went to Cambridge and several times sent for his Company." Jonas supposes that he went in response "twice or three times," and finally returned on the next day.   He used to tell his sons in after years, "I had hot chocolate for breakfast, cold lead for dinner and sore feet for supper."   Captain Nathan Barrett, also of Concord, was brought home slightly wounded, and Captain Charles Miles was wounded in the hand.   It was this Miles who said earnestly that he "went to the services of that day, with the same seriousness and acknowledgement of God, which he carried to Church." [4] Another Minute-man, Captain Levi Preston,[5] about 1842 told the Hon. Mellen Chamberlain that he fought "because we always had been free, and we meant to be free always."

[1] *Boston Evening Transcript*, April 6, 1909.
[2] *The Poetical Works of James Russell Lowell*, I.   Boston, 1848, 1876, 1890: Houghton, Mifflin and Company.
[3] *Lowell Daily Courier*, April 6, 1875.
[4] *Harper's Monthly*, May, 1875.
[5] *Story of Patriots' Day*, 77.   Geo. J. Varney.

Speaking for himself, Amos Baker [1] of Lincoln said, "I verily believe that I felt better that day, take it all the day through than if I had stayed at home." He was nineteen years old at the time, and his father and four brothers, beside a brother-in-law, Daniel Hosmer, were all in the fight. Nat Baker, one of the brothers, had been courting near the Lexington line when alarmed by Dr. Prescott, and took the news back to his father and brothers. Amos carried his father's old French war musket, and believed he was the only Lincoln man provided with a bayonet. At Flint's Pond, the source of Stony Brook, he loaded near Zach Smith's, with two-ounce balls. During the pursuit he lost all trace of his people and did not know if they lived or died, until reaching Lexington meeting-house that afternoon. Baker says it "was a mercy" they had the affair where they did in Concord, and not with the main body on the Common, for having powder-horns and no cartridge-boxes it would have been "presumptuous." Lieutenant John Barker [2] says in his diary, "Before the whole had quitted the Town we were fired on from Houses and behind Trees, and before we had gone $\frac{1}{2}$ a mile we were fired on from all sides, but mostly from the Rear, where People had hid themselves in houses till we had passed, and then fired." It was this circumstance, coupled with drink, which undoubtedly led to the subsequent plundering on the part of the British.

At noon the retreat had begun in earnest, in the same order as they entered: the Grenadiers and Marines in the road, flanking parties of Light Infantry, more numerous than before, on the Ridge and thrown further out from the main body. [3] These last Hawthorne has pictured as [4] forcing their way through a "dense thicket of birch trees, pitch pines, sumach, and dwarf oaks, scarcely yet beginning to bud into leaf."

[1] *Acton Celebration, 1835*, 20–1.
[2] *Atlantic Monthly*, April, 1877.
[3] *Harper's Monthly*, May, 1875.
[4] *Septimius Felton.* Nathaniel Hawthorne.

Thaddeus Blood,[1] of the Concord Militia, was one of a number who thought it best to go to the east part of the town and take the British as they came back. Each took his own station. "For myself," says he, "I took my stand south of where Dr Minot then lived and saw the British come from Concord, their right flank in the meadows, their left on the hill." By about half-past twelve the British had reached Merriam's Corner,[2] one mile on their road. Hearing the drums the housewife closed fast the door with chairs, but the hungry soldiers pushed in and drew her johnny-cake from the brick oven, while two of them went away to the barn looking for milk. The girls had meanwhile run across the road and crouched down amongst the quince bushes. There was a universal dread of fire that day and some of the household hastily removed thirty silver dollars from the cellar ash-pit. But the Billerica men drawing near, started the soldiers on in a hurry. With a readiness born of the hour, "slow Merriam" as he was called, one of the sons, took careful aim at an officer, remarking as he fired, "He has more stripes than any!" The lad had never been known to be first in anything before, but this shot was probably sped with sufficient promptitude to be effectual, as here Ensign Lester [3] of the 10th Regiment and several more officers were wounded. As they left, the British turned to fire back one more volley, a shot entering the east door. The hole it gouged has been filled in, but still shows.[2] Planted in the stone wall by the wayside one reads the inscription:

The British troops
retreating from the
Old North Bridge
were here attacked in flank
by the men of Concord
and neighboring towns
and driven under a hot fire
to Charlestown.

[1] *Boston Daily Advertiser*, April 20, 1886.
[2] *Old Concord*, 47, 48, 51. Sidney.
[3] *History of Sudbury*, 380. Hudson.

The Patriots from the North bridge had made a sweep across the northern Great Meadows and headed the British off in the upper flank.[1] They were helped in this by the men arriving at that instant from the Bedford road. Amos Barrett[2] says: "After awhile we found them amarching back towards Boston. We was soon after them. When they got about a mile and a half to a road that comes from Bedford and Billerica, they was waylaid and a great many killed. When I got there, a great many lay dead, and the road was bloody." Major John Brooks and the Reading Companies under Captain Bachelder, besides the Billerica men under Colonel William Thompson and a company from East Sudbury, probably Captain Joseph Smith's,[3] are all said to have been in season for a brush at this point.

The British flank[4] of about eighty to one hundred men came slow and steady, in silence, down the slope and, passing a little bridge near the corner by the Merriams', faced suddenly back and fired, over-shooting. The Americans were about twenty rods distant, and at their fire two of the Regulars were killed and several officers, as already stated, wounded. Of those that fell a little seven year old Merriam[5] boy remembered one was buried on the roadside near the well, opposite the school-house, and the other in the bank behind Deacon Mason's house. Here, Rev. Mr. Foster,[6] speaking for the Reading men, tells us, they "saw a wood at a distance which appeared to lie on or near the road where the enemy must pass. Many leaped over the walls and made for that wood. We arrived just in time to meet the enemy. There was on the opposite side of the road a young growth of wood filled with Americans. The enemy were now completely between two fires, renewed and briskly kept up. They ordered out a flank guard on the left to

[1] *History of Concord.* Shattuck
[2] *Journal and Letters of Rev. Henry True,* etc.
[3] *History of Sudbury,* 380. Hudson.
[4] *Harper's Magazine,* May, 1875.
[5] *Boston Morning Journal,* April 19, 1875.
[6] *History of Lexington,* 194–5. Charles Hudson. Boston, 1868.

dislodge the Americans from their posts behind the trees; but they only became better marks to be shot at." Lieutenant Barker [1] felt that the lay of the land was against the troops. "The country was an amazing strong one," he writes, "full of Hills, Woods, stone walls &c, which the Rebels did not fail to take advantage of, for they were all lined with People who kept an incessant fire upon us, as we did too upon them." The Lincoln men had the additional advantage that they were fighting in their own town, many of them on their own farms, where every feature was familiar.[2] Billerica heard about two in the morning through Woburn, that the country was rising. Among the first to get the news were the Ditsons, who naturally were keen to redress the tar and feathering of March 8th. Captain Jonathan Stickney led fifty-four men, Captain Edward Farmer thirty-five Militia, and Lieutenant Oliver Crosby twelve. Joseph Jaquith [2] did not belong to a company, but when he heard during the morning what was up, he left off ploughing in the Old Field behind the house, unhitched the oxen, took his gun from the wall over the door in "Aunt Abigal's room" and saying, "The redcoats are coming" went out to meet them. The Billerica men marched by way of Bedford, stopping to rest under the old oak near Fitch's tavern with the men from Reading. At Merriam's Corner they met the Regulars and kept on in pursuit; returning at last, their guns "slung over their shoulders," we are told, "in an easy-going manner." The death of Reuben Bacon of this town has been laid to fatigue undergone at this time. At Reading Dr. John Brooks,[3] afterwards General and Governor, was Captain of the Minute Company. He had been in the habit of watching the British at their drill in Boston and then repeating the manœuvres with his men in the parsonage kitchen of an

[1] *Atlantic Monthly*, April, 1877.
[2] *Beneath Old Roof Trees*, 224, quoting Mr. William F. Wheeler, 239, 245, 240, 246, 177. Brown.
[3] *History of Middlesex County*, II, 277. Drake.

evening. Until 1879 marks made in the ceiling by their guns were still to be seen. A claim was made as early as 1825 that this company was the first to drill. The day before the battle Dr. Brooks was in Boston and gathered that the troops were on the eve of moving. On his return to Reading he stopped at a patient's in the Hartshorn house, Pratt Row, now Haverhill Street, and by means of this visit and other calls supposed to be professional,[1] he was able quietly to pass the news on to one and another of his men. By this means many collected the latter part of the night at Weston's Corner in Wood End, under command of Lieutenant James Bancroft, and marched via Bedford. When the alarm first ran about Reading, the Rev. Edmund Foster,[2] then a divinity student, twenty-three years of age, hurried to Captain Brooks and asked, "Are you going to Concord and when?" The reply was "Immediately." Hastily borrowing a gun the young student went with him.

About eight A.M. the Wakefield [3] trainband of the First Parish was summoned and set out early, accompanied by the Rev. Caleb Prentiss, engaging, with the men of the Third Parish, at Merriam's Corner. The interest shown by the clergy was very real. Some are even said to have distributed the town ammunition from chaises to their parishioners in the field.[4] Noah Eaton's son Reuben, a good hunter, did not get off with the body of the Wakefield men, but waited to clean his gun, put in a new flint, and fill his bullet pouch as if to hunt ducks or deer.[3] At the Corner he caught up with the others and kept ahead of the British column, firing from cover. "Oh, it was glorious picking!" he said of it. Lingering on for another shot, he was once all but captured by the flank guard, having to run for dear life. Twice he threw himself flat and escaped. "See that Yankee," the British exclaimed, "we have killed him twice

---

[1] *History of Reading*, 700–1. Hon. Lilley Eaton. Boston, 1874: Alfred Mudge & Son.

[2] *Harper's Magazine*, May, 1875.

[3] *History of Middlesex County*, II, 726. Hurd.

[4] *Historic Mansions*, 369. Drake.

and he can run yet!"   The Rev. Isaac Morrill [1] of Wilmington is especially notable among the parsons who turned out. He had seized his gun and ridden off eagerly, and presently while resting a moment at his "Brother" Penniman's in Bedford, he could not forbear exclaiming, "Why are you here on such a Day!" "Oh, "pleaded Parson Penniman, "I can't go." "Yes you can. Seize your gun. Ride on with me!" "Oh, I can't," he protested, much to Morrill's chagrin. "You go and fight. I will stay and pray." Shortly after, it is interesting to note that the Rev. Joseph Penniman [2] prayed thus gently, "We beseech Thee to send the British soldiers where they will do some good; for Thou knowest, O Lord, that we have no use for them about here."

Captain Weston [3] of Reading was working on the site of the Lynnfield Hotel when alarmed by a rider. His house was the last in Reading, near Stoneham. Getting his gun he joined Thomas Sweetzer, who lived just over the line. They were firing from behind a rock near a wall when Sweetzer saw the flank guard, and warned his mate. Weston had his ammunition in his hat before him, and was too absorbed to heed what was said until he had been warned by Captain Nathan Parker as well, when all three sought cover in the woods near by.

In recalling the nineteenth, one Bedford [4] woman used to say that "all day long bells were ringing, men dashing back and forth on horseback, and all I could learn was that there had been an awful fight and numbers killed. I thought certain my husband must be one of them." Mr. William Parker [3] lived on a height in South Reading and always maintained that he heard the first volley. A Reading woman, Jerusha Emerson, later Mrs. Nat Cowdrey, [5] was busy frying doughnuts that morning. As the roads filled with men hurrying by to the fight she ran out time

[1] *Bedford Sesqui-Centennial Celebration*, 26.   Jonathan Stearns, D.D.
[2] *History of Concord*, 268.   Shattuck.
[3] *History of Reading*, 702–3, 704.   Eaton.
[4] *History of Middlesex County*, I, 245.   Drake.
[5] *American Monthly Magazine*, April, 1894.

and again with an apronful, much to the hungry fellows' content. Tewksbury sent two Militia companies. Captain Jonathan Brown led the Southeast and Lieutenant Thomas Clark the second.[1] Captain John Trull, who commanded the thirty-three Minute-men there, lived in the northerly part of the town, by the Merrimack, on a farm still owned in 1879 by descendants. About two A.M. his little eight year old son, sleeping in a trundle bed,[2] was roused by a rider shouting, "Captain Trull! The British are on their way to Concord, and I have alarmed all the towns from Charlestown to here." His father leaped from bed, lifted his gun from the peg where it hung, and fired an alarm from the window. Captain Varnum in Dracut, across the river, gave an answering shot; the men armed at the Centre and started on their fifteen mile march to Concord. They too are supposed to have joined in the fight at Merriam's Corner. In after years Captain Trull used to remark playfully that the Regulars "ran well" under fire. He kept warning his eager men to "Stand trim, boys, or the rascals will shoot your elbows off." Captain Moses Parker[1] led forty-three men and Captain Oliver Barron led sixty-one from Chelmsford. A boulder had been agreed on here as a rallying place. Sergeant John Ford[3] of East Chelmsford, now Lowell, was working at his saw mill when the alarm came. He hurried back to his little one-story home, ate a bowl of bread and milk standing by the window, and rode off to join Barron's Company. Young Oliver Richardson,[3] who lived two miles north of the Centre and was only sixteen, went with the rest. Parson Bridge[3] was on hand and wished to pray with the company before it left, but Sergeant Ford declared that they had more important business to take care of; and they were quickly on the road, coming up with the British at Merriam's Corner. The story is told of a young man, not enrolled,

---

[1] *History of Middlesex County*, III, 294; II, 257. Hurd.

[2] *History of Middlesex County*, II, 376. Drake.

[3] *Beside Old Hearth-Stones*, 267, 288, 250. Brown.

who begged to take the place of his more elderly employer. Given leave, he ran along beside Sergeant Ford's horse holding by the stirrup-strap.[1]

During the pursuit, Ford and an Andover man, named Charles Furbush,[2] are said to have been fired on by a British officer who was plundering in a house. They ran in and killed him. They were both French war veterans, but said the day was full of horror to them; the Patriots seemed maddened and beside themselves. Once they came on a poor fallen Grenadier whose blood was flowing from many holes in his waistcoat. As veterans they had fought beside the Regulars in the past, and they did not hesitate to raise gently the dying man, and give him the water he craved. That evening Parson Bridge[3] wrote in his diary: "The Civil war was begun at Concord this morning! Lord direct all things for his glory, the good of his church and people, and the preservation of the British Colonies, and to the shame and confusion of our oppressors. . . . [The] Lord only knows what will be the issue but I will hope in His mercy and wait to see His salvation." On the south side of Hardy's Hill, a short distance beyond Merriam's Corner, Captain Cudworth's[4] Sudbury men and the forementioned Colonel John Ford of Chelmsford made a spirited attack. Ford had been a Ranger in the French wars, and is said to have killed five soldiers during the day with his own hand. This, Parson Gordon of Roxbury says, "can be fully proved."[5] He also states that Oliver Barron and Deacon Davis of the same town "distinguished themselves" in the course of the day. There are 348 names recorded as serving from Sudbury.[6] Captain Aaron Haynes led the

---

[1] *Chelmsford proceedings at the Celebration of the 250th Anniversary of the Incorporation of the Town.* 1905. Report of the Committee, 51.

[2] *Historical Sketches of Andover,* 307–8. Sarah Loring Bailey. Boston, 1880: Houghton, Mifflin and Company.

[3] *Beside Old Hearth-Stones,* 253. Brown.

[4] *Harper's Magazine,* May, 1875.

[5] *American Revolution,* 485. Gordon.

[6] *History of Middlesex County,* II, 400. Hurd.

North Company of Militia from the West side, sixty men; Captain Joseph Smith led the East Company, seventy-five men, and Captain Moses Stone the South or Lanham Company of ninety-two from both sides of the river. Of the Minute-men, Captain John Nixon led the West side company, fifty-four men, Captain Natl. Cudworth the East side, forty, and Captain Isaac Loker (or Lover or Lake) twenty-one mounted troopers from both sides. The Old Men's Alarm Company was commanded by Captain Jabez Puffer. The East side companies went from the present Wayland. Captain Nixon had been at Louisburg in 1745, when only twenty years of age, and saw seven years in the army, first and last, dying at the age of ninety in Middlebury, Vermont.

Near Benjamin Tavern,[1] an unarmed man riding up, had his horse shot under him. North of the school-house was a tavern later called Brooks'. It had a sign [2] with the figure of an Indian on one side and King George on the other; the last being altered over into General George Washington in the course of the war that followed. From the foot of Hardy's Hill, the first considerable rise on the return route, so far as the tanyard near the foot of the next hill, the road formed the boundary between Lincoln and Concord. Eastward from the tanyard the road ascends and bends north, running all the while in a deep cut between high wooded banks. From a house at this point Major Loammi Baldwin [3] of Woburn saw some of his command and others running off the east end of the hill, and the Regulars following. A sharp fight ensued. Under cover of the trees and at Lincoln bridge, crossing Tanner brook, the Patriots galled the Regulars on both sides, raking them front and rear. A flanking party on the left tried to dislodge them and there was a fresh tussle. Two British were killed in the defile, and within a half mile from the brow of the hill, near

---

[1] *A History of the Fight at Concord*, 34. Rev. Dr. Ripley.

[2] *Harper's Magazine*, May, 1875.

[3] *History of Middlesex County*, I, 447. Hurd.

Jonas Mason's house, six or eight British and three Americans fell. A Regular wrote[1] home respecting the Yankees, "they fought like bears, and I would as soon storm hell as fight them again." At Hartwell's tavern,[2] a little beyond, two soldiers spied one of the old tavernkeepers at a window in the L and asked for a drink of water. The men were told to help themselves and made their way to the well, thanking him. A bit beyond another Grenadier fell on the green grass, beside a pair of pasture bars. When the "panting column" reached Samuel Hartwell's house, a detail was ordered to burn it, as the Tories had a spite against him for the service he had rendered to the Patriot cause as a gunsmith. However the soldiers were too closely pressed to carry out their purpose, and only succeeded in sending a few random shots into the garret and riddling a few window-panes. One of the Regulars thrust a damaged gun into a window and hurried on. Hartwell finding it there on his return home put it in repair and carried it for years when off hunting. His wife told her grandson, Mr. Samuel Hartwell of Lincoln, that after the British had gone past in the morning she had seen an occasional horseman dash by, but nothing very special happened until the afternoon, when she heard the musket shots at Brooks' tavern; then the troops stormed past in confusion, full of threats. "Oh, how glad I was," she used to say,[3] "when they all got by the house and your grandfather and our folks got home alive." She could not sleep that night, however, notwithstanding her relief, for thinking of the British soldiers lying dead down by the roadside. Next day the neighbors gathered the bodies in an ox-cart and Mrs. Hartwell and her children saw them buried, coffinless, in a trench in the burial yard back of Flint's. There was one amongst them, supposed to be that of an officer, which had lain near the brow of the hill just back of here, all through the "long hot afternoon

---

[1] *History of Middlesex County*, II, 623, 619, 830. Hurd.
[2] *Boston Evening Transcript*, April 18, 1900.
[3] *Beneath Old Roof Trees*, 221, 226. Brown.

in the dust, his head pillowed on the broad black [silk] ribbons [knotting] his cue, his ruffled shirt gleaming in the sunlight." [1]

Near Captain Wm. Smith's [1] another Grenadier fell mortally wounded, and was left by the wayside. He was found by the Lincoln men when gathering up the British dead and carried to the captain's house, where he lingered three or four days in great distress, imploring his attendants to end his sufferings. When he felt himself going he told a maid who had cared for him to look in his coat-lining and keep a gold sovereign she would find there. It was not forthcoming at first, but he stuck to it that it was there, and after his death Mrs. Smith succeeded in finding it. This poor fellow was buried in a field a little west of Folly Pond. A little beyond the Pond and the sharp bend northward, where Revere was taken, lie two fields on the north side of the road. The first,[1] "meadowy and ridged with long mounds and trenches," covered with coarse tufts of grass; the second, full of stones and boulders. A Lincoln man was busily firing on the King's troops from the first field here, when he was unexpectedly hemmed in between the main body of redcoats and the flank guard. Quick as thought he dropped down into one of the trenches and escaped their fire, thanks to the British practice of shooting breast-high, without taking careful aim. When the flank had gone on he took to his heels and gained the next field. Here he had cover from a large boulder which also served as a gun-rest, and fired several shots after the Regulars. Another Lincoln man named Childs [1] was caught the same way in a cross fire. The flank guard at this time were kept so near the main column that the British began to suffer from their own shots, and in the pause that followed, Childs ran along to the end of the lines. Once outside, he again became a target, but by dint of running, dropping to the ground, and making a fresh dash, he too gained the shelter of a rock, as he afterwards used to say, "verily holding his breath in

[1] *Boston Evening Transcript*, April 18, 1900.

his hands!" Across the road from the neighboring Nelson house [1] several British soldiers are buried in an orchard. The last house in Lincoln was the home of Samuel Hastings,[1] serving with the Lexington Company. A redcoat, who had been inside plundering, was mortally wounded as he came out by the front door here and was found lying across the step by the family on their return. Despite every care he died, when they discovered in his pocket one of their silver spoons! He was buried in the yard west of the house. Captain Nathan Cory [2] of Groton long kept an old powderhorn which he took from a redcoat lying by the roadside in Lincoln. It held just one pound and had a spring charger at the tip; at the large end, on its under side as it hung over the shoulder, was engraved the British Arms, on its upper side, the British Ensign. The small end of the horn was tipped with a saucer-shaped rim of brass perforated by a hole half an inch in diameter for convenience in filling, and the whole secured by a wooden stopper. The Regular's boots and clothes were stripped off by some others at the same time.

One redcoat was left midway in Lincoln Plain, another, we learn from Susanna Parker,[3] was found near their front gate. Altogether there are eleven British graves in Lincoln. Of these, five are in the old burying ground, three beside the road, and two in a field near Lexington line.[4]

February 10th, 1777, David Park [5] of Lincoln presented an order to Henry Gardner, treasurer of the Colony, for £2 16s. 9d. due for losses sustained April 19th. The nearer Concord families joined the Farrar [2] womenfolk in "Oaky Bottom" Wood, Lincoln, about half a mile behind the Farrar homestead. Captain Farrar's wife had loosed the cattle so that they need not perish in flames if the buildings were fired, and then bade the house farewell as she lugged

---

[1] *Boston Globe*, April 19, 1902.

[2] *Beneath Old Roof Trees*, 297, 222–4.   Brown.

[3] *Life of Amos A. Lawrence*, 1.   William Lawrence.

[4] *History of Middlesex County*, II, 619.   Hurd.

[5] *Mass. State Archives*, Vol. 139, p. 323.

off for safety baby Samuel, the great Bible, a loaf, and a looking-glass, besides all the silver. From time to time one or another crept up the hill to see if flames had broken out, rejoicing to find the house still safe and sound. The baby lived to be a trustee of Andover Seminary and died at ninety or more. The old Bible is said to be yet in the homestead, under glass. Samuel Farrar [1] did not, however, come off entirely unscathed, since it is on record that he applied February, 1777, to Henry Gardner, treasurer of the Colony, requesting that the compensation of £2 16s. 10d. allowed him, be paid through Colonel Brooks. Earlier in the day, Deacon Farrar,[2] a Lincoln man, had walked to Concord, three miles, and being old, gone into a house and sat down to rest. A British soldier looking in and seeing him armed cried, "What are you after, you old rebel?" "Come to fight," was the reply, upon which the soldier caught up the old man's gun and fired it into the air at the open door, cut the string of his powder-horn, scattered the powder, and made off.

Past noon, close by Cornet Ephraim Hartwell's house and barn, the Americans had lost three men — Captain Jonathan Wilson of Bedford in his forty-first year, Nathaniel Wyman of Billerica, and Daniel Thompson of Woburn, aged forty. The alarm had reached Woburn between two and three A.M. and the men marched before sunrise. Daniel Thompson [3] at that time had ridden bareback a mile to the north village to rouse his friends. But one man had hesitated, asking Thompson if he were not hasty and likely to run into danger, who answered, "No! I tell you our tyrants are on their march to destroy our stores, and if no one else opposes them, *I will!*" His brothers, Squire Samuel Thompson and Abijah, went with him. They had both taken part in the French and Indian War in 1758;

[1] *Mass. State Archives*, Vol. 139, p. 323.

[2] *Diary of C. C. Baldwin*, 287.

[3] *Memorial of James Thompson, of Charlestown, Mass., 1630–1642, and of Woburn, Mass., 1642–1682; and of Eight Generations of his Descendants.* Rev. Leander Thompson. Boston, 1887: press of L. Barta & Co.

the Squire, then but twenty-seven years old, serving as a lieutenant at Lake George. At Concord the Woburn men watched the enemies' motions, and some fired on the redcoats from the Bedford road at Merriam's Corner. The Squire said, at Tanner's brook in particular the Woburn men "greatly annoyed" the British. There were three times as many Regulars as Patriots, but the Yankees were so posted as to have the advantage. "The narrow road was filled with soldiers who stooped for shelter from the stone walls as they ran by the ambush." He himself shot at them some ten times at a distance of only ten rods, and thought that he killed or wounded several; after they had gone on the Squire found three or four lying where he had fired and took a gun and some small plunder, and then overtook the pursuit to fire once more. He said his brother Daniel "behaved very valiantly."

Daniel Thompson had posted himself just where a corner of Lincoln comes into the Lexington road behind the corner of the Hartwell barn, as there he had a chance to aim diagonally through the British ranks. A Regular, noticing his marksmanship, ran around the barn and shot him dead in the back, as he was reloading. This redcoat was killed a moment later by a Woburn bullet, always supposed [1] to have been fired by Thompson's brother. Daniel's body was carried back to his home on Central Street in Woburn — the house still standing, although altered. His brother broke the news to his widow and three children, Isaac Snow, fourteen years, Phœbe, thirteen, and Daniel, Jr., ten years of age. The oldest, Isaac, immediately went raving-distracted and remained in this state a number of days. He had been delicate from his birth, but had plenty of nervous energy, and the year following his father's death shipped in a privateer. Being captured by a British cruiser and imprisoned at the Barbadoes, he made his escape by a three mile swim to a French vessel. Abijah Thompson had then two children, Rhoda, twelve years of age, and Abijah, Jr., aged

---

[1] *Beneath Old Roof Trees*, 315. Brown.

seven. Squire Thompson had a lad, Jonathan, who was fifteen the following week. This boy determined to follow his father and uncles to battle. He had on hand a small quantity of powder, and now borrowing a musket, secretly took the leaden scale weights and ran them into bullets at a neighbor's shop. Once armed he hurried to Concord, arriving just as the retreat was begun. Jonathan noticed how the men headed the column off and peppered its whole length, and did the same. In one of these circuits, to their mutual surprise he and his father met. "Why, Jonathan, are *you* here!" the Squire exclaimed. "Well, take care of yourself. Your Uncle Daniel has been killed. Be prudent, my son, and take care of yourself." Then each parted for the pursuit.[1] Squire Thompson turned back at Lexington, being much fatigued, but Jonathan kept it up about thirteen miles, until having crossed from Arlington into Medford, he slept that night in a barn, dog-tired, and reached home early the next day. On Friday,[2] April 21st, the remains of Asahel Porter, killed early at Lexington, and of Daniel Thompson, who fell at noon in Lincoln, were "decently interred at Woburn, attended to the grave by a multitude of persons, who assembled on the occasion from that and the neighboring towns." Before the burial a "very suitable sermon and prayer was delivered by the Rev. Mr Sherman." Daniel Thompson's epitaph runs as follows:

> Here Passenger, confined, Reduced to dust,
> Lies what was once Religious, wise and just,
> The Cause he engaged did animate him high,
> Namely, — Religion and dear Liberty,
> Steady and warm in Libertie's defence.
> True to his Country, Loyal to His Prince,
> Though in his Breast a Thirst for glory fir'd.
> Although he's gone his name Embalmed shall be
> And had in Everlasting memory.

George Reed,[3] also of Woburn, in answer to his petition of December received a grant of £8 9s. 0d. in compensation

---

[1] *Thompson Memorial.*
[2] *Beneath Old Roof Trees*, 317–18. Brown.
[3] *American Archives*, IV, 4th ser., 1225. Force.

for his loss of three months' time in nursing and doctoring, while suffering from a ball in his side which prevented his caring for his family.

As we have seen, Captain Jonathan Wilson of Bedford was killed near Brooks' tavern; Lieutenant Edward Stearns succeeding him in command. Job Lane of the same town was badly wounded here. Some of the company helped Lane home, returning with loads of provisions for the others. In January, 1779, it was voted to [1] "abate half of Job Lane's war rates in consideration of his wounds;" the next year, it was further voted, to "abate his poll rate for every year since the war began." Two Billerica men, John Nickles [2] and Timothy Blanchard, were also wounded in Lincoln. In 1879 there was still shown a silver buckle given to Edward Flint [3] of Bedford by a wounded British drummer to whom he had shown kindness. Another wounded Regular gave a ring, still existing, to an American who had come to his aid. Cornet Nathaniel Page [4] was a very tall man, and helped capture several prisoners. Lieutenant Asa Spalding [5] of Billerica, having killed a Regular in the act of taking aim at him from behind a tree, carried a second home as prisoner. An idiot pauper, [6] boarded out in the Spalding household, was so incensed by the sight of this "specimen of a redcoat," he attacked him axe in hand, happily without effect.

Sudbury met with some losses that day: Isaac Reed's son Asahel, [1] who is said to have been bold even to rashness, was brought home dead; the family was well known, having been settled in the town since 1656. Thomas Plympton, [7] Esq., had a bullet through his coat, and Lieutenant Elisha

---

[1] *History of Middlesex County*, II, 833, 401. Hurd.

[2] *History of Billerica*, 236. Rev. Henry A. Hazen. Boston, 1883: A. Williams and Co.

[3] *Bedford Sesqui-Centennial Celebration*, 67. Rev. Dr. Stearns.

[4] *Beneath Old Roof Trees*, 169, 187. Brown.

[5] *Billerica Centennial Oration*, 20. Rev. Elias Nason. Lowell, 1876: Marden and Rowell.

[6] *Celebration of the Two Hundredth Anniversary of the Incorporation of Billerica*, 140. Lowell, 1855.

[7] *History of Sudbury*, 382. Hudson.

Wheeler[1] had a horse shot under him. They were both volunteers. Another old man, Thomas Bent[2] of East Sudbury, rode over to do what he could. He was wounded by a bullet in the leg so severely, he soon afterwards died. Riding slowly homewards he met on the road a young son, in his teens, with three of his brothers hurrying to bear a hand. Instead of holding the boy back to help him home, old Mr. Bent urged the lad to make haste forward and went on alone. John Wadsworth,[3] member of one of the Minute Companies, in spite of being ill, turned out, but was unable to proceed, and died within a year.

There was a private, Joshua Haynes, with Nixon, and a sergeant of that name with Captain Haynes. One of these two, styling himself Joshua Haynes, Jr.,[1] was so wounded as to be "unable to labor until the 20th of July following." Joshua Haynes[4] of the same neighborhood had a narrow escape. He was alone behind a stone wall when a squad of Regulars following the main body appeared to be marching right on him; he kept still and presently they wheeled at the curve of the road, following their mates. Then, resting his gun on the wall, Haynes fired and their sergeant fell. Running up he seized the sergeant's gun and tried to tear off his belt and cartridge-box, but the squad were only a few rods off and turned back to fire, so that he was glad to make good his escape. Old Deacon Josiah Haynes, eighty years old, had followed the British on from the South bridge, and at some time during the day, when within musket shot, drew up his gun and let drive among them. While reloading, the British turned and fired, literally shooting him to pieces as he received no less than fourteen wounds in his body.[5] One of the New Englanders said,[4] "I was

[1] American Archives, IV, 4th ser., 1388, 1352. Force.
[2] The Wayside Inn, Its History and Literature. An Address Delivered before the Society of Colonial Wars, 16–17. Samuel Arthur Bent. Boston, 1897.
[3] Bi-Centennial Celebration at Sudbury, 41. Published 1876 by the Trustees of the Goodnow Library.
[4] History of Sudbury, 381, 364–5. A. S. Hudson.
[5] Diary of C. C. Baldwin, 286.

Running across a Lot where there was a bend in the Road in order to get a Fair Shot, at the Enemy, in company with a Scotchman who was in Braddock's Defeat nineteen years Before. After we had Discharged our Guns I observed to the Scot who appeared very Composed I wished I felt as Calm as he appeared to be — He said its a Tread to be Larnt."

Another town actively engaged in Lincoln was Framingham. The alarm reached there before eight A.M. The bell was rung, guns fired, and in about an hour the men were off. The Centre and North Companies got away first; the South and West ones followed quickly. Captain Simon Edgell led seventy-five men; he had been in the Indian wars and went on foot with his gun all the way. Daniel Hemenway, who was wounded, belonged in this company. Captain Micajah Gleason, also a veteran, led forty-eight men, and Captain Jesse Eames led twenty-three. Left behind, unreasoning panic seized the women and children of the Edgell and Belknap district. A lingering memory of the Indian scares sent a rumor flying from one to another, "the Negros are coming to massacre us all!" and Mrs. Edgell and the others in great trepidation, after laying in an armory of pitchforks, axes, and clubs, bolted their doors.[1] The parson here, Rev. Samuel Haven,[2] was of a different fibre and ran bullets nearly all the following night.

Of the men who engaged, Ezekiel How and Benjamin Berry ran afoot the whole way to Concord, about twelve miles in two hours. How came right on a weltering redcoat the first thing and was so shocked he almost fainted. He said, "they pushed me along, and a few hours afterward I could see men dying with as much indifference as if sheep."[3] Near Merriam's Corner, Ebenezer Hemenway, of Captain Gleason's company, shot a British soldier named Thomas Sowers, and kept his gun. On the borders of Lexington, Noah Eaton, 2d,[1] one of two brothers in the fight, of Captain

[1] *History of Framingham*, 277–9, 275, 276–7. Temple.
[2] *Rambles about Portsmouth*, 321. Brewster.
[3] *History of Framingham*, 93. William Barry. Boston, 1847.

Edgell's company, having fired on the redcoats, squatted behind a knoll to reload. Just then a Regular came up on the other side for the same purpose. With ready wit Eaton raised his gun and took aim, demanding he should surrender. The redcoat laid his musket down in assent, and only then discovered that Eaton's piece was likewise unloaded. If he had suspected the truth, having cartridges, he might easily have turned the tables. Next day Eaton took the man back with him to Framingham, where he remained in his service. Just over the line,[1] on a hillside lying north of the road, in digging out an obstructing boulder a farmer lately uncovered, four feet below the surface, the rusted remnants of a sword and scabbard belonging to some hastily buried Regular.

Within the Lexington limits, near the boundary, stood the Bull Tavern, which is said to have been invaded and ransacked while some of the Regulars' wounds were being dressed.[2] It was kept by Daniel Child until 1820, when Joel Viles bought it and it acquired his name. In 1850, it was burned. An interesting photograph of this tavern was exhibited in 1897 through the Dorothy Q. Chapter D. R. by Mrs. Clinton Viles. Here Smith and Pitcairn had hoped to check the retreat long enough for the men at least to pull themselves together. For this purpose a detail was left behind near a bluff to hold the pursuit back, while the main body tried to form half a mile ahead in a woody defile. The tussle at this point is commemorated by the following inscription:

THIS BLUFF WAS USED AS A RALLYING
POINT BY THE BRITISH

APRIL 19 1775

AFTER A SHARP FIGHT THEY RETREATED TO
FISKE HILL FROM WHICH THEY WERE
DRIVEN IN GREAT CONFUSION

It seems, without their knowledge, a party of Provincials had already made their way through the woods, and were posted [3] close by the road behind some split rails, almost

---

[1] *Boston Globe*, April 20, 1902.

[2] *Boston Morning Journal*, April 19, 1875.

[3] *Lexington Hand Book*, 28.

opposite the point where the British were attempting to
rally. Consequently before anything could be effected the
British rear had been driven in and the confusion was
greater than ever. Pitcairn had been noticed by the Rev.
Edmund Foster "mounted on an elegant horse," [1] with a
drawn sword in hand, riding backward and forward, commanding and urging the troops with the view of restoring
order, when suddenly a shot hit him in the arm, breaking
it. He had pushed forward eagerly and, disabled by the
wound, could not control his horse, which plunged over the
piled wood [2] and threw him. The horse then leaped the wall
and made toward the Yankees, by whom it was captured
running in the fields, still carrying holster and pistols
attached to the saddle. The pistols were subsequently
sold at auction in Concord, and bought by Captain Nathan
Barrett,[3] who afterwards gave them to General Israel
Putnam, who carried them through the war. They were
placed, it is said, on the General's coffin when he died and
after passing through several hands, now rest in the Cary
Library, Lexington. In 1827 they were identified by Colonel
Munroe of Parker's company as having been used in the
initial shot. At this time Lieutenant Colonel Smith himself
received a wound in the leg, and a number of other officers
were disabled. Five wounded British were taken into the
red house of Benjamin Fiske [2] and in a corner of the field
opposite this house a number lie buried. In the yard of
the Fiske house may be seen a tablet inscribed as follows:

AT THIS WELL APRIL 19 1775

JAMES HAYWARD OF ACTON

MET A BRITISH SOLDIER WHO RAISING HIS GUN
SAID YOU ARE A DEAD MAN
AND SO ARE YOU REPLIED HAYWARD
BOTH FIRED   THE SOLDIER WAS INSTANTLY
KILLED AND HAYWARD MORTALLY
WOUNDED

[1] *Historic Pilgrimages in New England*, 385.   Edwin M. Bacon.
[2] "Wayside Happenings in 1775."   Rev. Edward G. Porter.
[3] *Harper's Monthly*, May, 1875.

Thomas Emerson,[1] an eighteen year old lad from Wake-field, it would seem was on the spot and saw the encounter. James Hayward was the son of Captain Samuel and Mary Hayward. He[2] was twenty-five years and four days old. He had been a schoolmaster, and was exempt from service through the loss of several toes on one foot by the cut of an axe. Despite this he was one of the first at Captain Davis's. Before leaving he had gone to the grindstone, saying, "I hope to have a push at them before night and want my bayonet *sharp*." Deacon Hunt's daughter Molly in after years used to tell [1] of having looked from the window that day and seen Hayward "walking along as fast as he could, with his gun in his hand. He seemed to be in a great hurry." Foremost throughout the morning in pursuit, he was going to the Fiske's well for some water when he was seen from the window by a plundering redcoat who stepped to the door to cut him off as he passed the corner of the house.[3] The soldier had pilfered jewelry from Mrs. Fiske's bureau drawers, and some pieces dropped from his knapsack into the pig's trough, which, when recovered, bore traces of the pig's teeth.[4] The Regular was killed at the first fire, but splinters from his powder-horn were driven into Hayward's body and he lingered eight hours in great torture. His mind was clear to the last and he told his father,[3] Samuel Hayward (Deacon,[2] the following September), that he was happy to die in defence of his rights. It[1] had been the greatest morning's work he had ever done and he was not sorry he had turned out. He sent his love to his mother and to one "dearer than his mother." His powder-horn[5] is preserved in Acton; out of a pound of powder but a few grains remained, and of the forty bullets with which he started only two or three were left. His epitaph runs:[6]

[1] *History of Middlesex County*, II, 726; I, 257, 271, 257. Hurd.
[2] *Acton Celebration, 1835*, 43, 8. Josiah Adams.
[3] *Lexington Address, 1835*, 62. Edward Everett.
[4] "Wayside Happenings in 1775." Rev. Edward G. Porter.
[5] *Lexington Hand Book*, 34.
[6] *Beneath Old Roof Trees*, 167. Brown.

This monument may unborn ages tell
How brave young Hayward like a hero fell,
When fighting for his countries liberty
Was slain, and here his body now doth lye,
He and his foe were by each other slain,
His victim's blood with his ye earth did stain;
Upon ye field he was with victory crowned,
And yet must yield his breath upon that ground.
He expressed his hope in God before his death,
After his foe had yielded up his breath.
O, may his death a lasting witness lye,
Against Oppressors' bloody cruelty.

The house from which he went still stands in West Acton. Mr. Benjamin Fiske's [1] losses include a "sash window, 4 fine Holland shirts, a black silk apron, a gold ring, one stone earing and pair of sleeve buttons, a black gause handkerchief, a Barcelona handkerchief, 6 shillings in cash and sundries." Forty Mexican dollars and a string of gold beads are also said to have been taken.[2]

Just beyond the bluff there is a fork in the road; the older way was to the left here down the steepest grade, and it was this which the British followed. Near the line Captain Parker [3] and his men met the British and fired briskly from woods on the south side of the road, and from the opposite hillside. Jedediah Munroe, wounded in the early morning, was now killed, at the age of fifty-four,[4] and Francis Brown, also of Parker's company, seriously wounded. He was thirty-seven years old and received a wound in the cheek by a musket-ball which passed nearly through his neck, and was almost a year later extracted from the back of the same. He lost about three months of his time and had a doctor's bill of £3 2s. 0d. to pay, besides nursing, in consideration of which he received a grant [5] of £12 2s. 0d. At the time [6] he was hit he had just

[1] *Mass. State Archives*, Vol. 138, p. 407.

[2] "Wayside Happenings in 1775." Rev. Edward G. Porter.

[3] *History of the Fight at Concord*. Rev. Ezra Ripley, D.D.

[4] "The Boys of '75." Clara Lee Bowman. *The Bristol Press*, June 6, 1895. Bristol, Conn.

[5] *American Archives*, IV, 4th ser., 1226. Force.

[6] *Reminiscences and Memorials*, 141. A. B. Muzzey.

stepped from behind a rock in Lincoln, near the boundary, when three Regulars fired, the ball passing under his ear. His granddaughter, Mrs. Pamela Fiske of Arlington, alive in 1894, as a child used to trace the scar with her finger.[1]

Among the other actors in the day's doings we find John Porter[2] of Littleton, a French war veteran, who reached Lexington in the morning, on his way home from Beverly. Borrowing a gun and ammunition from a farmer in town on the security of his horse, he too joined in the pursuit on the troops' return. Many strangers were about and some Lincoln women quickly got up a lunch of hasty pudding and milk for the tired Minute-men and served it at Leonard Hoar's, from a board resting on barrels beside the road.[3]

It had been agreed at Stoneham that no gun should be fired for private cause.[4] The first man to receive an alarm was to hasten to the Common before the meeting-house, when all were to rally[2] at Deacon Ebenezer Bucknam's. Getting under way, Captain Samuel Sprague's company of sixty men crossed the hills and met the British retreating. Before reaching Lexington they had scattered into little groups to shift for themselves in the pursuit. This threw[5] Edward Bucknam, Timothy Matthews, and James Willy together. In the running fight that followed a bullet narrowly missed Bucknam, passing between his left ear and skull, and both Matthews and Willy had bullet holes in their hats. Captain Benjamin Blaney led the Malden men; indeed, there was hardly a man left behind in North Malden. Thomas, Timothy, and Ezra Vinton lived at the Highlands, and went with Captain Sprague's Stoneham company. After the men had left, the women filled saddle-bags full of provisions and put them on an old horse of Phineas Sprague's and sent them along in Israel Cook's care. When near Concord, fearing that he might meet

[1] *Patriots' Day*, 101. Varney.
[2] *History of Middlesex County*, II, 869, 478. Hurd.
[3] *Beneath Old Roof Trees*, 225. Brown.
[4] *History of Middlesex County*, II, 344. Drake.
[5] *History of Stoneham*, 25. Silas Dean. Boston, 1843.

the British retreating, Cook chose a by-road. But before
he was safely out of reach they came in sight; he was spied
and a soldier crossing the field fired, killing the horse, after
which he returned to the ranks. Cook, nothing daunted,
shouldered the saddle-bags and trudged on until he met the
Stoneham boys, sadly in want of something to eat.[1]

Several anecdotes are told without any names being
attached; one respecting a Provincial who had received
a wound in the breast and lay resting his body against a
tree. To a fellow soldier who offered him help he said
earnestly,[2] "Pursue the enemy," and with these words on
his lips fell back and died. A big boy joined in the chase
and showed expertness in firing. At length a ball from a
return shot grazed his head and made a slight flesh-wound.
He soon recovered from the shock, bound up his head with
a handkerchief, and renewed [3] the battle. Running down
hill into Lexington, the redcoats alarmed an old man living
near, who in his turn startled Hancock. Soon after the
British had gone on that morning to Concord, Hancock,
as already related, sent a note to the parsonage asking his
aunt and Miss Quincy to drive over to his refuge at Madam
Abigail Jones's in Woburn Precinct, now Burlington, and
bring with them for dinner the salmon given him in Lexington. Accordingly they set forth, stopping on the way at
James Reed's for a moment, before the prisoners' arrival.
The reunited party were just sitting comfortably down to
enjoy the fish when the scared old man rushed in exclaiming,[1]
"The British are coming! My wife's in 'Eternity' now!"
Miss Quincy had driven to the parsonage in a coach and
four, and the great lumbering carriage still stood conspicuous
in the parsonage yard, painted probably a "stone yellow"
color, as was Hancock's custom.[4] Supposing themselves
attacked, Hancock and Adams slipped out by a by-road

---

[1] *History of Middlesex County*, III, 212; I, 393. Hurd.

[2] *American Archives*, II, 4th ser., 439. Force.

[3] *History of the American Revolution*, I, 485. Gordon.

[4] *John Hancock His Book*, 237. Brown.

into the swamp and were piloted by Madam Jones's boarder (and future son-in-law) Parson John Marett, twenty-eight years old, by one cart track and another to Amos Wyman's at Billerica. Meanwhile the tell-tale coach was hastily drawn aside into the thickets of Path Woods in the north-west precinct, near the road to Billerica, by the late parson Jones's slave, Cuff.[1] This negro, then twenty-nine years old, lived sixty years in the family and so won their esteem [2] he was at his death borne to the grave by the selectmen of the town. The Wyman lot, in the southeast corner of Billerica, owned latterly by George Bennett of Burlington, is marked as follows:[3]

Amos Wyman Homestead
Here
John Hancock and Saml. Adams
Found Refuge from the British Soldiers April 19, 1775.
This Inscription placed here by the Billerica Historical Society, 1898.

A goodly hot dinner had been left behind in Burlington, but the hungry Patriots, on reaching a safe place, thankfully ate a "cold boiled dinner" of salt pork and unpeeled potatoes, with brown rye bread, from a wooden platter. In after years, it is pleasant to read, Hancock gave a cow to Mrs. Seymour, Mr. Wyman's daughter, in testimony of his gratitude.[1] Miss Quincy, meanwhile, appears to have been again left behind to finish the meal with what appetite she might. Probably Hancock and Adams felt unwilling to embarrass her any longer with their presence during the day, for one account tells of their lurking about in the woods until night. After eleven, the story runs,[4] as Mrs. David Valette and her friend Mrs. Reed sat before the hearth talking over the incidents of that long day, both with infants in their arms, Mrs. Reed said, "Hark, I hear footsteps." "It's only the leaves rustling," Mrs. Valette answered; "we will not be needlessly alarmed." Then came a tap. "Who

---

[1] *Patriots' Day*, 99–100. Varney.
[2] *History of Middlesex County*, I, 664. Hurd.
[3] *John Hancock His Book*, 194. Brown.
[4] *Saco Valley Settlement*, 1010–11. Ridlon.

is there?" asked Mrs. Reed. "Friends," was the reply in a low tone through the hole from which the latch string was drawn in, and on the door being opened three men muffled in cloaks entered, one saying, "Do not be alarmed, ladies, we are friends to our country and are pursued by the enemy; we have hid in the woods all day and seek shelter for the night." "With all my heart!" cried Mrs. Reed, adding, "but here you would not be safe a moment. Why, the redcoats were here only yesterday eating up all my pies and bread and cheese and because they could not find enough at the neighbors' houses must need rip open the beds and leave the cider running. Oh, sir, these are dreadful times." "They are indeed," answered the spokesman, who proved to be Hancock. "But, gentlemen," turning to his companions, Samuel Adams and Paul Revere, he continued, "what shall we do? It is certainly unsafe to linger here." "Are there neighbors where we could be safe?" "Only my father's" said Mrs. Reed, "five miles off on the main road. But then it would be dangerous to go, except through the woods, and we haven't a man or boy to show you the way. They are all off fighting." Here crippled Mrs. Valette interposed that if Mrs. Reed would nurse her baby she would show them. "But you never walked a mile together in your life and could never go this wet night!" exclaimed Mrs. Reed. However, they started, Mrs. Valette resting on Hancock's arm and helped over the shallow rivulets in their course until, at three in the morning, the Reed house was reached. The family here arose, blazed the fire, and, even to the dog, made them welcome. At dawn Mrs. Valette drove home to her baby, John Hancock remarking as he handed her into the carriage, "Madam, our first meeting has been in troublous times. God only knows when these scenes will end; but should we survive the struggle, and you should ever need a friend, think of me." Hancock and Adams then went back to Madam Jones's, and from there on to the Wymans' again, where Paul Revere and Dorothy

Quincy [1] joined them.   There was quite a party of women and children from the neighborhood "roughing it" in the woods here, in dread lest they should be "murdered" or "carried off" by the redcoats if they stayed in their scattered homes.

When parting, the previous day, Hancock had urged on Miss Quincy the imprudence of returning to Boston; at first she had been inclined to dispute the point and felt that she must go to her father; now, however, she consented and, as it chanced, three years passed before she saw Boston. [2]

After several nights of enforced hiding — including a flying visit paid by Hancock and Miss Quincy at Shirley parsonage, [3] then occupied by his cousin, Lydia Bowes, wife of Rev. Phineas Whitney — on the evening of Monday the 24th, he reached Worcester in Adams' company and wrote to the Committee of Safety, desiring that depositions should be taken to establish the fact of the British beginning the attack, together with particulars as to who had been taken and killed.   "Are our men in good spirits?" he continues. [4] "For God's sake do not suffer the Spirit to subside, until they have perfected the reduction of our enemies. . . . Our friends are valuable, but our Country must be saved. . . . Where is Cushing?   Are Mr Payne and Mr J. Adams to be with us? . . . We travel rather as deserters, which I will not submit to.   I will return and join you if I cannot travel in reputation. . . . How goes on your Congress? . . . Are the members hearty?   Pray remember Mr S. Adams and myself to all friends.   God be with you.

I am, gentlemen,
your faithful and hearty countryman,
John Hancock."

Three days later Hancock purposed setting out for Philadelphia, while Mrs. Lydia Hancock and Miss Quincy

---

[1] *Henry Dunster and his Descendants*, 86.

[2] *Magazine of American History*, June, 1888.

[3] *Boston Globe*, April 20, 1903.

[4] *American Archives*, II, 4th ser., 383.   Force.

by slow stages journeyed to Fairfield, Connecticut, becoming the guests of Thaddeus Burr, Esq. A handsome young nephew, one Aaron Burr with a "pretty fortune," was also visiting there, but Mrs. Hancock "was very jealous of him" lest he should draw Miss Quincy's affections from her own nephew and "would not leave them a moment together." John Hancock, for his part, on leaving to take his place in the Continental Congress at Philadelphia, wrote, May 7th, from New York, a letter beginning "Dear Dolly," which concludes, "write lengthy and often. . . . Pray let me hear from you by every post." On the 28th of August following, — in brave defiance of General Gage's proclamation excepting her lover from pardon and declaring all such as harbored him to be traitors, — Miss Quincy was married to John Hancock (now President of the Congress through the illness and resignation of Peyton Randolph) at the house of Mr. Burr by the Rev. Andrew Eliot. The honeymoon that followed was a busy one, spent [1] in packing up officers' commissions and trimming the rough edges of the new bills of credit, until the bride's little fingers ached. However, since there was no clerk kept for some months to come, Mrs. Hancock and President John worked on happily together. As for Madam Lydia, we learn that she died at Fairfield, April 15th, 1776, "just on her return to the reënjoyment of an ample fortune." [2]

[1] *Magazine of American History*, June, 1888.
[2] A part of her epitaph. *John Hancock His Book*, 240. Brown.

DOROTHY HANCOCK

CHAPTER III

ON THROUGH ARLINGTON

TO return once more to the retreating British whose condition was now well-nigh desperate. Although[1] the men had started out with seventy-two rounds of cartridges each, within about one mile of the village they scarce averaged[2] two apiece; moreover the strain on the flanking parties had been so great they could hardly hold out longer in any case. It is supposed if Smith had found any one in command he would have surrendered[3] at discretion to save his men. The retreat was much hampered by wounded men, including eight of the officers. Three, it will be remembered, had been wounded at the North bridge, another at Merriam's Corner, and more recently Lieutenant-Colonel Smith and Lieutenants Baker, Cox, and Hawkshaw — the latter in the cheek. This last mischance occasioned especial regret, since he had been accounted "the greatest beauty of the British Army."[4]

They showed "amazing bravery," says DeBernière,[5] but little order, and in truth were running. A small fifer boy kept up with them pluckily until an old fellow hit him with wild goose shot, and he sat down with his fife stuck into the breast of his jacket, begging for help. This was given by one Lexington family, who received abuse right and left for their kindness.[6]

An attempt to check the retreat and form two deep

[1] *Memorial History of Boston*, III, 67, note.
[2] Henry Pelham writing to Copley. *Atlantic Monthly*, April, 1893.
[3] *Narrative*, appended to Parson Clark's Anniversary Sermon.
[4] *Historical Magazine*, March, 1869.
[5] *Mass. His. Soc. Coll.*, 2d ser., IV.
[6] *Beneath Old Roof Trees*, 40. Brown.

failed.   For the moment the confusion increased, but once down hill and in the town "the officers got to the front and presented their pistols and told the men if they did not advance they should die; upon this they began to form under a very heavy fire;"[1] happily for them, at this very instant they were joined by the First Brigade — the relief forces under Lord Percy.   These consisted of the 4th Battalion Royal Artillery, 23d Royal Welsh Fusileers, the 47th Regiment, and a battalion of Marines with two field-pieces, six-pounders.   This put a different face on everything.

Lieutenant Barker[2] says, "We had been flattered ever since the morning with expectations of the Brigade coming out, but at this time had given up all hopes of it, as it was so late."   They met "at half after two," half a mile below the church at Lexington.   Cæsar Ferrit and his son John, of the Natick company,[3] had just reached a house near the Green.   They fired on the flying British from the entry way and then hid under the cellar stairs, waiting until the retreat was resumed. Cæsar had a French and a Dutch grandfather, an Indian and African grandmother.[4]   John Bacon,[5] the father of Captain David Bacon of Natick, is said to have been killed during the day.   Captain Joseph Morse's company brought back several prisoners, who settled in Dover.   Lieutenant Mackenzie of the 23d Regiment states that they formed a line across the road as regularly as the stone walls would admit, upon a slight rise, whence they looked on toward the village and the hills back of it, and waited.   Seeing this welcome support, the Grenadiers and Light Infantry shouted repeatedly [6]

[1] *Mass. His. Soc. Coll.*, 2d ser., IV.

[2] *Atlantic Monthly*, April, 1877.

[3] *History of Middlesex County*, I, 523.   Hurd.

[4] *History of Middlesex County*, 194.   Drake.

[5] *History of Middlesex County*, I, 523.   Hurd.   Compare *History of Natick*, 42. Oliver N. Bacon.   1856.

[6] *Mass. His. Soc. Pro.*, March, 1890.

and made haste to come up. They had reason for fatigue, having been on the road at least sixteen hours, and marched between twenty-five and thirty miles, latterly disputing every inch of headway they gained. At the end of their strength, when enclosed by the hollow square of their comparatively fresh comrades, the stampeded redcoats flung themselves on the ground, "their tongues hanging out like dogs' after a chase." [1] Lieutenant Mackenzie [2] could not see above fifty Americans in a body at this time, but many lay concealed behind the field walls. The largest group was near the church, and a few cannon-shot were directed that way, clearing the road. Major Loammi Baldwin [3] of Woburn was then passing along between the meeting-house and Buckman's tavern, a prisoner before him, "when," as he tells it, "the cannon began to play, the balls flew near me, I judged not more than two yards off." He immediately went behind the meeting-house, and inside ten seconds was driven to fresh shelter by a ball which passed through the building and came out near his head. Lying in the meadow, north of the Green, he saw the balls strike the ground about him, but was not hit. The shot which passed out by the pulpit window fell at the door of a house occupied by one of Parker's company.[4] It was subsequently given to Harvard College, but has since been lost.[5] Most of the balls went high overhead, but the heavy plunging fire was disconcerting and kept the Yankees back. Chaplain Thaxter [6] says of it, "No cannon ever did more execution; such stories of their effects had been spread by the Tories through our troops, that, from this time, more went back than pursued." Jonathan Harris [1] of the Concord Minute Com-

---

[1] *Harper's Magazine*, May, 1875.

[2] *Mass. His. Soc. Pro.*, March, 1890.

[3] *History of Middlesex County*, I, 447. Hurd.

[4] *Historical and Genealogical Register*, October, 1877.

[5] *Lexington Hand Book to Points of Interest*, 34.

[6] *Historical Magazine*, March, 1869.

pany said that the falling branches in the woods were "full of alarm," until they gradually became accustomed to the sound.

The dress [1] of the Royal Artillery may not be uninteresting to note. The men wore white breeches, white stockings with black half-spatterdashes, and clubbed hair. The officers had their hair clubbed, when on duty, and a gold button and loop to their hats, which were cocked like the men's, with the front loop just over the nose. White stocks were alone permitted, for officers and men alike. Perhaps their white hose may have shown some traces of the Roxbury, Brookline, and Allston dust by this time, but as rescuers their comrades looked wholly good to the Grenadiers.

Near the fork where the Woburn and Boston roads meet stands the present high school, its yard, then a hill, marked by a memorial cannon in stone, pointed at the Green, bearing these words:

> ON THE HILL TO THE SOUTH WAS PLANTED
> ONE OF THE BRITISH FIELDPIECES
> APRIL 19 1775
> TO COMMAND THE VILLAGE
> AND ITS APPROACHES AND NEAR THIS PLACE
> SEVERAL BUILDINGS WERE BURNED

As the Patriots regained courage, a few crept near enough to fire on the Brigade. There was an open, "morassy"[2] ground to the left of the troops, opposite which were trees and walls yielding cover to the Yankees; a difficult spot to charge, but that was not thought of — only a breathing spell, and renewed retreat. Drawing up by the marsh, an officer was sent to bring up a six-pounder, and aided by some of their best marksmen endeavored to prevent the Yankees turning the British flank, as they had offered to do under protection

[1] *History of the Royal Artillery*, I, chapter XXIV. Captain Francis Duncan. London, 1879. 3d ed.

[2] Lieutenant Mackenzie. *Mass. His. Soc. Pro.*, March, 1890.

of the covered ground. During the halt the dead were collected, carriages were sought out for the wounded, and such articles in the way of bandages and bedding as might add to their comfort. Less legitimate plunder was taken in many instances, and wanton destruction done in the way of damaged furniture, while three houses, two shops, a barn, and a mill-house adjoining the latter, were in the end burned. This last may have been done with the view of detaining their pursuers to gain a little time. The losses were apportioned as follows.[1]

Deacon Joseph Loring	720	00	00
Mrs. Lydia Mulliken	439	08	00
Benjamin Merriam	233	04	00
Marrett Munroe	203	11	09
Joshua Bond	189	16	07
Thomas Fessenden	164	00	00
Jonathan Loring	103	07	00
Matthew Mead	101	00	00
Lydia Winship	66	13	04
Nathan Fessenden	66	10	00
Nathaniel Farmer	46	10	00
Benjamin Brown	42	00	00
John Williams	36	15	00
Margaret Winship	22	10	00
Amos Muzzey	18	04	00
Nathan Blodgett	18	00	00
John Mason	14	13	04
Jonathan Smith, Jr.	13	12	08
Robert Harrington	12	00	00
John Winship	12	00	00
Benjamin Estabrook	12	00	00
Jeremiah Harrington	10	14	11
Elizabeth Samson	10	00	00
Benjamin Fisk	9	06	00
William Munroe	9	00	00
Hepzibeth Davis	5	01	06
Samuel Bemis	4	08	08
£	2584	6	9

Jonathan Harrington's house was much exposed to the firing, and ninety-four squares of glass and forty-two wooden

[1] *Journals of Each Provincial Congress, 1774–5.*

sashes were broken to pieces, besides being overrun by plunderers who forced open two desks. His list of losses is much the longest that has been preserved. It runs: Account of things I lost by the King's troops.

1 eight day Clock Carried off almost new 15	00	00
1 fine India dark gown 2	08	00
1 striped English cotton do. 1	10	00
2 dozens of cotton & linen & 2 sheets 10	00	00
6 shirts, 6 shifts, to the value of 7	00	00
1 lawn apron; 1 doz. cambric, 1 doz. linen 2	10	00
4 new check aprons 1	10	00
1 doz. of handkerchiefs, part check, part printed 1	10	00
1 bed blanket	18	00
15 pr. Stockings, p't worsted, part thread & yarn 4	00	00
6 large diaper table cloths 4	10	00
1 doz. fine diaper cloths 2	08	00
1 doz. cotton linen diaper cloths 1	04	00
1 doz. napkins 1	10	00
1 scarlet riding hood 2	00	00
1 pr new boots & 2 pr shoes 2	04	00
1 new razee great Coat, 1 do. blue 6	00	00
2 new beaver hats 4	00	00
5 yds. of cotton & linen cloth 00	14	00
A No. of Womens' caps 1	10	00
1 muff & tippet	12	00
3 looking glasses, all large 6	00	00
2 large moose skins 4	00	00
3 Cartridge boxes; 3 bridles & Straps all new 3	00	00
3½ yds. of ratteen 1	15	00
2 cans, 1 trimmed with silver, 1 do. pinch-beek.........	18	00
1 doz. of stone plates, mugs, bowls, tea pots &c. 1	12	00
2 good razors, a No. of books, Latin History, &c. 2	00	00
1 doz. of spoons, porringers etc. 1	16	00
1 damask cloth, new buckskin breeches 2	08	00

Respecting the clock, the Rev. Theodore Parker [1] tells us that the weights and case were not carried away and the pendulum was afterwards recovered, having been dropped in the fields half a mile off. Young Jonathan Harrington, he adds, the fifer, then went to school to Pitt Clark, "a pretty man," who taught on the Common. Jonathan was studying Latin, but the soldiers took away his Latin books

[1] *Life and Correspondence*, I, 12.   Weiss.

— all, that is, except Young's dictionary. But for this he might have gone to college; as it was he went to school no more, and as the war went on it ruined his father's business, and "kind o' broke it all up." Jonathan Harrington,[1] Sr., just referred to, removed his family this memorable day to a house half a mile or more off the main street, on a lane leading to the Great Meadows from the present Lowell Street. His son Charles, twelve years old, saw from the house the British coming along, and ran up to the highway to watch them pass by. When the family returned in the afternoon a British soldier who had been resting on one of the beds took to his heels. He was ordered to halt, but ran on until fired at, wounded in the arm, and captured. For several years after he lived thereabouts as a laborer. From the Marrett Munroe house, still standing by the Green across from the tavern, was lost £83 11s. 9d. in the way of household effects, £90 worth of goods in the retail shop, and £30 damage was done to real property.

John Winship lost two suits of clothes; Margaret Winship, bedding, plate, and much of the fittings of two rooms. As her windows suffered, she probably lived near the Green. Nathan Fessenden[2] had damage "Don" his windows and furniture, besides losing the "Beding" and much of the "Warring apperil" of his "hole" family.

Thomas Fessenden, besides having damage done to his fence and windows and the furniture of four rooms, lost £20 of broadcloth from his trading shop, the wearing apparel of his whole family, consisting of seven persons, his plate, and a horse and chaise carried off to Boston. Nathaniel Farmer, it will be remembered, was wounded at daybreak; he heads his list:[2] "the Foalloaring is a Just and true Account of What Damages & Losses I sustained by the Wanton Ravages & Depradations of the troops of his Brittish Majesty under the Command of Lord percey on there Return from

---

[1] *Lexington His. Soc. Pro.*, II, 43–4, 46.

[2] *Mass. State Archives*, Vol. 138, pp. 377, 397.

Concord on the 19 of April, 1775," and speaks of his household of seven losing clothes and bedding, the fittings of three rooms more or less destroyed, and his house and shop windows being well wrecked.

Samuel Bemis had some dozen panes of glass to replace, and mentions the loss of a looking-glass and part of a timepiece. Natl. Blodget refers to the loss of two coats, one pair breeches, one beaver hat, etc. Amos Muzzey had no less than £6 14s. 0d. worth of broken glass.[1] A beaufet and the crockery belonging to it were also demolished here. Amos Muzzey was a cousin of Isaac, killed on the Green. He was the third generation to live on the spot, and in 1895 the place remained in the family.[2] It was supposed from the stains left in the house that some of the soldiers dressed their wounds here.

Jeremiah Harrington's list is very nearly as detailed as Jonathan's.

I lost on 19 Apr the following articles:

1 broad cloth great coat	3.	6.	0
1 pr goatskin breeches		19	
1 pr cotton & linen sheets	1	6	8
3 yds. Calico @ 6s		18	
1¼ yds tow cloth		1	10
4 linen handkerchiefs		8	
2 diaper towels		2	
10 yds tow cloth		15	
1 pewter platter		2	5
8 pewter plates	1	4	
6 pint porringers		16	
6 spoons		4	
1 pr hose		3	
1 pr shoes		9	

Jonathan Smith, Jr., had some finery carried off. A satin bonnet and cloak, silver sleeve buttons, silver buckles valued at eighteen shillings, and three silver spoons. Also one block-tin teapot and two pewter porringers. Hepzi-

---

[1] *Reminiscences and Memorials*, 362–3. A. B. Muzzey.

[2] "The Muzzey Family in the Revolution." Florence E. D. Muzzey. *American Magazine*, November, 1895.

beth Davis made her mark to a truly remarkable list and headed it: [1]

" to the town Clark

Lost at Concord fite

one paer of Shets	0	18	0
two paer of Piler Caes	0	8	0
three Napkins	0	4	0
two tabel Clothes	0	4	0
three Smockes	0	13	6
three Eaprns [aprons, bless her!]	0	6	0
hoes, Caps and other Artils	2	8	0
	£ 5	1	6

hepzibeth Davis

her

X

Marck

At the junction of the Boston and Woburn roads there still stands a house bearing the inscription:

HOUSE OF

BENJAMIN MERRIAM

ONE OF THE MINUTE MEN WHOSE FAMILY FLED
ON THE APPROACH OF THE BRITISH
WHO PILLAGED THE HOUSE
APRIL 19 1775

By the returns the loss here appears as a total of £6 real estate and £217 4s. 0d. personal property. The house was used as a hospital [2] for some of the wounded Regulars.

The afternoon was running on for soldiers with fifteen miles yet to march and only thirty-six rounds of ammunition in hand, so Lord Percy, at about a quarter past three, ordered the 23d Regiment to form the rear guard, and began collecting his men for a start. He had made his headquarters during the halt at William Munroe's tavern, a house already eighty years old, which still stands with the following inscription:

EARL PERCY'S

HEADQUARTERS AND HOSPITAL
APRIL 19 1775
THE MUNROE TAVERN
BUILT 1695

[1] *Mass. State Archives*, Vol. 138, p. 397.

[2] *Lexington Centennial*, 117.

Many soldiers had their wounds dressed in the south-east lower room,[1] the parlor. At the right of the front door was the barroom, tended by a lame old man whose name was John Raymond. The men swarmed in, eager for refreshment. One private dropped the butt of his musket on the floor, accidentally discharging the piece, as a shot hole in the ceiling still testifies. All was confusion inside; without, the cannon sounded. Unable to serve the liquors fast enough to please them, poor old John, in his fear and bewilderment, tried to escape by the back door, when he was overtaken by a shot and fell, as he ran across the yard. The moment for joining their ranks had now come, and the men hastily piled furniture before the bar and set it alight. The total damage was but £9 however, thanks to the innkeeper's father-in-law, Mr. Smith,[2] who put the fire out after the soldiers were gone on. In 1876 a platter used by the British and afterwards thrown on the fire was exhibited in the Old South collection of relics.

To the left of the tavern, on a hillside facing Lexington, stands a tablet inscribed as follows:

NEAR THIS SPOT
EARL PERCY
WITH REENFORCEMENTS PLANTED A
FIELDPIECE TO COVER THE RETREAT OF THE
BRITISH TROOPS
APRIL 19 1775

When ordered to protect the retreat, Lieutenant Mackenzie[3] states, the 23d Regiment "immediately lined the walls and other cover in our front with some marksmen, and retired from the right of Companies by files to the high ground a small distance in our rear, where we again formed in line, and remained in that position for near half an hour, during which time the flank Companies and the other Regiments of the Brigade, began their march in one column on the road toward Cambridge." This second position

[1] *Lexington Hand Book*, 25. Piper.
[2] *Under Colonial Roofs*, 153–4. Jones.
[3] *Mass. His. Soc. Pro.*, March, 1890.

lay southeast of the first, nearer Munroe Tavern, and about midway between the Mulliken and Bond houses. The first buildings burned by the British belonged to Deacon Joseph Loring, and stood on the sidehill, near the Boston and Woburn roads, close to the first position taken by the relief forces. When the main body of troops were on the way to Cambridge, it is conceivable that the rear guard felt the need of smoke to obscure their movements in taking up their second post. However this may be, the loss bore heavily on the village deacon. There were nine in his family and the loss as summed up comes to £720, including £3 in specie, eight featherbeds, pewter and brass ware, three cases of drawers, two mahogany tables, fittings of eight rooms, all the household tools and utensils, a barn seventy feet long, two calves, and five tons of hay, a corn house, cider mill and press adjoining the barn, and two hundred feet of stone wall overturned. The widow Lydia Mulliken lived in their very pathway, between the first and the second halting place. She had five in the family and lost upward of £400 worth of property through the firing of the house and her son's clock shop, many "valuable" clocks and tools being destroyed. Before leaving home she had hidden the silver safely in the well. Becky Mulliken,[1] thirteen years old at this time, used to regret that her embroidered pocket had not been hidden too, and so escaped burning. The following June, Nathaniel Mulliken[2] petitioned respecting a pair of silver shoe buckles then lost, which he had been told were in the possession of a sergeant of the 52d Regiment lodged in Concord jail. Joshua Bond's house and shop, somewhat in the rear of the second position, were also burned, causing a loss of nearly £200. One of these shops was joined to the house. Parson Gordon[2] writes to a friend: "You would have been shocked at the destruction which has been made by the Regulars, as they are miscalled, had you been present

---

[1] *Lexington His. Soc. Pro.*, I, 52–3.
[2] *American Archives*, II, 4th ser., 1353, 626–31. Force.

with me to have beheld it. Many houses were plundered
of everything valuable that could be taken away, and what
could not be carried off was destroyed; looking-glasses,
pots, pans, &c. were broke all to pieces; doors when not
fastened, sashes and windows wantonly damaged and
destroyed. The people say that the Soldiers are worse
than the *Indians;* in short, they have given the Country
such an early specimen of their brutality as will make the
inhabitants dread submission to the power of the British
Ministry, and determine them to fight desperately rather
than have such cruel masters to lord it over them."

Some [1] folks at "the Centre" hid their silver under a
heap of stones; in the afternoon, from her hiding place,
one of the family saw an officer unconsciously standing
on top of the pile! Lydia Loring,[2] the deacon's daughter,
took the church plate and hid it under a heap of brush
near the house.

The day's losses were crushing to those who lost their
all, especially at a time when the general loss was not inconsiderable. May 1st a petition [3] was presented in behalf
of Deacon Joseph Loring, Joseph Loring, Jr., the widow
Mulliken, and Joseph Pond, who "had their houses, furniture, and all apparel, burnt by General Gage's Troops in
the late battle, whereby they are reduced to a state of abject
poverty." One hundred and sixty pounds of pork, "in
order to prevent their Starving," was the burden of their
entreaty and the Committee of Supplies was authorized to
deliver for their use one barrel.

The Light Infantry and Grenadiers moved off first [4]
on the road toward Cambridge, covered by Lord Percy's
fresher men. Wagons [5] with the wounded formed the
centre, or they were carried in chaises, or rode horses found

---

[1] *Beneath Old Roof Trees*, 39–40. Brown.

[2] *Reminiscences and Memorials*, 380. A. B. Muzzey.

[3] *American Archives*, II, 4th ser., 779. Force.

[4] DeBernière's account. *Mass. His. Soc. Coll.*, IV, 2d ser.

[5] "The Old Men of Menotomy." Henry A. Kidder. *Young People's Magazine*, June, 1895.

standing by the way.[1] The rear guard was continually pressed upon in the pursuit and frequently relieved.

Below the tavern, toward Boston, the Sanderson [2] house was passed and Mrs. Sanderson's dowry-cow killed. When Mr. Sanderson called for his wife at night to bring her home she was so wrought up by the day's doings that it incensed her to learn that a wounded Regular had been left behind on her hands, and she chafed all the way back, asking her husband why he did not "knock him on the head," and declaring that she "would not have him in the house," she "would do nothing for him, he might starve." "The Satanish critters," she complained, had "stolen everything in the house and not left rags enough to bind up his wounds anyway." The soldier, rousing with the commotion, begged for tea, but in her state of mind, when this was reported, she said obstinately, "What should I gie him tea for? He shall hae nane!" But as the town authorities insisted upon his remaining, and her father offered to furnish his tea, she finally settled down to make the best of it. Even so, she used to admit to her grandchildren in after years, that now and again she "gie him a *divilish honing!*" Not reassured possibly by her manner, the soldier feared lest he should be poisoned and refused to eat or drink until one of the family had first tasted his portion.

The house nearly opposite, owned by John Mason,[3] suffered to the extent of £14 13s. 4d. For the next two miles, to the "Place of the Rocks," there was a little lull, and rapid progress was made.

Throughout the day the village parsonage was swarming with the rallying Minute-men, who camped down on the floor and partook so freely of Parson [4] Clark's cider, brown bread, and bacon that by four o'clock the supply gave out.

[1] *Essex Gazette*, Salem, April 25, 1775.
[2] *Lexington His. Soc. Pro.*, I, 61-2.
[3] *Under Colonial Roofs*, 153. Jones.
[4] *Life of Henry Ware, Jr.*, 5.

Eliza, a little girl of eleven, had helped her father feed the
men all day, and now they started to find Mrs. Clark and
the other children. It is said that some wounded were
taken in here and attended by Dr. Fiske,[1] whose house was
near by. This may, however, have reference to the morning
merely, as already noted. Most of the women and children
were gone from town. Elijah Sanderson,[2] having no arms,
saw what he could from Estabrook's hill. He says the
redcoats "hove fire" into several other buildings besides
these mentioned, but as Parson Clark[3] remarks, "the
flames were Seasonably quenched." Mr. Edmund Foster[4]
of Reading was in the village for a while, having taken a
wounded Regular prisoner near the almshouse, whom he
wished to lodge at the Buckman tavern. Two wounded
British indeed were left here, and two or three more beyond
at Thaddeus Reed's. One of the two left at Buckman's[5]
died, and was buried in the village burial ground. During
the halt at Lexington, the Acton men received their dinner
sent down by the boys. Francis Faulkner[6] and the other
lads on leaving Acton went first to Concord, where they
found all the able-bodied men gone, and those left behind
in great anxiety. They learned here that their neighbors,
Captain Davis and Mr. Hosmer, were killed and that young
Hayward was dying, but that, on the other hand, the
British were running before the Patriots toward Boston.
As they rode on to Lexington, Francis spied a man lying
beside a wall. Seized with a sudden fear he cried, "Oh,
boys, that is my father," and jumped off the horse to eye
him closer. Soon he called back to his waiting mates,
"That's not my father, boys, and I don't know who it is."
Again and again they passed men dead by the roadside.
At Lexington they heard the cannon and hunted up the

[1] *Under Colonial Roof Trees*, 149. Jones.
[2] Deposition. *History of the Battle at Lexington*. Phinney.
[3] *Narrative*.
[4] *A History of the Fight at Concord*, 35. Rev. Dr. Ezra Ripley. Ed. of 1827.
[5] *Lex. His. Soc. Pro.*, I, 75.
[6] *Col. Francis Faulkner*, 5–6. Rev. Dr. Cyrus Hamlin.

home company. To their surprise the Minute-men were in high spirits; they had "made the redcoats run for their lives." They only wished that they had the powder and ball the Regulars threw away. Many Minute-men indeed had run short of ammunition and were forced to turn home from this point. The Acton boys then started back with the news, getting home late after a thirteen mile ride each way.

Two more incidents belong to this part of the day, one laughable and the other romantic. Minute-man Thomas Cutler,[1] of the "west side," was off with the men fighting. The womenfolk fled for the woods, leaving in their haste the baby comfortably in its cradle. Or, as another version,[2] probably of the same tale, has it, hearing that the British were really coming the mother snatched up the baby as she supposed, only to find, when ready to drop, at a friend's house nearly a mile off the road, that she had blindly saved the old cat by mistake! Hurrying back she found her little one, luckily, all safe, and quickly regained shelter. The 19th of April, as it chanced, was the silver wedding anniversary of Peter and Anne Tufts,[3] who lived at Winter Hill. Paul Revere's alarm took Peter to the front, his son John, a lad of eighteen, being charged to stay behind and take care of things. The boy, however, could not be pacified at home and followed on, up beyond Lexington. While crossing one of the hills he met Elizabeth Perry, crying and running from her blazing home. He guarded her to her relatives and three years later made her his bride.

The reinforcements which alone saved the day were commanded by Lord Percy of the 5th Regiment. He is said to have slept the night of April 18th in the spare chamber of Mr. Andrew Cazneau's [4] house in Boston, and it is claimed that some of the red and white bed-hangings from

---

[1] *Beneath Old Roof Trees,* 39. Brown.

[2] *Col. Francis Faulkner,* 6–7. Rev. Dr. Hamlin.

[3] *Under Colonial Roofs,* 129. Jones.

[4] *Boston Evening Transcript,* November 21, 1897.

his chamber still exist.   There were serious delays in beginning their march.   One was occasioned by General Gage having addressed his order for the Marines to turn out to Major Pitcairn,[1] who was gone as a volunteer.   The letter naturally lay unopened and the Marines slumbered on undisturbed.   Again, Colonel Smith had left orders that the First Brigade should be under arms at 4 A.M., but the Brigade Major was out late the evening of the 18th and on his return, by some neglect, was not told of the letter awaiting him.[2]   An express from Colonel Smith, sent off at 5 A.M. to hurry the Brigade forward, covered the officers with dismay and immediately all was bustle.   Lieutenant Mackenzie[3] of the 23rd, or Royal Welsh, says, "at 7 o'clock this morning a Brigade order was received by our Regiment, dated at 6 o'clock, for the 1st Brigade to assemble at half past 7 on the Grand Parade.   We accordingly assembled the Regiment with the utmost expedition, and with the 4th and 47th [8 companies that is from each] were on the Parade at the hour appointed with one day's provisions [and 36 rounds apiece].   By some mistake the Marines did not receive the order until the other Regiments of the Brigade were assembled, by which means it was half past 8 o'clock before the Brigade was ready to march."

Harrison Gray Otis,[4] then a little boy about ten years old, was on his way from his home, in the neighborhood of the Revere House, to Master Lovell's school in School Street, while Percy's men were still drawn up along Long Acre, now Tremont Street, the column extending from near the site of the Scollay building, in the immediate neighborhood of the barracks in Cornhill, to the Mall on the Common. Otis had not gone far before he was stopped by a corporal and sent down Court Street out of the confusion.   Taking the Main Street (now Washington) a few feet southward

[1] *Memorial History of Boston*, III, 70.
[2] *Story of Patriots' Day*, 63.   Varney.
[3] *Mass. His. Soc. Pro.*, March, 1890.
[4] *Reminiscences and Memorials*, 28.   A. B. Muzzey.

he came to School Street and again turned his steps in the
direction of the gathering troops. Seeing that it was likely
to be a day of disturbance the teacher made no effort to
detain Otis and the other boys, exclaiming according to
tradition:

War's begun. School's done.
Deponite libros.

Master Carter, who kept the town school on the site
of the Scollay building facing Queen, now Court Street,
like Master Lovell, hastened to dismiss his scholars. It is
safe to conclude that the boys were soon in the thick of
the preparations and saw probably, amongst other things, a
wagon with 140 rounds of ammunition for the field-pieces
left behind on the Parade lest it should unduly retard the
march. As it was, twenty-four rounds apiece were carried
in the "side boxes;" an ample amount it was supposed.
At any rate Colonel Cleveland [1] declared afterwards that
plenty more was at hand if it had been deemed best to be
burdened with it. One soldier gives [2] the numbers com-
prised in the reinforcement as a total of something like
1,500 men, of which forty-seven were Marines and 1,423
ordinary soldiers. Before leaving, the troops understood [3]
they were to march out of town to support their comrades,
who had gone out the previous night.

At length, by a quarter before nine they were off in the
following order: Advance guard of a captain and fifty men,
two six-pounders, 4th Regiment, 47th Regiment, 1st Battalion of Marines, 23d Regiment or Royal Welsh Fusileers,
rear guard of a captain and fifty men; the whole under
the command of Brigadier General Earl Percy, who rode a
white horse.[4] They marched southward at first, over the
Neck by the present Washington Street to Roxbury, and
up the hill by the meeting-house and the parsonage, still

[1] *Evelyn Family in America,* 277. Scull.

[2] *Essex Gazette,* May 2–12, 1775.

[3] Lieutenant Mackenzie. *Mass. His. Soc. Pro.,* March, 1890.

[4] *History of Roxbury,* 315. F. S. Drake.

standing, built for the Rev. Oliver Peabody, 1750–52, soon to become General Thomas's headquarters. Roxbury, says the Rev. William Gordon[1] of the 3d Congregational parish, Jamaica Plain, had the alarm between eight and nine o'clock, before we had breakfasted. . . . The Country was in an uproar; another detachment was coming out of Boston; and I was desired to take care of myself and partner. . . . Having sent off my books, which I had finished packing up the day before, conjecturing what was coming on from the moment I had heard of the resolutions of Parliament, though I did not expect it 'til the reinforcement arrived, we got into our chaise, and went to Dedham." As the column approached, the grammar school master here, Joseph Williams,[2] dismissed his school also. The Roxbury Militia are thought to have gone to Dr. Gordon's church at Jamaica Plain [2] to attend service before starting in pursuit of the advancing troops; at any rate this would assuredly, under the circumstances, be wiser than remaining in the pathway of 1,000 men. Some quick-witted Roxbury boy shouted jeeringly [2] after the Redcoats, "You go out to Yankee Doodle but you will dance by and bye to Chevy Chase!" The old Border ballad runs:

> A woefull hunting once there did
> In Chevy Chase befall.
> To drive the deere with hound and horne
>
> Erle Percy took his way
> The Child may rue that is unborne
> The hunting of that day.
>
> . . . .
> This fight did last from break of day
> Till setting of the Sun
> For when they rung the evening bell
> The battle scarce was done.

It is said that the allusion laid heavily on Lord Percy all day. The tune of "Yankee Doodle" here referred to was played in contempt, it being frequently used when

---

[1] *American Archives*, II, 4th ser., 627. Force.
[2] *Memorial History of Boston*, III, 71.

offending soldiers were drummed out of camp. Since the tarring and feathering of young Ditson, according to a contemporary Worcester [1] paper, it had been a special favorite. To this well-known air the men came along by the "Parting Stone," where the road forked for Dedham and Rhode Island on the left and Watertown and Cambridge on the right. Taking the right-hand turn, down hill by the grist-mills, now the Providence railway crossing, on and on they went by the Puddingstone ledges; by the old Crafts house with the date 1709 on its chimney, lately removed; by the long Downer house in Brookline village; by the Edward Devotion house, now torn down, which stood beside the brick blacksmith's shop. On again by the Punch Bowl Tavern and its swinging sign of a bowl and ladle overhung by a lemon tree; by the old White house, which stood where Whyte's block is now, so to the right and over the brook.[2] At Harvard Square, where the road divides for Brighton and Cambridge, the King's troops were puzzled and asked a little boy the way to Lexington, who replied [3] saucily, "You may ask the way there, but damn it, you wont ask the way back!" Set right, the Regulars went on once more, along Harvard Street, by the old Davis house; by the old Aspinwall house, then 115 years old; past the old Sharp house nearly opposite Alton Place, and so on by Dr. Eliphalet Downer's house, since remodelled and occupied by Mr. Charles H. Stearns, and up beyond Edward Devotion's summer home, more recently known as the old Babcock house. Near the Coolidge Corner neighborhood Mr. Griggs, then a boy, was working on Corey Hill when he heard the drums and fifes, and, climbing a fence, sat there while the procession went by.[4] He was greatly taken with the glitter and the brass guns, and

[1] *American Archives*, II, 4th ser., 438. Force.

[2] "Old Brookline." Dr. Augustine Shurtleff in the *Brookline Chronicle*, August 8, 1891.

[3] Related by the late Mr. A. W. Goddard, 1895.

[4] "Brookline in the Revolution." Margaret Elisabeth May. *Brookline Historical Publication Society*, No. 3, note 8.

thought how fine they were! The Winchester [1] family,
living a little further on, are said to have kindly but unwill-
ingly given the men water.

Shortly after reaching Colonel Thomas Gardner's house,
on the Allston side of Brighton Avenue, the British were
at the river. "The two pieces of cannon made us very
slow," said one [2] of the men writing home. The route
taken as the roads then ran, made it an eight mile march
from School Street in Boston to the bridge across the Charles
at Allston. The men-of-war boats, however, were still at
Phipps' farm on the Cambridge side, and doubtless Gage
thought it good policy to awe the towns by a parade of
force. The river is at this point about 200 yards wide
and has been a crossing place since A.D. 1662. Two or
three hours had been spent on the road, bringing the time
to between twelve and one o'clock. General Heath had
ordered the bridge up, but unhappily the Committee of
Safety being loath to lose the planks had piled them beside
the shore [3] so that the main body was only temporarily
checked. John Montresor [4] of the Engineers, of Huguenot
descent, who had ridden on some miles in advance of
his corps with four volunteers, felt that it was largely
owing to him and his party that a passage was secured at
this point, failing which the troops must have taken a more
roundabout course through Watertown. Sending one of his
companions back to report how things stood to Lord Percy,
Montresor and the rest galloped ahead through the town of
Cambridge, already in arms. On the main body coming up,
men were sent across on the string-pieces of the bridge to relay
the boards and Lord Percy passed on.[3] The troops would
not have been stayed long in any case, as planks and [5] carpenters had been brought along to meet just such an emergency.

[1] *History of Brookline*, 121. Woods.
[2] Intercepted Letters, *Essex Gazette*, May 2-12, 1775.
[3] *Memorial History of Boston*, III, 72. |
[4] *Evelyn Family in America*. Scull.
[5] *The Pulpit of the American Revolution*, 236. John Wingate Thornton.
Boston, 1860.

Very few incidents are given of the march between here and Lexington. The houses largely appeared to be closed, and one of the officers argued from that they should meet with little opposition. But Percy thought differently and replied, "So much the worse, we shall be fired on from these very houses." [1] At Farwell's Corner, Harvard Square, on the Brighton side of Cambridge, a little 'prentice lad, Joe, watched the soldiers from an upper window as they swung past.[2] On reaching Cambridge cross-roads, Percy was bewildered and at first saw no one of whom he might ask the way until a tutor happened along, one Isaac Smith,[3] afterwards Preceptor of Dummer Academy. Instead of misleading the enemy, as the Patriots considered fitting, Smith gave them the right direction, and was treated so coldly in consequence, he shortly after sailed for England. On his return, in 1784, he seems to have been forgiven and was for a time Librarian at Harvard. Passing the colleges, Percy went on to Menotomy, or Arlington, by North (now Massachusetts) Avenue. Near Linnæan Street, on the easterly side of the turnpike, was the home of Deacon Gideon Frost,[4] where some of the soldiers gathered about a well-sweep to draw water.

Upon reaching the Concord road at Davenport's tavern,[4] another halt was made for water. After this, as the Regulars neared Spy Pond on their left, the road became more and more country-like, and it is said that the troops met little Nabby Blackington [5] watching her mother's cow browsing along the road. The cow wandered from side to side and the little girl followed it, the men saying, "We will not hurt the child," as she crossed their ranks. Deacon Ephraim Cutter [6] of Arlington, then a boy of eight, saw the troops going by. He used to say that their

[1] *Historic Mansions*, 398. Drake.
[2] "Ballade of Old Cambridge." John Holmes.
[3] *Memorial History of Boston*, III, 72.
[4] *Historic Guide to Cambridge*, 144, 148.
[5] "Nabby Blackington." Virginia L. Townsend. *St. Nicholas*, July, 1884.
[6] *History of Arlington*, 61. Cutter.

burnished arms and bright bayonets looked like a flowing river. About a mile and a half beyond Allston bridge Lord Percy sent the carpenters and lumber home.[1] It was not until quite one o'clock, at Menotomy, he heard that firing had taken place, his informant being possibly John Howe,[2] whose journal while a spy concludes: "when I arrived at Charlestown [Cambridge?] I met Lord Percy with a regiment of regulars and two pieces of artillery. I passed the troops and went on the ferry and crossed over to Boston; went to General Gage's headquarters and informed him of my route, and all that had taken place. He said he did not think the damned rebels would have *taken up arms against* His Majesty's troops etc. From this time I was determined to leave the British army and join the Americans." On learning that the Regulars were engaged Lord Percy "pressed [3] on to their relief as fast as good order and not blowing the men" would allow, and in less than two miles the interchange of shots was heard. About this time, between one and two, that is, in the afternoon, he met Lieutenant Gould [3] of the King's Own returning to headquarters and received fuller particulars. About a quarter of an hour later, something like a mile east of Lexington Green, he met the Regulars under Colonel Smith in full retreat.

Lieutenant Rooke [4] of the 4th Regiment, aid-de-camp to General Gage, just as the firing began was sent back by Lord Percy to inform the General of the situation of affairs, but as he was obliged to cross the country and keep out of the road in order to avoid the numerous parties of rebels who were coming from all parts, he did not arrive in Boston, by way of Charlestown, till past four o'clock.

Soon after the main body had gone forward, a mes-

---

[1] *American Revolutionary Pulpit*, 236. Thornton.

[2] *History of Middlesex County*, II, 584. Hurd.

[3] *History of Arlington*, Lord Percy to General Harvey, 81. Cutter.

[4] *Mass. His. Soc. Pro.*, March, 1890.

senger[1] rode post haste from Cambridge with word of the delayed convoy, waiting for repairs to be made at the bridge. A plan was quickly laid for its capture. The honor of leadership is disputed, but probably the Rev. Dr. Phillips Payson of Chelsea organized the attack, helped by the Rev. Edward Brooks of Medford. The old men of the neighborhood exempt from service, some dozen in all, got together hastily at Cooper's tavern and formed a plan of action. Among them were Jason and Joseph Belknap, James Rudge,[2] Israel Mead, Ammi Cutter, and an old French war veteran, David Lamson, a half-breed. Opposite the parish church, in a hollow, stood an old cider mill, near the present railroad. Here, behind a wall of earth and stone, they stood and waited. Dr. Payson was a Harvard man, about thirty-nine years old, and a native of Walpole.[3] With him were some of his own parishioners, under Captain Samuel Sprague from Chelsea. Naturally a "gentleman of the mildest manners," up to now he had been a friend to Government to such an extent certain Patriot preachers, like Parson Treadwell, had been unwilling to exchange pulpits with him.[4] Earlier that day, however, being at Lexington, Dr. Payson had with his own eyes witnessed the slaughter on the Green, and was now ready to head the attack, musket in hand. Captain Benjamin Blaney of Malden had early received word to report with his Militia company of seventy-five men at Watertown, where the Middlesex regiment under Colonel Gardner rallied. But on the way to the rendezvous a general officer had met him and diverted their march to Lexington.[5] At West Cambridge they met the provision train and, according to Bernard Green, who was present, had a chief part in its capture. Another who

[1] "The Old Men of Menotomy." Henry A. Kidder. *Young People's Magazine,* June, 1895.

[2] *Arlington Advocate,* March 27, 1875.

[3] *Diary of the Revolution,* 66. Moore.

[4] *Remembrancer or Impartial Repository of Public Events for the year MDCCLXXV,* 83. J. Almon.

[5] *History of Middlesex County,* 126. Drake.

fought on that day, Chaplain Thaxter,[1] already referred to, considers the head of the party to have been the Rev. Mr. Brooks, a great grandfather of the late Bishop Phillips Brooks, who, on this occasion, is remembered [2] as riding off to Lexington in his full-bottomed wig, carrying a gun on his shoulder. Whichever led, all acted with spirit and concert when the two wagons, one loaded with provisions and the other with ammunition, rumbled into sight. They were escorted by a guard of twelve Grenadiers under the command of a lieutenant, who is said to have ridden out for recreation [3] and to see the country. The call to surrender was met by a lash to the horses and the old men fired. A driver and four of the horses were immediately killed;[4] several other men, including one taken to be an officer, since all his buttons were quarter of a dollar pieces, also fell at this time.[5]

A London paper [6] refers to the commander of the convoy as being killed and gives his name as Captain Hogskie. Two more were wounded, while six men are said to have thrown their guns into Spy Pond and followed the westerly shore toward J. T. Trowbridge's old home, where, giving up all thought of escape, the story runs, they surrendered to an old woman, named Mother Batherick, out picking dandelions! [7] She took them to Captain Ephraim Frost's [3] house, and delivered them up to a party of Provincials with the words, "If you ever live to get back, you tell King George that an old woman took six of his grenadiers prisoners." A squib [8] went the rounds of the English Opposition papers that, "If an old Yankee woman can take six

[1] *Historical Magazine*, March, 1869.
[2] *Life of Francis Parkman*, 6. Charles Haight Farnham. Boston, 1900: Little, Brown and Company.
[3] "The Old Men of Menotomy." Kidder. *Young People's Magazine*, June, 1895.
[4] *Mass. His. Soc. Pro.*, April, 1878.
[5] *Arlington Advocate*, April 3, 1875.
[6] *Morning Chronicle and London Advertiser*, June 13, 1775.
[7] *Historic Mansions*, 403. Drake.
[8] *History of Arlington*, 63. Cutter.

grenadiers, how many soldiers will it require to conquer America?" One of the Regulars before surrendering bent [1] his gun over a stone wall to destroy it. This encounter took place so near the church, a ball passed through the door and the window glass was broken. Immediately after the firing ceased, all marks of a struggle were effaced, so as not to anger the returning Regulars. The wagons were removed to a hollow behind Captain William Adams' [2] house, east of the present railway station, together with the body of the fallen officer. Parson Cooke helped clear the highway of the bodies of the killed horses, which were dragged over by Mr. Trowbridge's, near Spring Valley. Later, the New Englanders carefully removed the horses' shoes. Rev. Dr. McClure [3], who happened to be on the spot at the time, remarked on them as fine British horses. Their bones were then left to bleach. Colonel Thomas Russell [1] remembered as a boy chucking them into Spy Pond in play. All could help themselves freely from the captured stores. One thirteen year old boy took a pack and blanket to his mother at the Whittemore house near Mystic River, but she would not let him come in for fear of reprisals.[1] As some of the company were going home they met Lieutenant Gould near Mill Street, who, it will be remembered, had been wounded in the ankle at Concord bridge, and was now riding slowly back to Boston. Owing to his wound, he was soon at their mercy, but through the intervention of Rev. Mr. Brooks [4] his life was spared. "Little Gould," as his friends called him, although he enjoyed an income of £1,900 and offered £200 ransom,[5] was closely guarded, first to the house of Mr. Ammi Cutter, the miller, and thence to Medford, where the living horses taken from the convoy were likewise driven. A tablet at Arlington Centre close to the first parish church commemorates these events. It runs as follows:

[1] *Arlington Advocate*, March 27, April 3, 1875.
[2] *History of Middlesex County*, III, 178. Hurd.
[3] *Mass. His. Soc. Pro.*, April, 1878.
[4] *History of Medford*, 450. Usher.
[5] *London Chronicle*, July 6–8, 1775.

AT THIS SPOT
ON APRIL 19, 1775
THE OLD MEN OF MENOTOMY
CAPTURED A CONVOY OF
EIGHTEEN SOLDIERS WITH SUPPLIES
ON ITS WAY TO JOIN
THE BRITISH AT LEXINGTON.

Sylvester Osborn,[1] of Danvers — later a major — then a lad of sixteen years, was one of a guard detached from Captain Eppes' company to take charge of one of the captured wagons and eleven prisoners. They had scarcely left the main body on this duty when they heard the rattle of the firearms as the British in full retreat drew near. The prisoners taken here were ultimately placed in Ipswich gaol.

Mrs. Hannah (Fayerweather) Winthrop,[2] wife of John Winthrop, F.R.S. and LL.D.[3] of Edinburgh University, Hollis professor of mathematics and natural philosophy at Harvard from 1738 to 1779, wrote concerning this day to Mrs. Mercy Warren of Plymouth, that her "partner" — sixty-one years of age at this time — had been confined to the house a fortnight by illness, but seeing a second brigade pass, "looking with the ferocity of barbarians," it seemed necessary to retire to some place of safety. After dinner they accordingly set out, not knowing whither to go, but were directed to a place called Fresh Pond, about a mile from the town, beyond "Elmwood." "But what a distressed house did we find," she writes, "filled with women whose husbands had gone forth to meet the assailants, seventy or eighty of these (with numberless infant children), weeping and agonizing for the fate of their husbands. In addition to this scene of distress we were for some time in sight of the battle; the glittering instruments of death proclaiming by an incessant fire that much blood must be shed, that many widowed and orphaned ones must be left as monuments of British barbarity." And where was Dr. Warren all this time? Early Wednesday morning a special messenger brought him

[1] *History of Danvers*, 217, 106. Hanson.
[2] *Mass. His. Soc. Pro.*, April, 1875.
[3] *Memorial History of Boston*, IV, 493.

word that the first blood had been shed at Lexington. Calling a pupil, William Eustis, then a lad of twenty-one, later Governor of Massachusetts, Warren asked him to "go round and take care of the patients" and rode himself to Charlestown ferry. This was at about eight in the morning. As the boat pushed off he spoke hopefully to a grandfather of the late John R. Adan,[1] saying, "Keep up a brave heart! They have begun it,—that either party can do; and we'll end it,—that only one can do." As Warren rode along on the Charlestown side he soon met a resident, Dr. Welsh,[2] who stopped to remark, "Well, they are gone out." Again he gave encouragement, "Yes, and we will be up with them before night." Affairs detained him until about ten, when Jacob Rogers,[1] another Charlestown man, tells us he met Warren riding "hastily" out of town. Rogers says, "We were alarmed with various reports concerning the King's troops, which put everybody in confusion. I asked him if the news was true of the men being killed at Lexington. He assured me it was. He rode on."

Meanwhile General Heath [3] had been roused from his bed by dawn, and set out early to meet the Committee of Safety.[4] From there he took a cross-road to Watertown, "the British being in possession of the Lexington road," and here he was joined by Dr. Warren and others. Frothingham [1] thinks it not unlikely that before noon the military officers had the advice of the Committee to guide them in the immediate emergency. This would seem to be the case in view of the orders despatched to change the route of the Malden men, as already noted. Moreover, we are told, that on some Militia applying in person for orders, they were sent by Heath [3] to Cambridge to take up the planks of the bridge at Allston again, barricade its south end, and take post awaiting the return of the British. When the meeting broke up General Heath and

---

[1] *Life of Warren*, 457, 459. Frothingham.
[2] *Memorial History of Boston*, III, 72.
[3] *Memoirs*, 12, 13. General Heath.
[4] *History of Arlington*, 65. Cutter.

Dr. Joseph Warren were companions on a by-road to Lexington. They seem to have first tried to pass up behind Percy's column, but had their way barred by bayonets. They then appear to have retraced their way by the main road into Arlington. Here they came on two soldiers, apparently stragglers, at Watson's Corner, who were trying to steal old Mr. Watson's [1] horse. He was pluckily holding on to the animal, while the redcoats tugged on the other side, when Warren came riding up and helped drive them off. Shortly after two British officers rode up to the group and asked the whereabouts of the troops. Dr. Warren replied he did not know. Dr. Welsh, who was of the party, describes them as "greatly alarmed." It was afterwards suspected that they were commanders of the baggage train who had fallen to the rear.[2] This would make it twelve or one at the time. Dr. Welsh then returned to Charlestown, leaving the doctor and Heath to discover a by-road which carried them at length to Lexington. "Our General" — as Heath always calls himself — joined the Militia at this point, as we know from his own words, just after Lord Percy had effected his conjunction. The valiant part taken by the doctor in the pursuit is thus alluded to in Boyle's Eulogy [1] published 1781:

> Again the conflict glows with rage severe,
> And fearless ranks in combat mixt appear.
> Victory uncertain! fierce contention reigns,
> And purple rivers drench the slippery plains!
> Column to column, host to host oppose,
> And rush impetuous on their adverse foes;
> When lo! the hero Warren from afar
> Sought for the battle, and the field of war.
> And bids the thunder of the battle rise.
> Sudden arrangement of his troops are made,
> And sudden movements round the plain displayed.
> Columbia's Genius in her polished shield
> Gleams bright and dreadful o'er the hostile field!
> Britons, astonished, tremble at the sight,
> And, all confused, precipitate their flight.

[1] *Life of Warren*, 457, 461. Frothingham.
[2] *Memorial History of Boston*, III, 72.

It was here in West Cambridge Dr. Warren had the pin [1] shot away from the hair of an ear-lock. One of the first things Heath [2] and Warren did was to "assist," the General tells us, "in forming a regiment which had been broken by the shot from the British field-pieces. (For the discharge of these, together with the flames and smoke of several buildings, to which the British, nearly at the same time set fire, open'd a new and more terrific scene.)" Before getting under way Percy appears to have addressed his men; at least the London *Gazetteer* [3] gives the following incident as "authentic." "On the retreat of the troops from Lexington, Lord Percy thought proper to make a speech to his corps, in order to encourage them, a young Lieutenant, who, it seems, entertained but an indifferent opinion of his Lordship's eloquence, could not forbear smiling. This was observed by his Colonel, who went up and struck him severely with his cane. The Lieutenant knowing, from the severity of the articles of war, that a challenge would be immediately punished with death, seemed to take no further notice, but represented the indignity he had suffered to many of his brother officers, upon which a meeting of the subalterns was called, and it was determined to address General Gage, and insist that the Colonel should be broke, or that in case of refusal, they would throw up their commissions."

A history of the Royal Artillery published so recently as 1872, by Captain Francis Duncan, serves to show that the dangers of the day are little known and still underestimated in the old country. The present regiment has a right to pride itself on its predecessor's endurance and not pass all over with a quiet allusion, "Under the fire of the guns, the troops were able to continue their retreat comparatively unmolested." For seven miles after leaving Lexington the 23d Regiment continued to form the rear [4]

---

[1] *History of Middlesex County*, III, 180. Hurd.

[2] *Memoirs*, 14.

[3] *The Gazetteer and New Daily Advertiser*, July 1, 1775.

[4] *Mass. His. Soc. Pro.*, March, 1890.

guard; then, having expended a great part of its ammunition, it was relieved by the Marines, the next battalion in the column. Armed men on foot and on horseback were continually coming up from all directions, bringing fresh strength and powder into the ranks of the pursuers; the British — being forced to retire for fifteen miles "under an incessant fire, which, like a moving circle,[1] surrounded and followed them wherever they went," — were taxed almost beyond endurance and showed good courage in holding out. "We were attacked," says Captain Evelyn [2] of the 4th or King's Own, "on all sides, from woods, and orchards, and stone walls, and from every house on the roadside (and this country is a continued village) so that for 14 miles we were attacking fresh posts." The fire from unseen enemies in certain houses so enraged them, writes one of their officers,[3] that they broke into them, killing all they could find. "If fire had been in them or there had been time to kindle any they would have been destroyed." "Our large flanking parties," says Evelyn, "scoured the woods and stone walls; and whenever we were fired on from houses or barns, our men dashed in and let very few of those they could find, escape." In some, Mackenzie tells us, seven or eight Americans were destroyed, in others, none were found, but after the Regulars in front had gone by they ran out from their hiding places and fell upon the rear guard.[3]

One intercepted letter remarks,[4] "When we found they fired from Houses, we set them on fire, and they ran to the woods like Devils." Another soldier [4] wrote word home: "we could not see above ten in a body for they were behind trees and walls, and fired at us and then loaded on their bellies. . . . As we came along they got before us and fired at us from the Houses and killed and wounded a great many of us, but we levelled their Houses as we came along. . . .

---

[1] *History of Arlington*, 81. Cutter, quoting Lord Percy to General Harvey.
[2] *Evelyn Family in America.* Scull.
[3] *Mass. His. Soc. Pro.*, March, 1890, Lieutenant Mackenzie.
[4] *Essex Gazette*, May 12, 1775.

The shot flew thick. I got a wounded man's gun, and killed two of them as I am sure of." Still another[1] reports to his "Honoured Mother": "The Rebels were monsterous numerous, and surrounded us on every side, when they came up we gave them a smart Fire, but they never would engage us properly. I received a wound in my Head."

When the Marines had borne all they could, covering the rear, they were relieved in their duty by the 47th, and that corps by the 4th. To spare Colonel Smith's exhausted men they were placed in the van, but as the day went on the fire here was almost equally severe. The flanking parties after the first were obliged by various obstacles to keep almost close beside the main body, and so could give less protection. Lieutenant Mackenzie[2] of the 23d says the redcoats threw away their fire very inconsiderately, emboldening the farmers to draw nearer; they pressed pretty closely at times, crying, "King Hancock for ever!" He says too, many houses were plundered in spite of the officers' efforts, and by all accounts he believes that several Regulars who had stayed too long in the houses were killed in the very act. One of the officers supposed that the pursuit was the sharper from the men's taking such spoil. "The plundering was shameful," writes Lieutenant Barker;[3] "many hardly thought of anything else; what was worse, they were encouraged by some Officers." It must be borne in mind, however, that by the capture of their provision convoy they were without the natural base of supply.

One or two prisoners taken by the British, according to Lieutenant Mackenzie,[2] were killed during the retreat by the fire of their own countrymen. The Regulars too, through "eagerness and inattention, are said to have killed many of their own side." The British were at the disadvantage of having the wind blow the smoke[4] directly back upon them all

---

[1] *Essex Gazette*, May 12, 1775.
[2] *Mass. His. Soc. Pro.*, March, 1890.
[3] *Atlantic Monthly*, May, 1877.
[4] *American Revolution*, I, 483. Gordon.

the time; they would load and fire over the stone walls, when there was not a man behind them, but, for the matter of that, the Yankees were constantly running from front to flank and from flank to rear, loading their pieces at one place and discharging them at another, so that they might quite easily mistake their whereabouts. Captain George Harris, afterward General Lord Harris, Baron of Seringapatam and Mysore, G.C.B.,[1] was then aged thirty, senior captain of the 5th Regiment, and captain of the Grenadiers. Being ordered to cover the retreat at one stage, he was so hard pressed by the Americans that twenty men, besides Lieutenant Thomas Baker, were either killed or wounded. This was his first essay on actual service. "The killed and wounded is sufficient evidence of the fire to which he was exposed, but it did not disturb his coolness or humanity, for in the retreat he filled his Grenadier cap with water for the relief of the wounded, and when found by Lord Percy administering it to them, would fain have had him partake of the precious beverage, which was gratefully declined." In writing to a favorite cousin May 5th he says, "How can I think I have nothing worth writing about? Wont my dear Bess be more pleased with hearing I am well and hearty, than with the account of all the world beside? That I am so, God alone can in His goodness account for; to him I have, and ever ought, to return grateful thanks for such protection. The tale would last a winter's night, so, some Christmas, when we have exhausted all our gambols, you shall have a history of our late frolic. . . . Thank you for the pocket-pistol (the bottle and cup); would that I had had it the 19th of April, for the sake of my friends and self."

Michael Jackson [2] of Newton, by one account, is said to have received the alarm from Wm. Dawes, who rode through Roxbury and Brookline and Brighton. However that may be, at early dawn John Pigeon [3] — whose home

---

[1] *Letters of Gen. Lord Harris.* Lushington.

[2] *History of Middlesex County,* III, 386. Hurd.

[3] *King's Handbook of Newton,* 273. M. F. Sweetser. Boston, 1889. Moses King Corporation.

MAJOR GEORGE HARRIS

was in Auburndale — fired an alarm gun from the gun-house near the church at the Centre. Corporal Timothy Jackson,[1] a lad not yet twenty, reported to his Captain at daybreak, and was sent on horseback to warn the men, and by eight that morning they marched. Captain Phineas Cook commanded the thirty-seven Minute-men; Captain Amariah Fuller led the West company of 105, including thirty-seven volunteers, exempt from service. Of these last, only one, Captain Edward Jackson, was under fifty; Captain Joshua Fuller was seventy-six, and Deacon Joseph Ward sixty-nine years old. The East company of seventy-six men was under Captain Jeremiah Wiswall; with him went his father, Noah Wiswall, seventy-six years old, as a volunteer, and another old man, Ebenezer Parker, aged seventy-three.

When the company of Minute-men was being formed by an orderly sergeant, in the absence of any commissioned officers, it became a question who should act as officer of the day. Michael Jackson,[1] forty years of age, a lieutenant in the French war, serving as private in the Volunteer Company, was called from the ranks and voted to the post by show of hands. Losing no time in words, he gave the order,[1] "Shoulder arms, Platoons to the right wheel. Quick time, Forward March!" and they were off. At Watertown they found the commissioned officers of the Middlesex Regiment, under Colonel Thomas Gardner, holding a council and discussing what course to pursue. Michael Jackson, captain *pro tempore*, was invited to take part in the debate, but declined with the words,[2] "The time for talking is gone by and I shall take my company the shortest route to the enemy," after which he again took the road. The council forthwith broke up, some companies following the Newton men; others dispersed, or lingered about awaiting orders. Captain Jackson's men met Lord Percy retreating, and at the first shot or two broke ranks, but rallied and

[1] *History of Newton*, 782, 334–8, 341. S. F. Smith, D.D.
[2] *History of Middlesex County*, III, 385–6. Hurd.

formed near by in a wood, together with part of the Watertown company,[1] and from this point kept after the British untiringly as far as Lechmere Point, receiving General Warren's thanks [1] at nightfall in the field.   Of their adventures several anecdotes are told.   Old Captain Noah Wiswall's home was on the northeast side of the Pond at the Centre. He had two other sons, besides Captain Jeremiah, out, and several sons-in-law were also engaged.   Despite his seventy-six years he "wanted to see what the boys were doing" and kept pace with the rest.   During the day he pointed out three redcoats, saying[2] to a comrade, "If you aim at the middle one you'll hit one of the three."   One indeed fell, but a ball from the British passed through the old man's raised hand at the same instant.   Captain Wiswall bound it up with his handkerchief and brought off the dead Regular's musket as a trophy.[1]   Joseph Ward[1] was master of a public school in Boston.   Hearing that the British were moving, he set out at daybreak for his father's house in Newton and rode from there with a gun to meet the troops. The following day, we are told, he was made aide-de-camp to General Heath.   A tradition exists that John Barber,[3] a tavernkeeper at West Newton, rode to the battle with his young son Samuel behind him, and that he was killed, the boy bringing the horse back alone.   One John Barber [1] served in the Minute Company and it is quite possible that he rode over in this way and remained behind wounded, without being killed.   Abraham Whitney [4] is said to have brought the alarm to Watertown.   The seventy men forming the company there were led by Captain Samuel Barnard. He was one of the officers moved by Captain Jackson's words to instant action.   Joseph Coolidge,[5] treasurer of Watertown, was ploughing at the "Vineyard" early that morning, when he heard of the King's troops being out.

[1] *History of Newton*, 342, 335, 343, 338.   S. F. Smith, D.D.

[2] *History of Newton*, 457.   Francis Jackson.   Boston, 1854.

[3] *Letter of E. D. Barbour*, February 8, 1896.

[4] *Boston Evening Transcript*.

[5] *History of Middlesex County*, III, 427.   Hurd.

Putting up his cattle, he left his wife and children and went to the village, where he fell in with a small company from Needham. Being more familiar with the way, he acted as their guide. At the High Rocks, on the edge of Lexington they were fired on by the British, and Coolidge fell. Nathaniel Bemis,[1] son of David, but nineteen years, fired on the retreating British and killed an officer whose sword he carried home. Phineas Stearns, another Watertown man, had an apprentice in the fight, named David Smith, whose gun burst. Besides inflicting a wound, this was "the Occation" of the following losses [2] as summed up by his master, March, 1776.

	£	s	d
one gun of the value of	2	14	0
Bayonet and Waist Belt		8	
Pouch		6	8
Haversack		2	
Powder Horn and 1¼ lb. of Powder		4	
40 Leaden Ball		1	
1 Dozen of Flints			8

Before leaving home Mr. Coolidge[3] had placed the town money in his wife's care and told her not to let any one enter the house. About noon or a little later two redcoats came and demanded entrance. Mrs. Coolidge refused them, but still they persisted. Finally she seized an axe which stood in the corner, and looking out of the second story window said, "The first one of you who dares pass this threshold, will get a deathblow from this!" This caused them to move on. It is possible that these men were stragglers from the convoy.

Lydia (Warren) Barnard,[4] the wife of David Barnard, also had an adventure. Her husband, father, and five brothers were taking part in the battle and she was at home

---

[1] *History of Middlesex County*, III, 386. Hurd.

[2] *Mass. State Archives*, Vol. 138, p. 382.

[3] Linda Coolidge. Brookline High School paper, presented 1895 in competition for the Murray Kay Prize.

[4] "She Captured a Redcoat." William Barnes Dorman. *Magazine of the Daughters of the Revolution*, October, 1893.

in her house, off the road, when a woman ran in crying, "A redcoat's coming!"   He was wounded, mounted, and supposed to be sent possibly for reinforcements, as he asked the way to Boston.   Lydia Barnard was a large, vigorous woman, and exclaimed impetuously, "How do I know but what you have killed some of my folks?"   He protested his innocence, but Mrs. Barnard, having discovered that several cartridges were missing from the box at his side, shook the man until he surrendered.   "He begged like a Trooper for his life," she used to say.[1]   The soldier was subsequently sent to the tavern for safe-keeping and later exchanged.   The horse was turned loose in the pasture, some distance behind the house, for the moment, and later given to a Mr. Stedman of Cambridge, who had ridden as messenger in the morning, and had his horse stolen from him by the advance pickets.   As for the saddle, it was thrown on the potato heap in the cellar and left with Mrs. Barnard. Beside her exploit on this occasion Mrs. Barnard was noted as a rare singer and a pleasant story is told of how, when she went to housekeeping, a Watertown man freely made her wooden ware on the understanding that she should sing evenings as he worked and always fresh songs.   Josiah Temple,[2] at this time living at Lechmere Point, later of Framingham, was out with a detachment of Militia and somewhere on the borders of Lexington and Cambridge received a ball in his shoulder which he carried to his grave.

Leaving the main road and turning down to the north by the Locke cottages — soon after crossing the railroad track — you come to the old Hill house on Forest Street. Facing toward the higher ground by "the foot of the rocks," it was well placed to command a view of the retreat.   As the tumult drew near the women and children made for Hutchinson's (or Turkey) Hill, 200 feet high, in the direction of Winchester.   In crossing the pastures they reached

---

[1] "She Captured a Redcoat."   Dorman.   *Magazine of the Daughters of the Revolution*, October, 1893.

[2] *History of Framingham*, 277.   Temple.

some bars which had to be let down; here, glancing back, the women were enraged by the rolling clouds of smoke, drawing from Nathaniel a little tot of three, the childish comment,[1] "Aren't they naughty!"

Cutler's or the Great Tavern still exists in a part of the present Russell house in upper Arlington. When the retreating British were at the "Foot of the Rocks," Mrs. Wm. Cutler [2] was told by a friend. She secured her husband's gold watch, his silver tankard, the spoons, and with all the household but black Ishmael, started up the opposite lane, toward Fillebrown's, across the Heights. They nearly met a detachment, but some Yankees coming up, headed the redcoats off and turned their course. Ishmael stayed inside until the troops came up, when he sprang out at a back window and kept watch from the hillside. The troops broke every window with their guns and drove a bayonet through the best mirror,[3] the frame of which was long preserved. They helped themselves to food, drank the cider, and left the taps of the molasses and spirit casks open. Finally, they emptied the drawers into sheets and made off with them and the bedding, setting fire to what was left. The household of twenty-one souls had not a change of shirt between them left, when they returned. The fire was put out before it did much harm through Ishmael's care; and he started for George Prentiss's house on the southern slope of the Heights with the news. Meanwhile rumors of a slave insurrection [4] had got abroad, and when the frightened women saw the faithful fellow coming, in their terror one cried, "Are you going to kill us, Ishmael?" Astonished enough, he answered good-humoredly, "Lordy Massy, no, Marm! Is my Missus here?" Little Lydia Prentiss became a Mrs. Peirce and lived to be over ninety. She remembered and used to speak of how full the house

[1] Traditional through Miss Lucy Stone of Somerville.
[2] Related by Francis H. Brown, M.D. *Arlington Advocate*, May 1, 1875.
[3] *Arlington Advocate*, April 3, 1875.
[4] *West Cambridge in 1775.* Rev. S. A. Smith.

was that day, of the peach trees being in bloom, and of hearing the cannon toward night. She also told of the Robbins [1] house being ransacked on top of Peirce Hill. The clock was set afire on the kitchen floor, but, as the story went, when the clothes-line caught alight the damp clothes fell down in a heap and put the fire out.

There were three Adams households within a quarter of a mile at this part of Menotomy. E. S. Thomas,[2] a child at the time, whose home was close by, writes: "In one of these Mrs. Adams was confined the night before; the enemy entered the house, took the bed on which she lay with her infant at the breast, and carried them into the yard, and left them there. A little boy, about four or five years old, had taken shelter under his mother's bed — his foot projected from beneath the drapery, a British soldier thrust his bayonet through it, and for a moment pinned it to the floor; the boy did not utter even a cry: this fact I had from his mother." Mrs. Hannah Adams was the second wife of Joseph Adams, deacon since 1759 and now sixty years of age. In 1864 the house remained as L to Henry J. Locke's. It stood on the opposite side from the present railroad station; a tree in front of the house was thickly spattered with lead, much prized by West Cambridge boys as time went on. Some accounts of the above incident make the infant a few days or even three weeks old, but all agree the mother was still weak, "scarce able to walk to the fire, and had not been to the chamber door since the baby was born." To follow it in detail, so soon as the firing was heard Mrs. Adams implored her husband to save himself by flight. Having been helped [3] into her clothes by her daughters, one a young woman of twenty, the other a girl of fourteen, she took her babe in her arms and awaited the soldiers, the children meanwhile creeping under her

[1] *Arlington Advocate*, April 3, 1875.

[2] *Reminiscences of the Last Sixty-five Years*, I, 10. E. S. Thomas. Hartford, 1840.

[3] *Christian Register*, October 28, 1854.

high four-post bed. Outside the uproar increased. Joined to the musketry was the sound of horses neighing, of men shouting and groaning. Suddenly the front door burst in and three redcoats came into the room where she lay. Drawing the bed curtains [1] one soldier pointed a bayonet at her breast. "For the Lord's sake, do not kill me," she cried. "Damn you!" was the retort, another soldier adding, "We will not hurt the woman, if she will go out of the house, but we will surely burn it." A letter [2] of that day says: then they "pulled off ye Cloths & told her to get out of ye way, or to use yir phrase to make herself Scarce." Wrapping the baby girl (afterwards Mrs. James Hill) in a blanket she crept with her to the corn barn, leaving five other little ones alone in the house hidden under the bed. The children [3] watched the soldiers' feet moving about, with keenest interest. At length nine year old Joel's curiosity got the upper hand of his fear, and he lifted a corner of the valance to get a better view. A soldier spying him said,[4] "Why don't you come out here?" "You'll kill me if I do," the boy answered. "No, we wont," was the reply, on which the child came out and tagged around after them. No objection was made while the family treasures and silver spoons were being packed up, but when they opened the cupboard [5] and offered to touch the communion silver in Deacon Adams' charge, Joel spoke out,[4] "Dont you touch them 'ere things. Daddy'll lick you if you do." In spite of his remonstrance, however, the pieces were dropped in a sack and carried off. One of the largest, a silver tankard, the gift of Jonathan Butterfield[6] in 1769, was redeemed at their own expense by the two deacons (Deacon Adams and Deacon Thomas Hall) through the information of a

[1] *History of Arlington*, 66. Cutter.

[2] *Henry Dunster and his Descendants*, 87. Letter from Rev. John Marrett to his Uncle Isaiah Dunster "att Harwich."

[3] *West Cambridge in 1775*. Rev. S. A. Smith.

[4] "Old Men of Menotomy." Kidder. *Young People's Magazine*, June, 1895.

[5] *Christian Register*, October 28, 1854.

[6] *Arlington Advocate*, April 3, 1875.

silversmith named Austin, to whom it had been pawned. This piece is still preserved by the First Parish (Unitarian) and may be seen at the Public Library.   The works of a tall clock were also carried off as spoil.   As they left the plunderers upset a basket of chips in the middle of the floor, thrust in them a brand from the fireside, and breaking up some flag-bottomed chairs, piled them on the kindlings.[1] A Bible [2] is spoken of as being partly torn helping to make them blaze.   One of these very outspoken children seeing a soldier beginning to tear its leaves, we are told, pushed his head out from under a table to cry, "My dad'll give it to you, if you spoil our best Bible."   A tale has grown up to the effect [1] as soon as the soldiers had gone, the children managed to put the fire out, using a pot of home-brewed beer and water from the cask outside, although some pewter was melted before they succeeded in their efforts!   In making his escape at the outset, balls flew whistling about Deacon Adams' head as he fled toward Parson Cook's barn on the side-road, where he covered himself in the hayloft.[3]   Happily for him the soldiers, although in close pursuit, dared not delay, and pierced the haymow hastily with their bayonets, missing him.   Perhaps but for Deacon Adams' running in this direction the parsonage might have escaped; as it was,[4] "yy broke ye windows of Mr. Cook's house & fired into it & ye kitchen, ye setty room & ye best room N. E.," and among the plunder of that day was carried off his clerical habit and wig.   From the "[5]Recollections of a Bostonian" in the *Centinel*, we learn that during the succeeding winter a Scotch sentry was scared by one of his mates, who had dressed up in Parson Cook's gown, supposing him to be the spectre of Parson Joseph Sewall of the Old South. Parson Samuel Cook had in 1762 married Lucy,[6] a daughter

[1] *West Cambridge in 1775.*   Rev. S. A. Smith.
[2] *Historic Mansions*, 404.   Drake.
[3] *Arlington Advocate*, April 3, 1875.
[4] *Henry Dunster and his Descendants.*   Letter of Rev. John Marrett.
[5] *Principles and Acts of the Revolution*, 129.   Niles.
[6] *History of Arlington*, 208, 29.   Cutter.

of the late Parson John Hancock and relict of the Rev.
Nicholas Bowes of Bedford, thus becoming an uncle by
marriage of John Hancock the Patriot. He himself was
born at Hadley and was at this time sixty-six years old.
He had shown great earnestness in the cause of liberty; and
in a sermon to the Minute-men,[1] from Nehemiah iv. 13–15,
he had said, "There at present appears no other choice
left us, but either tamely to sit down and surrender our
lives and properties, our wives and children, our religion
and consciences, to the arbitrary will of others, or trusting
in God, to stand up in our own defence, and of the British
Constitution." He was now eager to join in the fray and
could hardly be restrained by his more prudent son. When
a lookout on the Ridge behind the parsonage reported that
bayonets were in sight on the Lexington road, young Cook
set out with his father [2] and a white horse in the only chaise
owned in town, making for Mr. Clark's house on the outskirts of Watertown. A bullet hole [3] through one of the
parsonage shutters and a stain on the floor where a wounded
man was lifted in at a window remained to be seen in 1864.
The house was then occupied by his granddaughter. Since
its removal, the shutter has fitly found lodging in the Public
Library. A scrap of the old man's journal [1] shows how his
spirit was stirred. "Scatter, O Lord," runs his prayer,
"those who delight in blood! For the sighing of the
oppressed and needy, make bare thine Almighty arm for
their help! Teach our hands to fight, since in thy Providence we are called to this." In the Parish Register he sums
up the dead of 1775 as "47, besides some Provincials and
Hutchinson's Butchers [the Regulars] slain in Concord
Battle, near the meeting House buried here." There
is a tradition that one British soldier was buried between
the Rev. S. A. Smith's house on Academy Street, and
Pleasant Street, the rest, by some estimated as upward of

[1] *West Cambridge in 1775.* Rev. S. A. Smith.
[2] "Old Men of Menotomy." Kidder. *Young People's Magazine,* June, 1895.
[3] *Arlington Advocate,* April 10, 1875.

forty, near a wall close to a brook, in the slaves'[1] portion of the graveyard.

A newspaper[2] of 1847 speaks of the then "new" depot at West Cambridge taking the place of some venerable elms which stood before the house occupied by Captain Wm. Adams, already 130 years old in 1775. The westerly end of the house was cut off to make way for the railroad and disclosed many musket balls bedded in the brick filling of its walls. The portion still standing bore traces in its clapboards of how completely it was riddled with bullets. Two Danvers men[3] are said to have hidden in the chimney here, one in particular finding safety by supporting himself on the kettle lug-pole. A woman routed them out after a time, the story goes, with a broom and made them bear their part in what was doing. Mrs. William Adams,[3] on returning to the old home, had to step over a British soldier's dead body in order to enter her back door. In the front room she found another Regular lying mortally wounded and her white sanded floor all stained. She tried her best to bring the wounded man around by preparing nourishing food, but he only lingered a few hours. The front door panel here was pierced by a bullet, as may yet be seen in the section preserved in the Town Library. It was just about here, when the troops were at the centre of the town, that Landlord Cutler[4] got back from spreading the alarm. He put his horse in a barn, and without waiting to see what had happened at his own house above, ran down by the side of the new burying ground. In his haste he tripped, and as he fell heard a soldier cry, "There's another of the d—d Yankees gone!"

[1] *History of Arlington*, 70.   Cutter.
[2] *Farmers Monthly Visitor*, April 30.   Quoted by Cutter, pp. 146–7
[3] *West Cambridge in 1775*.   Rev. S. A. Smith.
[4] *Arlington Advocate*, May 1, 1875.

CHAPTER IV

THROUGH CAMBRIDGE AND SOMERVILLE

THE news that the Regulars were out reached South Danvers, now Peabody, about nine A.M. Samuel Eppes was captain here and immediately started, together with Gideon Foster. Foster was then twenty-six years old and had been chosen about ten days before captain of a Minute Company. Before leaving, the Rev. Mr. Holt[1] of the Middle Precinct, South Parish, gave the soldiers his blessing. Mr. Holt is quoted as saying, "I had rather live on potatoes than submit," and had drilled regularly in Captain Eppes' company. Captain Israel Hutchinson's men were from North Danvers, now Danversport, and Beverly. Hutchinson[2] was nearly fifty years old; he had been out in 1758 at Lake George and Ticonderoga, and again in 1759 with Wolfe against Montcalm. His home was at New Mills, named from Archelaus Putnam's wheat mills, running since 1754. But one man[2] remained behind here, Frank Brown, who was ill abed, and the women were kept in suspense, anxiously waiting at Captain Hutchinson's house[3] until Jonathan Sawyer, just at nightfall, arrived from the front with news. The Lynn men also had early word and lost no time in rallying. Sam Ireson,[4] then five years old, used to tell of his brothers, Edward and John — the one nineteen, the other seventeen — being called out by the neighbors' boys, who fired off a musket under the window as a summons.

[1] *Address on the Sixtieth Anniversary of the Battle*, 12. Appendix, 27, note A. Daniel P. King. Salem, 1835.

[2] *History of Danvers*, 185–6, 87. Hanson.

[3] *History of Essex County*, I, 448. D. Hamilton Hurd. Philadelphia, 1888: J. W. Lewis & Co.

[4] *Lynn in the Revolution. Compiled from notes gathered by Howard Kendall Sanderson*, I, 36–7. Copyright 1909 by Carrie May Sanderson. Boston, 1909: W. B. Clarke Company.

Andrew Mansfield, Jr.,[1] aged eleven, harnessed up and drove his father to the rendezvous at Gowing's tavern. From scattered stories we can picture the everyday occupations sharply interrupted by the call to arms. A house,[1] still standing opposite the Lynn hospital, already framed, was to have been raised that day, but the men who were to have put it up marched off on the alarm. Jotham Webb [2] was a brickmaker and busy in his yard at work. He had been married but a few days and hurried home to take leave of his young wife and put on his wedding suit, telling her, "If I die I will die in my best clothes." Abednego Ramsdell of Lynn was five-and-twenty, one of three brothers;[3] the other two were named Meshech and Shadrach, all sons of one Noah. He had been married a year and a month, to Hannah Woodbury, living in the eastern part of Essex Street. Ramsdell was out along the shore early gunning, when he heard the alarm. Dropping the two black ducks already shot he hastened to overtake his company, and was seen running through the town, his socks slipped down over his shoes. The story goes,[4] he was hailed by a woman who had a presentiment he would be killed, and replied to her warnings, "That may be, but I hope not before I get a shot at a redcoat to make the account square!" Captain Bancroft,[1] although over fifty years of age, had never seen fighting, and going along asked a veteran private, Zerubbabel Hart, if he was afraid. "No," Hart replied, "but I tell you to look out for the flank guard!"

The Common in South Danvers, where the company of that town mustered, was close to the tavern. Its innkeeper had been forced to confess in public:[5]

> I, Isaac Wilson, a tory I be,
> I, Isaac Wilson, I sells tea.

[1] *Lynn in the Revolution*, I, 36–7, 42.   Sanderson.

[2] *History of Danvers*, appendix, 296.   Hanson.

[3] *History of Lynn*, 339.   Alonzo Lewis and James R. Newhall.   Boston, 1865.

[4] *Centennial Memorial of Lynn*, 55.   James R. Newhall.   Lynn, 1876: Thomas B. Breare.

[5] *Beside Old Hearth Stones*, 193.   Brown.

It was known as The Bell Tavern, from its pictured signpost, and bore the motto:[1]

> I'll toll you in, if you have need,
> And feed you well and bid you speed.

While the men were mustering, a Quaker lady who lived opposite the Bell, the wife of Friend Edward Southwick, slipped some cheese into Haskett Derby's[2] knapsack observing, "We cannot assist thee and thy fellow-soldiers, but there is a long and painful march before thee, and as it is not right thee shouldst suffer,[3] if thee knows anyone who is hungry, there are twelve loaves of bread in my kitchen, which I have just taken from the oven, and I should not miss them if I never saw them again." Captain Jeremiah Page, over fifty years of age, bought here[4] four dozen biscuits and six pounds of cheese for his men, besides two yards of homespun tape, the last for use in bandaging possibly, or for wadding. He led[5] thirty-eight men, Eppes about seventy, and Captain Samuel Flint, also of Danvers, about forty. Captain Caleb Dodge's Beverly company engaged with them. Although they started independently of each other they made about the same time and met at Arlington. When asked by an officer as to a rendezvous Captain Flint[6] had replied, "Where the enemy is you will meet me." Captain Joseph Rea's Militia company from Beverly was later in starting. He had ridden down to the Farms with the alarm, but even so, before three that afternoon we find the men had gathered or marched. After they were gone a group of women met, and some despondingly exclaimed, "Our husbands and sons are gone, and none are left to protect us. If the Regulars come during their absence, what will become of us, what shall we do?" "Do?" cried

---

[1] *Beside Old Hearth-Stones*, 191. Brown.

[2] *Centennial Celebration of Danvers*, 24.

[3] *History of Danvers*, 105. Hanson.

[4] *Under Colonial Roofs*, 33. Jones.

[5] *Report of the Committee appointed to Revise the Soldiers' Record*, 149–50. Danvers, 1895. Published by the Town. Eben Putnam.

[6] *Danvers Address*, 23–4. King.

Hannah Batchelder,[1] the wife of Josiah Batchelder, Jr., "Do? Who cares for the Regulars? Let them come; and if they do not behave themselves, we'll take our brooms and drive them out of town."

At Woburn Gideon Foster learned of a short cut to the right of certain hills,[2] and in four hours his men had travelled on foot sixteen miles, fully half of the way on a run.[3] The companies when gathered together at Menotomy (West Cambridge) took post at Mr. Jason Russell's, one of the principal citizens thereabouts, whose land[4] extended along the present North Avenue, from Deacon Joseph Adams's to the Common by the meeting-house, stretching back on the Watertown Road beyond Parson Cook's. He was about to reshingle and the men made a rough barrier out of the bundles of shingles and barrels near his gate, west of the meeting-house. Mr. Russell was fifty-eight years old and had purposed stopping at George Prentiss's house over the hill, some distance from the highroad, where he had left his family. But on returning to bring away some valuables[5] he found the Danvers men in position, some back of the house, others behind the wall and barricade nearer the road, others again in the orchard.

Ammi Cutter, a neighbor on the north side of the road, seeing Russell among the soldiers crossed the brook and begged him to go to a safer spot, but he replied,[4] "An Englishman's home is his castle," and finding it too late for escape he joined the Danvers men in their ambush. Hutchinson, remembering the manœuvre of a flank guard, cautioned[6] young Foster to be prepared for an attack from that quarter. Foster accordingly was not in the enclosure, but took a place behind some trees on the hillside. The road bends, back of the ridge-like Heights, rising 310 feet — up

---

[1] *History of Beverly*, 62–3. Edwin M. Stone. Boston, 1843.

[2] *Arlington Advocate*, March 27, 1875.

[3] *Danvers Address*, appendix. King.

[4] *History of Middlesex County*, III, 179. Hurd.

[5] *Historic Mansions*, 402. Drake.

[6] *History of Danvers*, 107. Hanson.

toward Lexington — and thus favored the British approach. They were fairly on the Minute-men before discovered. So many men were rallying that day, at their first appearance even the veteran Hutchinson was misled, and said, "They are our own men," but Aaron Cheever [1] a moment later exclaimed, "No, they are Regulars, don't you see their red coats!"

The British were retreating by the highroad, but their strong flanks were coming down on either hand, guarding their centre. This exposed the Danvers men to a double fire, and instantly there was the greatest confusion. Mr. Cutter [2] was at the time returning to the north side of the road, and barely escaped the flank guard by throwing himself down flat amongst the logs at the neighboring mill. Bark was flying from the logs through the continuous fire and he had jerked silver [3] from his trowser pocket by his headlong fall, but he felt his only safety lay in remaining motionless. Meanwhile the flank guard on the south side of the road made a circuit along the foot of the hill and drove the Americans, lying in wait there, down upon the main body. Foster's men from the hillside now passed along the margin of the pond and crossed the road [4] in front of the troops. Jotham Webb of New Mills was shot through the body and killed by the first fire. Ramsdell of Lynn also soon fell dead. Captain Jeremiah Page [1] escaped by running through the orchard, bringing a row of apple trees between him and the enemy. His son, Samuel Page, twenty-two years of age, was one of the party in the yard; he was just driving a cartridge home with a wooden ramrod when the flank came up. In his eagerness, the ramrod snapped and he turned to his chum Perley Putnam [5] to borrow a fresh one, only to find his comrade killed by a ball. Foster's men from the cover of a ditch wall across the road continued

[1] *History of Danvers*, 213. Hanson.
[2] *History of Middlesex County*, III, 179. Hurd.
[3] *History of Arlington*, 69. Cutter.
[4] *Danvers Address*, 13. King.
[5] *Beside Old Hearth-Stones*, 180. Brown.

firing as long as their shot lasted.   Foster said that he fired
eleven times himself and two balls each go, taking sure
aim.   He was unhurt, but Nathaniel Cleaves of Beverly, who
stood by his side, had a finger and ramrod shot away.[1]

The most desperate part of the struggle was at the house,
where many had rushed for shelter.   Being lame Mr.
Russell [2] was the last to reach the door and was killed by
two balls in his body, receiving eleven bayonet stabs from
the exasperated enemy as they passed in and out.   Eight
of the Danvers, Beverly, and Lynn men had poured into
the house and secured themselves in the cellar; they were
followed by the Regulars and one redcoat [3] was shot at the
head of the stairs; a dozen bullet holes in its head beam
long testifying to the briskness of the encounter.   Daniel
Townsend of Lynn, aged thirty-seven, was with his comrade
Timothy Munroe [4] behind the house firing at the main
body of the troops.   Townsend had just fired and cried,
"There is another redcoat down!" when Munroe saw the
flank guard coming down the field at their back, hemming
them in.   They ran inside the house, but could not find a
cellar or closet door.   The back windows were raining in
bullets.   The nearness of the troops, however, precluding
any other outlet, Townsend [4] leaped through the end window,
carrying sash and all with him, and instantly fell dead.
Munroe followed and ran for his life between the double row
of British.   As he passed the last one he heard a redcoat cry
"Damn the Yankee!   He is bullet-proof, let him go."   He
had a ball in his leg and thirty-two bullet holes through his
clothes and hat.   Even the metal buttons of his waistcoat
were shot off.   At this time he was thirty-nine years old.
Nine months later [5] he was still unable to support his family.
During the day at some time he used his handkerchief to
bind up a British soldier's wound, and was given in grati-

[1] *Danvers Address*, 13 and appendix.   King.
[2] "Old Men of Menotomy."   Kidder.   *Young People's Magazine*, June, 1895.
[3] *History of Middlesex County*, III, 180.   Hurd.
[4] *History of Lynn*, 330–40.   Lewis and Newhall.
[5] *American Archives*, IV., 4th ser., 1418.   Force.

tude a pair of silver knee-buckles, reported as still existing.[1] The soldier, it is said, died in his arms.[2] His own riddled clothes were preserved as a souvenir of his narrow escape until he wearied of showing them.

After the engagement, Job Wilson[3] of Danvers, on examining his coat, found that a square foot of gingerbread in his pocket had been pierced by a bullet. Dennison Wallis,[4] also of Danvers, aged nineteen, was taken prisoner, but seeing that despite the officers' efforts the redcoats were killing their prisoners he attempted escape and received twelve bullet wounds, falling beside a wall in the act of leaping it. He was left for dead, but recovered. The day following the battle, as we learn by his bill against the Province, old Dr. Holyoke[5] of Salem dressed Wallis's thigh, charging 3s. for his journey and service. He had been stripped when he fell of his gun, bayonet, cartouch-box, watch, and fifteen dollars, but the following January received £8 11s. 0d. in compensation[6] from the General Court, inclusive of "nursing." The Russell house still stands on the south side of North Avenue, near Jason Street, about opposite Mill Street, on the left-hand side as you go toward Lexington, being across the street from the Baptist church. At the time of the battle it is said to have stood nearer the road. An inscription reads:

SITE OF THE HOUSE OF
JASON RUSSELL
WHERE HE AND ELEVEN OTHERS
WERE CAPTURED
DISARMED AND KILLED
BY THE RETREATING BRITISH
ON APRIL 19, 1775.

Some of the wounded[7] were taken to the tavern, others

---

[1] *History of Lynnfield*, 106. Wellman.
[2] *Lynn in the Revolution*, I, 44. Sanderson.
[3] *History of Danvers*, 107. Hanson.
[4] *History of Arlington*, 67. Cutter.
[5] *Essex Institute His. Coll.*, July, 1876.
[6] *American Archives*, IV., 4th ser., 1420. Force.
[7] *West Cambridge in 1775*. Rev. S. A. Smith.

to the meeting-house, parsonage, and nearer houses. Two
British were killed here.[1] One of the Regulars, mortally
wounded, begged to be killed outright.[2] This last Regular
may have been encountered by two of the Lynn men.
Harris Chadwell [3] and Ephraim Breed were near the Russell
house, but escaped capture. While on a sidehill the flank
guard tried to surround them, but they plunged over a stone
wall and again escaped, although in getting over Chadwell's
knee was injured. The main body of the British was
nearly on them and Chadwell, to avoid capture while bearing arms, threw his gun and equipments into a small
pond. However, he was not noticed and presently felt
emboldened to take a peep over the sheltering wall. The
Regulars were then still at hand, but had gone past when
he stole another look, and a shot was sent after them.
The return volley knocked the stones from the wall,
but left him untouched. He and Breed soon after met a
wounded redcoat who begged to be put out of pain. Breed
would have fired, but Chadwell struck his gun from his
hands, exclaiming, "Don't fire! He is our prisoner."
Thomas Newhall of Captain Rufus Mansfield's company
broke a leg in his eager pursuit. Abednego Ramsdell,
aged twenty-four, who had just fallen, had been a near
neighbor of Joseph Richards, a youth of twenty-one, where
the present Essex Street enters Swampscott. After his
friend's death a soldier very nearly finished Richards also
with a bayonet. Felling him before he could strike, the
lad continued in hot pursuit. When the battle had passed
on the bodies of twelve Americans were laid out in the south
room of the Russell house. Daniel Townsend's brother
had already taken his body home. Those remaining are
thought to have been Abednego Ramsdell, William Flint, and
Thomas Hadley of Lynn; Jason Russell, owner; Benjamin
Pierce of Salem; Lieutenant John Bacon, Nathaniel Cham-

---

[1] "Old Men of Menotomy." Kidder. *Young People's Magazine*, June, 1895.
[2] *Historic Mansions*, 402. Drake.
[3] *Lynn in the Revolution*, 45–6, 48. Sanderson.

berlain, and Amos Mills of Needham; Elias Haven and Jonathan Parker of Dedham; and Jabez Wyman and Jason Winship of Menotomy. Two days later Russell and the rest were placed on a sled and drawn by a yoke of oxen on the bare ground to the burying place and laid "head to point" in a wide trench without coffins, clothed as they fell.[1] Captain William Adams, a younger brother of the deacon, exclaiming that he could not have his neighbor buried before his eyes without a winding sheet,[2] hurriedly brought one from his house. The gravestone[3] is inscribed:

"M[r]. Jason Russell was
barbarously murdered in his own
House by Gage's bloody Troops
on ye 19th of April 1775 Ætat 59
His body is quietly resting
in this grave with Eleven
of our friends, who in like
manner, with many others were
cruelly slain on that fatal day.
Blessed are ye dead who die in y[e]
Lord."

Of the eleven, two are certainly known, these being Jabez Wyman and Jason Winship. Seventy-three years later Peter C. Brooks of Medford raised a shaft to mark the spot; at which time some bits of clothing, brass buttons, an old shot pouch, and two flints were found mingled with the bones.[4] A Bible given to the Widow Russell is preserved in that family, inscribed,[5] "Purchased with the money given her by some unknown friend in England in consideration of the loss of her beloved husband, on the 19 of April, 1775, who was inhumanly murdered by the British troops under the command of General Thomas Gage to the eternal infamy of the British nation."

At sunset the evening of the nineteenth, the women of

[1] *West Cambridge in 1775.* Rev. S. A. Smith.
[2] *History of Arlington,* 70. Cutter.
[3] *Historic Mansions,* 407. Drake.
[4] *History of Middlesex County,* III, 180. Hurd.
[5] *Story of Patriots' Day,* 103. Varney.

New Mills gathered together (in a house occupied in 1848 by a Mrs. Reed) with the children. At dusk, Jonathan Sawyer[1] came slowly home with his heavy tidings, and Lydia Webb, the young bride, learned that she was become a widow. The Danvers men spent that night at Medford and returned next day to bring home the bodies of their comrades who had fallen. It would appear that the following vivid little touch has reference to their journey home. Joanna Mansfield,[2] then a young girl living on Boston Street, near Park, in a house later known as Bubier's, had again and again on the previous day helped in drawing well-water for the thirsty lads hurrying to Arlington. Now as the cart carrying the seven bodies passed she recognized that they belonged to members of the same company by their gray homespun stockings. We are told that on the return of the Danvers men they were met by the townspeople, and the sexton[3] of the south parish drove the carriage containing the slain to the house of Mr. Samuel Cook, Sr., on Central Street. These were:

SAMUEL COOK, JR., thirty-three years, who fell by the side of his brother-in-law, Jonathan Tarbell.
GEORGE SOUTHWICK, twenty-five years.
HENRY JACOBS, JR., twenty-two years.
EBENEZER GOLDTHWAIT, twenty-two years.

The other Danvers men who fell belonged to Hutchinson's company and their bodies were carried the evening of the 20th to their captain's house to rest that night at Danversport; the railroad station now occupies its site.[4] Their names were:

BENJAMIN DALAND, JR., twenty-five years.
PERLEY PUTNAM, twenty-one years.
JOTHAM WEBB, twenty-two years.

The next day, Friday, they were buried from the Old

---

[1] *History of Danvers*, 87. Hanson.
[2] *Lynn in the Revolution*, I, 41–2. Sanderson.
[3] *History of Essex County*, II, 1011. Hurd.
[4] *Beside Old Hearth-Stones*, 188. Brown.

South Church, Danvers, the Rev. Mr. Holt[1] making a "well adapted prayer." Armed men filled the gallery, two Minute companies from Salem acted as escort with reversed arms and muffled drums, while soldiers from Newburyport, Salisbury, and Amesbury — going to besiege Boston — formed in single ranks along the road as the funeral passed. Three volleys were fired at the grave.[2]

Captain Flint[2] of Danvers had been reported killed, so that his return occasioned great rejoicings. He lived then — to fall two years later at the head of his company at Stillwater. Captain Flint's men are credited with marching forty miles and one of them, Nathaniel Smith,[3] who carried a prisoner to Ipswich, with marching a total of sixty miles. Of the Danvers killed, Daland and Southwick left families; the town generously supporting[4] the latter's family after his untimely loss. Dennison Wallis of Danvers, undeterred by his wounds, went privateering for a time. Dying childless in 1825[4] he endowed a school with $2,250. Joseph Bell[2] of Danvers, likewise taken prisoner, was kept two months by his captors on a frigate. Nathan Putnam[1] of Captain Hutchinson's company, a brother of Perley, received a severe shoulder wound and nine months later was still unable to do a day's work at his trade.[5] During June he advertised in the Essex *Gazette*[6] for a French fire-lock marked D. No. 6. with a marking iron on the breech, which he had carried to a cross-road near the mill and subsequently lost. He desired it might be returned through Colonel Mansfield of Lynn or to the Danvers selectmen. In February, 1776, several grants[5] were made to Captain Eppes for the use of petitioners who had met with losses. Henry Jacobs, Sr., whose son was killed, received £3 8s. 0d. in compensation for gun, bayonet, and clothing

[1] *History of Arlington*, 68, 67. Cutter.
[2] *Danvers Address*, 15–16, 14–15, 13. King.
[3] *Danvers Soldiers' Record*, 112. Putnam.
[4] *History of Danvers*, 106. Hanson.
[5] *American Archives*, IV., 4th ser., 1420, 1327, 1435. Force.
[6] *Essex Gazette*, June 8, 1775.

then lost. The widow Mary Daland for a "gun &c" was allowed £2 14s. 0d. Samuel Cook's father mentions a gun and bayonet as being lost, and received £2 12s. Nathaniel Goldthwait's son Eli lost a gun and bayonet, and had a grant of £2. Thomas Gardner, Jr., lost his gun in the battle and his father had £1 4s. 0d. allowed. Jonathan Tarbell prayed consideration for the loss of his servant's time, gun, and clothing and received a grant of £2 11s. 0d.; £3 14s. 4d. was also granted to Jotham Webb's widow [1] for "sundries" lost at that date. The neighboring towns had likewise met with losses. Cleaves, besides being wounded, lost a horse which he had ridden as far as Menotomy, also the saddle and bridle valued at £12, or $40, as Captain Hutchinson certifies,[2] for which he was allowed [1] £2 12s. 0d. Benjamin Shaw,[4] of Captain Dodge's company, likewise petitioned for consideration, having lost a fine horse valued at the lowest computation at $45, which he had used on the way from Beverly. With regard to Cleaves' wounds we learn further from Dr. Holyoke's bill: [3]

The Colony of the Massachusetts Bay to Dr. Edward Augustus Holyoke.

To Surgery, to sundry medicines administered & attendance on sundry Persons as follows:

> Nathaniel Cleaves of Beverly
> wounded in Lexington Battle
> To Amputating his finger, sutures &c
> To 5 dressings Do.

Dr. Holyoke, as we learn from the same source, while caring for Wallis in Danvers, dressed the leg of a wounded Regular, making the same charge 3s. Another doctor busy at this time was Martin Herrick,[4] a pupil of Dr. John Brooks of Medford.

Beverly had two others wounded,[5] Wilson Dodge and

[1] *American Archives*, IV, 4th ser., 1448, 1435. Force.

[2] *Mass. State Archives*, Vol. 180, p. 415, and Vol. 185, pp. 307, 308.

[3] *Essex Institute Hist. Coll.*, July, 1876.

[4] *History of Lynnfield*, 113. Wellman.

[5] *History of Essex County*, I, 700. Hurd.

Samuel Woodbury; and Reuben Kennison, killed. His body is said to have been brought home on an ox-cart and buried in the old Leach lot on Brown's Folly Hill.[1] His widow, Apphia Batchelder, later married Uriah Wright. A piece of his striped homespun shirt, a foot square in size, has been lately placed in the rooms of the Beverly Historical Society by Mrs. Elizabeth Tucker, a grand-niece; the part which was bloodstained is now decayed away.

Lynn had four men killed. Ramsdell's widow, Hannah, petitioned [2] for consideration and allowance for her husband's gun, accoutrements, and hat. Of the others, Thomas Hadley [3] was a widower, his wife Rebecca having been accidentally drowned the winter of 1771. His home was at South Lynnfield,[4] where William Flint also lived. Flint had married Sarah Larrabee in 1770 and it was doubtless a similarity in name which led to the report of Captain Samuel Flint's loss. Daniel Townsend of Lynnfield Centre left a widow and five children; when taken home his body lay at the Bancroft house the night before burial, the floor, it is said, still showing traces of bloodstains a hundred years later. He was descended,[1] through Thomas Townshend, from an old Norfolk family near King's Lynn in England, and is spoken [5] of as "a friend to the poor, a good adviser, a mild, sincere, and able reprover." In February, 1777, £2 14s. 1d. compensation was paid through Mr. Edward Johnson, representative for Lynn, to Daniel Townsend,[6] a minor, his mother having died in the interval.[4] Joshua Felt of Lynn was wounded,[2] and Josiah Breed [3] both wounded and taken prisoner. The latter was an old man with a large family; he was exchanged the following May, and afterwards petitioned for loss of his gun. While prisoner he was taken to New York.

[1] *History of Essex County,* I, 700, 383. Hurd.
[2] *American Archives,* IV, 4th ser., 1422, 1378. Force.
[3] *History of Lynn,* 339, 340. Newhall.
[4] *History of Lynnfield,* 105, 117. Wellman.
[5] *Essex Gazette,* May 2, 1775.
[6] *American Archives,* IV, 4th ser., 1422. Force. And *Mass. State Archives,* Vol. 139, p. 323.

Needham suffered severely, losing many men in Arlington. One of the killed, though credited to this town, seems to have belonged in the present Wellesley. The news reached there about nine A.M. The tavernkeeper, Bullard,[1] fired a signal gun from a hill, great fires were built up indoors, and the women ran bullets, the minister of the east neighborhood dealing out ammunition from the stores in his care. They marched by way of Watertown, getting off by ten. Lieutenant John Bacon [1] rode till near Newton Lower Falls and then sent his horse home. He was a native of Natick, at that time a part of Needham, and had been at Annapolis Royal between 1745–48. He was now fifty-four years of age, serving in Captain Caleb Kingsbury's company. Soon after he rode off the men from Framingham passed through, Nero Benson, a negro, trumpeting at each house as they went along by. David Mills,[2] of Needham, was getting up a big stone from his pasture when the alarm came. He never wished it touched upon his return, but left it partly unearthed as a memento. In the flurry of getting away his wife could only put her hand on some cold fried potatoes to slip in his pocket for lunch. All the morning the firing was heard and the retreat could be traced by clouds of smoke. Some "expected the enemy at their door," wrote the Rev. Mr. West.[1] The suspense was great and Mrs. Mills worried so over her husband that in the afternoon, to ease her anxiety, she went to a neighbor's for news, leaving the baby, Joseph, in its cradle. The little one woke while she was gone and fell a-screaming so long and loud as to give rise to a chronic infirmity.[2] Next day an old French war veteran, named Hawes,[1] had a story to tell. He and Bacon were on a ledge of rock in Menotomy behind a stone wall, Hawes on the watch for the flank, while Bacon, his powder in his hat, lay behind the wall with another man. Suddenly Hawes cried, "Run, or you are dead, here's the side guard." It was too late as far as Bacon was concerned and he was

[1] *History of Norfolk County*, 518, 520, 521, 520. Hurd.
[2] Traditional. Related 1895 by Miss Sarah Kilmer of Boston.

shot near the third button. He had with him when he fell, and then lost,[1] a gun worth eight dollars, or £2 8*s.* 0*d.*, a powder-horn valued at 1*s.* 7*d.*, a pound of powder 2*s.*, a pound of bullets 5*d.*, 4 shillings in cash, and clothing worth eleven shillings. He left a widow and nine children. A son[2] went over seeking news, only to find his father had already been buried at West Cambridge. Some of his clothes were lying in the school-house there; he knew the old striped hat on top of the pile, and carried them home the night of the 20th. Amos Mills,[2] a private in the same company, was forty-three years old; he left a widow and six children. His home was in the west part of the town. Sergeant Elisha Mills,[2] his cousin, was a blacksmith, forty years old. He was 1st sergeant of Captain Robert Smith's company. At West Cambridge he stepped outside a barn to fire on the flank and received six balls. He also left a widow and six children. The 23rd of April Mrs. Deborah Mills petitioned that the "Bearer" might be paid "what is aloud me for what my husband Lost when he was killed."[1] Later she married Aaron Smith, Jr.,[2] who brought Mills' body back on the 20th.

Jonathan Parker and Aaron Fisher were surprised in a barn by the flank guard. Parker[2] was killed; he was twenty-eight years old that very day and left a widow and three children. He and Elisha Mills belonged to the same company, the men of which are described as "fighting on their own hook." Natl. Chamberlain,[2] likewise killed, was a native of Roxbury, serving as private in Captain Kingsbury's Needham company. He was fifty-seven years old and had enlisted, 1760, "in his Majesty's service for the total Reduction of Canada."

John Tolman,[3] aged twenty-two, — while lying flat under a wall, with three or four more, their guns pointed over it

---

[1] *Mass. State Archives*, Vol. 138, p. 383ᵃ; Vol. 139, p. 300.

[2] *History of Norfolk County*, 520. Hurd.

[3] *History and Directory of Needham for 1888–9.* "War of the Revolution," 30. C. C. Greenwood. Boston, 1888. Copyright A. H. Foss & Co., Needham.

awaiting the advancing redcoats, — was surprised by the sudden fire of the flank guard, which apparently carried off the cue of a man by his side, for he "saw his hair drop;" the name of the man so narrowly escaping (Tolman's grandson thinks) was Smith (probably either Aaron, Jr., or William, both of whom served). The Needham men sprang to their feet and Tolman's gun flashed in the pan. Clearing the vent with a pin from his shirt collar, he primed, but again it missed fire, leaving him exposed to the crossing shots of the flank guard and main column. A ball entering between his shoulders, he was left for dead, but it was subsequently extracted from the breast, where it had lodged; and recovering, in 1778 he married Elizabeth Fisher of the well-known Needham family, and wrote to a son [1] in his old age with regard to these days: "What could be more pleasing to ambition than to knock off the shackles of despotism? Freedom or independence was the hobby I mounted, sword in hand, neck or nothing, life or death. I will be one to support my country's rights and gain its Independence. Lexington was the spot where we were first call'd to defend our rights by force of arms. The company that I belonged to met the British troops in front, fix't as fate, to repell their force, we played the man, or rather, we meant to act the soldier, but inexperience operated against us, we were soon convinced of our error; we suffered much in consequence of our inexperience and enthusiasm. The tenfold force that we met bore us away like a mighty torrent: a no. k. & w., myself amongst the latter, drop'd in the field incapable of action, wallowing in my blood." Far from being daunted the old man adds that this "prov'd a seal to my father prosecuting my first intention," and accordingly, January 3d following, so soon as he was able to shoulder his musket, he joined the American army.

Lieutenant Eleazer Kingsbury [2] was struck in the leg by a musket-ball and, but for his leather breeches, it is said,

---

[1] *Dedham Historical Register*, July, 1894.
[2] *History of Norfolk County*, 521. Hurd.

would have received more injury than he did. The following June, Nathan Newel of [1] Needham petitioned with regard to a bayonet then lost. The Rev. Mr. West [2] of Needham wrote concerning "this memorable day," that it had "a surprising effect on the spirit of the people in general; and from being, as I had supposed them, and as they were actually, mild and gentle, they became at once ferocious, cruel, — at least towards all those whom they suspected as unfriendly to their cause." Dedham [2] got the alarm about nine o'clock by a rider who came through Needham and Dover. Not less than 300 men all told marched from the several parishes. The First Parish sent sixty-seven, commanded by Captain Aaron Fuller, and seventeen under Lieutenant George Gould; the South sent sixty under Captain William Bullard; the Third Parish, thirty-one under Captain William Ellis; the Fourth Parish, sixty-seven under Captain Ebenezer Brattle. A company of French war veterans also served under Hezekiah Fuller and Nathaniel Sumner. A hatter named James, or Henry, Tisdale [3] was so excited by the news he gave the hat he was finishing a toss in one direction and sent the brush flying in another as he made haste to join his company. Joshua Whiting, Jr., [3] seventeen years old, left his plowing to turn out. A team is said to have been left in the highway while the driver, mounting his horse, galloped after his arms. [2] Captain Ephraim Cheney [3] of Medfield also left his plow in the furrow, unhitched his oxen, and started; Silas Mason [3] of the same town left his plowing on Pine Street and hastened away. Captian Joseph Guild, [3] leaving a wife and seven children behind him, started off, and met on the road a croaker, who called it all a false alarm. Fearing he might deter volunteers, Guild gagged the man with his own hand and left him in guard. At the East Parish meeting-house the Rev. Mr. Gordon [4] of Roxbury, who had just driven up, made a prayer standing on

[1] *Mass. State Archives*, Vol. 139, p. 301.
[2] *History of Norfolk County*, 522, 54. Hurd.
[3] *Dedham Historical Register*, July, 1891, July, 1897, April, 1896.
[4] *250th Anniversary of Dedham*, 78.

the steps of the east porch, before the men moved off.   Captain Ebenezer Brattle,[1] of the Fourth Parish Company, led the Dover men to Watertown, and from there they followed the highway on to Menotomy.   Elias (not Charles) Haven, in his command, said to be of Springfield Parish,[2] Dover, was shot by a redcoat who came around the corner of the First Church at West Cambridge.   He was standing beside his brother-in-law, Aaron Whiting,[2] at the time.   He was thirty-three years old and is buried near the Arlington monument. When summoned about eight that morning Whiting, aged thirty, left his plow in the field, where his wife unhitched the oxen and drove them to pasture.

Sergeant Jabez Baker [1] of Dover killed a British soldier and stripped him of his coat, which he brought home.   As late as 1866 a part of it still existed and was used on Strawberry Hill in the east end of the town, 200 feet above Charles River, to scare the crows!   This story suggests another of a powder-horn[3] said to have been carried by a Yankee that day and found not long since in the possession of a guide in the Adirondacks, who referred to it as "a useful thing around the barn.   What do I do with it?   Why I measure medicine for my horses in it.   That's what my father used it for, and it answers first rate."   Israel Everett, Jr.,[4] belonging to a Dedham company from the present town limits of Norwood, was among the wounded.   Dr. Nathaniel Ames of Dedham, who went to the fight and helped in caring for the injured, left recorded on the fly-leaf of his ledger a copy of the following bill:[5]

Israel Everett to Dr. Nath.l Ames, Dr. 1775, April 19th. To extracting a Bullet from the Cubitus of Israel Everett, Jr., which he received at the Battle of Lexington, the first of the War with Great Britain . . . . . 3 *s*

To sundry visits and dressings of the wound. . . 12.

[1] *History of Dover*, 92, 93.   Smith.
[2] *Dedham Historical Register*, July, 1891, January, 1892.
[3] *Boston Evening Transcript*, August 10, 1895.
[4] *History of Norfolk County*, 502.   Hurd.
[5] *250th Anniversary of Dedham*, 210.

On the opposite side of the street from Jason Russell's, not far above the railroad station, was a store kept by Thomas Russell.[1] It still stands, somewhat altered, on the corner of Water Street. The thirsty troops broke in here, and on resuming their march left the spigots out of the molasses and liquor casks. A member[2] of the family was watching at a safe distance and prevented a total loss. Beyond this point the soldiers burst into Cooper's tavern, on the corner of Medford Road, and killed two men, both unarmed, Jason Winship and Jabez Wyman. At the same time more than a hundred bullets came pelting in through doors and windows. An account,[3] by one who was then a child, states there were three old men, "of seventy years and upwards each," killed, who were Tories in their sympathies. The old men had gone up to the tavern for news. A letter[4] of that day says "they had not been in the engagement but were solacg themselves at ye tavern ye chief of ye day, they were drinking flip — Wyman, who used to work for Mr Cook, was warned of ye Danger, but says he 'let us finish ye mug yy wont come yet' — he died as ye fool dieth." The landlady, Rachel Cooper, who was mixing flip at the bar, hurried with her husband, Benjamin,[5] to the cellar and so escaped injury. On the following Sunday, April 23d, Jason Winship,[6] "a son of Jason killed the 19th," was baptized, also Anna,[6] infant granddaughter of Jason Russell. This last little one was born the 19th and soon died. A manuscript sermon of Parson Cook's[7] bears this marginal note, "This prepared for April 23, 1775, Lexington battle & plunder prevented." So we may suppose something most appropriate took its place. A tablet on Massachusetts Avenue

---

[1] *Arlington Advocate*, April 10, 1875.

[2] *Beneath Old Roof Trees*, 251. Brown.

[3] *Reminiscences of the Last Sixty-five Years*, 10. E. S. Thomas.

[4] *Henry Dunster and his Descendants.*

[5] *History of Cambridge*, 412. Paige.

[6] *History of Arlington*, 327, 298. Cutter.

[7] *West Cambridge in 1775.* Rev. S. A. Smith.

on the corner of Medford Street, in front of the present
Arlington House, is marked:

HERE STOOD COOPER'S TAVERN
IN WHICH
JABEZ WYMAN
AND
JASON WINSHIP
WERE KILLED BY THE BRITISH
APRIL 19, 1775.

On the north side of Main Street, in the eastern part of
the town, lived Samuel Whittemore. The house was not
far from the great elms near the Cambridge boundary, on
the Arlington side of the brook. The family was descended[1]
from William Whittemore of Hitchen, Herts. Samuel
Whittemore, born 1696, in his young days had been a
Captain[2] of the Royal Dragoons and was yet a dangerous
man to rouse. In 1741 he had expressed the opinion that
Colonel Vassell[3] was no more fit for a selectman than his
horse was. Colonel Vassell began action of defamation,
claiming £10,000 damages. On trial the words were found
not actionable, and Whittemore, turning on Vassell for
false and malicious imprisonment, recovered £200 damages.
Whittemore knew that the Regulars were out, for he had
seen them march by in the moonlight, and he was bent on
"going up in the town." His grandson Amos, then sixteen,
— the future inventor of the carding machine, — brought
out two or three French muskets, whose broken locks he
had tinkered into shape. But the boy was told he must
remain[4] and take care of his mother and the younger children.
Samuel Whittemore's wife urged him to go over to their
son's[2] house Mystic River way, but his blood was up and
he refused, continuing to oil his musket and pistol. Again
his children prayed him to go over to Hill's, where many had
fled for safety, but he sat knocking his flint, and said he should

[1] *History of Arlington*, 77. Cutter.
[2] "Old Men of Menotomy." Kidder. *Young People's Magazine*, June, 1895.
[3] *Mass. His. Soc. Pro.*, June, 1858.
[4] *Arlington Advocate*, March 20, 1875.

not go, he meant to get a shot at the redcoats when they came back. His daughter said imploringly, "Father, they will take you." Still rapping his flint and not raising his head he answered, "They will find it hard work to do it." He[1] took his post behind a stone wall in the rear of Cooper's tavern by a cross-road to Woburn and had just loaded when he heard[2] the wall rattle and saw the flank guard, five redcoats shoulder to shoulder, bearing down. As they came on, a friend drew off, but Whittemore refused to run, saying, "I am eighty years old, and I will not leave, for I shall be willing to die if I can kill one redcoat." His lameness too put it out of the question, and he set himself to selling his life dearly. Lying behind the wall he shot at one with his gun, and saw him clap[3] a hand to his breast. Taking aim with a pistol he brought down a second, and was firing a third time when a ball from the enemy carried away part of his cheek-bone. The remaining soldiers, exclaiming,[1] "We have killed the old rebel!" sprang over the wall and bayoneted him. When found four hours later he was faint from loss of blood and life but just perceptible. He was carried into Cooper's tavern, then in use as a hospital, and Dr. Simon Tufts of Medford,[4] "a perfect Chesterfield," at first feared to dress his wounds. Doctors Welch and Spring, however, finally[1] ventured to care for his gun-shot wound and some thirteen bayonet holes. He was a large, athletic man and recovered. The Arlington people said[3] that he "bled like an ox," and received a new lease of life. After some weeks he was well enough to recognize his family, and one of his daughters asked, "Are you not sorry that you went out?" "No," said he stoutly, "I should do just so again!"[1] Turning to his wife, he repeated, "I would run the same chance again."[3] He died February, 1793. His cartridge-box and bayonet were still preserved in 1896.[5]

[1] *History of Arlington*, 77, 76. Cutter.
[2] *West Cambridge in 1775.* Rev. S. A. Smith.
[3] *Arlington Advocate*, April 10, 1875.
[4] *Medford Historical Register*, October, 1898.
[5] *Beneath Old Roof Trees*, 263. Brown.

A Boston woman heard the soldiers say after their return,[1] "We killed an old devil there in Menotomy, but we paid almost too dear for it, lost three of our men, the last died this morning."

As W. D. Howells has [2] remarked, "There can be but one opinion concerning his resolution and physical toughness." The site is now marked by a tablet on Mystic Street, to the north of Main Street, behind the Russell school-house.

NEAR THIS SPOT
SAMUEL WHITTEMORE,
THEN 80 YEARS OLD,
KILLED THREE BRITISH SOLDIERS
APRIL 19, 1775
HE WAS SHOT, BAYONETTED,
BEATEN AND LEFT FOR DEAD,
BUT RECOVERED AND LIVED
TO BE 98 YEARS OF AGE.

Below Cooper's tavern was the Butterfield house, on the north side of the road. About a year before, Elizabeth Bemis of Watertown had married Samuel Butterfield and gone to housekeeping. With other women she had left the line of march for greater security. When the battle had rolled past she returned home to find her best bed covered with blood and occupied by a British officer, a wounded Provincial in the other.[3] Some of the neighbors upbraided her for sheltering an enemy, but she replied,[1] "only cowards would want to kill a dying man." The officer's name was Edward Hall or Hull, 1st lieutenant of the Royal 43d Regiment. He was wounded in the arm at Concord and brought down in a chaise in the centre of the troops. The horse was not so swift as the men, however, and falling into the rear, Hull was wounded again, this time mortally.[3] It is probable that an advertisement in the Essex *Gazette*, the following August, has reference to

[1] *Arlington Advocate*, April 10, 1875.
[2] *Three Villages*, 60. Howells.
[3] *History of Arlington*, 78. Cutter.

this. "Lt. Joseph Hayward of Concord gives Notice that on the 19th April last, in the Fight, he took from the Regulars in Menotomy a Horse and Chaise. The Chaise was owned by Mr Reuben Brown of Concord. What remains in his hands is a mouse coloured horse, near 13 hands high, old, poor and dull; a good Bed quilt, Tammy on both sides [a woollen stuff, that is, glazed like alpaca]; a good Camlet Riding hood, brown color; one pillow; and a piece of bed tick. The owner may have them by telling the marks and paying the Charge of this Advertisement." [1] This chaise was pierced with bullet holes and much stained with blood.[2] Lieutenant Hayward, who was a French war veteran, took a second chaise in West Cambridge, killing a man in each.[3] Lieutenant Isaac (or James) Potter of the Marines was made prisoner in the second chaise. He was confined some time at Reuben Brown's in Concord, as previously stated. Rev. Dr. McClure,[4] who saw Lieutenant Hull as he lay ill, describes him as being "of a youthful, fair and delicate countenance. He was of a respectable family of fortune in Scotland. Sitting on one feather-bed, he leaned on another, and was attempting to suck the juice of an orange which some neighbors had brought. The physicians of the place had been to dress his wounds, and a woman was appointed to attend him. His breeches were bloody, lying on the bed. I observed that he had no shirt on, and was wrapped in a great coat with a fur cap on his head. I inquired of the woman why he was thus destitute of clothing. He answered, 'When I fell, our people [the British] stripped me of my coat, vest and shirt, and your people of my shoes and buckles." How inhuman, his own men! I asked him if he was dangerously wounded. He replied 'Yes, mortally;' that he had received three balls in his body. His countenance expressed great bodily

[1] *Harper's Magazine*, May, 1875.
[2] *Concord Gazette and Middlesex Yeoman*, April 24, 1824.
[3] *History of Concord*, 114. Shattuck.
[4] *Mass. His. Soc. Pro.*, April, 1878.

anguish." He lingered, as we learn elsewhere,[1] until May 2d, then died. On the 3d, in deference to his request, his body was brought to town. Lieutenants Farnum, Johnson, and Walker, Adjutants Febijer, Warner, and Fox, were detailed as escort[2] as far as Charlestown Ferry, whence a barge from the *Somerset*[3] carried the coffin to Boston. It has been supposed that the burial took place on Copps Hill.

A letter[2] from Lieutenant Hull's younger brother, probably received after his death, has been preserved. It runs:

HILLSBOROUGH, IRELAND, April 12, 1775,

Dear Ned,

I have often heard you say that when you went abroad you would keep a journal of your life and actions. It is now one year since you left England. I suppose the reason you did not write was to wait until the year was expired, and then you would send us the whole year's journal, which my father, mother, and sisters beg you will do. It must be a large one; and send it in different letters directed to different persons in the family, paging it, and that will afford you subjects enough to write one to every person here, which will please them, and which is so much longed for. As there is a dispute between England and America, and you are in the only place where the greatest dispute is, you must surely know every occurence that happens there, being one of the persons under pay to prevent any further disputes with the Americans. The above journal is sincerely wished for here; and, if sent, would cure all past neglects, and also inform us that you are alive, which some persons think you are not, as you never write.

He was succeeded, according to the London *Gazette* of July 8th, by Ensign Henry Dawson of the 43d. Rev.

---

[1] *Atlantic Monthly*, May, 1877. Lieutenant Barker.
[2] *Mass. His. Soc. Pro.*, April, 1878.
[3] Rev. Dr. McClure.

Dr. McClure[1] saw in the same room with Lieutenant Hull a wounded Provincial, Daniel Hemenway of Framingham. McClure's diary, already quoted, has been preserved in a fragmentary form and opens abruptly: " . . . that it was flattened on one side by the ribs as if it had been beaten with a hammer. He was a plain, honest man, to appearance, who had voluntarily turned out with his musket at the alarm of danger, as did also some thousands besides, on that memorable day." Further particulars are gathered from the Massachusetts Archives[2] as follows and are now published for the first time, so far as I know:

To the General Assembly of the Massachusetts Province,— The Petition of Daniel Hemenway of Framingham humbly Sheweth that your Petitioner Agreeable to the Advice & Order of Congress, enlisted for the Service of the Province and equipped himself with all necessary requisites to be ready on any Sudden emergency. And on the 19th Day of April last Your Petitioner by Alarm with the Company he belonged to engaged the British troops: At Lexington &c in which engagement was wounded at Cambridge, received a ball from the enemy that first passed through his right thumb & broak the bone to shivers then penetrated his body at the lower part of the rib & made its way through the midreff & was cut out at his back, which after hath put him into great pain, his being at such a distance from his Family when wounded, the pain & expense of getting home, his cost for providing necessary comfortable things for his support, the constant attendance Day & Night in the time of his extremity, the entire loss of four months time in a Season of the year when everything for the Support of a large Family was depending, the Surgeons Bills. Doctr. Hemenway for dressing his wounds seventy-seven times & necessary Topical & Internal remidies, Charges Ten Pounds eight shillings. Doctr. Stone for advice, Dressing &c Three Dollars and although the wounds are

---

[1] *Mass. His. Soc. Pro.*, April, 1878.

[2] *Mass. State Archives*, Vol. 207, pp. 16–17.

healed, at the present time is unable to perform any hard Service, & is ever likely to have the misfortune in a good measure to lose the use of his right thumb &c; your humble Petitioner begs your wise and attentive consideration in his Case that you would in your goodness administer such relief as shall in some manner compensate the great misfortunes he hath met with in boldly defending the Cause of his Country's rights & your humble Petitioner as in duty bound shall ever pray,

Daniel Hemenway.

Framingham, August 15, 1775.

October 16th in the House of Representatives: Resolved that the Receiver General of this Colony be and hereby is ordered to pay out of the Publick Treasury to Capt. Josiah Stone for the account of the Petitioner the sum of £17, 12s., 6d., including Dr. Ebenezer Hemenway's account of £6, 2s., 4., in full.

The heavy firing at Cooper's tavern brought Mrs. Thomas [1] to her door, her home being less than half a mile below. Her husband was a Minute-man and had been roused by the tread of the British on their outward march and stood at the window to count the platoons as they went past, and afterwards he had succeeded, by going 'cross lots, in heading them off and reaching Lexington first. Alarmed by the firing and fearing to remain unguarded in the enemy's path, Mrs. Thomas hastened indoors again for a bag of coin and a few small articles. She then started to escape, carrying a child of two years, with two older children "hanging to her apron." Her aim was to reach Captain Whittemore's, about two miles across the fields on the banks of the Mystic, where something like a hundred women and two or three hundred children were in hiding. They had barely started when one child cried for bread; turning back she cut a slice from the loaf, giving him some

---

[1] *Reminiscences of the Last Sixty-five Years*, I, 8, 11–12. E. S. Thomas. He tells this of his mother.

to eat, and putting the rest in her apron. By this time the troops were close on her. As they made off a whole volley was fired and two balls passed through her cap. The Patriots shouted encouragingly, "Run, good woman, run," and she got away. A flanking party sent to get between her and her goal lodged bullets in the house and a large elm, twenty-five feet from the house, was thickly spattered with shot, which served the village boys with keepsakes for many a year. The Regulars meanwhile entered the Thomas house and took every article of clothing and bedding, ripped the beds open, split up the furniture, and set the building afire, but it was saved after they had gone on. They also killed a horse in the stable, and some hogs in a pen. Before coming to the Cambridge line the troops passed a Tory tavern, which received inadvertently some shot, and four Winship houses, commemorated in the rhyme [1]

> Jed and Jeth, Jason and Joe
> All lived in Menotomy Row.

Somewhere along the line of the British retreat through Arlington, Jonathan Whittemore,[2] thirteen years old, and his brother Josiah, aged eleven, sat on a fence to see all that was going on. They thought it a "big Show" until a bullet hit the rail, when Josiah dropped off wailing, "I'm dead" — much to the family's amusement in after years. Thoroughly frightened, the children took to the nearest swamp for the night and, becoming bewildered, strayed as far as Watertown[1] before they fell into friendly hands and were taken home.

At the Molly[3] or John Cutter house, next above the Universalist Church on Massachusetts Avenue in Arlington Centre, the soldiers trampled on a year's stock of candles just made, smashed a bookcase panel,[2] still existing in

---

[1] *Beneath Old Roof Trees*, 263–4. Brown.

[2] *Arlington Advocate*, April 10, 1875.

[3] *Historic Houses and Spots of Cambridge, Mass., and Near-by Towns*, 36. J. W. Freese. Boston, 1897: Ginn and Company.

1864, and set it alight, building their fire in a closet.   The house of Gershom Cutter, Jr.,[1] who married Rebecca Crosby, was also fired; a Regular killed here being buried in the meadow, forty rods distant.   Nehemiah Cutter, a tanner, lived on Arlington Avenue; the family here did not take flight, as one of the girls was too ill to be moved.   Mrs. Cutter[2] used to tell how hard it was in her worry to be called off down cellar to draw mug after mug of cider for the soldiers.   A bullet is still shown bedded in a section of a banister taken from Lieutenant Bowman's front hall.

Indeed throughout Menotomy Plains the fire was especially brisk.   One musket-ball carried away the pin of Dr. Joseph Warren's[3] ear-lock as it whizzed past.   Soon after, the right flank was exposed to the fire of a fresh body of Militia which had come from Roxbury, Brookline,[3] Dorchester, and Milton.   To withstand this attack the British again brought their field-pieces into use.   The Militia were so close on the British rear at the time, Dr. Eliphalet Downer of Brookline, "an active and enter-prising man,"[3] came to single combat with a British soldier, whom he killed by a bayonet-thrust through the body. Shortly after two British plunderers came out of a house and met him; one was killed from a shot in the rear, the other and Downer both fired and each missed.   Then they "scuffled" with their muskets; in the struggle the breech of Downer's gun broke, but he got the redcoat under. He begged for quarter, but Downer would not give it. "The Brookline men blamed him for this.   He should have been held for exchange."   Downer used to say,[4] "It was not ten minutes before I got another shot."

William Polly of Medford, aged eighteen, is said to have been shot by the flank guard while on horseback[1] a dis-tance from the main road in Menotomy.   He was brought

---

[1] *History of Arlington*, 210, 72.   Cutter.
[2] Traditional.   Through Miss Lucy Stone of Somerville.
[3] *Memoirs*, 14.   General Heath.
[4] Related by the late Mr. A. Warren Goddard.

home alive [1] to his widowed mother Hannah, but died on the 25th of his wound. Richard Francis [2] of the same place, also a weaver, is said to have killed five redcoats during the day. The Town History [3] mentions two Medford men as killed — Francis and Smith — of whom no particulars are learned. Mr. Henry Putnam,[4] a Louisburg veteran, sixty-three years of age, was exempt from service, but "showed his Putnam spunk" and went to meet the British. He fell at the same time and place as Polly and is credited to Medford, although he came of Danvers stock. A drummer-boy grandchild and five sons went with him to the fight; one, Henry Putnam, Jr., of Danvers, being wounded, as we have seen. He was nursed at Medford by his wife [2] — a Putnam by birth — who had three brothers in the fight, of whom one was killed and one wounded. It is told of the old man that once on a journey he put up for the night at Bolton and fell so in love with the host's daughter that he proposed to her in the morning, married her forthwith, and cheerfully drove home her dowry of two cows and twelve sheep.[4]

Two Cambridge men were made prisoners, Seth Russell,[5] a relative of Jason Russell's, and Samuel Frost.[5] By way of deterring the latter from escape they put him on horseback with his waistband strings cut. He may have been Samuel Frost, Jr., the eldest of ten or eleven children, aged thirty-two, whose sister Rebecca had been married [6] within a week to Solomon Prentice. Seth, we find, was the son of Jeremiah Russell, forty-three years of age and the father of six children. They were both exchanged June 6th. Elijah Seaver of Roxbury was also captured. The London press could not credit the first accounts of

---

[1] "Medford in the War of the Revolution." Helen T. Wild. *Medford Historical Register*, January, 1899.

[2] *Medford Historical Register*, July, 1900, January, 1899.

[3] *History of Medford*, 162. Usher.

[4] *History of Essex County*, I, 449. Hurd.

[5] *Arlington Advocate*, March 27, April 10, 1875.

[6] *History of Cambridge*, 554. Paige.

the retreat, and on June 7th the *Gazetteer* had a paragraph satirically worded, " . . . after such behavior as this, no account of barbarity, that may for the future come from that quarter, can appear too exaggerated; and we may expect to hear, that Mr. Samuel Frost and Mr. Seth Russell, the two militia gentlemen who are missing, have been eaten up by these cannibal regulars, and that an affidavit will be made by some persons, that they saw Lord Percy and Colo. Smith make an hearty meal of them." Among the Cambridge Militia under Captain Samuel Thatcher were numbered two negroes,[1] Cato Stedman and Cato Boardman; and three students[1] from the college, John Haven, class of 1776, Edward Bangs and Daniel Kilham, class of 1777. Of the Harvard boys Bangs[2] only, aged nineteen, is supposed to have engaged, since he was spending the Easter recess at college. He is said to have saved the life of a wounded Regular when threatened by his pursuers. The British took one unarmed man prisoner and required him to help them bring off their wounded; dismissing him on reaching Boston. From him it was learned that two prisoners taken that day were confined in the British barracks. He had personally heard Lord Percy order the troops to fire the houses. He also noticed a Boston barber with the troops as a guide, one Warden, as he supposed.[3] A breeches maker from Boston named Mansfield[4] is likewise mentioned as going with the Regulars and in the rout meeting a just reward, for being mistaken for a Provincial — a ball entered his neck and came out at his mouth. At about this point an old gray-haired hunter from Woburn, named Hezekiah Wyman,[5] riding a fine white horse, hung on the British rear to their sore annoyance. Riding within gun-shot he would dismount, rest his gun on the saddle, and *hit* his mark every time. "Look out," the redcoats would cry, "there is the

[1] *History of Cambridge*, 409. Paige.
[2] *History of Middlesex County*, I, 343. Drake.
[3] *American Archives*, II, 4th ser., 439. Force.
[4] *Diary of the Revolution*, 67. Moore.
[5] *Arlington Advocate*, April 10, 1875.

man on the white horse again." James Russell, then a
boy of twelve, lurking behind a house on Charlestown Street,
saw Wyman gallop across the brook and up the hill, pursued
by the flank guard. He turned in his saddle and one fell;
riding on, he again shot his man. Old Timothy Fuller,[1]
of Middleton, also caused panic in the British rear. They
spoke of him as "Death on the white horse." He would blaze
away and then ride back to his mates for a fresh gun. Such
unwonted exertion left him so chafed that he preferred
walking home when all was over and letting Daniel Brown,
a Danvers boy, ride his old horse back.

From the centre to the eastern limits of the town the
fighting was continuous. Some of the Danvers men who
escaped at Jason Russell's took up a new position here and
slew many. Leaving their dead and wounded behind, the
Regulars crossed the brook into Cambridge. Some twenty-
two Americans, and probably twice as many British, were
killed while passing through Arlington.[2] Some of the
wounded are said to have been carried to the Cochran
house [3] on the River or old Waltham Road.

The Brookline men — ninety-four Militia under Captain
Thomas White, beside two companies of volunteers under
Colonel Thomas Aspinwall and Squire Isaac Gardner —
mustered on the Green beside the First Parish Church (Unitarian) on Walnut Street. There were no Tories in town and
every man is said to have turned out, except Mr. Ackers,
who "could not get ready." [4] Mrs. Gardner [5] and her older
daughters, like other Brookline women, had been busily
employed in running bullets and getting an early dinner,
which when ready they felt too moved to make away with,
much to the children's wonder. On leaving his home on
the present Chestnut Hill Avenue, Isaac Gardner went up

[1] *History of Essex County*, I, 939. Hurd.

[2] *History of Middlesex County*, III, 180. Hurd.

[3] *Historic Houses and Spots*, 115. Freese.

[4] *Nathaniel Goddard a Boston Merchant*. Pickering.

[5] "Brookline in the Revolution." Margaret Elizabeth May. *Brookline Historical Publication Society, No. 3.*

to his wife "and kissed her silently;" then, as he reached the door, he turned and looked at her and said "Farewell." "Oh Mr. Gardner," she exclaimed, "don't say that word!" Then he went up to her again — again he silently kissed her, and left the house — never to return." On the way to the Green he passed Mrs. Ebenezer Davis,[1] with the children in her chaise, seeking a place of safety, and besought her to comfort his wife. Mrs. Captain Corey[1] and her children took shelter in the woods at this time, in the "upper part" of the town. The whole neighborhood was in motion and one of the Kendrick family[1] on South Street remembered seeing men leap fences back of Walnut Hill, going through Newton to Lexington. Once off, the Brookline companies headed for Cambridge, "going as the bee flies"[2] across the fields, trying to reach the pickets at Lexington while the troops were halted. As the day went on they scattered, to fight as they best could. Dr. William Aspinwall,[2] a brother of the Colonel, was starting in his usual red coat, when it was suggested that its color might expose him to the American fire, so he hastily made a change. During the pursuit, it seems, the doctor preferred posting himself against a tree and chancing the British fire to running the risk of a ball from his excited countrymen. He was blind of an eye and forced to aim from the left shoulder, but did good service notwithstanding, and when Ebenezer Davis[2] called attention to the effect of one shot, and pointed out the soldier's weapons as fair spoil, Aspinwall continued in hot pursuit, leaving the stripping of the fallen to other hands.

When the Brookline men first came in sight of the main body of the British, Colonel Aspinwall is said to have ordered[3] them to defile over the stone walls. Squire Gardner posted himself with a few others behind some dry water-casks, his son, Isaac Sparhawk, a lad of seventeen

---

[1] *History of Brookline*, 201, 181–2, 393–5. Woods.
[2] *Boston Evening Transcript*, June 15, 1857.
[3] "Brookline in the Revolution." *Brookline His. Pub. Soc., No. 3.* May.

DR. WILLIAM ASPINWALL
From the painting by Gilbert Stuart

years, fifer in Captain White's company, being near.
This spot was on the south side of North Avenue, east of
Spruce Street, commonly known, from its being in Mr. Jacob
Watson's neighborhood, as Watson's Corner. Here the
flank guard surprised Gardner, as it had so many more, and
was "like to have scooped up"[1] all the Brookline men. One
story makes the Squire drinking at a well[2] when attacked.
He received twelve ball and bayonet wounds, and next day
his body was found under an apple tree by his cousin,
Mr. John Heath, and Dr. Aspinwall, who "went to Lexington[3] to see what had become of Mr. Gardner." He was
the first Harvard[4] graduate killed in the War. His loss
to Brookline at the early age of forty-nine could not be
replaced. He bore many offices, being justice of the peace,
school committeeman, town surveyor, and town clerk.
He left a widow and eight children, one daughter subsequently marrying Dr. Aspinwall. His eldest son alone, of
his family, saw "the dear remains," which forty years after
it affected him to allude to. The body was brought across
the trestles of Brighton bridge and taken to the old Aspinwall house, opposite the present St. Paul's church. On
the second night after the battle he was secretly buried
in the Walnut Street cemetery, not far from the Unitarian
Church, to prevent the agony the sight would have occasioned his townsmen. Close by the place where Gardner
fell stood Snow's tavern, later known as Davenport's,
a portion of which still stands, having been removed to
Eustis Street near Beacon. Edmund Foster,[5] who had not
checked in the pursuit since Merriam's Corner and indeed
Reading, was fairly worn out on reaching here and glad
to put up for the night despite the house being emptied of
furniture. From the tavern he could see one of the enemy

[1] The late Mr. A. W. Goddard of Brookline.

[2] *History of Brookline*, 201. Woods.

[3] "Brookline in the Revolution." *Brookline His. Pub. Soc., No. 3.* May.

[4] "The First Harvard Graduate killed in the Revolution." Charles Knowles
Bolton. *New England Magazine*, March, 1895.

[5] *A History of the Fight at Concord*, 36. Ripley.

lying on the same side of the road, and Gardner of Brookline directly opposite. A British deserter is said to have taken shelter in Jacob Watson's cellar, and the Abraham Watson house in the same lot was used as a hospital.[1] Three Cambridge men were also killed near the easterly end of Spruce Street. John Hicks,[2] fifty years of age, is said to have been shot through the heart. He had taken part in the Boston Tea Party two years previously. The house he built and occupied is still standing on Dunster Street, at the corner of Winthrop, close by the colleges. When he failed to come home his fourteen year old son was sent by his mother to look for him, and found him lying by the others. William Marcy[2] was a laborer employed by Dr. William Kneeland. Being but half-witted, he sat on a fence to enjoy the supposed sham fight, until shot by the flank guard. Moses Richardson, fifty-three years old, a housewright, lived in a house still standing on the northeast angle of Holmes Place. He and Hicks were both exempt from service by their age, but both actively engaged as volunteers. Hicks and Marcy and Richardson were all buried the same night by torch-light in a common grave, without coffins. Moses Richardson's[2] son Elias thought it too bad that the earth should fall directly on their faces and, getting into the trench, spread over his father's face the cape of his coat. A tablet to their memory is inscribed:

AT THIS PLACE
APRIL 19, 1775
FOUR CITIZENS WERE KILLED
BY BRITISH SOLDIERS
RETREATING FROM LEXINGTON.

Lieutenant Bowman[3] met at North Cambridge a soldier who had straggled from the ranks. Neither had loaded guns and the Regular charged with his bayonet fixed. Bowman awaited him with clubbed musket and warded off the thrust, then felled him with a blow and took

[1] *Historic Guide to Cambridge*, 147.
[2] *History of Cambridge*, 412–4. Paige.
[3] *History of Arlington*, 78. Cutter.

him prisoner. The troops had taken too much liquor during the retreat to be any longer manageable. Lieutenant Barker [1] of the King's Own says, "they were so wild and irregular, that there was no keeping 'em in any order." This was shown again in North Cambridge, at the Blue Anchor, [2] Ebenezer Bradish's tavern, known in later years as Porter's, which stood on the westerly side of Boylston Street, midway between Harvard Square and Mount Auburn Street. The innkeeper had apparently withdrawn that day from Cambridge to Boston [3] on the presumption that his sympathies and his wife's delicate health would insure protection. Hannah Bradish, his wife, was a daughter of Timothy Paine, Esq., of Worcester and made a deposition [4] at that place a week later. By which it appears that at five o'clock in the afternoon of Wednesday the 19th she was in her bedroom, with an eight day infant. And being still weak, upon hearing the troops' tumultuous approach, rose from her easy-chair to retire from the front of the house to the kitchen and was scarce gone before a bullet was bedded in the back of the chair she had just quitted. The house was soon surrounded and some seventy bullets shot at the front. Several lodged in the kitchen. Then the street door was forced in; she did not actually see soldiers inside, but the noise sounded like it, and when they were gone she missed a rich brocade gown, called a negligee, a lute-string gown, a white quilt, a pair of brocade shoes, three shifts, light white aprons, three caps, a case of ivory knives and forks, and several small articles. One David Dutton [5] later heard Saml. Paine of Worcester, chatting in a garden, say that these losses were due to the Provincials' pilferings. This tale, Bradish [3] declared publicly in the most positive terms, on the 11th of May, never came from him. He was in a coil of trouble aside from this, and several

---

[1] *Atlantic Monthly*, May, 1877.

[2] *Historic Guide to Cambridge*, 37.

[3] *Essex Gazette*, June 8, 1775.

[4] *Journal of the Proceedings of the Congress held at Philadelphia, 1775.*

[5] *Mass. State Archives*, Vol. 138, p. 43.

appeals for consideration are on record. The fifteen cords of wood which lay piled in his yard on the day of the fight had been gradually walked off with, a few logs at a time, by the Militia rallying to the siege.[1] We have the awed testimony of his servant, Abraham Hasey, "I was there when the House was in possession of the Hampshire Troops, and see all the Eatables Consumed daily by them, . . . I frequently saw the Provisions Brought from the Cellar and piled upon a Large Mahogany Table in one of the Rooms," ending with the lament, "when the aforesaid Troops Left the House Every Atom of Provisions Belonging to it was Utterly Exhausted."[1] A bill[1] presented in December is too suggestive not to be given entire and is now, I believe, published for the first time.

COLONY OF THE MASSACHUSETTS BAY

To EBENEZER BRADISH

1775

April & May	£	s	d
To 8 Cords Wood delivered for the use of the Army	8	0	0
To 20 Days Board, 3 wounded Regulars, fire, Watching, Candles, destruction of two Feather Beds	6	–	–
To Burial of 2 Regulars, Blanketts & Sheets, Expenses to Sextons & Pall Holders	2	–	–
To a Horse to Jos. Warren, Esq. 4 times express to Concord, (the Horse look upon to be damaged 30 dollars)	4	–	–
To a Horse & Sulkey to Mr. Henshaw to Brookfield	1	12	–
To a Horse to Capt. White to Piscatequea on express	1	–	–
To Horses & Chaise sundry times Impres[d]. for the Colony Service	3		
To 1 Blanket, 1 sheet, delivered to Doctr. Foster for Hospital	1	4	–
To 1 hh[d]. Jamaica Rum de[d]. at the Alarm	0	0	0
1 hh Cyder	0	0	0
1 hh Cherry Rum	0	0	0
To 6 small arms & ammunition to the poor of Town of Cambridge	0	0	0
To Enter[g]. 30 Minute Men eating & drink[g]. 24 Hours	0	0	0
To Capt Leason & Drury Barricking at my House & Chaise House a Month	2	0	0

To Supplys to New Hampshire Troops at my House at Menotomy Capt. Willson's Comp[g].

2 Bl Pork @ 8 .... 8 0 0——

1 bb Beef 3 0 0

30 bushills Rye @ 4 .... 6 0 0——17 0 0

[1] *Mass. State Archives*, Vol. 180, pp. 263, 261, 264.

	£	s	d
Wine, Bacon, Cyder &c	6		
To Use of that House for Poor of Boston Col°. Legatte desire, from April to August..	2		
To Expenses paid moving one of those familys from sd. House to Northborough, with their Effects by Mr Gill's desire	3		
To my Assistance to the Minute Men at the Alarm &c.................	0	0	

56.16.0

Cambridge,
22^d Decr. 1775.

In November of the same year William Barker [1] of Sudbury advertised in the Salem *Gazette* the loss of a gun captured from the Regulars, marked number 30, and 66 Stand of Arms. It had been taken from Bradish's house the day after the battle, and Barker promised a reward of six dollars for its return or information leading to its recovery. It is also stated that some wounded Patriots were carried into the Stephen Goddard [2] house opposite Porter's and cared for. General William Heath had, as we have seen, ordered the Brighton bridge to be again dismantled, barricaded, and guarded by a company he found at Watertown. Lord Percy, however, did not attempt returning by the road he went out, but took the direct road for Charlestown by way of Prospect Hill, this route being shorter and more open, besides avoiding the Allston bridge, which he feared might be up, as was indeed the case. Lieutenant Barker [3] remarks on the luckiness of their taking this "short cut" since it "threw" the Americans, who in great numbers lined the road by the bridge. Dr. William Aspinwall [4] at the College Road found Captain Gridley and six or seven score men. He had just suggested the Regulars might take this turn, and had mounted a wall for a better view, when they crossed the northern extremity of the road in full flight. Crying, "There they go! Now, boys, whoever wants to do good work follow me!" he was again at their heels. It was perhaps in reference

[1] *New England Chronicle or Salem Gazette,* November 2–9, 1775.
[2] *Historic Guide to Cambridge,* 144.
[3] *Atlantic Monthly,* April, 1877.
[4] "Brookline in the Revolution." *Brookline His. Pub. Soc., No. 3.* May.

to this encounter Lord Percy [1] wrote that he did not "perceive any body of [Patriots] drawn up together, exc. near Cambr, just as we turned down towards Chastown, who dispersed on a cannon shot being fired at them, & came down to attack our right flank in the same straggling manner the rest had done before." Before reaching the Milk Row Road from Beech Street the redcoats were bewildered and on the point of going astray. Their danger was extreme and might have been fatal, but for their being set right by a "young gentleman [2] residing at the College." From the westerly border of Menotomy to this point "their passage was through a flame of fire." During the afternoon Dr. Downer [3] of Brookline, chancing to enter a barn by the wayside, met a wounded Regular who had crawled in there out of the way. Seeing his state, the Doctor offered to care for his leg, when the man surlily replied, "Damn ye, I'll dress your wound," and fired; upon which he was immediately despatched by the squad in attendance. Downer was a "zealous man" and had yet another adventure. On his way home he came upon two plundering Regulars; one was killed by a shot from the rear, the other and Downer exchanged shots at close range, but missed. Then they "scuffled" with their muskets. Downer got the redcoat under, and he begged for quarter, but Downer would not give it. "The Brookline men blamed him for this. He should have been held for exchange." Dr. Wm. Aspinwall testified in after years that Mr. Elijah Jones [4] was surgeon's assistant and helped him and Dr. Downer dress and care for the wounded soldiers from April 19th to August 12th, "before the Regular Appt.mt of surgeons to ye Reg.ts."

John Goddard of Brookline, on leaving home, had armed and brought along with him his hired man, Joel Hager, [5] and five small-arms which he had no difficulty in lending.

[1] *History of Arlington*, 81. Cutter.
[2] *American Revolution*, I, 483. Gordon.
[3] The late Mr. A. Warren Goddard of Brookline.
[4] *Mass. State Archives*, Vol. 183, p. 178.
[5] *Nathaniel Goddard a Boston Merchant*. Pickering.

Joel fired constantly, while the British were passing, from behind a tree, which was found afterward spattered by seven balls. Mr. Goddard,[1] himself, saw a ball flattened near him on a stone wall, and next day "had the curiosity" to go back and bring it away; it was about the size of an old copper cent. In the excitement of the day a neighbor of Mr. John Goddard's to whom he had lent a fowling-piece contrived to lose it. Years after, going up to visit a relation in Worcester, Mr. Goddard recognized his piece on a rack above the hearth at the Wayside Inn at Sherborn, and proving his property, received it back. At the end of the day the Brookline men "came home the nighest way.[1]"

The "Damages [2] to Buildings in Cambridge after view by Committee was

	£	s	d
valued at	75	5	6
Value of Goods & Chattels destroyed or taken out, estimated by owner under oath	1036	6	3
The same, unsworn through absence	72	6	10
To meeting house and school house of north west precinct	13	4	
Church vessels, linen and cash from Deacon Joseph Adams 16	16	8	
	£1202	8	7 "

It is interesting to note in this connection that the Essex *Gazette* of May 12th had the following inserted: "Lost out of a House in Cambridge, between the 19th and 26th inst. A woman's gold watch, with two miniature Pictures among it other appendages, also a Mourning ring." The late Hon. John W. Candler [3] of Brookline, of West Cambridge stock, used to hear as a child how an old nurse, Phœbe Bathrick, who lived sixty-two years in the family, was wakened by the British passing his grandmother's in the early morning, and of the children crowded into the ox-cart seeking shelter with many more at Spot Pond off the line of retreat, and of her seeing the Regulars and

[1] Related by his grandson the late Mr. A. Warren Goddard.
[2] *Journal of each Provincial Congress, 1774–5.*
[3] *250th Anniversary of the Settlement of Cambridge,* 100–101. Cambridge, 1881. Printed by order of the City Council.

Provincials sweep confusedly by, in the distance, and then passing a dead soldier in the ditch as they all returned at sunset to a sacked house.

At 6 P.M. the Regulars, almost on a run, entered Somerville, pushing back through Beech Street into Elm, hotly followed by the Yankees. At the westerly corner of these streets was a grove from which the Minute-men galled the Regulars. The troops here planted their cannon on the northerly spur of Spring Hill, behind Timothy Tufts'[1] house, and won a short respite. This house, already alluded to, still stands on Elm Street at the corner of Willow, marked by a tablet.

> A SHARP FIGHT OCCURRED HERE
> BETWEEN THE PATRIOTS AND THE BRITISH,
> APRIL 19, 1775.
> THIS MARKS BRITISH SOLDIERS GRAVES.

Leaving a few dead, now buried in Mr. Tufts' lot,[1] just inside the fence, the troops crowded on down Elm Street into Somerville Avenue. One Regular was killed near Walnut Street, another by the present Middlesex Dye Works, and shortly after a volley was fired into an unlet house belonging to Mr. Rand on the northeast corner of Central Street. At dusk some one chancing to stumble over the soldier's body, threw it inside the vacant house;[2] it is possible that a grave accidentally disturbed at the corner of Somerville Avenue and Park Street in 1853 was his. From the soldier buttons, this was supposed to hold the remains of a Regular, which were then transferred to the Somerville Avenue cemetery opposite School Street. It had been "a wonder of a winter," "so moderate and unfreezing," and this day was particularly warm, so that on reaching the lower ground at the foot of Laurel Street some redcoats threw themselves down and drank like dogs from an old pond.[1] Down Washington Street they went, skirting the foot of Prospect Hill. Here possibly

---

[1] *History of Middlesex County*, 312. Drake.
[2] Traditional, through Miss Lucy Stone of Somerville.

the hottest fire of the day was received, forcing Lord Percy again to unlimber his field-pieces. Samuel Shed, Sr., lived in a gambrel-roofed house on the north side of Washington Street; the roof still remains on an otherwise altered house, on the north side of Washington Street nearly opposite Mystic Street, where the road turns to the west not far from the Charles G. Pope school-house. A soldier ransacking the drawer of a highboy here was killed by a shot aimed through the window and found by the family on their return lying dead across the open drawer. This highboy, which has a curved front and brass handles, is (1903) in the possession of Miss Martha Tufts of Medford Street. It bears several bullet marks, and one of the drawers formerly showed stains of blood.

Some ten rods in front of Mrs. Gilson's on Prospect Hill, James Miller, a Charlestown Minute-man, stationed himself with a comrade. Their fire was so effective a platoon was detached to drive them back. As it mounted the hillside his friend said, "Come, Miller, we've got to go," but Miller, who was sixty-five, answered, "I am too old to run," and fell, pierced by thirteen balls. His wife was Sarah Lane of Bedford; she had fled to her people and there heard of his death. A tablet on Washington Street next the Pope School commemorates the incident:

> On this hillside
> James Miller,
> minuteman,
> aged 65
> was slain by the British,
> April 19, 1775.
> "I am too old to run."

Miss Martha Tufts' grandfather Miller, then a boy, made his home with the old people, his grandparents. It is said that the occupants of a house on Bow Street hid their silver spoons in the brick oven, where they remained undiscovered.[1] Others were less successful in preserving

[1] Traditional, through the Rev. Henry H. Barber of Meadville, Penn.

their property, as appears by the "Original Petitions,"[1] to which reference is made in Hunnewell's History of Charlestown. These petitions concern the losses sustained at Charlestown on the 17th of June as well as on the 19th of April; but in copying from the manuscript an attempt has been made to confine the statements to the latter date only.

Joseph Adams:

To Loss in Concard Fite

```
to twó Glass windows ...........................................  1 16  0
to a Gun ......................................................  2
to a Bever Hatt ...............................................  1 10
```

An accompt of the Loss Mr. James Call [2] sustained in April the 19, 1775, Containing the following articles:

> Such as one Broad Cloth Coat
> a new Lamb skin setute
> three Broad Cloth jaccoats
> one Small Cotton Velvet Do.
> one ankeen   Do.
> two homeSpun   Do.
> two Long gowns Womans
> four Childrens gowns
> a Black Calliminco Petecoat
> A white Linning   Do.
> a Black sattin Cloak new
> two white Aprons
> two Check.   Do.
> four yards of check
> six new shifts
> seven shirts
> one pair of sheets
> six new plats
> six old   Do.
> two Dishes
> One Looking glass
> two new porringers
> one table Cloath
> one pair Stais
> two pair of Britches
> one pair of Shoes new

---

[1] Vol. I, p. 4. Original Petitions concerning Losses at Charlestown June 17 and April 19, 1775. *City Hall Archives.*

[2] *Ibid.* 39. Figures omitted.

Caps and hankerchiefs
three fans
one pair Mitts silk
one pair worsdad Do.
three pair cotton stockins mens
three pair of white yarn Do.
four pair of Childrens Do.
three skirts
a new psalm Book
a new Book the Death of Abel
a Dwelling house
a pair of chist draws
a cupboard
a table
thirteen chairs
one Bedstead
a pair of Curtains Rods and Rails
one half a sute of curtains
one pair of tongs
one pair of handirons
two hogsheads and one terce
three Barrels and five tubs
a Cradle
a Chast
four duzon Bottles
one ax
a Dung fork
two spits
one cord and a half of wood
two Bottles of gin and spirits
four pound of cofe and one pound chocolate
seven pound of Sugar
two pound of hard Sope
two ounces of indego
one trammel
a fender
a powdering tubb
three flour Barrels
one iron bound and three small cask

	£	s	d
Damage done to me Sam.l Chote [1] upon the 19 Day of April Last, 1775....	1	4	0

John Edmands [1] of Charlestown Lost at Lexenton in time of Concord fight.

	£	s	d
To 1 Silver can £4. To 2 Large Silver spoons 25/4	5	5	4
To 5 small Spoons 15s. To half a Dozen Garlia Shifts @ 10s.	3	15	
To 2 Cotton linnin shifts 12/		12	
To 6 pair of Cotton Stockings @ 3/		18	

[1] *City Hall Archives*, Vol. I, pp. 52, 72.

	£	s	d
To a new Calliminco Gown 26/	1	6	
To 2 Pair of Sheets 2.4.0. To a Pair of Britches 12/	2	16	
To 1 Looking Glass 8/		8	
To Deplh ware 6/ To a pair of earrings 20/ To a Pair	1	6	0
Buttons 6/8		6	8
To 1 Stay hook 3/ To 2 pair Pillar Bears 10/8		13	8
To a Rudg 12 To 1 Blankett 8/	1		

also John Edmands
a Merandom of Things not put into the firs account at Lexington

a Bibel 60/ silver clasps and Corners 80/	7		
a Gridiron 30/ a frying pan 30/ a Colender 22/6	4	2	9

the Dammeg don to my whof

Damages done by the Ministerial Army to Abraham Frost[1] on the —
day April, 1775
To 54 Sqrs Glass
To Sundry Cloths yous of the Army

James Frost[1] An acount of a Number of Articles which I James Frost Lost at Lexington and Bunker Hill Battle Being then an Inhabitant of Charlestown . . . what was Taken from mee at Lexington Battle was

one pair of Broad Cloth new Bretches at 1/8 pr yard	1	12	0
one New Fine Shirt		12	
Two Pair of worsted Hose		9	
a New Pair of Stone Sleeve Buttons		6	
a New Black Silk Handkirchief		4	8
Lining handkerchief		2	
to a Pair of shoes not half worn		3	
To A new Cotooch Box & Belt		6	4
To Books		3	4
	3	18	4

To takeing care of a regeler left at my hous the 19 of April 10 days
1 pound

Stephen Goddard.[1]

The folowing sum is an Estimate of what John Kettle[1] Lost in Charlestown Last April viz. Household Furniture 5. 6. 8. L.M.

Eunis Miller[1] los at charlestown on the 19 da of April 1775 by the meletery oprosions — to many sorts of Clothing and beden and sundry sorts of hous furnetuer, £23. 9. 0.
Charlestown, April 19, 1775.

This may Cirtefy that I, James Miller[1] of Charlestown, then being an Inhabitant of said town, did on the said Nineteenth day of April loose and have not as yet Recovard any of the aforesaid Articles heretofore annexed.

A Valuable Gun and sundry other articles	£3	12	0
1775, April the 19, Lost in Concord fight	£6	2	2

Ebenezer Shed [1]

[1] *City Hall Archives*, Vol. I, pp. 85, 86, 101; Vol. II, pp. 5, 32, 33, 80–1.

old tenor 1775
Charleston Apael the 19
lost when the reglers came back from Concord

two barrels and half a syder	15	
forty weat salt pork	7	
one galond rum	13	6
my great cot	9	10
one bever hat	3	
one cutlash	2	10
one sash winder	9	

Ebenezer Shed.

In connection with the " wido Abigal [1] Sheds thirds " allusion is made to "apil, loces, ockwood, chire and plum tres " being injured.

An Account of Damage done by the ministerial Troops in their Excursion on the 19 April 1775 to the Estate of Samuel [1] Shed

one Silk Gown (Grogram) almost new	6	
1 pair of sheets	2	
2 Pillow cases 14/	14	
4 Napkins 10/8	10	8
2 Towells 5/	5	
1 pair of woman's Shoes a 3/	3	
1 Do. men's Do. 5/	5	
1 pair black Hose	4	
1 black Handkerchief 3/	3	
1 white Cambrick Do. 8/	8	
Black & Red Lace 17/	17	
White Do. 5 yards & ½ 10/	10	
Cap & Ribbons to the value of 6/	6	
1 Sword 1 10 a piece of Lace for a hat 12/	2	2
Case of Drawers Shot thro & damaged to ye amt.	1	10
1 Barrel of Cyder	12	
2 Shifts	1	10

Samuel Shed

	£	s	d
To Cash paid for 20 squares of sashes		5	4
To 11 Acres of pasture Laid open all the season of the summer for which i was offered by Mr Honeywill	2	15	4

And carried of a quantity of stone wall to the amount of 20 Load as nigh as I can tell
Charlestown April 2 1776

Jeremiah Snow [1]

70 windows broke at Lexington fight.

[1] City Hall Archives, Vol. II, pp. 81, 82, 85.

"this is to Sartefy the Selectmen of Charlestown that I, Esther Spafford,[1] inhabitant of Charlestown, have lost in the time of Concord fight one Bed and Beding valed at ten pounds Lawfull money, two low Cases of Draws, one pound sixteen shillings Lawfull money

	L.	M.
two tabels at	1	
six Seting chares a 3s a piece		
two tramels 12s L.M.		
one frying pan & one spider 7s L.M.		
two bedsteads and three bed-cords	1	2 10
half a Dos[son]. of Whitesone plates		3
tow spining whels		12
one bras kettell		8
two doz glas bottles and three Case Ditto	8	
one barel of Sope	1	1
one side Sadel	1	10
ten Puter Poringers		3
one bible and one psalm book		4
one fire shovel and one Iron skillet		5
one yeard Russet		2 5

In addition to the above there is a list of losses occasioned by the "Rugalars" on the "17th" of April to the estate of Richard Foster, Esq., which, from the nature of the items, probably has reference to June 17th. Also "Envantaries" made the following February at Andover by Samuel Hutchinson of "things Lost in Charlestown by Reson of the Kings troops in April last &c" and another by Susannah Hutchinson, which appear to have reference to a later date. Joshua Hooper at Haverhill on the same date sums up "what I left in Charlestown last April." Abigail Parker dates from the same town, the following month, respecting the "principle things I left in Charlestown in April last." Nath. Souther had already entered a claim from Haverhill in December to the same effect. Many must have taken flight that April day never to see their homes again until after the firing of the town at the time of the Bunker Hill fight, and so necessarily have been unable, like the widow Esther Rand, to separate their statements. From John Stanton's return we get a notion

[1] *City Hall Archives*, Vol. II, p. 88.

of the cost of removal. In his case, "carting my goods to the edge of

Woburn 3

up to Worcester .... 18" etc.

The Malden Company[1] were witnesses of the risk attending the gathering of loot, coming, as they went along the foot of Prospect Hill, upon a dead redcoat lying on the grass before a house which he was about to enter when checked by a shot through the window, and bayoneted. Lieutenant Wm. Tay, Jr.,[2] of Woburn had been roused from sleep very early in the day and had kept up the pursuit the whole stretch of the way from Concord to Charlestown. Here at the end of the afternoon, he says, as he and others were passing a house they were fired on from within by three of the "ministerial troops." Two redcoats fell by the return fire and Tay, rushing into the house, seized the survivor, Matthew Hayes,[3] sergeant of the 52d Regiment, in his arms and, in his own words, "gave him sundry cuffs" so that he straightway surrendered. While busy securing his prisoner Tay lost sight of his captured arms and could not learn in the bustle what became of them. Understanding later that they had come into the possession of Lieutenant Joseph Howard of Concord, he made an attempt in May, and again in September, to establish a prior claim.

[1] *History of Malden*, 747. Corey.

[2] *Siege of Boston*, 368–9. Frothingham.

[3] *Mass. State Archives*, Vol. 180, p. 144.

CHAPTER V

CHECKED BY THE CHARLES AT NIGHTFALL

EVERY moment now was regarded as precious and the Patriots pressed close on the British heels for a parting shot. At this point Colonel Bernard[1] of the Royal Welsh was struck by a ball and wounded in the thigh, "which," to quote a soldier's letter, "all the regiment was sorry for." Lord Percy [2] also had a narrow escape, a middle waistcoat button being shot away, the ball coming, it was supposed, transversely and glancing off again. A private letter from an officer on board the *Somerset* given in the London *Chronicle* (May 30–June 1) says Lord Percy likewise "very narrowly escaped being taken by the corps assembled from Marblehead." A naval lieutenant, Philip D'Auvergne,[3] Duke of Bouillon, from the *Asia*, who had volunteered to go on the expedition, was also all but taken prisoner. Lord Percy,[4] throughout the day, is said to have behaved with great spirit and coolness and "shown himself [5] a worthy descendant of the race of soldiers from whom he came." He wrote to General Harvey in London, "I have myself, fortunately, escaped very well, having only had a horse shot [one, by the bye, for which he had paid the excessive price of £45]. Poor Lt. Col.s Smith and Bernard are both wounded, but not badly." [6] During the retreat the soldiers had enclosed Percy and General Haldiman on all sides, serving as a body guard.

[1] Intercepted Letters. *Essex Gazette*, May 12, 1775.

[2] *The London Chronicle*, June 10–13, 1775.

[3] *Historic Mansions*, 358. Drake.

[4] *Mass. His. Soc. Pro.*, March, 1890.

[5] *History of Middlesex County*, III, 179. Hurd. "Arlington," by James P. Parmenter, A.M.

[6] *History of Arlington*, 82. Cutter.

Captain Charles Miles,[1] of the Concord Company, was wounded about this time in the hand; and Major Buttrick [2] and others of that town spent the night at Charlestown. Charlestown had had an anxious day of it; that afternoon General Gage had sent and warned the Hon. James Russell [3] that if a single man went out armed the most disagreeable consequences might be expected, for in truth the town — containing perhaps 250 houses — would be laid in ashes. When the judge had announced this threat in front of his mansion house in the Square, one of the bystanders swore,[4] "I'll go out and fight the regulars if Gage does burn the town!" As the afternoon wore on it became known that the Cambridge bridge had been taken up and that the troops were bound to return through their midst. At once the alarmed inhabitants thought of seeking shelter elsewhere, "some ran along the marsh" towards Medford; and at Penny Ferry, along the line of the present Malden bridge, many boat-loads crossed the Mystic River to the farther shore. Those living at the further end of the town rushed toward the Neck. As the late Dr. Prince [3] of Salem was standing in the midst of an armed group at this point, a person wrapped in a cloak rode up on horseback and asked the news. He did not pause for an answer, but immediately put spurs to his horse, the animal started forward suddenly, the rider raised his arms and, the cloak thrown out of place, revealed a uniform. The men levelled their guns and would have fired, but Prince struck them up exclaiming, "Don't fire at him, he is my friend Small, a fine fellow." It was Major Small, riding as express from the army, who thus daringly got safely through to Boston. *The Morning Chronicle and London Advertiser* of June 21st states that Major Small was dangerously wounded in the neck during the day; "they have not put him among the wounded in

[1] *American Archives*, IV, 4th ser., 1378. Force.
[2] *Harper's Magazine*, May, 1875.
[3] *Siege of Boston*, 79. Frothingham.
[4] *History of Charlestown*, 318. Richard Frothingham, Jr. Boston, 1845.

the *Gazette;* yet the fact is so." If this was the case he had so far recovered as to take an active part at Bunker Hill.

Just before sunset distant firing was heard, and soon the British troops were seen in the Cambridge Road. At some stage of their return poor Gibson had been killed, whose wife, it may be remembered, worked for Mrs. Stedman; just before he fell he told a mate, although an old campaigner he had never seen so hot a day.[1] About six P.M. the van filed across the Neck. John Hay[2] lived at this time at Crafts Corner, where Warren Street joins Main, opposite Austin, with a full view up Main Street in the direction of the British approach. Mercy Hay, a little girl of ten, later Mrs. Thomas Boylston, was hurried by her mother to the shelter of the great chimney arch in the cellar as the rout poured on down hill toward the house. Encouraged at length by the lull in the trampling of feet, she crept up garret and looked out, to find the soldiers had come to a halt, with stacked muskets, under their very windows. Frightened and sore at heart, the child, scarce knowing what she did, flung corn cobs about their heads. Startled in their turn, a couple of soldiers sprang to arms and turned their pieces toward the house, but some of the officers, standing in front of Mr. Hay's bakery on the opposite sidewalk, called to them just in time, "Don't fire, it's only a little girl's freak!" A story told of Mrs. Mallet,[3] whose home was on Charlestown Neck, probably relates to this time. She is said to have been startled with the cry "the British are coming!" in the very act of filling her brick oven for a baking, and started at once on foot for Salem with her own children and a neighbor's child who was playing there. Mary Mallet, a seventeen year old girl, was separated from her parents at this time and took refuge in Woburn.

Not far from Harvard Street corner, on Main Street,

[1] *Memorial History of Boston,* III, 68.

[2] *Old Charlestown,* 307–8, 310. Timothy T. Sawyer. Boston, 1902: John H. West Company.

[3] *Boston Evening Transcript.* Notes and Queries. November 10 and 17, 906.

lived Sergeant Timothy Thompson,[1] a native of Woburn.
He was engaged with his company, his wife, Mary, having
sought protection with her father, Joseph Frothingham, in
the same street. During the afternoon the old gentleman hurried in to say that the Regulars must pass through
Charlestown, the sergeant could not leave his post, but
there would be time, if Mary was quick, to run home and
pick up any little valuables. Mrs. Thompson, acting on
his suggestion, filled a small bag and turned her back on
her home, leaving beans and loaves in the brick oven and
a quarter of spring veal hanging in the cellarway. Her
flight was none too soon. Even before she had secured
passage to the Malden shore word ran about that a youth
had been fatally shot. The townspeople had been told
that the British would not harm them unless fired upon.
Unfortunately[2] an excited negro could not restrain his
impulse to shoot, and the return fire killed Mercy Hay's
cousin, Edward Barber, Captain William Barber's son, a
lad of fourteen, who was looking out of a window at the
corner of the road leading to Malden bridge. Lieutenant
Mackenzie,[3] of Percy's Brigade, says this was the only
negro seen to fire on the King's troops and that he was
wounded. The Charlestown people who were flocking that
way toward the Neck to make their escape turned back,
panic-stricken. Word ran through the crowd that women
and children were being massacred; the turmoil and distress increased. Captian Jacob Roger's [4] experiences may
be taken as a type.

I got my chaise, took my wife and children; and as I
live near the school-house, in a back street, drove into
the main street, put my children in a cart with others
then driving out of town, who were fired at several times on
the common, and followed after. Just abreast of Captain

[1] *Old Charlestown*, 49–50. Sawyer.
[2] *Beneath Old Roof Trees*, 307. Brown.
[3] *Mass. His. Soc. Pro.*, March, 1890.
[4] *Siege of Boston*, 371–2. Frothingham.

Fenton's, on the neck of land, Mr. David Waitt, leather-dresser, of Charlestown, came riding in full speed from Cambridge, took hold of my reins, and assisted me to turn up on Bunker's Hill, as he said the troops were then entering the common. I had just reached the summit of the hill, dismounted from the chaise, and tied it fast in my father-in-law's pasture, when we saw the troops within about forty rods of us, on the hill. One Hayley, a tailor, now of Cambridge, with his wife, and a gun on his shoulder, going towards them, drew a whole volley of shot on himself and us, that I expected my wife, or one of her sisters, who were with us, to drop every moment.

It being now a little dark, we proceeded with many others to the Pest House, till we arrived at Mr Townsend's, pump-maker, in the training field; on hearing women's voices, we went in, and found him, Capt. Adams, tavern keeper, Mr Samuel Carey, now clerk to Col. Mifflin, quartermaster general, and some others, and a house full of women and children, in the greatest terror, afraid to go to their own habitations. After refreshing ourselves, it being then dark, Mr Carey, myself, and one or two more, went into town, to see if we might, with safety, proceed to our own houses. On our way, met a Mr Hutchinson, who informed us all was then pretty quiet; that when the soldiers came through the street, the officers desired the women and children to keep indoors for their safety; that they begged for drink, which the people were glad to bring them, for fear of their being ill-treated. Mr Carey and I proceeded to the tavern by the Town House, where the officers were; all was tumult and confusion; nothing but drink called for everywhere. I stayed a few minutes, and proceeded to my own house, and finding things pretty quiet, went in search of my wife and sisters, and found them coming up the street with Capt. Adams. On our arrival at home, we found that her brother, a youth of fourteen, was shot dead on the neck of land by the soldiers, as he was looking out of a window. I stayed a little while to console them,

and went into the main street to see if all was quiet, and
found an officer and guard under arms by Mr David
Wood's, baker, who continued, it seems, all night; from
thence, seeing everything quiet, came home and went to
bed. . . . The next morning with difficulty I obtained to
send for my horse and chaise from off the hill, where it had
been all night, and found my cushion stole, and many other
things I had in the box. Went to wait on Gen.l Pigot,
[43rd Reg.t] the commanding officer, for leave to go in
search of my children; found Dr. [Isaac] Rand, ˙ Capt.
[Joseph] Cordis [whose home was on Main Street opposite
Union Street], and others, there for the same purpose, but
could not obtain it till he had sent to Boston for orders,
and could not find them till next night, having travelled
in fear from house to house, til they got to Captain Waters
in Malden.

Captain Rogers subsequently took refuge in Reading.
Here some Stoneham persons, on the suspicion that he had
given the British refreshment, threatened to raise a mob and
drive him away, but on appealing to General Washington
he was entirely acquitted.[1]

The Militia had continued to hang on the rear of the
British until they reached Bunker Hill in Charlestown and
it had become so dusk as to render the flashes of the muskets
very visible. At this instant an officer [2] on horseback came
up from the Medford Road and inquired the circumstances
of the enemy; adding that about 700 men were close behind,
on their way from Salem, to join in the attack. Had this
force arrived a few minutes sooner, the left flank of the
British must have been greatly exposed and suffered con-
siderably; possibly their retreat would have been cut off.
Dr. Thomas Welsh [3] was on Prospect Hill, taking part in
the pursuit, when he saw Colonel Pickering's Essex Regiment of 300 men on top of Winter Hill, nearly in front of

[1] *Mass. State Archives*, Vol. 180, pp. 166, 195–8.
[2] *Memoirs*, 14–15. General Heath.
[3] *History of Charlestown*, 317. Frothingham.

Mr. Adams' house. They had marched twenty miles in less than six hours; another portion arrived later and slept at Malden. Despite his efforts, Colonel Pickering was blamed by some for "want of alertness. Had he pushed on, so as to head the British off" — so the charge ran — "(and he was near enough) they must have clubbed their firelocks." [1] Colonel Pickering, twenty-nine years old at this time, was at his office, the Registry of Deeds, in Salem that morning when, between eight and nine Captain Epes [2] (Eppes) of Danvers reported for orders and brought the first word of the affair at Lexington. Captain Epes's company lived two miles nearer Boston and they were told to set out at once, not waiting for the Salem men. Colonel Pickering, who was chairman of selectmen and a member of the Committee of Safety, hastened to Webb's tavern in School Street (the present Court Street), where the leading men of the town having gathered, it was felt that the distance from Boston was too great for them to do any material service, beyond testifying their interest in the cause. After awhile, however, four companies started by way of Danvers, Lynn, Malden, and Medford. Dr. John Warren,[3] brother of Joseph, twenty-two years of age, is said to have accompanied them as surgeon. A story is told that when some Provincial troops, possibly these, marched by the "King" Hooper [4] house in Danvers the lead of the gate-post ornaments was seized on, and a remonstrance answered by a reckless shot, still denting the front door. At the Bell Tavern,[5] Mrs. Anna Endicott is said to have exclaimed to Colonel Pickering, "Why on earth don't you march! Don't you hear the guns in Charlestown?" Soon after this they halted near a fork in the road about twenty minutes, expecting to hear the British were gotten back to quarters. More talking followed, and it was decided that they should at

[1] *American Revolution*, 484. Gordon.
[2] *Life of Col. Timothy Pickering*, I, 69–70.   Octavius Pickering.   Boston, 1867.
[3] "Boston Doctors of a Century ago," II.   *Boston Sunday Herald*, May 7, 1899.
[4] *Under Colonial Roofs*, 44.   Jones.
[5] *Beside Old Hearth-Stones*, 191.   Brown.

least go on until something definite was learned. At Newell's tavern in Lynn, seven miles farther, the men halted long enough to refresh themselves with drink, and kept on steadily the next nine miles. This brought them to Medford[1] in the late afternoon. While his men stopped here for necessary refreshment, it was learned that the British were strongly reinforced and aiming for Charlestown. It was not known, however, how keen the pursuit had been, or the small amount of ammunition remaining for use. It seemed a desperate chance that the Salem men could effect much, but they hurried forward, sobered, as some recalled later, by the thought of a possible encounter. At length, from the top of Winter Hill, they were in time to see the British rear guard retreating in order toward Charlestown, and "the smoke of musketry discharged at them by some scattered militia from so great a distance as to be of no avail." [1]

At the first sight of the Regulars, Pickering halted [1] his companies and ordered them to prime and load, in full expectation of coming to an engagement. While they were in the act, or at the moment of its completion, a person arrived with a message from General Heath, the superior officer on the field, stating that the British troops had artillery in their rear, and could not be approached by musketry alone, and that the General desired to see Colonel Pickering. Leaving the companies in that position, he went across the fields with the messenger and met General Heath somewhere on the ground between the Cambridge and Medford roads to Charlestown. While they were together, the Regulars made their way over the neck between Mystic and Charles Rivers and posted themselves on Bunker Hill, to the left.

The following August the town of Salem sent a memorial [2] to the General Court, urging that the Militia of said town, "near 300, marched off, and directed their course according

---

[1] *Life of Col. Pickering*, I, 71–2.
[2] *American Archives*, III, 4th ser., 337. Force.

to the intelligence they were continually receiving;" and concludes: "Why the inhabitants of Salem should be so highly censured for their conduct on this occasion, the town cannot conceive. Thousands of men, nearer, much nearer, the scene of action, either stayed at home or arrived no sooner than the Salem militia. From Milton and its environs in particular, the militia got as far as Cambridge only, at the same time that the Salem militia arrived at Charlestown."

Colonel Pickering on returning to his men led them back to Medford, where a guard was posted at the bridge, and the rest slept. Next day they returned home. The Salem side of the story is rather borne out by a London newspaper,[1] which speaks of three expresses being despatched to Lynn, the first for aid, the second countermanding this since the British were in retreat, and a third upon finding that Lord Percy had come out. It concludes, "they were just so much too late as they had halted."

One Salem man was killed during the day, Benjamin Pierce, a baker;[2] his nephew and namesake was a Librarian of Harvard College, and father of the famous mathematician.[3] It is said that Pierce came on ahead of the Essex Regiment and stopped on horseback at Waite's[4] tavern in "Scadan," south of the Salem road, to greet the innholder, his uncle by marriage. A contemporary writes:[5]

> We sore regret poor Pierce's death,
> A stroke to Salem known,
> Where tears did flow from every brow
> When the sad tidings came.

Deacon Tudor, who lived on the southeast slope of Nonantum Hill in Newton, notes in his diary:[6] "By 6 the firing was hear'd on the Hills & the smoke seen near my

[1] *Lloyds Evening Post*, May 29-31, 1775.
[2] *New England Chronicle or Essex Gazette*, May 2-12, 1775.
[3] *Essex Institute Coll.*, July-September, 1881.
[4] *History of Malden*, 679. Corey.
[5] *History of Arlington*, 73. Cutter. From the *Salem Gazette*.
[6] Page 52.

House on sd Hills. By 7 they were drove by our gallant Countremen near to Charleston Neck, on Charleston Hill, the Genarl (Gage), had planted som canon on sd Hill to preserve his Troops in their retreat; here our people halted very prudently as sd Cannon mite have kil'd many & night coming on put an end to this terable days work."

Several skits appeared in reference to the rapid marching. One entitled "The British Grenadier"[1] was in the form of a song.

> For fifteen miles they followed and pelted us, we scarce had time to draw a trigger;
> But did you ever know a retreat conducted with more vigor?
> For we did it in two hours, which saved us from perdition;
> 'Twas not in *going out* but in *returning*, consisted our *expedition*.
>
> Says our General we were forced to take to our arms in our own defence;
> (*For arms read legs*, and it will be both true and sense.)
> Lord Percy (says he) I must say something of him in civility,
> And that is I never can enough praise him for his great agility.

Benjamin Franklin,[2] after reaching Philadelphia, makes this allusion in a letter to Edmund Burke, May 15th, "You will see by the papers that Gen. Gage called his assembly to propose Lord North's pacific plan; but before they could meet, drew the sword and began the war. His troops made a most vigorous retreat — 20 miles in 3 hours, — scarce to be parallelled in history. The feeble Americans, who pelted them all the way, could scarce keep up with them."

As soon as the British gained Bunker Hill, they immediately formed in a line opposite to the Neck; General Heath, seeing any further attempt upon the enemy would be futile, ordered the Militia, who were at the Common, to halt and give over the pursuit.[3] Gathering the officers about him at the foot of Prospect Hill, he then ordered a guard to be formed, and posted near that place, sentinels to be planted down to the Neck, and patrols to be vigilant

---

[1] *Historic Mansions*, 393, 405. Drake.

[2] *Mass. His. Soc. Pro.*, April, 1858.

[3] *Memoirs*, 15.

in moving during the night.   Lieutenant Hamilton,[1] of the 64th, returning to his regiment at Castle William, was shortly after stopped and made prisoner by those on duty. General Heath further ordered that he should be immediately informed in case the British made any movements.   The Militia were then sent to Cambridge, where, after forming and sending off another guard to the points below the town, the whole were ordered to lie on their arms.

One result of the communication with Boston being broken was that several of Master Carter's school-boys, who had started off with three cheers to see the fight, now found that they could not return to their homes.   However, the soldiers gave them quarters at Cambridge and kept them busy.   Benny Russell,[2] then a thirteen year old lad (later, a well-known newspaper editor), being skilfull with his pen, was made clerk to one of the companies.   The following August, while on duty, his father, who had escaped from town, came up unexpectedly and was about to shake him for leaving his family in suspense, when the soldiers present interfered, saying, "Leave that boy alone, he's our clerk."   Explanations took place, Ben was discharged, and next day taken to Worcester and apprenticed to Isaiah Thomas, printer.

The July following the battle, Samuel Alleyne Otis,[3] of Watertown, made petition respecting the doings of his apprentice, who had taken his horse and chaise April 19th "unpermitted by him or his friends, . . . and only to gratify a childish curiosity became a Spectator of the tragical occurences of that day."   Though unarmed, he found himself in danger and retreated to Charlestown when, hearing a ship of war was about to fire upon the town, he retreated back for that night to Malden; "from there the next morning, the indiscreet youth, by the help of Mr Henry Bass of Boston again got to Charlestown," where

---

[1] *Mass. His. Soc. Coll.*, IV, 2d ser.

[2] *Pictorial Views of Massachusetts for the Young*, 51–2.   Warren Lazell.   Worcester, 1845.

[3] *Mass. State Archives*, Vol. 180, p. 107.

he left the team in the care of a Mr. Goodwin, soon after
which "a then assistant of the late worthy General Warren,
and now Dr Eustis, got possession of the same, and they
have ever since been in the service of the Colony." This
Otis felt peculiarly hard, as he might at any moment be
in "absolute need of Horses and Carriages to transport his
distressed Family inland."

The British were all at Charlestown between seven and
eight P.M. under cover of the guns in the river, with scarce
a cartridge left. They brought [1] in with them about ten
prisoners, some of whom were taken in arms. The Selectmen [2] at once sent word to Lord Percy that if he would not
attack the town, they would take care the troops were
not molested and do all in their power to help them across
the ferry. The troops then drew up on the Heights above
Charlestown Neck, i.e., on Captain Fenton's or Bunker's
Hill, and remained there about half an hour. It must
have been grateful to stand at ease, as the Yankees had only
suffered them to halt three or four times during the last
fifteen miles, and then in open plains. After this breathing
spell Lord Percy [1] ordered the Grenadiers and Light Infantry
to march down into Charlestown; they were followed by
the Brigade, which marched off by the right, the 4th Regiment leading, with the 23d in the rear. Boats were ready
to receive them, the wounded men crossing first; this took
until ten at night, then the flank companies of the 4th and
47th embarked, the boats returning with the pickets of
the 2d and 3d Brigades, the 10th Regiment, and 200 men
of the 64th, who had been called up from Fort William.
These troops were under the command of Brigadier-
General Pigot, and were ordered to take possession of
Charlestown and the Heights commanding the Neck. Here
they accordingly threw up a work to secure themselves.
As these movements necessarily took considerable time,
leave was asked of the town, and the 23d and the Marines

---

[1] Mass. His. Soc. Pro., March, 1890. Lieutenant Mackenzie.
[2] Mass. His. Soc. Coll., IV, 2d ser.

ordered into the Town-house, others into the meeting-house,[1] where they remained some two hours awaiting transportation. It was past midnight, indeed, before they were landed at the North End and marched to their barracks. One soldier in Chatham's division of Marines says,[2] "We got back to Boston about 2 next morning, and them that were able to walk were forced to mount Guard and lie in the Field. I never broke any Fast for 48 Hours, for we carried no Provisions, and thought to be back next morning. I had my Hat shot off my Head three Times, 2 Balls through my Coat, and carried away my Bayonet by my side, and near being killed." The Rev. Mr. Gordon of Roxbury wrote,[3] "the British officers are astonished, chagrined, and mortified beyond measure at what has happened." An anecdote [4] was current at the time, that on their return to Boston one British officer asked another how he liked the tune of "Yankee Doodle" now. "D— them [returned he], they made us dance it till we were tired!" Lieutenant Colonel Smith [1] reported to Governor Gage that the Patriots' fire "continued without the intermission of five minutes altogether, for, I believe, upwards of 18 miles; so that I can't think but it must have been a preconceived scheme in them to attack the King's troops the first favorable opportunity that offered, otherwise, I think they could not, in so short a time as from our marching out, have raised such a numerous body and for so great a space of ground. Notwithstanding the enemy's numbers, they did not make one gallant attempt during so long an action, though our men were so very much fatigued, but kept under cover." Lieutenant John Barker [5] remarks rather sorely, "We got to Charlestown between 7 and 8 o'clock at night, took possession of the hill above the Town, and waited for the Boats to carry us over, which came some time after; the

---

[1] *Mass. His. Soc. Pro.*, April, 1870, May, 1876.
[2] Intercepted Letters.   *Essex Gazette*, May 12, 1775.
[3] *American Revolution*, I, 484.
[4] *Historic Mansions*, 397.   Drake.
[5] *Atlantic Monthly*, April, 1877.

LORD PERCY

Rebels did not chuse to follow us to the Hill, as they must have fought us on open ground and that they did not like. . . . Thus ended this Expedition, which from beginning to end was as ill-plan'd and ill-executed as it was possible to be."

Lord Percy [1] in a private letter was more generous to his opponents and wrote, "During the whole affair the rebels attacked us in a very scattered, irregular manner, but with perseverance and resolution, nor did they ever dare to form into any regular body.   Indeed they knew too well what was proper to do so.   Whoever looks upon them as an irregular mob will find themselves much mistaken.   They have men amongst them who know very well what they are about, having been employed as Rangers against the Indians and Canadians; and this Country being much covered with wood, and hills, is very advantageous for their method of fighting.   Nor are several of their men void of a spirit of enthusiasm, as we experienced yesterday, for many of them concealed themselves in houses and advanced within 10 yards to fire at me and other officers, though they were morally certain of being put to death themselves in an instant.   You may depend upon it that as the rebels have now had time to prepare, they are determined to go through with it, nor will the insurrection turn out so despicable as it is perhaps imagined at home.   For my part, I never believed, I confess, that they would have attacked the King's troops, or have had the perseverance I found in them yesterday."

With regard to the repeated statements that the Yankees fought under cover of their farm walls, Dr. Franklin [2] long ago observed that "Walls have two sides!"   General Heath [3] considered the fact that the British flanks were covered, almost to the height of their shoulders, as they ran in the road, accounted for the relatively small loss to the British.   Another quite probable reason why fewer

[1] To General Harvey.   *History of Arlington*, 82.   Cutter.
[2] *Historic Mansions*, 356.   Drake.
[3] *Memoirs*, 17.

British were killed than wounded may be because of the small buck-shot[1] used by the Yankees, since it was much smaller than the army bullets. Again David Green[2] tells us, in an account of the late action written May 6 to Gardiner Green, Copley's future father-in-law, at Demerara — "Many of their wounds were slight, owing to the people's firing from a very great distance." A British surgeon in writing home took exception[1] to the American balls, which he states were slit almost into quarters, and these, breaking apart when fired, did execution generally. The wounded Patriots did not bear the usual proportions to the killed, since the British did not choose to encumber themselves with prisoners.[3] They had enough to look after in getting themselves back to town. When one considers the fatigues and risks gone through, hour after hour, by both pursuers and pursued, admiration for their common Anglo-Saxon stock is increased. And one feels Lord Percy's commendation[2] of the redcoats is not misplaced, when he reports (as "Acting Brig. Gen."), "His Majesty's Troops during the whole of the affair behaved with their usual intrepidity and spirit." And one understands the standpoint from which Pelham[4] wrote to Copley: "It was almost a Maricle that they were not entirely destroyed. When the battle ended they had not near a Charge a Man: . . . an insessant fire was supported on both sides for 7 hours till sunsett, during which time the Regulars made a Retreat which does Honour to the Bravest and best Disciplined troops that ever Europe Bred. The fatigue & conduct of this little Army is not to be paralleled in History. They march'd that day not less than 50 Miles, were constantly under Arms part of them at least from 11 o'Clock at night till an hour after Sunsett the next Even'g, the whole of the time without any Refreshment, attack'd by an Enemy

[1] *Diary of the Revolution*, 121, 100–1. Moore.

[2] *Mass. His. Soc. Pro.*, June, 1873, May, 1876.

[3] *Memoirs*, 17. General Heath.

[4] "Some Pelham-Copley Letters." Paul Leicester Ford. *Atlantic Monthly*, April, 1893.

they could not see." David Green[1] adds, "The light infantry and grenadiers, you will observe had been up all night, and had been fighting all day; the brigade had had a long march through Roxbury, and no refreshments for any of them. Taking the whole together, it was the most fatiguing day's work that I ever heard of." Several British officers are reported to have said they "never were in a hotter[2] engagement." "Many are killed on both sides," we read in a private letter,[2] "and were left on the road, neither side having time to collect their dead." A Boston merchant,[2] writing the next morning to a friend in New York, reported Major Moncrieffe, Captain Parsons, and Mr. Haines as "safe returned." The Major had only come to Boston from New York the previous Monday. John Andrews[1] wrote in part, to a friend near Philadelphia, as follows:

"BOSTON, April 20,
Yesterday produc'd a scene the most shocking that New England ever beheld." Respecting the rumors current in town, he tells us, "the first advice we had was about eight o'clock, in the morning, when it was reported that the troops had fired upon and killed five men in Lexington; previous to which an officer came express to his Excellency Gov. Gage, . . . About 12 o'clock it was given out by the Gen.'s Aid-de-Camp that no person was kill'd, and that a single gun had not been fir'd, which report was variously believed; but, between one and two o'clock, certain accounts came that eight were killed outright, and fourteen wounded of the inhabitants of Lexington."

Parson Gordon[3] states, Gen. Gage "had early intelligence of the rising of the country, but the slaughter of the Militia men was carefully concealed from him until late in the afternoon."

Mr. Andrews continues by giving the story of the morn-

---

[1] *Mass. His. Soc. Pro.*, June 1873, July, 1865.
[2] *American Archives*, II, 4th ser., 361. Force.
[3] *The American Revolution*, I, 481.

ing's encounter as he heard it. The Lexington people, to the number of about forty, were drawn out early, he says, "near the meeting house to exercise. The party of Light Infantry and Grenadiers, to the number of about eight hundred, came up to them, and order'd them to disperse. The Commander of 'em repli'd that they were only innocently amusing themselves with exercise, that they had not any ammunition with 'em, and therefore should not molest or disturb them, which answer not satisfying, the troops fir'd upon them, & kill'd three or four, the others took to their heels, and the Troops continued to fire. A few took refuge in the meeting, when the soldiers shov'd up the Windows and pointed their Guns in & kill'd three there. Thus much is best account I can learn of the beginning of this fatal day.

You must naturally suppose that such a piece [of cruelty] would rouse the country. . . . The troops continued their march to Concord, enter'd the town, and refresh'd themselves in the meeting and town house. In the latter place they found some ammunition and stores belonging to the country, which, they found they could not bring away by reason that the country people had occupied all the posts around 'em. They therefore set fire to the house, which the people extinguish'd. They set fire a second time, which brought on a general engagement at about eleven o'clock. The troops took two pieces [of] cannon from the peasants, but their numbers increasing, they soon regain'd 'em, and the troops were oblig'd to retreat towards town, which they did," he adds, "with the bravery becoming British soldiers; but the country was in a manner desperate, not regarding their cannon in the least. . . . The last Brigade was sent over the ferry in the evening to secure their retreat." Another,[1] writing on the same date to New York, conveys a similar impression of the affair at Lexington Green, making Captain Parker reply that he was on his own ground, that his company were without ammunition, and had no intent

---

[1] *American Archives*, II, 4th ser., 361. Force.

but that of improving in the military art. After some altercation, the report says, the captain and his men turned to go off, and that the Light Infantry fired on them, killed six, and wounded mortally two others.

Another letter [1] of the 19th, to New York, contains this reference to the capture of the convoy: "There were two wagons, one loaded with powder and ball, and the other with provisions, guarded by seventeen men and an officer going to the Army, when six of our men waylaid them, killed two, wounded two, and took the officer prisoner; the others took to the woods, and we brought off the wagons. . . . I have endeavored to give you a few of the particulars, as near as I am able, considering the situation we are in, not knowing but the Troops may have liberty to turn their revenge on us. We have now at least 10,000 men round this Town. It has been a most distressing day with us; but I pray God we may never have reason to be called to such another."

Deacon Tudor,[2] already referred to as living on Nonantum Hill near Brighton, records in his diary: "April 19, fine Weather, but terable News from Lexinton, just after 6, this morning we had a rumer that the 1000, some said 1200 Regular solders, that marched oute of Boston privately last night had kil'd 30 men of sd Lexenton who where exercising: by 7 that there was but six: by 9 but three & 3 wounded; that the regulars were gon to Concord &c. &c. Rumor on Rumor: men & horses driveing post up and down the Roads; by 10 that the News got to Boston by 7. By 10 we heard of 2 or 3 ridgements marching from Boston under the Command of lord Percy, with field peices, to get to the Assistance of those who ware fiting with our people of Concord, Lexinton, &c. By 11 we hear'd [that] Percy's troops took Old Camb.g Road, that they where 1,000 at least; people were in great perplexity, Women in distress for their husbands & frends who had march'd arm'd after them on the 1st & 2d rumor." Indeed we can hardly realize

---

[1] *American Archives*, II, 4th ser., 359. Force. [2] *Diary*, 51-2.

what the anxiety of that day was. Mr. Samuel Appleton[1] remembered his father leaving home on horseback and hearing a neighbor, Mrs. William McClary, say consolingly to his mother, "You are fortunate in not having boys old enough to go." There were four McClarys out. Returning to Charlestown, we find that some families spent[2] the night after the battle in the clay pits behind Breed's Hill. When it was supposed that the town was quiet, word was sent to Mr. Temple's, where many had taken shelter. Two Mr. Russells, with their wives, thereupon ventured back, only to find another regiment had been landed, together with 200 men of the 64th, who at once encamped on the hill, throwing the people again into a panic. A letter, supposed to be from Dr. Isaac Foster[3] of Charlestown to his sister Eleanor, wife of Dr. Nathaniel Coffin of Portland, Maine, gives expression to the general dismay: "In the morning, Mr Temple got a pass for as many as would to return Home. I went with him, but oh, I can't describe to you the Melancholy Sight, to behold the preparations that was making on the Hill, and before I reached home met 500 more marching up to the Hill. The town I thought was gone, before night I thought it would be so fortifyed that we must give up or Die. But through the goodness of God in three Hours every soldier was out of the Town and we in Quiet. They were frightened and fled as If pursued; but no man pursued them; they heared an Army was come against Boston. This but an imperfect account but cant do more at present."

A letter written on the 20th to New York from Boston says:[4] "Our people came to no regular battle, but annoyed their whole passage back. We could see the flashes and hear the reports of the guns for hours; the warmest fire being about 2 miles from the Town, where only water

---

[1] *The Hundred Boston Orators from 1770 to 1852.* Preface, edition of 1855. James Spear Loring. Boston, 1853.

[2] *Siege of Boston,* 80. Frothingham.

[3] *Mass. His. Soc. Pro.,* April, 1870.

[4] *American Archives,* II, 4th ser., 361. Force.

parted us." John Andrews,[1] already quoted, wrote to his brother-in-law, "I stood upon the hills in town and saw the engagement very plain. . . . They were till ten o'clock last night bringing over their wounded, several of whom are since [dead], two officers in particular. When I reflect, and consider that the fight was between those whose parents but a few generations ago were brothers, I shudder at the thought, and there is no knowing where our calamities will end." One of the officers, mentioned as dying on the day following the battle, was Lieutenant Joseph Knight of the 4th Foot. He had been wounded in Menotomy and "was," as we read in the Salem *Gazette*,[2] "greatly regretted, being esteemed one of the best officers among the King's troops." The *Morning Post and Daily Advertiser*, London, June 24th, has the following notice: "Lt. Joseph Knight, a gentleman of Ireland, who fell in the late unhappy action in America, was one of the worthiest men and bravest officers in His Majesties Service. He served with great honour in the last war, and received many wounds but no promotion. Adverse fortune seems to attend particular men. Mr. Knight was the only officer killed [news of Lieutenant Hull's death had not then reached England] upon the occasion: he was mortally wounded; after which he lived 3 hours [13 hours?], and died with the greatest composure. One of his brother officers writes home, 'No man lived more beloved, or died more lamented.'"

Captain William Glanville Evelyn,[3] thirty-three years of age, of the same regiment, wrote home to his father, the Rev. Dr. Evelyn, Dean of Emley, Tipperary, and Chancellor of Dromore, Ireland, the 23d of April: . . . "Considering the circumstances, we should have thought our loss inconsiderable, were it not for the death of one, the most amiable and worthy man in the world. You will be grieved to hear that my poor dear friend, Joe Knight, received a

[1] *American Archives*, II, 4th ser., 360.   Force.

[2] May 5, 1775.   *History of Arlington*, 53.   Cutter.

[3] *The Evelyns in America*.   Scull.

ball through the body, of which he died next day, to our unspeakable grief, and the general loss of the whole army."

In a letter of June 6th Captain Evelyn writes to his cousin, respecting her brother in his charge, a seventeen year old lad, Ensign Boscawen: "In a letter to Mrs Boscawen shortly after the 19th of April, I hinted to her a desire of looking out for a Lieutenancy to purchase for George in some Regiment lately gone home. This desire arose purely from the anxiety and uneasiness I was under all that day lest an unlucky ball should involve us in fresh distress, and complete her misfortunes; [she had, it will be recalled, recently lost her husband, Admiral Boscawen and her elder son] and what might we not apprehend, when the most amiable young man I ever knew, Mr Knight, fell by the hands of a rebel. We shall no doubt commence an active campaign; and though, were he my brother, I should wish him engaged in all the busiest scenes of it, yet knowing how much your mother is wrapt up in him, I confess I cannot be without uneasiness at his being subject to the Chance of war; and what could I say to her, should any accident befall her only remaining son? But if you are all satisfied to commit him, I declare I think his present situation the most desirable and most fortunate one he could be thrown into; and you would think so, could you see how much he is improved; and I know he would be far from wishing to exchange it."

After the battle of Bunker Hill, June 17th, 1775, Captain Evelyn, when making his will, "as the fatal experience of this day shews us how particularly precarious a tenure of life has a soldier," enters among other bequests the following item, "I have further to desire, that if my Books should be sold, the three volumes of Hudibrass in French and English, the Legacy of my amiable and unfortunate Friend Joe Knight, may be reserved and by some means transmitted to my Father." Memo., Staten Island, August 20th, 1776, "I only beg that my amiable Friend Captain [Thomas?] Knight will accept of the Ring left me

CAPTAIN WM. GLANVILLE EVELYN

by his incomparable and dearly beloved Brother." November
6th, following, Captain Evelyn died of a battle wound.

Lieutenant Knight was succeeded[1] in command by Ensign
James Goddard Butler, 4th Regiment. The Salem *Gazette*
of May 5th alludes to the recent death of 23 wounded
soldiers at Castle William, and it is probable that the loss
on either side will never be fully known. An intercepted
letter[2] from a soldier's wife begins:

May 2nd, 1775,

Loving Brothers and Sisters,

The 19th of April the Engagement happened, and my
Husband was wounded and taken Prisoner, but they use
him well, and I am striving to get to him, as he is very
dangerous, but it is almost impossible to get out or in, or
to get anyThing, for we are forced to live on Salt Provisions
entirely, and they are building Batteries round the Town
and so are we, for we are expecting them to storm us. Are
expecting more Troops every Day. My Husband is now
lying in one of their Hospitals, at a place called Cambridge,
and there is now 40 or 50,000 of them gathered together, and
we are about 4000 at most. It is very troublesome Times,
for we are expecting the Town to be burnt down every Day.
And I believe we are sold, and I hear my Husband's Leg
is broke and my Heart is almost broke."

About a week after the battle the Rev. Dr. McClure,[3]
already quoted, saw three Regulars abed in a Cambridge
house, one being mortally wounded. In his diary he says:
"Conversed with them on their melancholy situation. One
of them refused to answer, and cast upon me a revengeful
look. Perhaps he was a Papist, and his priest had pardoned
his sins. The houses on the road of the march of the
British were all perforated with balls, and the windows
broken. Horses, Cattle, and swine lay dead about. Such
were the dreadful trophies of war for about twenty miles."

---

[1] *London Gazette*, July 8–11, 1775.

[2] *Essex Gazette*, May 12, 1775.

[3] *Mass. His. Soc. Pro.* April, 1878.

A private letter [1] of May 6th reports Lieutenant Hawkshaw as "badly wounded but like to recover." A British soldier [2] wrote home on the 28th of April, "I am well all but a Wound I received through the Leg by a Ball from one of the Bostonians. At the time I wrote you from Quebec I had the strongest assurance of going Home, but the laying the tax on the New England people caused us to be ordered for Boston. . . . I can't be sure when you'll get another Letter from me, as this extensive Continent is all in Arms against us: These people are very numerous, and full as bad as the Indians for Scalping and Cutting the dead men's Ears and Noses off, and those they get alive, that are wounded and can't get off the Ground."

Henry Pelham,[3] a Tory, has left an account of his attempt to drive to Newton with his Sister Copley, in order to suggest to his brother, Charles Pelham, that at the rate events were moving he would be safer in town. However, finding a disturbance in the country, on the eve of starting this plan was altered and Mr. Pelham set out alone with the Copley's horse and chaise. To use his own words: "I went to the ferry. The ferryman refused to carry me over, the Wind being high, tho there was a Chaise passing over. This I considered as a great disapointment & scolded at the Ferrymen who I thot acting out of their line of Duty. I here lost an hour, being obliged to Return thro the town and go over the Neck. This in the sequel will appear a very fortunate Circumstance as it detered from attempting to return the same way. I found my brother unable to move being confined with the Gout. Anxious for my Friends, as the Country was now in the utmost Confusion my attention was drawn to our Amiable Friend Miss Sally Bromfield who was then at Cambridge. I went & took her into my Chaise. The people hav.g taken up the bridge

---

[1] *Mass. His. Soc. Pro.*, June, 1873.

[2] Intercepted Letter. *Essex Gazette*, May 12, 1775.

[3] "Some Pelham-Copley Letters. Paul Leicester Ford. *Atlantic Monthly*, April, 1893.

at Cambridge to Stop the Troops in their Retreat and fear.g another Disapointment at Charlestown I thot it most prudent to Return home by the Way of Watertown tho it was 13 Miles, which I happyly effected by Sunsett, after hav.g Rid apost a Circuit of 30 miles. Had we Returned through Charlestown we should have been in the midst of the Battle and have remaind a fortnight involuntary exiles from our Friends who as it was were very uneasy for us. This is evident, Mr Harry Bromfield having gone the same afternoon to fetch his Sister down but finding she had just left her Uncle's with me, hastened immediately back to the Ferry where he found the boats stopped by order of the Gen.l. The Armies fast approach.g and that being a very unsafe place he had but just time to escape over Charlestown Neck before the retreat.g army entered it. He was forced to Remain 13 days in the Country unable to see his Friends, before he could obtain a pass to Return home. Amidst the Horrors of that fatal Day I feel myself happy in being instrumental in rescuing my very lovely Friend from such a Scene of Distress and Danger."

About midnight on Wednesday, the 19th, the Patriots were startled by an alarm that the enemy were coming up Charles River. It proved, however, to be an armed schooner, and not a man-o'-war, probably sent to make discovery. She got aground, and stuck fast until the next tide; only the lack of a field-piece prevented her being taken. Small arms alone were insufficient for the purpose as the marsh was too deep to get very near.[1] With reference to this alarm, James Stevens of Andover states in his journal,[2] "Thursday, ye 20th, this A.M. we had alarm about day, we imbodied as soon as possible & march into the comon; we herd that the regerlers was gon to Boston, we staid on the Comon a spel & . . . herd severl small arms & one or two swevels from a tender. We staid awhile, ten or aleven a clock, & then come down & got some refreshments, & men come in very fast."

[1] *Memoirs*, 15. Heath. [2] *History of Andover*, 309. Bailey.

This was the last incident of that long and trying day. With Thursday morning came the fresh problem of feeding the rallying army, and the sad duty of caring for the fallen. Cambridge had become a camp and all the eatables that could be spared were collected for breakfast and cooked in the college kitchen.   Beef and pork prepared on Tuesday for the Boston market were brought from Brighton and a large quantity of ship bread at Roxbury, said to belong to the British navy, was taken for the Militia.[1] Rations being thus scarce, Daniel Vose of Milton[2] agreed to care for a regiment from Saturday until Monday morning.   Hurrying back to Davenport, the Milton baker, he sent messengers to the farmers asking them to fetch in sheep.   In the basement of his store was a fireplace for eight-foot wood; here he hung up three kettles and made chocolate by the gallon. The soldiers were quartered in the attic above and elsewhere, drinking from tin dippers in the absence of canteens.

Thursday was a cloudy day with fresh gales.[3] Having slept off part of their fatigue, the Dedham Militia — fifty-six men — under Captain John Battle,[1] were sent over the scene of action to bury the slain.   In case the British "should come out in superior force and scatter" the Americans, it was arranged that a general stand should take place on the high ground toward Watertown.

Mrs. Hannah Winthrop, after an uncomfortable night spent near Fresh Pond, where many had taken refuge, "some nodding in their chairs, some resting their weary limbs on the floor," received word in the morning that it would be useless to attempt returning to Cambridge, for the British were moving up the river and firing on the town.   She continues in her letter[3] to Mrs. Mercy Warren:

Methinks in that hour I felt the force of my Mother Eve's soliloquy on being driven out of Paradise, comparing small things with great:

[1] *Memoirs*, 16, 15. Heath.
[2] *History of Milton*, 431.   Rev. A. K. Teele.   Published by the Town, 1887.
[3] *Mass. His. Soc. Pro.*, August, 1860, April, 1875.

Oh, unexpected stroke, worse than of death!
Must I thus leave thee, Paradise. Thus leave
Thee, native soil? these happy walks and shades,
Fit haunt of gods, where I had hoped to spend,
Quiet, though sad, the respite of that day
That must be mortal to us both?
How shall I part, and whither wander down
Into a lower world, to this obscure
And wild? how shall we breathe in other air
Less pure, accustomed to immortal fruits?

and could only be consoled by the mild reply of Michael, her guardian angel:

Lament not, Eve, but patiently resign
What justly thou hast lost, nor set thy heart,
Thus over fond, on that which is not thine;
Thy going is not lonely; with thee goes
Thy husband; him to follow thou art bound;
Where he abides, think there thy native soil. '

His benign words to Adam must also afford consolation to the lonely soul:

His omnipresence fills land, sea, and air.
Surmise not, then,
His presence to these narrow bounds confined.

Thus with precipitancy were we driven to the town of Andover, following some of our acquaintance, five of us to be conveyed by one poor, tired horse-chaise. Thus we began our [pilgrimage] alternately walking and riding, the roads filled with frightened women and children, some in carts with their tattered furniture, others on foot fleeing into the woods. But what greatly added to the horror of the scene was our passing through the bloody field at Menotomy, which was strewed with the mangled bodies.

We met one affectionate father with a cart, looking for his murdered son, and picking up his neighbors who had fallen in battle, in order for their burial. I should not have chose this town for an asylum, being but twenty miles from seaports, . . . our situation . . . is rural and romantically pleasing, seated in a truly retired spot, no house in sight, within a mile of neighbors . . . the house, decent and neat, stands under the shade of two venerable elms, . . . a spacious meadow before it, a small rivulet meandering through it, . . . several little mounts rising in a conic form intersected with fertile spots of waving grain, the horizon bounded by a thick wood . . . nothing is heard but the melody of the groves and the unintelligible language of the animal Creation . . . instead of losing my fondness for society, I shall have a higher relish for the pleasure of friendly converse and social endearment, though the family we live with are very obliging.

In Boston, no less than in Cambridge, the thought also was of flight. Mrs. Sarah Winslow Deming relates in her journal:[1]

Towards morning I fell into a profound sleep, from which I was waked by Mr Deming between 6 and 7 o. c. informing me that I was Gen. Gage's prisoner all egress & regress being cut off between the town and the country. . . . No words can paint my distress—I feel it at this instant (just eight weeks after) so sensibly that I must pause before I proceed.

This was Thursday, 20th April. About 9 o. c. A.M. I was told that the way over the neck was opened for foot passengers but no carriage was permitted to cross the lines. I then determined to try if *my feet* would support me thro, tho I trembled to such a degree that I could scarce keep my feet in my own chamber, had taken no sustenance for the day & very sick at my stomach. I tyed up a few things in my handkerchief, put on my cloak and was just setting out upon my march with Sally & Lucinda [her niece and negro slave] when I was told that carriages were allowed to pass. By this time I was so faint that I was obliged to sit down. Mr Scollay, Mrs Sweetzer, and who else I remember not, advised me to stay where I was, reconing Boston the safest place for me, but I had no faith in their opinion. I had been told that Boston would be an Alceldama as soon as the fresh troops arrived, which Mr Barrow had

[1] *American Monthly Magazine*, January, 1894.

told me were expected every minute. I therefore besought Mr Deming to get a carriage for me. I had then heard that carriages were permitted to pass, and carry me off with my frightened girls: and set me down anywhere out of Boston. He went out . . . awhile & returned and told me there was not a carriage . . . to be got for love or money: ah, can any one one that has not felt it know my sensation. Surely no. Mr. D. threw himself into the easy chair, & said he had not strength enough to move another step. I expected to see Sally fall into hysterick fitts every minute. Lucinda holding herself up by anything she could grasp. I bid her however git us some elixer drops, & when we had taken it in a little wine mixed with water which happened to be boiling, I prayed Mr. D. once more to let us try to get off on foot. He said he would presently and see me out but positively he would come back again. There is no describing my sensations. *This moment* I thot the *crisis*, the *very crisis*. — I had not walked out at the top of the Court [*i.e.*, Central Court, Avon Street] since last October — I went down and out to the edge of the street [Washington] where I saw and spoke with several friends near as unhappy as myself, in a few moments the light of a chaise, which I engaged to take me off when it returned from Roxbury where it was going with women and children, this somewhat lightened me. Before this chaise returned Mr. Deming engaged another, & while we were waiting I might have packed up many necessaries but no body had any business that day — there was a constant coming and going; each hindered the other: some new piece of soldier barbarity that had been perpetrated the day before, was in quick succession brought in — I was very ill — but to cut short about 3 o'clock P.M. the chaises returned (for they both went to Jamaica Plain with Mr. Waters wife, children and maid, he having first engaged them, one of 'em being his brother Thompson's, which he, Mr. Thompson, offered to Mr. D. while it was out & promised we should have it on its return). We set out immediately, Mr. D. and I in one, Sally, Lucinda

with Jenny Church to drive in the other.   We were stopped
and inquired of whether we had any arms &c by the first
and second sentinels, but they treated us civily and did not
search us.   The third & last sentinels did not chalenge us,
so we got safe thro ye lines.   We had not yet resolved where
to go.   In that respect we resembled Abraham & I ardently
wished for a portion of his faith.

John Rowe [1] tells us in his diary that he dined at home
the evening of the 19th "with the Rev. Mr. Parker, Mrs.
Linzee, Mrs Rowe, and George Inman" (his nephew).
Three years before, when only eighteen years of age, Mrs.
Rowe's favorite niece, Sucky Inman, had married [2] Captain
John Linzee of the Royal Navy.   This was their first
visit since, bringing with them a fine little son, not quite
two years old, who lived to become a British Admiral.
Captain Linzee's sloop, the *Falcon*, had arrived at Clark's
"wharff" the previous Sunday, Easter Day, from Spit-
head and Falmouth.   Thursday, both Captain Collins of
the *Nautilus* and Captain Linzee were guests at Mr. Rowe's,
Captain Linzee remaining into the evening.[1]   The London
Morning Post and Daily Advertiser of July 13th gives part
of a letter sent home by one F. M—h, midshipman on the
Lively.   From it we find at five o'clock that very afternoon
Captain Linzee had ordered all on this frigate to clear for
action and renew the attempt to come up the river.   At
2 A.M. accordingly after this family dinner the *Lively* dropped
anchor in the Charles within a mile of Cambridge near the
bridge, and about daybreak had a brush with 200 Liberty
men.   For half an hour four swivels and two six-pounders,
double charged, were turned on the Yankees, causing them
to withdraw.   She then sailed back to Boston.   Captain
Linzee was present at this engagement, two of the British
being wounded and many on the other side, by the middy's
account.   The people of Boston were greatly disturbed.
One wrote to New York, "I have yet an opportunity of

---

[1] *Mass. His. Soc. Pro.*, March, 1895.

[2] *Letters and Diary of John Rowe.*   Introduction, 10–11, 291.   Ed. Cunningham.

writing to you from my own house, but how long that privilege is to continue God only knows." *Lloyd's Evening Post and British Chronicle* of June 16–19 gives what is "literally the Conclusion of a letter from a Tradesman at Boston, dated April 23: 'Perhaps this is the last letter you will ever receive from me; for before the return of Captain Brown I may be buried in the ashes of Boston, should not a pitying Providence interfere, and save it from destruction. I have a sick mother, a lying-in wife and five children, all completely wretched. It would soften the most brutal nature to behold children crying to their parents, and mothers weeping over their children.'"

Still another letter, states the *Morning Chronicle and London Advertiser* of July 4th, "received about a fortnight ago, by a considerable tradesman at Chester, from his son now at Boston, has the following passage in it: 'Now for a word or two about the present appearance of this country, which I cannot do better than in the words of my favorite Dryden:

> The neighbo'ring plain with arms is cover'd o'er
> The vale an iron harvest seems to yield,
> Of thick sprung lances in a wav'ring field;
> The polish'd steel gleams terribly from far,
> And every moment nearer shows the War.

"'This you may be sure can yield no pleasure to those peaceably and loyally disposed.'"

The wildest rumors ran about and appeared in the press of both countries. The *Morning Chronicle and London Advertiser*, a twopenny ha'penny paper, under date of June 14 quotes from an American letter: "Such is the barbarity of the king's troops, that seven of the Mercenaries, with their bayonets fixed, entered the house of one Hindman, a husbandman near Concord, and inhumanly murdered his wife, who had laid in but a few days, by stabbing her several parts of the body, after which they plundered the house of cheese, some bread, and whatever eatables they could find."

In *Lloyd's* paper of June 19–21 appears the following:

"There is said to be a letter in town from a young Scotch Gentleman, who was one of the party on the Expedition to Concord, in which he informs his friend 'that with his small detachment he forced open one or more houses, and put the inhabitants, being thirteen in number to the sword.' This Gentleman bears ample testimony to the courage of the Americans and observes, that out of the thirteen, one only pleaded for his life alleging, that he could not possibly have annoyed the Troops, being confined to his bed with a broken thigh." A letter in the *Pennsylvania Journal*[1] of August 2d says: "The cruelty of the king's troops, in some instances I wish to disbelieve. They entered one house in Lexington where were two old men, one a deacon of the church, who was bed-ridden, and another not able to walk, who was sitting in his chair; both these they stabbed and killed on the spot, as well as an innocent child running out of the house."

An extract purporting to be "from a Letter of a Gentleman of Rank in New England," given in *Lloyd's*, June 19–21, runs, "I saw some houses that had been set on fire, and some old men, women and children that had been killed." "There was a number of women and children burnt in their houses," says an intercepted letter.[2] The absurdity of these assertions at least shows the speed of their retreat and the narrow escape of some of the inmates of the fired homes, who to all appearances were overtaken by the flames.

The London *Chronicle* of May 30–June 1 has a letter from an officer on board the *Somerset*, man-o'-war, at Salem, with additional "circumstances, which for particular reasons are not made public," but may be depended on as facts. "To the list of killed you may add Lt. Col. S—h . . . . Neither our seamen or soldiers enter heartily on the service. Our Marines are almost in arms. . . . eighteen have deserted . . . The *Morning Post*[3] adds to the above: "P.s. The Salem Packet

---

[1] *Diary of the Revolution*, 66. Moore.
[2] *Essex Gazette*, May 12, 1775.
[3] June 1, 1775.

James from Dublin is just arrived with an account that troops were shipping there for America. Pray Heaven they come soon or not at all." On July 5th there was published an "Extract of a Letter from one of the Surgeons of H. M. Ships at Boston," dated May 26th. It runs [1] as follows:

"My curiosity led me to make use of the privilege of my profession to visit the New England camp, and some acquaintances in it, who had formerly been my fellow students at Edinborough. Among others I saw——, who attends a number of those that were wounded on the 19 of April, I did not think it fair to ask him the particulars of that day, as we are on different sides; but be assured their loss greatly exceeds that of the regiments; there is a large body of them in arms near the town of Boston. Their camp and Quarters are plentifully supplied with all sorts of provisions: and the roads are crowded with carts and carriages, bringing them rum, Cyder &c. from the neighboring towns, for without New England rum, a New England army could not be kept together. . . . I had the honour to see several of their great Generals, and among the rest, Gen. Jedediah Priddle [of Falmouth, *i.e.*, Portland]: he is a stout-looking old fellow, seems to be turned of seventy. I could not help thinking that his head would make a very good figure on Temple Bar."

The London *Morning Post and Daily Advertiser* of June 21st evidently discredits the rumors of atrocities committed by the troops, and makes game of the whole affair by a so-called Extract of a Letter from a friend near Boston: "several small Parties were sent forward to discover if any Provincials lay in ambush, to ransack houses, &c., &c.: Some of which entered a farm house near the road between Lexington and Cambridge, where lay an old woman, a native of Ireland, who came over in Charles II. reign with her father, and was one hundred and sixteen years old, had been bed-ridden for the last thirty-three years, retained perfectly her senses, and supported nature by linen rags, which she kept con-

[1] *Morning Post and Daily Advertiser.*

stantly dipping in milk and sucking them; she was wantonly murdered by a soldier who plunged his bayonet through her body; her granddaughter who sat by the side of the bed aged seventy-five, and blind, was also stabbed, but not mortally; her grandson, master of the farm aged fifty-nine, and son to the blind woman, had been with two of his sons assisting at Concord &c. and just entered his own farm-yard, time enough to prevent the murder of his wife, who was running from a soldier through the garden. The Murderers fled on seeing the farmers, who instantly fol-lowed; and what is very remarkable, they all fired together at the villains, only one fell, and on examining, they found that each had placed a ball through his body, although they had the same aim at each of the others, yet it seems something directed the balls at him, as he was certainly the murderer of the old woman, for his weapon was yet reeking with her antient blood. She had been thrice married, and all her husbands were born in England: in her first husband's time she lived at the Settlement at Casco Bay, had seven children, was taken captive by the Indians, who killed and scalped her husband and two sons; she made her escape, and had six children by her second husband, and two by her last, all dead, and all her grandchildren except the blind woman, who heard her groan her last; there remains five great grandchildren, and fifty-six great great grandchildren, to curse the memory of your cruel ministers, and lament the untimely death of their venerable ancestor."

A youth from Gloucester, England, midshipman on the *Nautilus*, gives his experiences in the *British Chronicle* of July 3–5: "My situation here is not very pleasant, for I am stationed in an open boat at the mouth of Charles river to watch the Americans, who are busily employed in making fire stages, to send down the stream to burn our ships. I have a command of 6 men, and a six pounder is fixed to the bow of our boat, which we are to fire to alarm the Camp and Fleet, as soon as we observe the fire stages. The woods on both sides the River swarm with People as cruel as the savage

Indians, so that it is impossible to go on shore without being scalped. The Inhabitants of Boston are delivering up their arms, and leaving the Town. The *Somerset* of 74 guns lays between Boston and Charlestown, which are only separated by a channel about a mile broad, and our ship lays about half a mile above her, and if she sees a particular signal hung out, she is to fire on Charlestown."

The day after the battle Dr. Warren, President of the Committee of Safety, engaged Paul Revere [1] to ride messenger for that body. Revere met Dr. Church in Cambridge that same day, and was shown blood on his stocking which Church said was "spirted" on him from a man who was killed close by. Up to then Revere had felt some misgivings because Dr. Church had been so intimate with a half-pay British officer, one Captain Price, and Commissioner Robinson. He thought, however, as he says, "If a man will risk his life in a cause, he must be a friend to that cause; and I never suspected him after, till he was charged with being a traitor." On the Friday, April 21st, about sunset, as many of the Committee were sitting at Mr. Hastings' house (more recently known as the old Holmes house), Revere continues, "Dr. Church,[1] all at once started up — Dr. Warren, said he, I am determined to go into Boston tomorrow. — Dr. Warren replied, Are you serious, Dr. Church? they will hang you if they catch you in Boston. He replied, I am serious, and am determined to go at all adventures. After a considerable conversation, Dr. Warren said, If you are determined, let us make some business for you. They then agreed that he should get medicine for their and our wounded officers. He left the next morning; and I think he came back on Sunday evening. After he had told the Committee how things were, I took him aside, and inquired particularly how they treated him. He said, that as soon as he got to their lines, on Boston Neck, they made him a prisoner, and carried him to Gen. Gage, where he was examined, and then he was sent to

[1] *Life of Revere*, 208–9, 210. Goss.

Gould's barracks, and was not suffered to go home but once. After he was taken up, for holding a correspondence with the British, I came across Deacon Caleb Davis; — we entered into conversation about him; — he told me, that the morning Church went into Boston, he (Davis) received a billet for Gen. Gage — (he then did not know that Church was in town) — when he got to the General's house, he was told that he was in private with a gentleman; that he waited near half an hour, when Gen. Gage and Dr. Church came out of a room, discoursing together, like persons who had been long acquainted. He appeared to be quite surprised at seeing Dea. Davis there; that he (Church) went where he pleased, while in Boston, only a Major Caine, one of Gage's aids, went with him. I was told by another person, whom I could depend upon, that he saw Church go into Gen. Gage's house, at the above time; that he got out of the chaise and went up the steps more like a man that was aquainted, than a prisoner. Sometime after . . . I fell in company with a gentleman who studied with Church (Dr. Savage, now of Barnstable); . . . he said he did not doubt that he was in the interest of the British; and that it was he who informed Gen. Gage, that he knew for certain, that a short time before the battle of Lexington (for he then lived with him, and took care of his business and books), he had no money by him, and was much drove for money; that all at once, he had several hundred new British guineas; and that he thought at the time, where they came from."

Dr. Church was born in Newport, Rhode Island, 1734, and it is said that he built too fine a house in Raynham, which brought on money difficulties which led to his defection and receiving bribes.[1] September 13th, 1775, when called before a Council of Generals, he made no defence. The Court held its sittings at Watertown Meeting-House, where he was conducted, by chaise, under guard of General Gates and twenty men. The galleries were crowded throughout the trial,

[1] *One Hundred Boston Orators*, 39, 43.   Loring.

the bar being set in the middle of the broad aisle. October 3d, he was found guilty.[1]

On Brattle Street in Cambridge, at the corner of Hawthorn, nearly opposite the Episcopal Divinity School, stands a house, sometimes known as the Governor Belcher house. Built about 1700, it had been lately vacated by Major Henry Vassal's widow,[1] Penelope Royall, who is said to have fled so hastily at the first rumor of open hostilities that a young guest was carried off in her train. This left the house available as a place of confinement for Dr. Church, who occupied a room on the second floor lit by two north and two south windows. A trace of his presence is said to remain in the letters "B. Church, Jr.," deeply cut on a closet door.[1] He was subsequently imprisoned in Norwich, Connecticut, and finally banished. Setting sail May, 1776, in a brigantine for Martinique, he was lost[2] at sea, and in 1788 his widow Sarah died an exile in England.

The seizing of horses was not all on one side. Some little time after the battle the Rev. William Emerson[3] of Concord requested "the use of a horse," taken from the Regulars at that time by Mr. Isaac Kitteridge of Tewksbury; two Concord men, Captain Nathan Barrett and Henry Flint, reporting favorably in committee. Parson Emerson expressed himself ready to pay a "reasonable price for keeping" the horse, and wished an order for its delivery. After some debate it was accordingly agreed, on June 5th, that Thomas Reed of Woburn should turn over to Mr. Emerson a "certain Sorrel Horse that was taken by the guards at Roxbury, from an officer of Gen. Gage's Troops, on the 20th of April."

[1] *Historic Mansions*, 287, 286. Drake.
[2] *Historic Pilgrimages*, 442. Bacon.
[3] *American Archives*, II, 4th ser., 1382, 1390. Force.

CHAPTER VI

ON Thursday, April 20th, Dr. Warren wrote an urgent letter to the towns, which was sent out as a circular from the Committee of Safety. "We conjure you, therefore," he pleads,[1] "by all that is dear, by all that is sacred, that you give all assistance possible in forming the army. Our all is at stake. Death and devastation are the certain consequences of delay. Every moment is infinitely precious."

On the same date, he wrote [1] to General Gage from Cambridge, ". . . I think it of the utmost importance to us, that our conduct be such as that the contending parties may entirely rely upon the honor and integrity of each other for the punctual performance of any agreement that shall be made between them. Your Excellency, I believe, knows very well the part I have taken in public affairs: I ever scorned disguise. I think I have done my duty: some may think otherwise; but be assured, sir, as far as my influence goes, everything which can reasonably be required of us to do shall be done, and everything promised shall be religiously performed. I should now be very glad to know from you, sir, how many days you desire may be allowed for such as desire to remove to Boston with their effects, and what time you will allow the people in Boston for their removal. . . . I have many things which I wish to say to your Excellency, and most sincerely wish I had broken through the formalities which I thought due to your rank, and freely told you all I knew or thought of public affairs; and I must ever confess, whatever may be the event, that you generously gave me such opening, as I now think I ought

---

[1] *Life of Warren*, 466. Frothingham.

JOSEPH WARREN

to have embraced: but the true cause of my not doing it was the knowledge I had of the vileness and treachery of many persons around you, who, I supposed, had gained your entire confidence."

The New Hampshire and Maine companies were rallying rapidly, numbers crossed the Merrimac at the upper ferries, and four companies passed through Newburyport this same Thursday, causing Mr. Greenleaf [1] to write for advice, since the massing of every available man in the Cambridge and Roxbury camps left the seaports unguarded. Special instructions in the event of a cutter putting in were earnestly desired. On Saturday, having heard from headquarters in the interval, Mr. Greenleaf wrote to the Committee of Correspondence in Hampton that there were enough soldiers about Boston and the local companies must be reserved for local occasions. He then alludes to the famous Ipswich Alarm which had thrown the whole countryside into distress the day before.

It seems some small vessels were seen near the mouth of Ipswich River, and the townsfolks, having the convoy-prisoners [2] in custody, grew nervous, until finally the story grew that the soldiers had landed and were murdering right and left. The women and aged men were still in the first excitement of receiving news from the battle, and did not stop to reason about the alarm, which it has been supposed was encouraged by British sympathizers.

When the news reached Newbury at midnight, that the clash had come, Parson Toppan, from boards laid across an ox-cart, spoke encouragement to the men of the upper parish, the company leaving by sun-up. Two ox-carts followed with luggage and rations. Next day more supplies were sent. [3]

At about the same time Friday that Ipswich was thrown

[1] *American Archives*, II, 4th ser., 374. Force.

[2] *Danvers Address*, 24. King.

[3] *Reminiscences of a Nonagenarian*, 171. Sarah Anna Emery. Newburyport, 1879: Wm. H. Huse & Co., printer.

in a panic, Beverly heard [1] that the Ipswich folk were being massacred, and the report had spread to Newbury, ten miles north, in the middle of the afternoon. Parson Thomas Cary of the First Parish had just opened with prayer the town meeting gathered in consultation upon the alarming accounts from Lexington, when in burst Ebenezer Todd,[2] an express from Rowley. Panting, his cue ribbon flying and hair loosened from haste, he rushed up the staircase and cried, "Turn out, for God's sake, or you will all be killed! The regulars are marching on us; they are at Ipswich now, cutting and slashing all before them!" The meeting broke up in disorder, all hurried home in confusion. Men and boys ran about the streets and increased the panic declaring that the redcoats "by this time were at Old-town bridge." Near sunset, at Crane neck, "Aunt Sarah," [3] then sixteen years old, spied a horseman waving his hat and shouting, "The regulars are coming! They have landed at Plum Island and have got to Artichoke bridge, burning and killing all before them." "Neither Grandfather Smith or Grandsir Little believed his tale, but most folks did," Aunt Sally used to say. At one house, having hidden their valuables, the horse was put in the chaise and stood at the door all night, an old lady sitting in an armchair, wrapped in a coverlet, ready to drive off to "South End" in case of an attack. Old Mr. Joshua Bartlett yoked his oxen and took his family to the Platts' place, a lonely, unoccupied farm where others found shelter. Colonel Stephen Bartlett, then an infant just weaned, cried lustily for a forgotten jug of milk until some of the party — beside themselves with fright — suggested "killing the brat." Hannah Eastman, an old asthmaticky woman, breathed so hard she was covered with a blanket, buried in leaves under a stone wall, and abandoned. One youth fled to the pasture

[1] "Ipswich Alarm." *Literary Recreations and Miscellanies.* John G. Whittier. Ticknor and Fields. Boston, 1854.

[2] *History of Newbury,* 245. Joshua Coffin. Boston, 1845.

[3] *Reminiscences of a Nonagenarian,* 172-3. Emery.

with a gun, powder-horn, junk of salt pork, and a half loaf of brown bread. Here he climbed an oak and tremblingly awaited daylight, when, being missed, he was routed out by his friends. One gentleman hid his papers in a hollow tree and had great trouble in regaining them. His wife lowered her silver spoons into the well, from which they were easily recovered, but the maid in her excitement had pulled her "nuts and drops" from her ears and flung them down, never to be seen more! The same informant adds:[1] "I have often heard Mrs. Moses Colman, then Betty Little, tell how she fancied the wind in the chimney and the sizzling of the woodfire — the drums and fifes of the British." One old lady,[2] fancying she had gold, lugged a leather bag, full of lead weights, several miles, only finding out her mistake as she sat panting by the roadside. Another[2] caught up a cat from the cradle and supposed it her babe until stopping to nurse it on the steps of Belleville Meeting-house! One man,[2] perhaps in the trick, rode furiously through Tappan's Lane and spread consternation by saying, in reply to the question, "Are any killed?" "Why, I've rode over more than twenty dead bodies since morning!"

There was talk of destroying Thurla's and Parker River bridges. Large numbers crossed the Merrimac, and spent the night in the deserted houses of Salisbury,[3] whose inhabitants, stricken by the strange terror, had fled across the line into Hampton, New Hampshire, to take up their lodgings in dwellings also abandoned by their owners. One man[4] took his children off in an ox-cart. One hid valuables under a great stone,[4] locked his doors and windows, and loaded his musket. One woman hid her pewter and silver in the well, and filled a bag with pies.[4] The plate may have been recovered, but the bag of food, being left a moment unguardedly by the wayside, was caught up

---

[1] *Reminiscences*, 173. Emery.
[2] *History of Newburyport*, 86. Mrs. E. Vale Smith. Newburyport, 1854.
[3] "Ipswich Alarm." Whittier.
[4] *History of Newburyport*, 246. Coffin.

by some of the stragglers. An old man, C— H—, too
unwieldy to fly, seated himself in his doorway with a gun,
and upbraided his more nimble neighbors, advising them to
do as he did, and "stop and shoot the devils." [1] One man
got his family into a boat to go to Ram Island for safety.
Fancying they were pursued in the dusk of the evening, he
was so annoyed by the crying of an infant in the after part
of the boat, that he called out nervously to his wife, "Do
throw that squalling brat overboard, or we shall all be
discovered and killed!" [1]

The same afternoon saw John Tracy [2] of Marblehead
riding bareback through Haverhill with word that the
British were coming. Some people put their children at
once to bed, others fled from home. The women gathered
around the pump and Meeting-house, while horses were
saddled and oxen yoked. Many from the East parish spent
the night at the Hemlocks, on the east side of Kenoza
Lake, with posted sentinels. [3] At midnight a rider, clad only
in his shirt and breeches, dashed up to the house occupied
by the poet Whittier's grandfather, twenty miles up the
Merrimac River, shouting, "Turn out! Get a musket!
Turn out! The regulars are landing on Plum Island!"
"I'm glad of it," answered the old gentleman from his
chamber window; "I wish they were all there, and obliged
to stay there," Plum Island being little more than a naked
sand ridge! [1]

Amidst the general dismay, one is glad to read of the
old lady, whose home was "on the seaboard about one day's
march from Boston." When the alarm came that the
British were right on them — within three hours' march —
instead of being "frightened from propriety" like the
neighbors, she set to work arming her two sons — her
husband being gone on a coasting trip to Virginia. The
elder lad, of nineteen years, had nothing better than his
father's fowling-piece to carry. Objecting to duck and plover

---

[1] "Ipswich Alarm." Whittier.   [2] *History of Haverhill*, 387.   Chase.
[3] *History of Essex County*, II, 1999. Hurd.

shot, the energetic old lady took a chisel, cut up her pewter spoons, and hammered them into slugs, giving him these in a bag. He set off to the minister, who encouraged him with a: "Well done, my brave boy, God preserve you." The second son, about sixteen, had only a rusty sword left, and hesitated at the door, when his mother cried, "You John H. . . . , what will your father say if he hears that a child of his is afraid to meet the British. Go along; beg or borrow a gun, or you will find one, Child. Some coward, I dare say, will be running away, then take his gun and march forward, and if you come back and I hear you have not behaved like a man, I shall carry the blush of shame in my face to my grave." She then shut the door, and he went.[1]

When the people had crossed the river they feared to continue their flight by frequented roads, and took to the swamps and wooded hills, where the snow had scarcely melted. The tramp and outcry behind them was supposed to come from a pursuing host, so that those in advance pressed on, frightening others in their turn. Houses were deserted, and the village streets strewn with household stuffs.[2] Toward morning, beginning to get the better of their fears, some of them, armed with long poles, sharpened and charred at the end, turned back. A young man of Exeter, New Hampshire, Eliphalet Hale, who had awaited the onslaught at Ipswich, was by this time satisfied that the alarm was baseless, and started on horseback to undeceive all whom he could overtake. Late on the Saturday night he got to Newburyport, greatly to the relief of the sleepless inhabitants, and crossed the river with his welcome tidings.[2]

A rhyme commemorating the panic closes:[3]

> Returned safe home, right glad to save
> Their property from pillage;
> And all agreed to blame the man,
> Who first alarmed the village.

---

[1] *Concord Gazette and Middlesex Yeoman,* August 14, 1824.
[2] "Ipswich Alarm." Whittier.
[3] *History of Haverhill,* 388. Chase.

A letter from Alexander Scammel [1] at Portsmouth, N. H., to John Sullivan in Philadelphia is full of contemporary color.

Honored Sir. . . .

When the horrid din of civil carnage surprised us on the 20th of April, the universal cry was — Oh! if Major *Sullivan* was here! I wish to God Major *Sullivan* was here! ran through the distressed multitude. April Court, which was then sitting, adjourned immediately. To arms! to arms! was breathed forth in sympathetick groans.

I went express to Boston, by desire of the Congressional Committee, then sitting at Durham, proceeded as far as Bradford, where I obtained credible information that evening. Next morning I arrived at Exeter, where the Provincial Congress was assembling with all possible haste. There I reported what intelligence I had gained: that the American Army at Cambridge, Woburn, and Charlestown was more in need of provisions than men; that 50,000 had assembled in 36 hours; and that the Regulars, who had retreated from Concord, had encamped on Bunker's Hill, in Charlestown.

The Congress, upon this report, resolved that the Durham company, then at Exeter (armed complete for an engagement, with a week's provisions), should return home, and keep themselves in constant readiness. All the men being gone from the westward and southward of Newmarket, and Men of War expected hourly into Portsmouth, it was with the greatest difficulty your Durham soldiers were prevailed upon to return. Six or seven expresses arrived at Durham the night after our return; some desiring us to march to Kittery; some to Hampton; some to Ipswich, &c., which places, they said, sundry Men of War were ravaging. The whole country was in a continual alarm; but suspecting that the Marines at Portsmouth might take advantage of the confusion we were in, and pay Durham a visit, we thought proper to stand ready to give them a

[1] *American Archives*, II, 4th ser., 501-2. Force.

warm reception; and supposing that your house and family would be the first mark of their vengeance, although I had been express the whole night before, I kept guard to defend your family and substance to the last drop of my blood. Master Smith being under the same apprehension, did actually lay in ambush behind a warehouse, and came very near sinking a fishing boat anchored off in the river, which he supposed heaped full of Marines: Men, women, and children, were engaged day and night in preparing for the worst. . . .

In longing expectation, your safe, happy, and speedy return &c., &c.

Although the community was in general opposed to the King's measures, yet, on the very day of the battle, a corps of Loyalists was formed in Boston, 200 strong. They were called the Gentlemen Volunteers, and Timothy Ruggles, Jr., one of the Mandamus Councillors, put in command.[1] He was the son of the Rev. Timothy Ruggles, for nearly sixty years settled at Rochester[2] in Plymouth County, and himself sixty-four years of age at this time. He had been a general in the French and Indian war of 1755, and found difficulty in adjusting himself to the new order of things.

In the week just closed the American losses had been as follows:

ACTON
Killed

Captain Isaac Davis, *at the North Bridge*, shot in the heart, thirty years.
Abner Hosmer, *Ibid.*, shot in the head, twenty-two years.
James Hayward, at Fiske House, *Lexington boundary*, twenty-five years.

Wounded

Luther Blanchard, *at the North Bridge*, shot in his side and neck, eighteen years. Enlisted in the army but soon died, according to tradition, as a result of the wound.[3]
Ezekiel Davis,[4] head grazed.

[1] *Memorial History of Boston*, III, 77.
[2] "Old Rochester and her Daughter Towns." Mary Hall Leonard. *New England Magazine*, July, 1899.
[3] *Memorial to Luther Blanchard*, 95–6. Hudson.
[4] Thomas Thorp's deposition, 44. *Acton Celebration, 1835.*

BEDFORD
Killed

Captain Jonathan Wilson, *in Lincoln*, forty-first year.

Wounded

Job Lane, *in Lincoln*, and crippled.
Solomon Stearns[1] and Reuben Bacon are said to have died as a result of the day's exertions.

BILLERICA
Killed

Nathaniel Wyman,[2] *in Lincoln*, in the afternoon, credited to Lexington.

Wounded

John Nickles, *in Lincoln*.
Timothy Blanchard, *Ibid*.

BROOKLINE
Killed

Justice Isaac Gardner, Esq., *at Watson's Corner, Menotomy*, twelve ball and shot wounds, forty-nine years.

BEVERLY
Killed

Reuben Kenyme or Kennison.

Wounded

Nathaniel Cleves, *at Menotomy*, finger shot off.
Samuel Woodbury.
William Dodge 3d.

CONCORD
Wounded

Captain Charles Miles, *at Charlestown*,[3] in the hand.
Captain Nathan Barrett.
Captain George Minot, in the afternoon.
Jonas Brown, *at the North Bridge*. Shot in the shoulder near the neck.
Abel Prescott, Jr., aged twenty-five, non-combatant, in his side, *at Concord*.

CHELMSFORD
Wounded

Deacon Aaron Chamberlain.
Captain Oliver Barron.[4]

---

[1] *Beneath Old Roof Trees*, 177. Brown.
[2] *History of Middlesex County*, II, 619. Hurd.
[3] *American Archives*, IV, 4th ser., 1378. Force.
[4] *American Revolution*, I, 485. Gordon. Here called Barns.

CAMBRIDGE
Killed
William Marcy, *in Cambridge.*
Moses Richardson, *Ibid.*, aged fifty-three.
John Hicks, *Ibid.*, shot in the heart, fifty years.
Jason Russell, *in Menotomy*, by two balls and eleven stabs, aged fifty-nine
Jabez Wyman, *at Cooper's Tavern, Ibid.*, sixty-five years.
Jason Winship, *Ibid.*, forty-five years.

Wounded
Captain Samuel Whittemore,[1] *in Menotomy*, shot wound and thirteen bayonet wounds, aged seventy-nine or eighty.
Josiah Temple,[2] in the shoulder. Later of Framingham.

Prisoners
Samuel Frost.
Seth Russell, aged forty-three.

CHARLESTOWN
Killed
James Miller, *in Somerville*, by thirteen balls, sixty-five years.
Edward Barber, *on the Neck*, fourteen years.

Wounded
A Negro.[3]

DANVERS
Killed
Samuel Cook, *at Menotomy*, in the heart, thirty-three years.
Benjamin Daland, Jr., *at Menotomy*, twenty-five years.
George Southwick, *at Menotomy*, twenty-five years.
Perley Putnam, *at Menotomy*, twenty-one years.
Jotham Webb, *at Menotomy*, twenty-two years.
Henry Jacobs, *at Menotomy*, twenty-two years.
Ebenezer Goldthwait, *at Menotomy*, twenty-two years.

Wounded
Nathan Putnam, *at Menotomy*, in the shoulder.
Dennis Wallace [or Wallis], *Ibid.*, twelve wounds, aged nineteen.

Prisoner
Joseph Bell.

DEDHAM
Killed
Elias Haven, *at Menotomy*, aged thirty-three.

Wounded
Israel Everett, in cubitus.

---

[1] Apparently given as Williams by Gordon in *American Revolution*, I, 485.
[2] *History of Framingham*, 277. Temple.
[3] Lieutenant Mackenzie. *Mass. His. Soc. Pro.*, March, 1890.

FRAMINGHAM
Wounded

Daniel Hemenway, *at Menotomy*, in his ribs and right thumb.

LEXINGTON
Killed A.M. *on the Green*

Jonas Parker.
Robert Munroe, sixty-four years.
Samuel Hadley.
Jonathan Harrington, in the chest.
Isaac Muzzey, thirty-one years.
Caleb Harrington.
John Brown.

P.M.

Jedediah Monroe, previously wounded in the morning, fifty-four years.
John Raymond, *at Munroe Tavern.*

Wounded A.M. *on the Green*

John Robbins, and crippled.
Solomon Pierce.
John Tidd, in the head by a cutlass.
Joseph Comee, in the left arm.
Ebenezer Munroe, Jr., elbow of right arm.
Thomas Winship.
Nathaniel Farmer, right arm.
"Prince" Estabrook, a negro.

In the afternoon

Francis Brown, in the cheek, thirty-seven years.

LINCOLN
Wounded

Joshua Brooks,[1] in the forehead, *at the North Bridge.*

LYNN
Killed

Abednego Ramsdell, *in Menotomy*, aged twenty-five.
Daniel Townsend, *Ibid.*, thirty-seven.
William Flint, *Ibid.*
Thomas Hadley, *Ibid.*

Wounded

Joshua Felt.
Timothy Munroe, *in Menotomy*, by a ball in his leg, thirty-nine years.

Prisoner

Josiah Breed, wounded as well.

---

[1] Amos Baker's deposition, 21. *Acton Celebration, 1835.*

MEDFORD
Killed

Henry Putnam, *in Menotomy*, aged seventy. A Danvers [1] man.
William Polly, *Ibid.* (mortally [2] wounded).
—— Smith.[3]
—— Francis.[3]

NEEDHAM
Killed

Lieutenant John Bacon, *at Menotomy*, near heart, fifty-four years.
cousins { Sergeant Elisha Mills, *Ibid.*, six balls, forty years.
{ Amos Mills, *Ibid.*, aged forty-three.
Nathaniel Chamberlain, *Ibid.*, aged fifty-seven.
Jonathan Parker, *Ibid.*, aged twenty-eight.

Wounded

Captain or Lieutenant Eleazer Kingsbury.
John Tolman, ball through him, twenty-two years.

NEW SALEM

Amos Putnam,[4] died of exhaustion from his rapid march.

NEWTON
Killed

John Barber, by family tradition.[5]

Wounded

Noah Wiswall, in hand, aged seventy-six.

ROXBURY
Prisoner

Elijah Seaver.

SUDBURY
Killed

Deacon Josiah Haynes, in afternoon, aged seventy-nine.
Asahel Reed.

Wounded

Joshua Haynes, Jr.
Thomas Bent,[6] non-combatant, bullet in the leg, died from the effects.

STOW
Wounded

Daniel Conant.

---

[1] *History of Essex County*, I, 449. Hurd.
[2] *Medford His. Reg.*, January, 1899.
[3] *History of Medford*, 162. Usher.
[4] *Danvers Soldiers' Record*. 157. Putnam.
[5] Letter of E. D. Barbour, Esq., February 8, 1896.
[6] *The Wayside Inn*, 16. Samuel Arthur Bent.

SALEM
Killed
Benjamin Pierce.

WOBURN
Killed
Asahel Porter, *at Lexington*, in the morning.

Wounded
Daniel Thompson, *in Lincoln*, in the back, by the flank guard, aged forty or forty-one.
George Reed, ball in his side.
Jacob Bacon.[1]
—— Johnson.[2]

WATERTOWN
Killed
Joseph Coolidge, *in Menotomy*, forty-five years.

Wounded
David Smith,[3] by explosion of his gun.

WESTFORD
Wounded
Captain Oliver Bates, fifty-four years,[4] died July 4 from effects of wound.

NATICK
Killed
Captain David Bacon, by some accounts.[2]

Approximately, fifty-five Americans lost their lives, forty-six were wounded, and five taken prisoners. Parson Gordon [5] wrote: "The persons who have fallen, are regretted with the deepest concern, and are honored not only as patriots, but as martyrs, who have died bravely in the cause of their country. . . . If the contest is to become general between the Colonies and the Mother Country, it may be deemed a happiness for them that it has commenced in the Massachusetts, where all the inhabitants are so connected with each other by descent, blood, uniformity of manners, similarity of civil and religious sentiments, mediocrity of circumstances, and a general equality, that the killing of a

[1] *American Archives*, IV, 4th ser., 1425. Force.
[2] *History of Middlesex County*, I, 393, 523. Hurd.
[3] *Mass. State Archives*, Vol. 138, p. 382.
[4] *History of Westford*, 110. Hodgman.
[5] *American Revolution*, I, 485–6.

single individual interests the whole Province in the event, and makes them consider it a common cause."

The list of killed and wounded as given in a Salem paper [1] closes: "The Publick most sincerely sympathize with the friends and relations of our deceased brethren, who gloriously sacrificed their lives in fighting for the liberties of their Country. By their noble and intrepid conduct, in helping to defeat the forces of an ungrateful tyrant, they have endeared their memories to the present generation, who transmit their names to posterity with the highest honor." On the Sunday following, those who had been in the fray stood in the aisles, many with bullet holes in their clothing, while thanks were publicly returned for their safety.[2]

The Rev. John Marrett [3] of Burlington says in his diary under this date, "April 23 Preached at home. Soldiers traveling down and returning; brought their arms with them to meeting, with warlike accoutrements. A dark day. In the forenoon service, just as service was ended Dr. Blodget came in for the people to go with their teams to bring provisions from Marblehead out of the way of the men of war. Considerable number at meeting. 24th Monday, At home. A dull time. Packing up my most valuable effects to be ready to move on any sudden occasion."

We now come to the British losses, on which the following comment has been made:[4] "The English lost at Argincourt but four gentlemen 'none else of name, and of all other men, but five and twenty.' Plassy, which gained India to England, cost the victors seven Europeans and sixteen native soldiers, killed, thirteen Europeans and thirty-six native soldiers, wounded. The Americans lost but twenty-seven at New Orleans. There were more Englishmen slain on the retreat from Concord than fell of Wolfe's army who captured Quebec, more than were slain on the Greek side at Marathon;

[1] *American Archives*, II, 4th ser., 393. Force.

[2] *Historic Mansions*, 369. Drake.

[3] *History of Middlesex County*, I, 675. Hurd.

[4] *History of Middlesex County*, II, 583. Hurd. Quoting Senator Hoar.

more men fell on both sides that day than at the first battle of Bull Run."

RETURN OF THE BRITISH [1] LOSS

Killed

One lieutenant, one sergeant, one drummer, sixty-two rank and file.

Wounded

Two lieutenant-colonels, two captains, nine lieutenants, two ensigns, seven sergeants, one hundred and fifty-seven rank and file.

Missing

One lieutenant, two sergeants, twenty-four rank and file.

Total of 65 killed.   180 wounded.   27 missing, distributed as follows:

4TH CORPS

Lieutenant Joseph Knight mortally wounded at Menotomy, died April 20th in Boston.

Lieutenant Edward Thoroton Gould wounded in the foot at the North Bridge, made prisoner at Menotomy by the old men.   Exchanged.

Three sergeants wounded.

One drummer wounded.

Seven rank and file killed.

Twenty-one rank and file wounded.

Eight rank and file missing.

Total, forty-two.

Of these last we have the names Alexander Campbell,[2] wounded, taken prisoner and exchanged, and James Marr,[3] likewise taken prisoner.

5TH CORPS

Lieutenant Thomas Baker wounded in the hand near Lexington.

Lieutenant William Cox wounded in the arm near Lexington.

Lieutenant Thomas Hawkshaw wounded in the cheek, *Ibid.*

Five rank and file killed.

Fifteen rank and file wounded.

One rank and file missing.

Total, twenty-four.

[1] The list as given in *History of Arlington*, 53–4, Cutter, is essentially the same as published in the *Gazette* of June 10 and the London *Town and Country Magazine* for June, 1775. Additional particulars are drawn from Lieutenant Mackenzie's account. *Mass. His. Soc. Pro.*, March, 1890, and DeBernière's report to General Gage, *Mass. His. Soc. Coll.*, IV., 2d ser.

[2] *Essex Gazette*, June 8, 1775.

[3] Rev. Wm. Gordon in *American Archives*, II, 4th ser., 627.

10TH CORPS

Lieutenant-Colonel Francis Smith wounded in the leg near Lexington.

Captain Lawrence Parsons wounded in the arm, contusion.

Lieutenant Waldron Kelly wounded in the arm at the North Bridge.

Ensign Jeremiah Lester or Lister wounded in the arm near Concord, *i.e.* Merriam's Corner.

One rank and file killed.

Thirteen rank and file wounded.

One rank and file missing.

Total, nineteen.

A gun was taken from this corps at the North Bridge.

18TH CORPS, ROYAL IRISH

One rank and file killed.

Four rank and file wounded.

One rank and file missing.

Total, six.

This last may possibly be Samuel Lee,[1] referred to above.

23D CORPS

Lieutenant-Colonel Berry Bernard wounded in the thigh at Menotomy.

Four rank and file killed.

Twenty-six rank and file wounded.

Six rank and file missing.

Total, thirty-seven.

Of these last we have the names of Evan Davis and George Cooper, taken prisoners.[2]

38TH CORPS

Lieutenant William Sutherland, slight wound in the breast at Concord bridge

One sergeant wounded.

Four rank and file killed.

Eleven rank and file wounded.

Of these, William McDonald, taken prisoner,[2] was one.

43D CORPS

Lieutenant Edward Hull wounded in the arm at the bridge, later in the body at Arlington, when he was made prisoner. Died May 2 at Arlington.

Four rank and file killed.

Five rank and file wounded.

Two rank and file missing.

Total, twelve.

A gun was taken from one of the first group of prisoners, belonging to this corps.

[1] *American Archives,* II, 4th ser., 627. Force.

[2] *Essex Gazette,* June 8, 1775.

47TH CORPS

Lieutenant Donald McCloud wounded in the breast, near Lexington.
Ensign Henry Baldwin wounded in the throat near Lexington.
One sergeant wounded.
Five rank and file killed.
Twenty-one rank and file wounded.
Total, twenty-nine.

Of these last, John Hilton, wounded, made prisoner [1] and exchanged, was one.

52D CORPS

One sergeant missing. This would be Matthews Hayes.[2]
Three rank and file killed.
Three rank and file wounded.
Total, six.

59TH CORPS

Three rank and file killed.
Three rank and file wounded.
Total, six.

MARINES

Captain Souter wounded in the leg near Lexington.
2d Lieutenant —— McDonald, slight wound.
2d Lieutenant Isaac Potter, slight wound, made prisoner in Menotomy. Exchanged.
One sergeant killed.
Two sergeants wounded.
One sergeant missing.
One drummer killed.
Twenty-five or thirty rank and file killed.
Thirty-six or thirty-eight rank and file wounded.
Five or two rank and file missing.
Total, seventy-four or eighty-one.

ARTILLERY

Two wounded.

The following names of British prisoners appear, not assigned by regiment:

John Bateman, wounded and buried at Concord.
John Tyne, wounded and exchanged.[1]
Samuel Marcy,[1] *Ibid.*
Thomas Parry,[1] *Ibid.*
Thomas Sharp,[1] *Ibid.*

---

[1] *Essex Gazette*, June 8, 1775.
[2] Captured by Lieutenant Tay.

John Tingle, wounded and enlisted [1] in the American army, deserted 1778.
John Maddin, settled in Gazeboro'.[2]
Daniel Green, made prisoner.[3]
Thomas Sowers, whose gun was taken on the edge of Concord.

The letter given below, written in the heat of the moment, throws some additional light on the day's doings. It is addressed to Colonel Freeman of Sandwich by W. Watson [4] of Plymouth.

PLYMOUTH, April 24, 1775.
Dear Col. Freeman,

I congratulate you and our good friends in Sandwich on the grandest event that ever took place in America; I mean the late battle at Concord, &c. That 700 poor, despised Yankees (I glory in the name) should have put to flight and totally defeated 1700 of Lord North's best picked troops, consisting of grenadiers and Earl Percy's regiment of Welsh Fusileers, is a circumstance deeply mortifying to those who thought themselves invincible. One of our Kingston friends was in Boston when the vanquished troops returned, and was at the Ferry when they were brought over, who says he cannot express the mortification, disappointment, and chagrin that appeared in their countenances. Cartloads of the wounded were hurried to the Hospital, (many of whom are since dead), their mouths belching out curses and execrations. We have disarmed our tories, and they are in a melancholy situation — suing and begging for reconciliation on any terms. We are in high spirits, and don't think it is in the power of all Europe to subjugate us; for it is evident that the Lord of Hosts has declared in our favor, and to this God let us ascribe all the glory and all the praise. The poor, wicked, mandamus party are fled to the ships; and to what can they fly next? I am sure they have not a good conscience to fly to. I wish

[1] *Mass. State Archives*, Vol. 211, p. 243, and *Mass. Soldiers and Sailors in the War of the Revolution*, Vol. 15, p. 762.
[2] *Mass. State Archives*, Vol. 182, p. 324.
[3] *American Archives*, II, 4th ser., 1503–6. Force.
[4] *History of Cape Cod*, I, 471. Frederick Freeman. Boston, 1869.

them future happiness; but I cannot in conscience wish them much good in this life.   I sincerely wish and most heartily pray that a proper sense of this very remarkable intervention of Providence in our favor may have a proper effect on the minds of a much injured and greatly insulted people.   Ned Winslow was in the action, and had his horse shot under him.

I am sir, with much esteem, and most sincere affection,

in great haste,

Your humble servant,

W. WATSON.

Col. Nathaniel Freeman, Sandwich.

P.S. Please forward this to Col. Otis of Barnstable, after Col. Freeman has read it."

Winslow, to whom allusion is here made, was one of the Tory guides.

A diary kept in Chesterfield, west of the Connecticut, by a native of Deerfield is filled with rumors of the day concerning the other Tory guides.   On the same date, (April 24) he writes:[1]   "Men from Northampton told me Daniel Bliss [of Concord] was killed and Samuel Murray was wounded."   They were both intimate friends of the writer and had lived at Deerfield.   The report continues: "Murray was shot through ye Hips & when the People came to take him he told ym he was determined not to take or give quarter and yy were obliged to run him through both arms with a Bayonet before they could.   Bliss and Murray went to pilot ye Regulars out."   Four days later more news came: "Colt who had been as far as Brookfield told me Murray not Bliss was dead.   The people had taken one [?] Murray and had him confined in Concord Goal and that he was as well as ever he was, and that Bliss was now in Boston unhurt."   Finally a Post that rode from Charlemont to Boston "in order to get ye true state of Facts," has it, "one Bliss was killed, but not Daniel."

---

[1] MS. Diary in the possession of the Hon. George Sheldon of Deerfield.

The following letter [1] to a gentleman in New York shows how Connecticut received the tidings:

Weathersfield, Connecticut, April 23.

The late frequent marchings and countermarchings into the Country, were calculated to conceal the most cruel and inhuman design; and imagining they had laid suspicion asleep, they pitched upon Tuesday night for the execution. A hint being got, two expresses were sent to alarm the Congress. One of them had the good fortune to arrive; the other (Mr. Revere) is missing, supposed to be waylaid and slain. In the night of Tuesday, the company of Grenadiers and Light Infantry from every Regiment were transported to Charlestown in long boats, and at day-break began their march for Lexington, where a number of the inhabitants were assembled peaceably, without arms, to consult their safety. The Commander called them rebels, and bade them disperse. On their refusal, he fired; killed and wounded nine. They then proceeded towards Concord, marking their way with cruelties and barbarity, never equalled by the savages of America. In one house a woman and seven children were slaughtered, (perhaps on their return). At Concord, they seized two pieces of cannon, and destroyed two others, with all the flour &c.

By this time, about four hundred (no accounts make them more than five hundred) of our men assembled, and placed themselves so advantageously, without being perceived, that when the enemy were on the return, they received the full fire of our men. A heavy engagement ensued; the enemy retreating, and our men pressing on them with constant reinforcements. At Lexington, they retook their two pieces of cannon, seized the enemy's wagons and baggage, and made about twenty prisoners; continuing to press the Regulars close to Charlestown, where they were on the point of giving up, (one account says this Brigade was almost all cut off), but a

---

[1] *American Archives*, II, 4th ser., 362. Force.

reinforcement, under the command of Lord Percy, having been detached that morning from Boston, they joined the first detachment in the retreat, and retired with it to Bunker's Hill, where they intrenched, and night parted them. Our number increased, and next morning would have surrounded the hill, had it not been for the situation near the water, where, on one side, they were exposed to the fire from a Man-o-War.

We lost thirty men in the action. The lowest account of the enemy's loss is one hundred and fifty. Lord Percy, Gen. Haldimand, and many other officers, are said to be among the slain. A gentleman of veracity assured me that he numbered, within half a mile from the place where the fight began, one hundred and fifty. The post confirms the same account.

We are all in motion here, and equipt from the Town yesterday one hundred young men, who cheerfully offered their services; twenty days provisions, and sixty four rounds, per man. They are all well armed, and in high spirits. My brother is gone with them, and others of the first property. Our neighboring towns are all arming and moving. Men of the first character and property shoulder their arms and march off for the field of action. We shall, by night, have several thousands from this Colony on the march.

The eyes of America are on New York; the Ministry have certainly been promised by some of your leading men, that your Province would desert us; but you will be able to form a better judgement when you see how this intelligence is relished. Take care of yourselves; we have more than men enough to block up the enemy at Boston, and if we are like to fall by treachery, by Heaven we will not fall unrevenged on the traitors; but if balls or swords will reach them, they shall fall with us. It is no time now to daly, or be merely neutral; he that is not for us is against us, and ought to feel the first of our resentment. You must now declare most explicitly, one way or the other, that we may know whether we are to go to Boston or New York. If you desert, our men will as cheerfully attack New York as Boston; for we can but perish, and that we are determined upon, or be free. I have nothing to add, but am,

Your friend and countryman &c.

P. S. Col. Murray's son, one of the Tories, undertook to guide the Regulars in their march to Concord, and on their retreat was taken prisoner; but attempting to escape from our people, they shot him, a death too honorable for such a villain! They have made another of them prisoner, but I do not recollect his name; none of ours were taken. Will Col. Grant believe now that New England men dare look Regulars in the face? Eighteen hundred of their best men retreating with loss, before one third of their number, seems almost incredible, and I think must be called an omen for good. In every Struggle Heaven has, as yet, given us Strength equal to the day; its hand is not shortened, nor its arm weakened. We are now called upon to show the world "that whom we call fathers did beget us," and that we desire to enjoy the blessings they purchased for us with their lives and fortunes. We fix on our Standards and Drums, the Colony Arms, with the motto "*qui transtulit sustinct*," round it in letters of gold, which we construe thus, "God, who transplanted us hither, will support us."

To quote Parson Gordon [1] again:

"The proceedings — of April 19, have united the Colony and Continent, and brought in New York to act as vigorously as any other place whatsoever; and has raised an army in an instant, which are lodged in the several houses of the Towns round Boston till their tents are finished, which will be soon. All that is attended to, besides ploughing and planting, &c., is making ready for fighting. The Non-importations and Non-exportations will now take place from necessity, and traffick give place to war.

[1] *American Archives*, II, 4th ser., 626–31. Force.

We have a fine spring, prospects of great plenty; there was scarce ever known such a good fall of lambs; we are in no danger of starving through the cruel acts against the New England Governments; and the men who had been used to the fishery, (a hardy generation of people,) Lord North has undesignedly kept in the Country to give strength to our Military Operations, and to assist as occasion may require; thanks to a superior wisdom for his blunders. The General is expecting reinforcements, but few have arrived as yet; the winds, contrary to the common run at this season, instead of being easterly, have been mostly the reverse. When the reinforcement arrives, and is recovered of the voyage, the General will be obliged in honour to attempt dislodging the people, and penetrating into the country; both soldiers and inhabitants are in want of fresh provisions, and will be likely to suffer much, should the Provincial Army be able to keep the Town shut up on all sides, excepting by water, as at present.

The General engaged with the Selectmen of Boston, that if the Town's people would deliver up their arms into their custody, those that chose it should be allowed to go out with their effects. The townsmen complied, and the General forfeited his word, for which there will be an after reckoning, should they ever have it in their power to call him to an account. A few have been allowed to come out with many of their effects; numbers are not permitted to come out, and the chief of those who have been, have been obliged to leave their merchandise and goods (linen and household stuff, cash and plate, excepted) behind them. You must look back to the origin of the United Provinces, that you may have an idea of the resolution of this people. May the present struggle end as happily in favour of American liberty, without proving the destruction of Great Britain. We are upon a second edition of King Charles First's reign, enlarged. May the dispute be adjusted before the times are too tragical to admit of it. Both officers and privates have altered their opinion of the Yankees very much since the 18th of April."

Rev. William Gordon, D.D.

The Rev. John Marrett [1] opens a letter, — dated from Shushan to his uncle Isaiah Dunster, "Att Harwich," "Rev.d Hon.d and Dear Sir," saying in the course of it, "As to ye British Parl.nts having ye supremacy over ye American Colonies, as now contended for by yt Body I hope yt through ye help of Divine Providence by next September great Britain will be convinced she never did, nor will hold such a Power in her hands. . . .

Our Army appear in good Spirits . . . our chief General is much admired. Wish him Good Speed . . . there is likely to be plenty of Cyder and Indian Corn. . . . I have got good Bottle Cyder and pipe and tobacco. Will you come and see me? My Dutiful regards to Mrs. Dunster and love to your Children."

The Worcester newspaper [2] concludes its account of the day: "Immediately upon the return of the Troops to Boston, all communication to and from the Town was stopped by General Gage. The Provincials, who flew to the assistance of their distressed countrymen, are posted in Cambridge, Charlestown, Roxbury, Watertown &c., and have placed guards on Roxbury Neck, within gun-shot of the enemy; guards are also placed everywhere in view of the Town, to observe the motion of the King's Troops. The Council of War, and the different Committees of Safety and Supplies set at Cambridge, and the Provincial Congress at Watertown. The Troops in Boston are fortifying the place on all sides, and a Frigate-of-War is stationed up Cambridge River, and a 64 gun ship between Boston and Charlestown."

In connection with the above the following letter [3] from Captain John Jones, "a son of Dover," who settled in Princeton in 1765, is of interest:

CAMBRIDGE, April 22, 1775,

Loving Wife:

There was a hot battle fought between the Regulars

[1] *Henry Dunster and his Descendants.*
[2] *American Archives,* II, 4th ser., 439. Force.
[3] *Dedham His. Reg.,* July, 1891.

that marched to Concord and our people on Wednesday, the 19th of this instant, in which many on both sides were slain (but most of the enemies) as we heard before we marched. As we marched to Concord we were often informed that the enemy had marched from Boston a second time and had got as far as Lincoln. We hurried on as fast as possible expecting to meet them in Concord but when we arrived there we were informed that they had returned from their first engagement to Charlestown, from which they are gone to Boston. We are now stationed in one of ye Colleges as are many more of ye Army all in good health through ye Divine goodness and hope of ye blessing of Heaven. In ye first combat among those that were slain were Lieut. John Bacon of Needham, two Mill's, Nat. Chamb'n and two others from Needham. Elias Haven from Springfield [parish of Dover]. If you have an opportunity you may send brother Hapgood a shirt and pair of stockings. Tis uncertain when we shall return, may we all be enabled to repent and turn to our God that he may save us from ruin.

> I am with the greatest respect,
> Your affectionate and loving husband till Death,
> John Jones.

As already noted, the College buildings of that day, still standing, are Old Massachusetts, Stoughton and Harvard Hall, little Holden Chapel and Hollis. The students were removed temporarily to Concord. About this time Lieutenant Barker [1] remarks, "The Rebels have erected the Standard at Cambridge; they call themselves the King's Troops and us the Parliament's. Pretty Burlesque!" Another name [2] applied to the Regulars was Lord Bute's troops, so loath were the Provincials to consider that matters had gone beyond a party issue, in which they still flattered themselves they had the support of a powerful body of home-born Britons.

"April 22," says Deacon Tudor [3] in his diary, "No

---

[1] *Atlantic Monthly*, May, 1875.   [2] *Remembrancer*, 82.   Almon.

[3] *Diary*. Ed. Tudor.

persons allow'd to come oute & our army at Roxbery
Suffer'd none to go in, so that the people in Boston Suffer'd
greatly for want of fresh provision, milk &c but by the
25, 26 [Tuesday and Wednesday, that is, of the following
week] people was permitted by a pass from Governor Gage
to com oute, but not suffer'd to bring oute any provision,
or Merchandise whatever. For as the report is the Admiral
[Graves] claimes a Right, as plunder, to all merchandise &c,
on a Supposition that the people are in Rebelion & should be
treated as Rebels, as he and som others call 'Em."

Meanwhile, on the 23d, John Rowe [1] heard that his
skipper, Captain Brown, had been "Stop'd at Charlestown
by the Country People." Next day, Monday, he writes, "I
Rose very early, and got away Mr Nun [a Lieutenant in the
Royal Navy, bearing despatches], John Inman, Mr. Sparks,
Thos Knights, Jos. Taylor & John Head on board Mr
Sheriff's Sloop for Salem. Between one & Two Capt. Brown
got to Town. I soon despatched him." April 26th he
adds, "John Inman is come to Town & tells me that my
Brigg.n Sucky [which had been named for his niece Susanna
Inman Linzee] sailed from Marblehead yesterday towards
night — in her went the following Passengers Lieut. Nun,
Mr Sparks, Jos. Taylor, Thos. Knight, John Head, Mr
Sherlock, Young Paine of Worcester, Mrs. Brown & her
Child."

On the 25th many of the Townsmen gave up their arms
to the Selectmen of Boston; something over 3400 being
collected[2] which were never returned. Two days later Governor Gage announced that permits to pass the lines might
be had, after eight, on the morning of the 28th, from General
Robinson. The men, upon leaving, were required to pledge
themselves that they would not "take up arms[3] against
the King's troops, should an attack be made;" the women
and children were passed unquestioned. About the same

---

[1] *Letters and Diary*, 293–4. Ed. Cunningham.
[2] *Memorial History of Boston*, III, 77, 76.
[3] *Evacuation Memorial*, 118.

time an advertisement appeared in the Essex *Gazette*[1] signifying that such persons as desired permits to enter Boston should apply at the Sign of the Sun, Charlestown, or at John Greaton's house in Roxbury.

"On the 29th," continues Deacon Tudor,[2] "My Daughter Savage with three of her Children took their flight from Boston to my House [at Nonantum Hill] for safety, two of my daughter Thompson's children from Brookline was with us before, many others who can gett a pass are dayly leaving Boston, from those terable times, Good Lord deliver us." Jane Tudor, one of the old gentleman's daughters, had married William Thompson; another, Elizabeth, was the wife of Habijah Savage. Their brother William was courting a Miss Delia Jarvis,[2] a Boston Tory, who is said to have given tea to the exhausted troops returning from Lexington fight.

Edmund Quincy's[3] diary furnishes another picture of the times: "Saturday, April 29, Left Boston with Katy Sewall to go to Lancaster. Lodg'd Saturday and Saturday night with my good friend Mr Richard Cary—on Monday went to Cambridge and lodged at Mr Jon'than Sewall's [the husband, that is, of his daughter Esther], proceeded next day to Watertown and lodg'd Tuesday, Wednesday and Thursday nights at Mr E. Hall's, K. S. at Mr Remington's, and having sent two negroes and goods to L., followed next day, on Friday eve'g reach to son Greenleaf's" [*i.e.*, William Greenleaf of Lancaster].

To his son Henry he writes:[3] "I was from noon Saturday till Friday eve'g getting up hither with much difficulty by reason of scarcity of carriages. Cost me near £20, besides quartering on some of my friends who were very kind and generous. Your sister Dolly with Mrs Hancock came from Shirley to your Brother Greenleaf's and dined

[1] May 2.

[2] *Diary*, appendix, X, XI.

[3] "Story of an Old House." S. H. Swan. *New England Magazine*, October, 1897.

and proceeded to Worcester, where Col. H. and Mr A[dams] were on their way, [*i.e.*, Tuesday, April 25th]. This was ten days before I got hither so that I missed seeing them. As I hear she proceeded with Mr H. to Fayerfield, I don't expect to see her till peaceable times are restored."

The following letter [1] indicates what an undertaking it was to transfer one's family and goods and to pluck up well established interests for an uncertain future. It is from Paul Revere in Charlestown, addressed to his wife, without date:

My dear Girl,

I receiv'd your favor yesterday. I am glad you have got yourself ready. If you find that you cannot easily get a pass for the Boat, I would have you get a pass for yourself and children and effects. Send the most valuable first. I mean that you should send Beds enough for yourself and Children, my chest, your trunk, with Books Cloaths &c to the ferry tell the ferryman they are mine. I will provide a house here where to put them & will be here to receive them. after Beds are come over, come with the Children, except Paul. pray order him by all means to keep at home that he may help bring the things to the ferry. tell him not to come till I send for him. You must hire somebody to help you. You may get brother Thomas. lett Isaac Clemmens if he is a mind to take care of the shop and maintain himself there, he may, or do as he has a mind. Put some suger in a Raisin cask or some such thing & such necessarys as we shall want. Tell Betty, My Mother, Mrs Metcalf if they think to stay, as we talked at first, tell them I will supply them with all the cash & other things in my power but if they think to come away, I will do all in my power to provide for them, perhaps before this week is out there will be liberty for Boats to go to Notomy, then we can take them all. If you send the things to the ferry send enough to fill a cart, them that are the most wanted.

---

[1] *Life of Revere*, I, 261–5. Goss.

Give Mrs Metcalf [torn] in, their part of the money I dont remember the sums, but perhaps they can. I want some linnen and stockings very much. Tell Paul I expect he'l behave himself well and attend to my business, and not be out of the way. My Kind love to our parents & our Children, Brothers & Sisters, & all friends."

My Son.[1]

It is now in your power to be serviceable to me, your Mother and yourself. I beg you will keep yourself at home or where your Mother sends you. Dont you come away till I send you word. When you bring anything to the ferry tell them its mine & mark it with my name.

Your loving Father

P. R.

It may be interesting to note here that Revere was twice married, his second wife, Rachel Walker,[1] being now about thirty years of age, with a five months baby, Joshua.[1] There were six children living by his first wife, Sarah Orne, viz., Deborah, seventeen years of age, and Paul, already mentioned, fifteen years old, Sarah, thirteen years, Frances, nine years, Mary, seven years, and Elizabeth, five years.

The next letter is from Mrs. Revere and is dated:

Boston, 2 May, 5 o'clock afternoon, 75,

Dear Paul[1]

I am very glad to hear you say you are easy for I thought you were very impatient but I cannot say I was pleased at hearing you aplyed to Captain Irvin for a pass as I should rather confer 50 obligations on them than to receive one from them. I am almost sure of one as soon as they are given out I was at Mr Scolays yesterday and his son has been here today and told me he went to the room and gave mine and Deacon Jeffers name to his Father when no other person was admitted I hope things will be settled on easier terms soon I have not received a line from you to say till this moment Why have you altered your mind

---

[1] *Life of Revere*, I, 263, 111, 109; II, 605. Goss.

PAUL REVERE

in regard to Pauls coming with us? this Capt. Irvin says he has not received any letter and I send by this 2 bottles beer 1 wine for his servant. do my dear take care of yourself. . . .

Yours with affection,

R. Revere.

We learn from Niles [1] of a young man sent a few weeks later to Major Cain with a schedule of effects to demand a pass. Such a throng was gathered, he tells us, it was some hours before he could reach the door, and when he did, the press behind sent him headlong over the threshold, and though the Major must have perceived the act was involuntary, he relates, "yet he had the brutality to exclaim, ' Hoot, hoot, Mon! Are you going to murder me?' I was obliged to bear this insolence in silence, though my countenance must have exhibited marks of indigna-tion, and I walked to a window which looked into the courtyard, where my feelings were still more excited by a view of my fellow citizens, who, with countenances almost bordering on despair, were waiting for a favorable moment to obtain admission. The first reflection which presented itself to my mind was, what must be the indignation of our King, if he knew how his faithful, loyal, and affectionate subjects, were abused, insulted, and driven into acts of reluctant resistance. . . . But to return . . . after waiting nearly an hour the Major accosted me with, 'Well, young man, what do you want?' I handed him a schedule of my father's family, including that of his sister's (the widow of a clergyman). He examined a small book which contained what the tories called the 'black list,' when slowly raising his scowling eyes, he said with great asperity, 'Your father, young man, is a d—d rebel, and cannot be accommodated with a pass.' Not at all intimidated by his brutality, I asserted with much vehemence, that my father was no rebel, that he adored the illustrious house of Hanover, and

---

[1] *Principles and Acts*, 115–16. Niles.

had fought for good King George the 2d, in forty-five. Whether . . . he himself had been a *real rebel* in Scotland, in 1745, . . . whatever may have been the cause of his irritation — the moment I had finished speaking he rose from his chair, and with a countenance foaming with rage, he ordered me out of the room with abusive language. The sentinel at the door had an English countenance, and, with apparent sympathy, very civily opened it for my departure, which I made without turning my back on my adversary." It appeared later that his offence was, his father had been a fellow member in the Whig Club with Otis, Dr. Warren, Dr. Church, Dr. Young, Richard Derby of Salem, Benjamin Kent, Nathaniel Barber, William Mackay, Col. Bigelow of Worcester, and half a dozen more who met to discuss civil liberty and the British Constitution; maintaining a correspondence with Wilkes, Saville, Barré, and Sawbridge.

It was not only the Tory party that exercised vigilance where suspicions had been roused. The Selectmen of Waltham reported May 23d the result of an inquiry into Mrs. Melliquet's conduct,[1] and find the charge of her conveying intelligence not borne out by facts. In short, notwithstanding that Mr. Melliquet was on the half-pay list, they were convinced that his integrity might be counted on. As for Mrs. Melliquet, she "went only once to Boston to bring her little child out which was at Mrs. Newman's before the Engagement." The Essex *Gazette*, printed in Stoughton Hall at the College, reports May 1st, in detail by county and town, the arrangements made for the removal of 4903 persons to specified townships, as, "36 to Deerfield," etc., the countrymen accommodating the refugees with the use of their teams. Even so the removal was not without hitches; as witness an open letter in the Boston *Gazette* of June 8th:

"To the perfidious, the truce-breaking Thomas Gage. It is difficult to know how to address such a monster . . . and yet you have the impudence to tell this downright lie to

---

[1] *Mass. State Archives*, Vol. 193, p. 135.

the world, *i.e.* That you have found examples of tenderness (in those Dogs of War) after you had let them loose, and cried havoc. . . . When Mr Pierpont carried you a bill of the goods, which you robbed him of on Boston Neck, and demanded of you either pay for them, or a return of them, did you not refuse to comply with either? . . . Nay, have not you, and your associates, by your orders, been mean enough to steal rum and sugar from a poor teamster, half a cake of gingerbread, a nutmeg, and half a bisket from a poor woman who was flying half famished out of Boston." Before this, Dunlap's[1] Pennsylvania *Gazette* reports April 26, via New York, "We have no Papers from Boston by yesterday's Post. The report is that as the printers were moving their types out of town, the packages were stopt and broke open by the Soldiery, and the letters Scattered or thrown into disorder, so that no Paper could be got ready." Robert and Mary Rand[2] of Boston had buried in the Granary their first child, Mary, two days before the battle. Now that others were leaving home, they also removed to Chelmsford, carrying with them a pincushion, still in existence, which had been daintily prepared for the baby and lettered "Welcome, little stranger, to Boston, though the Port is blocked up. 1774."

Even when a place of safety was reached, it proved but a spot, often, in which to die, as a Billerica gravestone bears record: "Here lies ye body of the Widow Lydia Dyer,[3] of Boston, the place of her nativity, where she left a good Estate and came into ye country May 22, 1775, to escape ye abuce of ye Ministerial Troops sent by George ye 3d to subject *North America*. She died July 28, 1776, aged 80 years." Any one suspected of strong sympathies with the Colony found it difficult to leave the town however much they might desire to. Mrs. Abigail Adams,[4] the following

[1] *Lloyds*, June 19–21, 1775.

[2] *Beside Old Hearth-Stones*, 334, 338. Brown.

[3] *Historical Collections of Every Town in Mass.*, 352. John Warner Barber. Worcester, 1848.

[4] *Letters*, 69–70.

October, tells of a man — "one Haskins — who came out the day before yesterday [*i.e.* the 19th]. I learn that there are two thousand five hundred soldiers in Town. . . . He had been in irons three weeks, some malicious fellow having said that he saw him at the Battle of Lexington; but he proved that he was not out of Boston that day, upon which he was released, and went with two other men out in a small boat, under their eye, to fish. They played about near the shore, while catching small fish, till they thought they could possibly reach Dorchester Neck; no sooner were they perceived attempting to escape, than they had twenty cannons discharged at them, but they all happily reached the shore."

Lieutenant-Colonel Abercrombie [1] on the 2d of May wrote from Boston to his friend the Lieutenant-Governor of New York expressing his surprise on finding the town blockaded upon his arrival, April 23d. He concludes:

I cannot commend the behaviour of Our Soldiers on their retreat. As they began to plunder and payed no obedience to their Officers, fortunately for the Grenadeers & Light Infantry Lord Percy's Brigade were Ordered Out to support them or the flower of this Army would all have been cut off. By report they have thirty pieces of Cannon and two Mortars at Cambridge, altho' they threaten yet I cannot believe they will raise Batteries against the Town, if they do I am certain I can take them, the Whigs are all leaving town and such of the Torys as pleases Come in, but they are few, Parties run as high as ever they did in Cromwels time, and was there not a Red Coat in the Country they would cut one anothers throats. I cannot pretend to say what Our Generals will do, but I think it is in the power of the Congress to prevent the horrors of a Civil War. The Colony of Connecticut have sent two of their Assembly with a letter to the General the purport of the letter is to prevent hostilities & hoping a method of pacification may yet be adopted.

I am sorry to hear the Phrenzy of the people has shewn

---

[1] *Mass. His. Soc. Pro.*, April, 1897.

itself in your Province, as a particular mark of distinction
was Shewn them in the Fishing Bill I flattered myself they
would have been quiet.

The Whigs have plundered the Houses of Judge
Auchmuty, Col. Vassal's, and Hatche's, and Captain
Loring's, what other devastations they have committed
We have not heard.

I am glad to hear you are in good health and I have the
honor to be

> Dear Sir,
>> Your most obedient, humble Servant,
>> James Abercrombie.
>>> Lt. Col. 22d Regt.

P.S. since writing the above I am appointed Adj. Gen.l.
Lt. Gov. Colden, New York.

On the 24th of June following, Adjutant-General Abercrombie died of a mortal wound, received in the battle of
Bunker Hill, the previous week.

A few Tories lived in Jamaica Plain at this time, one of
whom, Commodore Loring,[1] is probably referred to in the
above letter. He had been made prisoner at Louisburg,
taken part in the capture of Quebec under Wolfe, and served
under Amherst. After receiving a severe wound on Lake
Ontario he was retired on half pay, and now occupied the
two-story house with a portico and fluted columns on three
sides, still standing[2] opposite the Soldiers' Monument, near
the intersection of Centre and South Streets. He was sorely
distressed at the turn events were taking, but the habits
and associations of a lifetime in loyal service to the Crown
could not be sundered, and after talking and consulting
nearly the whole night of the 18th with Deacon Joseph
Brewer, he ended by riding away for Boston the next day,
leaving all his belongings. An old friend, meeting him
on the road, stopped to ask if he were leaving for good.
"Yes," said he, "I have always eaten the King's bread and

---

[1] *History of Roxbury*, 416–17.   Drake.

[2] *Historic Houses and Spots*, 104.   Freese.

always intend to." He received a pension in exile and died 1781, aged sixty-five, at Highgate. His widow, Mary, daughter of Samuel Curtis, also died in England at the age of eighty. A grandson, Sir John Wentworth Loring, born in Roxbury, became a British Admiral; another, Henry, died 1832, Archdeacon of Calcutta.

On May 4th Mrs. Abigail Adams[1] wrote to her husband, who had just left home to attend the Second Continental Congress, "I want very much to hear from you, how you stood your journey, and in what state you find yourself now. I felt very anxious about you; though I endeavoured to be very insensible and heroic, yet my heart felt like a heart of lead. The same night you left me, I heard of Mr. Quincy's death, which, at this time, was a most melancholy event; especially as he wrote in minutes, which he left behind, that he had matters of consequence intrusted with him, which, for want of a confidant, must die with him. I went to see his distressed widow last Saturday, at the Colonel's; and, in the afternoon, from an alarm they had, she and her sister, with three others of the family, took refuge with me and tarried all night. . . . Poor afflicted woman; my heart was wounded for her." In this same letter Mrs. Adams exclaims respecting "that forlorn wretch," Ex-Governor Hutchinson, a portion of whose correspondence was making a great stir, "May the fate of Mordecai be his!" On May 7th she again wrote to her husband, "The distresses of the inhabitants of Boston are beyond the power of language to describe; there are but very few who are permitted to come out in a day; they delay giving passes, make them wait from hour to hour, and their counsels are not two hours together alike. One day, they shall come out with their effects; the next day, merchandise is not effects. One day, their household furniture is to come out; the next, only wearing apparel; the next, Pharaoh's heart is hardened, and he refuseth to hearken to them, and will not let the people go. . . . They have taken a list of all those who they suppose were concerned

[1] *Letters*, 30–1, 32.

ABIGAIL ADAMS, WIFE OF JOHN ADAMS

in watching the tea, and every other person whom they call obnoxious, and they and their effects are to suffer destruction."

David Green,[1] in a letter of May 6th to Gardiner Green, writes:

On Friday all communication with the Country was stopped. Nobody since can leave the town by land or water without leave of the General or Admiral; and no one can come in by land without a pass from General Ward. An agreement was made in a few days by General Gage with the inhabitants of the town that they should deliver up their arms, and then should be suffered to go out. Accordingly the arms have been delivered (mine with the rest), and many of the people have left the town, but it is a slow business. Many difficulties have arisen about it, which have retarded the giving of passes to them. They say the Gen.l promised they should carry their *effects*, and therefore want to take their *goods*, &c. The General, it seems, if he did use that word, meant only *furniture*, and he does not allow merchandise to go out. The passes have been stopped several times, too, on this account. It is said if the Whigs go out, the Tories ought to be suffered to come in, and the General suspected or was informed they were prevented. Your good old friend and neighbor, T. Chase, is at Roxbury; several passes have been seen here signed by him as Major-Brigade. You may well suppose, from this situation, we have been in a constant alarm; many have been in expectation that the provincials would attack the town, and have therefore been in great consternation, and the General has been strengthening his fortifications and making new ones. A breastwork is thrown up across the Neck; another by Hewes' Works in Pleasant Street; another on Fox hill, Beacon, and Fort, and Copse Hills; and we are in daily expectation of six or seven thousand troops from England. What will be done when they come, God only knows!

[1] *Mass. Hist. Soc. Pro.*, June, 1873.

The present confusion is like to scatter us over the face of the earth. My mother, Mrs. Townsend, Mr Hubbard's children, Mr John Amory's children, &c. are gone to Norwich; N. G. and his family are gone to Passatuxet; your particular connections stand fast in town, likewise D. H. and wife, and Betsey and Charles.

I am going to London with Captain Calahan, and expect to have for fellow-passengers Mr J. Green and wife of School Street, Mr J.[oseph] Barrell and lady [of Summer Street], Mr John Amory and lady, Mrs Callahan, Mr Balch, Mr S. Quincy, D. Sears &c.

Joseph Green,[1] writing four days later to his brother Gardiner, adds: "Mr Amory and wife and David, and about a dozen more are going to London in the *Minerva*. . . . There has upwards of two thousand persons left town. . . . Callahan and our dear Lucretia, &c sail in about a week." The following letter belongs to a much later date and gives a last unenviable glimpse of the Loyalists in exile. It is from a letter of John Perkins[1] to the same Gardiner Green, dated, "Halifax, August 2, 1776. About the middle of March past, Gen. Howe, with his army, consisting of about seven or eight thousand men, with women and children, inhabitants of Boston, refugees from the Country, &c. quitted the town of Boston . . . and came down to this hole, the dregs of the earth, where they all remained till the 10th of June, when they went away again for action to some part of the Continent. . . . Almost every one who came from Boston to this place have gone away again: some for England, some for headquarters, and the remainder will go as soon as they can learn where the army is gone to, and whether they have made their landing good, for this is without exception the most despicable place ever I knew. The price of living here is exceeding high: . . . if I'm not much mistaken, there will be an example made for rebellion in future, notwithstanding there appears much lenity in every step taken

---

[1] *Mass. His. Soc. Pro.*, June, 1873.

on government side, — too much in my opinion. It is certainly a happy thing to live under so mild a government as the present English government; . . . Your old friend, Jack Coffin, arrived here a few days past from London, . . . your Uncle Chandler sailed a few days past for London, together with John Powell and his family, our old friend Frank Johannot, John Erving and family, Mr Lechmere and family, the Commissioners &c., &c; in short, one half of Boston is now in England, and they tell me the Bostonians are so thick about the streets of London that it is imagined Selectmen, wardens, &c, will be chosen there, according to the old Bostonian method."

The London *Chronicle* [1] gives an Extract from a Halifax letter dated May 8th which says, "On the 22d of April we received the news here of the skirmish that had happened three days before. . . . Almost every day since has brought some fugitives hither from New England. . . . There are two vessels ready to sail with 100 fat oxen on board, besides poultry, hogs &c. . . . We hear there are 10 or 15 sail of sloops and schooners lading in the Bay of Fundy, with live stock for the Army. Though the Newspapers I send you says that the Americans felt bold, and fought at Lexington, yet I believe their loss has been very great; for the people that have come down here are in the utmost fright, and lament the loss, and mention here ten times as many deaths as appears by the Newspapers."

Early in April Mr. Oliver Wendell, being ill, left his house in School Street, opposite the King's Chapel, and took shelter with his brother-in-law, Jonathan Jackson, in Newburyport. James Lovell, master of the grammar school, living where the Parker House now stands, was debarred by lack of strength from active service in the trenches, where, he writes, his 'whole Soul lodges nightly.' Hence he undertook the helpful office of making suitable provision for the protection of his friends' abandoned homes. Early in May we find him applying to General Gage for a pass for the

[1] June 17–20, 1775.

removal of several trunks belonging to his old neighbor, itemizing small articles of especial value, as "a number of large Spoons, a Pepper Box, Sugr. Tongs, a Porringer and pair of open work Shoe Buckles."[1] For the rest he writes Mr. Wendell: "Yr. Bedding & Trunks with *useful* Furniture rather than the *best* must be chosen. The best will be grossly abused. . . . My Family is yet with me. 4 Children are prepared to go away, and Mrs Lovell with the rest will follow when able, if I so judge proper. . . . I shall tarry if 10 Seiges take place. . . . Newbury is not a place for you. The people there are in Fears like Boston Folks. . . . Think as little as you can about any other Thing but the future happy Days of America which are fast coming up the great wheel. . . . Will Britain see that we count Seaports and all the Merchandize they contain of no value in Comparison of our Rights; that we fly to the Country with them and dare her to invade them there; and will she madly persist in the present Humor? What is America to her more than the habitable Moon if Commerce ceases? 3 times 30 days will inform us of her Recovery. Why should Boston be the Seat of Government? Why not the great Menodnock? We act as if Commerce and not Acres was our Foundation." Again, "I feel happier on water Gruel, with the present glorious publick Prospect, than I ever did full of roast Beef & Wine, while there remained a Chance of the Establishment of Tyranny on the horrid ministerial Plan." May 10: "Mrs Lovell begins to mend, . . . 'Tis a miserable little Baby in comparison of her former ones; but that is not to be wonder'd at, considering it as hitherto nurtured by Anxiety." Presently he writes that an army surgeon, "Doct. Morris . . . a very grave Gentleman with a very small Family," has been admitted as tenant as the surest means of protecting Mr. Wendell's property. He then concludes: "I had the House swept from Garret to Cellar removing every Thing new & old but the following." A portion of his memorandum follows: "In the *front room.* a Look.g Glass, a marble slab,

[1] *Essex Institute Hist. Coll.*, July, 1876.

a Card Table, a Japan Tea table, a mahog.y stand, Desk & Case, 10 Chairs, 2 China Vases, 2 Family Pictures, a Lamp Tea Kettle. In the *Entry*. A Glass Lanthorn. On the *Stairs*. An oval Japan Tea Table. *Middle Room.* A Clock, a Breakfast Table, a Desk, a Look.g Glass, 1 Family Picture, 8 Metzitintos, 1 Fudling, 4 small red leather Chairs, 1 Hearth Brush. *Kitchen.* 3 Trammels, 1 pr. H^d. Irons, 1 Jack, 2 Spits, etc. 1 Checker Board, 1 Barn Lanthorn, a large and small Pine Table, 1 Brass Kcttle, etc. 1 large wooden mortar, 1 flat tin & 2 iron Candlesticks, salt-Box, 1 pr. Snuffers, 1 Tobacco Jar, etc. In the *front Chamber.* 1 Chest of Drawers, looking Glass, 6 Chairs covered with Check, the Family Coat of Arms, 1 folding screen, Mr Jackson's picture. In the *Entry*. Chest of Drawers, Mehogony Fire Screene. In the *middle Chamb'.* Chest of Drawers, Lookg. Glass, 5 Chairs red covered with Callicoe, 1 Hearth Brush, 1 Family Picture. *Kitchen* Chamber. Lookg. Glass, 1 pr. Hd. Irons. In the Closet a View of the Colledges. In the three upper Chambers sundry beds etc. 32 metzitintos, 4 painted on Glass, 1 Sampler. On the *Cellar Stairs*, a Candle Box. In the *Cellar* a Bread Trough, pickling Tubs, Beer Barrell, etc. In the *Shed* 1 Fish Kettle. In the *Wood House*. I Washing Bench, etc."

By way of consolation Lovell once more expresses his confidence that the Country "nay this very Town will soon rise to Glory and Peace." Tories were as anxious to be within the protection of Boston as the Whigs to make their escape. May 15th, Lady Frankland (Agnes Surriage, born 1726) of Hopkinton (now Ashland) made application [1] for a pass for Thursday, stating that she wished to carry in with her six trunks, one chest, three beds and bedding, six wethers, two pigs, one small keg of pickled tongues, some hay, and three bags of corn. When the day arrived, however, she had so increased the quantity of effects it occasioned complaint;[2] there being no less than four horses, two

---

[1] *Memorial History of Boston*, III, 77.
[2] *American Archives*, II, 4th ser., 810. Force.

chaises, one phaeton, six oxen, two carts, five sheep, one swine, about four hundred of hay, two barrels, and one hamper filled with bottled wine, one keg of tongues, the trunks, bedding and linen mentioned above, besides one gun, one pistol, one sword, one flask, with a small quantity of powder and lead; about ten bushels of Indian corn and a canister with a small quantity of tea. The matter was brought before the Committee of Safety and permission finally granted[1] for her to bring seven trunks, the beds and belongings, all the boxes, crates, barrels, the hamper and sundry small bundles; a basket of chickens and a bag of corn; two horses and two chaises, the phaeton, some tongues, ham and veal, but no arms and ammunition.

The *British Chronicle*[2] prints a portion of "A Letter of a respectable person in New England," dated May 27, running as follows: "Never was there a more dismal prospect than is now before us. Grim visaged war has taken entire possession of this once flourishing, peaceable and happy country. The barbarities committed by the Soldiery we imputed to the rage and shame of their disappointment and defeat. The burning houses, and slaughtering old men, and children, though done in hot blood, were bad enough. But we regard the deliberate denial of it by Gen. Gage, in his letter to Gov. Trumbull, as infinitely worse. It is a most outrageous violation of a truth, to which thousands of us have been eye witnesses. The horrid scene has been viewed over and over again by multitudes. This induces us to believe that our enemies mean to preserve neither faith nor humanity towards us. We have endeavored however to set them an example in the tenderest treatment of our prisoners."

Referring next to the "thousand obstacles" thrown in the way of those wishing to seek safety outside Boston, the writer concludes sadly, "These violences and impositions sink deep in the minds of the people. Such conduct will soon eradicate those principles of love and respect which they have been

---

[1] *Memorial History of Boston*, III, 77.   [2] July 5–7.

taught to feel for Englishmen, and make that name odious *which was honorable.*"

Chief Justice Peter Oliver, writing to Mrs. Elisha Hutchinson at her father's house in Plymouth, says:[1]

BOSTON, May 26,

My Dear Polly, —

The only satisfaction that absent friends can receive from each other is by intercourse in an epistolary way: this intercourse hath been interrupted by the Sons of Anarchy, and is like to be a short time to come, but I have great reason to think, not much longer, for yesterday arrived [by the *Cerberus,* Capt. Chad, April 18th, from Spithead] three approved Generals—Howe, Clinton, and Burgoyne, who are to be followed (and who are to be expected in a few days) by 5 or 6000 troops from Ireland, with a Regiment of Horse; so that we shall have here 13 or 14000 well-disciplined troops, when the campaign will be opened by 5 as fine General officers as perhaps are in the King's service. . . . What miseries must attend a conquest or no conquest! . . . A person who hath been active for years past in the defection, sent to me to-day to intercede for him, and is almost distracted: another of the like stamp sent to me to get his house excepted from the ravages of the troops when they go out, but he is fled himself out of the Province.

I feel the miseries which impend over my country. . . . The God of Order may punish a community for a time with their own disorders; but it is incompatible with the rectitude of the Divine Nature, to suffer anarchy to prevail. Observe, my dear, the course of Providence: the first, and grand incendiary, [Otis] is now marked out as a mad man: Molineaux is supposed to have died an unnatural death: Mr Bowdoin is not far from dying: Pitts is not likely to continue long: Denny, it is said, is ill with a mortification in his leg: Hancock is tho't to be ruined in his large fortune: Lee, of Marblehead, is dead; and after the Battle, was frightened, and continued so 'till he died: . . . All this is striking. . . .

[1] *Diary,* I, 457. Hutchinson.

General Thomas, of Kingston, wrote to a gentleman in town, that your father voluntarily offered and advanced money to support their cause. I am sorry for it. . . .

The letter that follows [1] is from Dr. Peter Oliver, son of the Chief Justice, to his brother-in-law, Elisha Hutchinson.

BOSTON, June 1st, 1775.

. . . By the time this reaches you havock will begin, and whether we shall ever see one another in this world, I am not clear in, but hope we shall meet in another quite different from this, free from storms, from Battles, from fire and famine, from *Rebellion*, the worst of *crimes*, where all serenity, peace, and concord prevails, where parents and children will be of one mind and one heart. . . .

7th instant. Yesterday Major Dunbar, who has been prisoner at Cambridge, and other officers, with 6 Marines, who all were prisoners, were exchanged at Charlestown. Major Dunbar was Town Major at Quebeck, and was sent by Governor Carlton express to Gen. Gage soon after the Battle; not knowing of any difficulty happening, was by land seiz'd by the common people back of Cambridge and remained with them ever since.

The Chief Justice writes to Elisha, himself, on the 10th, and makes this reference [1] to the exchange of prisoners: "Mr Hamilton, of the 64th Regiment, was taken prisoner 6 or 7 weeks ago, going to the Castle, and was liberated this week; as was also Major Dunbar, who came on a visit from Quebec, and has been a prisoner 4 or 5 weeks. . . . May the God of Armies send us better times!"

Major Dunbar [2] was taken prisoner April 29th at Cambridge, as we learn elsewhere, and kept on parole at Woburn and Newbury. Some of his letters are said to have been preserved among the family papers of Mr. Samuel Osgood, aide-de-camp to General Ward.

[1] *Diary*, I, 458, 469. Hutchinson.
[2] *History of Andover*, 305–6. Bailey.

CHAPTER VII

MANY scattered stories of the Nineteenth linger on in town and county histories and in family tradition, which, slight in themselves, serve to round out the day where the details are familiar.

We learn a little more of the confusion reigning in Jamaica Plain from a petition of Benjamin Pemberton,[1] bearing date June, 1779, preserved in the State Archives; wherein he states that early on Wednesday morning "when the men on the Plain were in great hurry" to be gone to the battle, he met a young man of Roxbury who had no gun and asked the loan of his flintlock.   He was not known to Pemberton even by sight, but well known to his negro servant who was with him, and he let the gun go, and that was the last he ever saw of it.   By the current valuation it was worth £16.

The next morning the Petitioner left his house to two of his servants, and retired to Dedham; the Troops immediately took possession and all the malt and meal on the premises was speedily consumed. . . . "The Petitioner had (as he was wont to do) pickt out of Twenty Cords or more, about six cords of the best large round Walnut wood, sawed and piled up, in order to Splitting, for the Spring, Sumer and fall Season, all of which the Soldiers burn't, before they were supplied other ways." This wood he values at £18 a cord, or £108, that "being no more than I gave last week for very ordinary comon wood, not half as valuable."   It concludes: "Necessity obliges your Petitioner, at this time, humbly to address this honourable Court, on this matter, from the difficulty of his raising wherewith to pay said Taxes, occasioned by his several Debtors, almost all of them having

[1] *Mass. State Archives*, Vol. 185, p. 195.

discharged their debts and mortgages in the present circulating currency, in lieu of silver lent them, insomuch that the yearly interest of said debts, which, when formerly paid in silver, afforded a comfortable and handsome support, will now scarsly supply one tenth part of one; Your Petitioner is hereby so much reduced, as obliged to sell a house and one of his horses, live without any man servant, let out his Land at halves, and Expose his Chariot and other things for sale." The total claim presented was for £151 and but £13 15s. 0d. allowed.

The women and children of Roxbury in many instances left their homes; Mrs. Greaton,[1] whose husband was afterward a General, started in a cart for Brookline, the little ones inside, the rest walking beside it. Three Minute Companies [1] turned out under Moses Whiting, William Draper, and Lemuel Child. The last-named kept the Peacock Tavern on the westerly corner of Centre Street and Allandale Road in West Roxbury. Later in the day the tired men were fed under a great tree at the Scarborough homestead, as they returned from the battle.[1] Draper, like many others, is said to have left his plough in the furrow. Dr. Thomas Williams,[1] a Roxbury Tory, remarked to Edward Sumner, apropos of the outbreak, "Well, the nail is driven," who replied resolutely, "Yes, and we'll clinch it too."

We have already seen that the Rev. William Gordon,[2] D. D., drove to Dedham for safety. He was a man of about forty-five years, born in Hitchin, Herts., and before coming to America, in 1770, had been successively settled over the Independent Congregational Chapel at Ipswich, Suffolk, and Gravel Lane, Wapping. About 1793, having returned to the Old Country, he was settled at St. Noel's, Huntingdonshire, finally dying at Ipswich in 1807. It is to him we are indebted for sundry inquiries made, soon after the battle, of those who took part, both villagers and prisoners.

The towns to the southeast of the line of march between

---

[1] *History of Roxbury*, 156, 31, 435, 229, 117. Drake.
[2] *Historical Magazine*, February, 1862.

Boston and Concord, notwithstanding their distance, responded to the alarm and some incidents are still remembered.

Captain Ebenezer Tucker[1] and fifty-one Milton men are
credited with marching eight miles from and to their homes.
Andrew Kennedy,[1] tavernkeeper at Scott's woods, and his
three sons turned out, and William Sumner, of Brush Hill.
Parson Robbins[1] had two brothers in Captain Parker's
Lexington company. On getting the alarm, Captain Lemuel
Robinson[1] set off to Weymouth for General Lovell's marching orders; his first Lieutenant, Daniel Vose, meanwhile
marching directly to Cambridge. Finding the bridge across
the Charles destroyed, they retraced their way, learning
later that the planks had been piled on the Cambridge side.
Captain William Bent[2] of Canton received word to join
Captain Asahel Smith's company about meal-time; his
favorite dish of fried smelts was preparing, but he did not
stop for a bite.

Wednesday Lecture was taking place at Stoughton, and
Parson Dunbar, who had been Chaplain at Crown Point
in the French War, was holding forth to his people. Suddenly Henry Bailey[2] threw open the door and tramped up
the aisle, shouting, "There's an alarum!" Little Lemuel
Bent seized on the bell rope, while Captain James Endicott
told Israel Bailey to mount his colt and ride through the
town, giving May's tavern as the rendezvous. This house
stood on the Post road to Taunton at the corner of Washington and Pleasant Streets, its site long marked by a large
blackheart cherry tree. The day after the men marched,
Captain Endicott's[2] eleven year old son, John, was despatched with food for the company. At Roxbury he was
directed on to Prospect Hill, where at length he safely
delivered his load. Sharon was then called Stoughtonham;
several companies went from here and from Foxborough, be-

---

[1] *History of Milton*, 430, 260. Teele.

[2] *History of Canton*, 412, 348, 349–50. Daniel T. V. Huntoon. Cambridge,
1893: John Wilson and Son.

sides Stoughton proper; no less than 470 men in all. Daniels Carpenter,[1] of Foxborough, was working on a ditch when he heard that the Regulars were out. Dropping his tools, he ran for his musket, took some bread and meat in his knapsack, and started to join his company at Wrentham. Not coming up with them there, Carpenter pluckily footed it on alone to Dedham, where he met fellow-soldiers, finally overtaking his comrades at Roxbury. Samuel Haws [2] of the Wrentham company has told the story of their march, which may be taken as typical of others.

April the 19th About one a clock the minute men were alarmed and met at Landlord Moons We marched from there [32 miles from Boston] the sun about half an our high towards Roxbury for we heard that the regulars had gone out and had killed six men and had wounded Some more that was at Lexington then the King's troops proceded to concord and there they were Defeated and Drove Back fiting as they went they gat to charlestown hill that night We marched to headens at Walpole [21 miles from Boston] and their got a little refreshment and from their we marched to Doctor cheneys and their we got some victuals and Drink and from thence we marched to Landlord clises at Dedham [13 miles from Boston], and their captain parsons and company joined us and we marched to Jays and their captain Boyd and company joined us and we marched to Landlord Whitings we taried their about one hour and then we marched to richardes and Searched the house and found Ebenezer aldis and one pery who we supposed to Be torys and we searched them and found Several Letters about them which they were a going to cary to Nathan aldis in Boston but makeing them promis reformation We let them go home then marching forward we met colonel graton returning from the engagement which was the Day before and he Said that he would be with

[1] *History of Norfolk County*, 683. Hurd.

[2] *Soldiers Journals, 1758 & 1775.* Poughkeepsie, 1855. Published by Abraham Tomlinson at the Museum.

us amediately then we marched to jamicai plain their we heard that the regulars Were a coming over the neck then we striped of our coats and marched on with good courage to Colonel Williams and their we heard to the contrary We staid their sometime and refreshed our Selves and then marched to Roxbury parade and their we had as much Liquor as we wanted and every man drawd three Biscuit which were taken from the regulars the day before [possibly convoy stores] which were hard enough for flints. We lay on our arms until towards night and then we repaired to Mr. Slaks house and at night Six men were draughted out for the main guard nothing strange that night.

The 20th of April nearly 100 men halted at Colonel Pond's in West Dedham. They had marched all night and wanted food. Mrs. Pond [1] was alone at the time with the hired man and a young girl. She at once set on the crane a brass kettle holding several pails of water and some Indian meal, which the soldiers helped stir; others milked the ten cows in the yard. Meanwhile the man and girl hurried off to beg supplies from the neighbors. Brown crockery ware, and pewter spoons, tied up into dozens, were hastily procured from the neighborhood store, and inside an hour the whole company were fed and on the march.

Dedham originally had four parishes, *i.e.*, the first, or present Centre, the second, now Norwood, the third, now West Dedham or Westwood, and the fourth, Springfield, now Dover. This last at the time of the Revolution had a population of about 350, of whom in 1774 no less than sixty-six were enrolled in Captain Ebenezer Battle's company; Elias Haven, who fell, being one.

Mrs. Mary Draper,[2] aged fifty-six, lived on Centre Street in Dedham, that being the highroad to Roxbury. Her husband had died the preceding January, her oldest son, Moses, was 2d Lieutenant of the West Roxbury company, the youngest was a boy of thirteen. As the tired and hungry

[1] *The Women of the Revolution*, I, 117. Elizabeth F. Ellet. New York, 1850.
[2] *American Monthly Magazine*, March, 1902.

volunteers came thronging past the door on their way to besiege Boston, it occurred to her she might offer them refreshments. A couple of forms were set by the roadside in charge of a couple of boys. Old John,[1] a French war veteran, living in the family, brought crackers, brown bread, and cheese from the kitchen, and cider from the cellar, which the lads served out by the dipperful from tubs. Two large ovens did a great baking within doors, where, by one account, she was helped by her daughter Kate.

From Sherborn,[2] fifty Minute-men marched, under Captain Benjamin Bullard. Walpole [3] sent 157 men from a population of less than 800. The distance, however, was too great for them to engage. Medfield [3] responded with a total of eighty-one men, of whom twenty-seven were Minute-men under Captain Sabin Mann. Many of these companies would naturally pass through Dedham on their way to Roxbury Camp.

Sixty-one Minute-men from Attleborough,[4] under Captain Jabez Ellis, received orders to march directly for Roxbury. They started the evening of the 19th and stopped a short time at Maxcy's, later known as Hatch's tavern. From there they went forward to Dedham, where they breakfasted hastily at two wayside tables, possibly Mrs. Draper's, and reached camp early on the 20th. Here their company was marched round and round the meeting-house on the high land to make a great show of numbers. One of the men, Henry Richardson, as they came along, had sworn that he'd have a redcoat before he got back. At the first chance after reaching headquarters he charged his musket, went down in front of the lower guard, and let fly at the opposite British sentinel, wounding him severely. Much to his disgust and bewilderment, Richardson found himself immediately put under arrest. However, in consideration

---

[1] *Women of the Revolution*, 113–15.   Ellet.
[2] *History of Middlesex County*, I, 699.   Hurd.
[3] *History of Norfolk County*, 711, 445.   Hurd.
[4] *History of Attleborough*, 130.   Dagget.

of his "good intentions," he soon regained liberty, and shortly after meeting another of his company exclaimed innocently, "There, I told you, I'd have one of them 'ere British rascals." At Weston,[1] 100 men having gathered at Captain Samuel Lamson's, the Rev. Samuel Woodward offered prayer, then fell into the ranks and marched with his people. They came up with the Regulars at Lincoln and followed them to Charlestown. The Artillery company also turned out under Captain Israel Whitemore.

Joseph Stedman[2] lived in Weston about a mile from Newton Corner. He had one daughter, Lucy, a fifteen year old girl at this time, and seven sons, the youngest being playfully known as "the Doctor." On the morning of the 19th Mr. Stedman said to his boys, "The ground is too wet to plough until it dries a little, let's shingle the shed." As they worked, a man galloped by, beating a drum and shouting, "Turn out! turn out! the regulars have gone to Lexington and fired on our men." Instantly all was bustle while they made ready for the march. As the day dragged on, Lucy and her mother prepared a hearty meal against their home coming and listened to the distant firing with beating hearts. Night fell without their return and the two crept into bed together listening to the slow "tick-tick, tick-tick" of the eight-day clock as the hours slipped on. At last, at the dead of night, Lucy used to say, "We heard the door open and one by one our men tiptoed into the house, whispering. Presently all but the 'Doctor,' the youngest, were safe home and we trembled, fearing that he was hurt. But just then we heard his merry whistle as he came from the barn where he had stopped to feed the cattle and when he opened the door and we heard his voice, what rejoicing there was! Well earned was the bountiful supper and the eight hungry ones eat and talked and told how the proud regulars had been driven on-the-run into Charlestown."

---

[1] *History of Middlesex County,* I, 490. Hurd.

[2] "As it was in April, 1775." Horace N. Fisher. *Boston Evening Transcript,* April 18, 1903.

During the winter, stores had been kept at Waltham.[1] When the troops were known to be preparing for a raid, it was not clear whether Concord or Worcester would be the goal, or even if Lord Percy brought reinforcement or was intended to march on Worcester. Since Waltham would be the direct route in the latter case, the local company very naturally was kept on the spot. Many families sought shelter with their belongings elsewhere. The town had twelve officers and 109 privates on duty three days, under Captain Abraham Pierce, who states respecting "Lexenton fite," "These lines may sartifie my company was keept upon gard til Saturday" and they are credited with marching 28 miles, but the route is not known.

Josiah Smith[2] had moved to Lexington from Waltham in 1760 and now lived on Blossom Street, on the east side of a high hill, two miles from either township. He was not on the Green, but marched toward Concord later in the day and joined in the pursuit. Back of the Smith house are two parallel ledges, rising abruptly ten to twenty-five feet in height and stretching north and south some one to two hundred feet, with a span of twenty or thirty feet. The westerly crag was known as Josh Rock. A. A. Smith tells of his grandmother climbing this rock in the afternoon and listening to the musketry and seeing the smoke of the guns. Many women and children took refuge here. Josiah Smith, Jr., then of Waltham, reached Lexington just after the British had gone on to Concord and picked up a gun on Concord Hill which he hid behind a wall to take away later. When he went back after it, however, it was gone. Common Street, Belmont, leads to Watertown; here on the right is an old house set on a knoll with a stone wall in front, the home of Peter Clark,[3] who had all his belongings packed on a wagon, so the story goes, ready to be off if the regulars should go by the Turnpike to Concord.

[1] *History of Middlesex County*, III, 712. Hurd.

[2] *Lexington His. Soc. Pro.*, II, 112, 117, 114, 113.

[3] *Walks and Rides in the Country round about Boston*, 227. Edwin M. Bacon. Cambridge, 1897. Published for the Appalachian Mountain Club by Houghton, Mifflin and Company.

A diary, supposed to be that of Paul Litchfield,[1] a member of the class of 1775, at Harvard College, has the following entries: April 11th, "Rode from Cambridge [at the Easter Recess] to Braintree in Company with Otis and Sever, and from thence alone to Scituate." Here "April 20th very early in the morning [they] received the news of the engagement between the King's troops and the Americans at Concord the day before, upon which our men were ordered to appear in arms immediately. I was upon the guard on the third cleft the night ensuing [there are four sandy cliffs] and about eight o'clock took two Tories as they were returning from Marshfield, who were kept under guard that night. Exceeding windy." April 21st he adds, "About day took four Tories, and sprained my ankle. Then marched to the meeting house with our prisoners."

At Kingston Seth Drew,[2] Lieutenant of the Minute-men, a shipwright, was cleaning a ship's bottom at the Landing when summoned. He had just lit a tar barrel, to pass under the ship in the process of cleansing, when his brother James rushed into the yard with the exciting news. Without a word he passed the burning barrel to a fellow workman and joined his company.

Fired by the tidings, the Minute-men of Kingston and thereabouts determined to drive Captain Balfour's "Queen's Guards" from Marshfield, without loss of time. Captain Wadsworth,[2] of Kingston, was so keen, he pushed on ahead of the rest, and the Regulars withdrew by Cut River to their ships, which lay off Brant Rock. They got away easily then, but are all said to have fallen save five and their Captain in the Bunker Hill fight.

Word of the battle at Lexington reached Wareham[3] by a rider from Boston on the 20th of April. On receipt of the news a company of Militia started for Boston, and

[1] *Mass. His. Soc. Pro.*, September, 1882.

[2] *History of Plymouth County*, I, 280, 263. D. Hamilton Hurd. Philadelphia, 1884: J. W. Lewis & Co.

[3] *Colonial Times in Buzzards Bay*, 182–3. 2d ed. Wm. Root Bliss. Boston, 1889: Houghton, Mifflin and Company.

another for Marshfield, where there was quite a settlement of Loyalists living under special protection of the King's troops. The latter company was commanded by Major Israel Fearing, whose wife, Lucy Bourne, was an ardent Loyalist. The tradition is that as the Major passed out of his door to lead the men who were waiting for him, she, desiring to prevent his going, seized fast to the skirts to his military coat. But, "like Captain Sir Dilbery Diddle in the Song, —

> Said he to his lady, 'My lady I'll go;
> My company calls me, you must not say no.'

and he broke away, leaving a part of his uniform in her hands."

Even from so far down the Cape as Barnstable [1] a company set forth to the relief of Boston. On the skirts of the village the men passed the home farm of their drummer boy. He was an only child, and his father, as they came to a halt, said, "God be with you all, my friends! And John, if you, my son, are called into battle, take care that you behave like a man, or else let me never see your face again."

By the 20th a rumor had reached Rochester [2] that hostilities had begun, and Abraham Holmes, a youth of twenty-one, was sent to Middleborough to learn its truth. On finding there was no mistake about it, the lad returned, so he records in his diary, "as gay as a lark."

Governor Wanton, of Rhode Island, was a Tory and sent a messenger after the Kentish Guards, already on the march, recalling them. Nathanael Greene, [3] later a General in Washington's army, had, at the cost of forfeiting his religious privileges as a "Friend," bought a musket in Boston, in 1774, smuggled it out of town in a wagon under straw, and perfected himself in the Manual. He was now in the ranks as a volunteer, and not being subject to Wanton's control, he rode on, followed by his brother and several more.

[1] *Historical Magazine*, September, 1862.

[2] "Revolutionary Records of a Country Town." Mary Hall Leonard. *New England Magazine*, November, 1898.

[3] *Life of Gen. Nathaniel Green*, 51, 70. George Washington Greene. New York, 1867: G. P. Putnam and Son.

Other stories are told of the towns lying north and west of the line of march.

From a vote taken at Haverhill, [1] March 21st, 1775, we learn that the uniform of Captain Greenleaf's company consisted of a "Blue Coat turned up with Buff, and yellow, plain Buttons, the Coat cut half way the thigh; and the Pockets a Slope." The waistcoat and breeches were to be buff or nankeen, stockings white with half gaiters, and the "hats all cocked alike." "A Bright gun," with bayonet and steel ramrod, completed the equipment, which was to be ready not later than the first Monday in May.

The Cambridge Minute-men,[2] as we learn through a member, wore at this period dull reddish, homespun coats with knee breeches of the same. The coats were cut long and single breasted and crossed by a double belt, to which was attached a bag for bullets and flints, priming wire, and brush. The privates wore shoes with large square buckles, the officers had top boots; both had cocked hats, powder-horns were hung by a cord about the neck and they carried a flintlock "King's arm," if they could come by one, if not, light fowling-pieces. Naturally as yet there was no uniformity amongst the various companies.

April 13th, Thursday, Captain James Sawyer's "minit men," went from Haverhill [1] to Andover for "Exsise;" forty-six out of a total of sixty-four were present, little suspecting that it was their last opportunity for preparatory "training."

On the 16th, Sunday, a disastrous fire broke out in the main street here. There was but one engine with which to fight it, and it raged from Court Street to White's Corner, sweeping away seventeen houses, including a tavern.[1] On the afternoon of the 19th news of the battle reached the town. Nehemiah Emerson [3] was on a roof at the time, helping to check the flames, but hastened to join his company

---

[1] *History of Haverhill*, 375, 383, 386. George Wingate Chase. Haverhill, 1861.
[2] *Boston Evening Transcript*, through a Deacon Walton who died 1823.
[3] *History of Essex County*, II, 1999. Hurd.

and, but for a single visit home, stayed in the army until the close of the war. One hundred and five men, nearly half the Militia, left before night, Captain Daniel Hills'[1] company soon following. At seven in the morning James Stevens,[2] of Captain Poor's company, tells us the alarm reached Andover "that the Reglers was gainst Conkerd." His company gathered at the meeting-house and marched through Tewksbury and Billerica. "We stopped to Polerds," he goes on, "and eat some bisket and ches on the common." At Lexington they came "to the destruction of the Regelers. They killed 8 of our men and shot a cannon-ball through the metin-house. We went along through Lexington and we saw several regerlers ded on the rod and some of our men, and 3 or fore houses was Burnt, and some horses and hogs are kild, they plundered in every house they could get into, they stove in windows and broke in tops of desks, we met the men a coming back very fast."

Lieutenant Benjamin Farnum,[2] of the same company, says in his account, "April 19th, 1775, This day, the Mittel men of Col. Frye's regiment were Alarmed with the Nuse of the Troops marching from Boston to Concord, at which Nuse they marched very quick from Andover, and marched within about 5 miles of Concord, then meeting with the Nuse of their retreat for Boston again with which nuse we turned our Corse in order to catch them. We retreated that Day to Notme [Menotomy] but we could not come up with them. The nit coming on, we stopped; the next day we marched to Cambridge."

Thomas Boynton,[2] of Captain Ames' Andover company, gives their route a little more fully. "Andover, April 19, 1775. This morning, being Wednesday, about the sun's rising the town was alarmed with the news that the Regulars was on their march to Concord. Upon which the town mustered and about 10 o'clock marched onward for Concord. In Tewksbury news came that the Regulars had fired on

[1] *History of Essex County*, II, 1999. Hurd.
[2] *History of Andover*, 307, 308. Bailey.

our men in Lexington, and had killed 8. In Bilricke news came that the enemy were killing and slaying our men in Concord. Bedford we had the news that the enemy had killed 2 of our men and had retreated back; we shifted our course and persued after them as fast as possible, but all in vain; the enemy had the start 3 or 4 miles. It is said that their number was about 1500 men. They were persued as far as Charlestown that night; the next day they passed Charles River. The loss they sustained as we hear were 500; our men about 40. To return, after we came into Concord road we saw houses burning and others plundered, and dead bodies of the enemy lying by the way, others taken prisoners. About eight at night our regiment came to a halt in no time. The next morning we came into Cambridge and there abode."

While the Andover men were gone to the fight a house caught fire and old Mrs. Johnson [1] used to tell how the women climbed on the roof and put it out. At North Andover [2] the women were seized with a dread that the Regulars were coming to plunder the town. Valuables were hastily bundled up and they were about to fly for the woods at Den Rock when it was proved to be a false alarm. Colonel James Fry's eldest son lived at Methuen [2] across the Merrimac River. He was ploughing near home when the word came to march. His wife, knowing that he would lose no time, hastened out of the house to bid him good-by, but on reaching the field found the oxen and plough standing alone. Hurrying down the road toward the town, she could, from the top of the hill, just descry her husband in the distance running at full speed. At her loud call he waved his hat and was soon out of sight.

Benjamin Pierce, [3] an eighteen year old Lowell lad, was ploughing in a field when he heard the firing of alarm guns and met messengers with news of the fight. He chained

---

[1] Informant, a granddaughter, in 1895.
[2] *History of Andover*, 313, 301. Bailey.
[3] *Beside Old Hearth-Stones*, 275. Brown.

his steers to a stump and went to his uncle Robert Pierce's house, on the road to Chelmsford. Getting a gun here, he footed it to Concord, arriving after the British had retreated.

Lieutenant Peabody,[1] of Boxford, heard the North Andover church bell sound the alarm, and left home, as it proved, for months. The east parish here sent fifty-seven Militiamen under Captain Jacob Gould. The west parish thirty-three, under Captain John Cushing.[2] Captain William Perley led fifty-two Minute-men; these last appear to have arrived in time to join in the pursuit. At this time Captain Cushing's company received three days' provisions from the townspeople; later, when he asked in their behalf for compensation, he had leave to withdraw his petition.[3]

Captain Edward Payson and Captain Thomas Mighill of Rowley [2] marched on the alarm, arriving on the morning of the 20th.

At Hamilton [2] Rev. Dr. Manasseh Cutler spoke to the rallying Minute-men and, joined by the Rev. Joseph Willard of Beverly — afterward President of Harvard College — rode in their company to Cambridge. Robert Dodge [2] of this town was sowing barley on a hill when he got the alarm. Riding down to the village, he seized on a drum, and tore up and down the country road, beating it, until his company had mustered; in two hours more they were at Charlestown. Next day his wife, who had listened anxiously to the cannon, drove down alone with a horse and chaise to see what had become of him.

Early in the morning of the 19th a horseman rode along Medford road crying, "The Regulars are out!" At this time there was no one stirring at Kettle's tavern, which stood on the corner of the Salem and Reading roads. Soon, however, the west room was full of village folk, the Malden [4] company mustering on the Green outside. When, during

[1] *History of Andover*, 301. Bailey.
[2] *History of Essex County*, II, 963, 1142, 1223. Hurd.
[3] *Mass. State Archives*, Vol. 180, p. 339.
[4] *History of Malden*, 743. Corey.

the morning, by order of Colonel Thomas Gardner, they set off for Watertown, stepping briskly forward to the tap of Winslow Sargeant's drum, they were followed over the bridge and to the brow of the hill by a group of women and children. At Medford bridge the Minute company was halted and near noon ordered to Menotomy, which they reached in time to be of assistance in the taking of the convoy.

The North Malden men were led by Captain Benjamin Blaney. John Edmunds,[1] whose home was in northeast Malden, near the Chelsea line, started out early, an eighteen year old unarmed lad, named Breeden, who belonged probably near Black Ann's Corner in Chelsea, bearing him company. The boy had begged to be taken along, saying, "If only I may go I'll soon find a gun!" In the afternoon he was so venturesome in the pursuit Phineas Sprague kept saying, "Look at the boy, he'll get killed." Mindful of his purpose, however, Breeden followed hot on the track of a flagging redcoat and at last, getting the loan of a gun, overtook the man, when both fired. Neither was hit and the Regular, quickly reloading, again fired, and missed. Breeden was more successful, killing him on his second fire as he made over a wall, and, securing his piece, was eating the Britisher's rations when the rest came up.

An anecdote is told of an old Mr. Sprague,[2] who was deaf as a post, but turned out, notwithstanding, with his son. At some stage of the encounter, when the rest of the company were making for cover in every direction out of the path of the advancing enemy, he was seen standing calmly on a mound, swinging his hat and shouting, "Victory!" Captain Naler Hatch[3] and sixty more Melrose men threw up defences at Beacham's Point.

Captain Isaac Hall[3] led fifty-eight men from Medford. A farmer here, whose home was at the west end of the town, ran home for his gun and was hurrying off again

---

[1] *History of Malden*, 747. Corey.

[2] *Bi-Centennial of Malden*, 177. Boston, 1850.

[3] *History of Middlesex County*, II, 127. Drake.

when his bewildered wife exclaimed, "Why, husband, you are not going without your dinner!" "Yes, I am," he replied, "I am going to take powder and balls for my dinner today, or to give the redcoats some!" [1]

From its nearness to Boston, Medford sheltered many strangers that night and was in a continual bustle with men coming and going. The Essex *Gazette* of May 2–12 has an advertisement inserted by David Felt, of Salem, respecting his horse, "strayed or stolen," from a Medford tavern on the day of the battle. It stood about fourteen hands high, he writes, "was black," the neck "something short and main thick, and poor withal." The bridle and saddle had disappeared at the same time. September 14th Mr. Samuel Tufts, of Medford, advertised[2] that a basket of crockery ware had been taken up in that town, some time after the battle, which the owner might reclaim.

Nearby where the Mystic River issues from Mystic Pond stands an ancient hickory with a spread of sixty-two feet, a height of sixty-seven, and a girth of seven and a half feet. Under this tree, the story runs,[3] a slave, named Pomp, met Peter C. Brooks, Parson Edward's son, then a boy of eight, hurrying to what he supposed was a muster in Arlington, and told him the redcoats were out. In the same neighborhood, beside the Francis Brooks'[4] house at West Medford, stands an old elm, beneath which chocolate and coffee, made "in the big and little kettle," were served by Mrs. Abigail Brooks,[5] the Parson's wife, to the tired Yankees at the day's end.

The Marblehead[6] Militia, under Captain Russell Trevett, were handicapped by the presence of two men-o'-war, the *Lively*, twenty guns, and another, of sixteen, in their harbor. Many of the inhabitants were away fishing

[1] *History of Medford*, 162.   Usher.
[2] *New England Chronicle or Salem Gazette*, September 14–21.
[3] *Boston Globe*, September 27, 1898.
[4] *Boston Evening Transcript*, March 23, 1897.
[5] *Medford His. Reg.*, January, 1899.
[6] *Life of Col. Timothy Pickering*, I, 541.

and the selectmen and Committee of Safety delayed the company's march until ten that night, when they stole off without making an avoidable sound.

Captain Andrew Masters of Manchester[1] marched his company as far as Medford, where they were recalled. One of these Manchester men, David Annable,[2] had a son born the day of the battle.

Newbury received word too late to take part that day, but started two companies off the same night.

The call to arms was not even confined to the length and breadth of the state, but ran beyond its bounds and out to sea. Some twenty Rockport[1] boats were on the inshore fishing grounds when they received news that the troops had marched on Concord. They weighed anchor and sailed for home and before night almost every man aboard was in arms at Gloucester harbor ready to march.

Shortly before this, Captain John Cochran,[3] a native of Londonderry, had been put in charge of a fort in Portsmouth Harbor. On the 20th a party of volunteers made him and his family prisoners of war on parole. Later, when Governor Wentworth sought shelter at the fort, Cochran broke his parole, the two escaping together. Continuing his connection with the army after peace was declared, he settled down in St. John's, New Brunswick, where he died.

After the Captain had made his escape there remained at the fort Mrs. Cochran, her four children, the hired man, and a maid. At this time all outbound vessels were required to show their passes to the officer in command at the fort. Sometime after this a vessel failed to present its papers. "You must hail her," said Mrs. Cochran to the man. "Ma'am," he answered, "I have but one eye and can't see the touchhole." At this Mrs. Cochran herself made shift to fire, the vessel hove to, and the papers were produced. On learning the circumstances, suitable acknowl-

---

[1] *History of Essex County*, II, 1264, 1370. Hurd.

[2] His silhouette was exhibited July 17, 1895, at Manchester.

[3] Loyalists of the American Revolution, 320-1. Sabine.

edgment was made by the British Government.   Governor Wentworth's disappearance soon became known, and a party of Patriots arrived to overhaul the fort.   After a fruitless hunt, upstairs and down, some one proposed looking down cellar.   "O yes," assented one of the Cochran girls, "I will light you."   The "little Tory," much to her satisfaction, then proceeded to guide the men into a low-studded corner, where, blowing out her light, as if by accident, she beat a retreat.   Left to themselves, the men blundered about, bumping their heads and swearing roundly, while, to exasperate them the more, the child, with apparent innocence, inquired from time to time, "Have you got him?"

At Harvard Jonathan Barnard [1] was clearing land when the news came.   A ten year old girl, little Martha Atherton, came running, to tell him, across a piece of ground but lately burnt over; in that way scorching her feet so badly she was nearly crippled for life.   In after years Barnard made her his wife, and both lie buried in North Bridgton, Maine.   An old lady in the Oak Hill region here was rendered so nervous by the agitation of the time, she mistook the red tips of young maple trees, fringed out since last noticed, for redcoats rising the hill, and, hastening indoors, set on her large kettle to boil, in order to give them a warm reception.[2]

In December James Perry,[3] of the same town, had leave to withdraw a petition for compensation, his wife having — as therein stated — "out of great pity" sent down some provisions to the Camp.   As the horse was being ridden home, April 21st, it was killed by a chance shot.   "For which horse," says Perry, "your petitioner had divers times been offered Ten pounds Lawful money, one of which offers was the week before."   He further explains, "were it a possibility to lay the loss of the Horse on said man who rode the said Horse, yet it would be impossible to recover the same

[1] *The Spirit of '76*, December, 1896.
[2] Traditional through Rev. Henry Barber of Meadville, Penn.
[3] *Mass. State Archives*, Vol. 180, p. 253.

of him, he being an aged man and his labour done (in a manner) and he has not estate wherewith to make restitution." In spite of which plea no allowance was made.

Eighty men marched from Shirley,[1] leaving but seven behind, who were disabled by extreme age, or other infirmities.

William Longley,[1] known as Old Will the miller, an aged man, bent over on his staves, protested that he should march whether or no. When told he was too infirm, he brandished his canes saying he knew he could not use a musket but he might fight with his sticks. He had a son, Joshua,[2] in the company. James Dickerson[2] was planting corn when he heard the news, dropped his hoe, and hurried off. His wife, Priscilla, twenty-six years old, took up the hoe, finished out the row, and carried on the farm duties until her husband's return. Her father, Francis Harris, was eleven times selectman, town clerk, treasurer, and the like.

Amos Holden's[2] ten year old Johnny was a good fifer and begged hard to go with his father, but was told, "You are too young; wait awhile, and if they don't get enough of it to-day when we meet them, you may have a chance later," and he did.

Samuel Hazen, Jr.,[2] another Shirley man, was ploughing, and, on hearing what had taken place, at once ran to the house, took down his gun and powder-horn, saying briefly to his wife (Elizabeth Little), "Betty, you take care of the children and cattle, I must go." There were five children here under ten, the baby not quite two months. In the hasty distribution of ammunition several of the balls rolled away and a full century later were unexpectedly found in the upper gallery of the meeting-house.[2] About eleven o'clock the Shirley men reached Acton and marched on as far as Cambridge.

Lancaster[3] sent off 257 men the same day, General

---

[1] *History of Middlesex County,* I, 460. Hurd.

[2] *Beside Old Hearth-Stones,* 80, 84, 88–9, 81, 94, 96. Brown.

[3] *History of Worcester County,* I, 27. D. Hamilton Hurd. Philadelphia, 1889: J. W. Lewis & Co.

John Whitcomb coming up before the running fight was over and sharing its direction. Colonel Abijah Willard,[1] of Lancaster, was more than fifty years old, having served as a captain before Louisburg in his youth, and, being conservative in temperament, his sympathies were with England. The day the alarm came he had set out for his farm in Beverly, taking seed in his saddle-bags and intending to oversee his spring planting. Finding the countryside risen, he diverted his steps to Boston. He was three times married, his first wife, Elizabeth, being a sister of Colonel Prescott. On the 17th of June following he chanced to recognize his brother-in-law on the redoubt at Bunker Hill, and in reply to Gage's question, "Will he fight?" answered: "Prescott will fight you to the gates of Hell!" Willard died in 1789, an exile in the Provinces, his family returning to Lancaster as pensioners of the British Government; a son and daughter lived to be over ninety, one, indeed, surviving until 1858.

Captain John Joslin led the Minute-men of Leominster, and the following January £11 18s. 2d. was allowed in compensation [2] for supplies furnished to the volunteers at this time. When the alarm guns were fired, they surprised Joshua White,[3] crossing the mill-pond. He had two girls in his boat, and all three listened so intently that the boat, left to drift, shot over the dam, end foremost! An old rhyme continues the tale:

> But White being strong and meeting no harm
> He took a Miss Wheelock under each arm
> And carried them both safely ashore;
> Then bid them goodbye and said nothing more,
> But hastening home he snatched his gun
> And travelled off for Lexington.

On Tuesday, April 18th, the Lunenburg [4] Minute-men, having drilled, were afterward entertained at a dinner

---

[1] *Bay State Monthly*, June, 1884.
[2] *American Archives*, IV, 4th ser., 1417. Force.
[3] *History of Leominster*, 51. David Wilder. Fitchburg, 1853.
[4] *History of Worcester County*, I, 771. Hurd.

provided by their officers and then marched to the Meeting-house, where the Rev. Zabdiel Adams preached from Psalms XXVII, 3. The following day the farmers were sowing and ploughing when called to arms. The selectmen of this town were allowed [1] £13 for food furnished to the soldiers. On Cushing Street in Fitchburg there is a stone inscribed:

> Near this spot
> in 1775 stood the store of
> Ephraim Kimball.
> It was the rendezvous of
> Fitchburg's minute men.
> Here, at 9 o'clock, a.m.,
> on the 19th of April, 1775,
> the Alarm gun was fired
> and a Company of forty-two men, under
> Captain Ebenezer Bridge,
> marched for Concord,
> where they arrived the same evening.
> Another company under
> Capt. Ebenezer Woods,
> followed, the same day.

Kimball's store was used as an armory, and a wagonload of provisions followed.

Townsend [2] sent two companies, seventy-five men in all, under Captain James Hosley and Captain Samuel Douglas. The alarm here was sounded at noon from cannon planted on Meeting-house Hill. Ephraim Warren [2] lived a little southeast of Townsend Harbor, so called. On hearing the firing he left his plough in the furrow, mounted one of the horses, and set off full speed to "have a shot at the Regulars." As he neared home, he called to his wife, Mary Parker, [3] of Chelmsford, "Molly, the Regulars are coming, and I'm going. Give me my gun." He got to Concord early in the evening and saw the dead and wounded redcoats. This company [3] was recalled to take care of the Tories at home. The Townsend [4] selectmen had a grant of £7

[1] *American Archives*, IV, 4th ser., 1417. Force.
[2] *History of Middlesex County*, II, 384. Drake.
[3] *History of Middlesex County*, I, 581–2. Hurd.
[4] *American Archives*, IV, 4th ser., 1417. Force.

10*s*. 0*d*. allowed for supplies furnished. Ashby[1] heard about nine in the morning. Captain Samuel Stone led forty-six Minute-men, and Captain John Jones thirty Militia. The alarm is supposed to have been fired in front of Lieutenant Jonas Barrett's inn, he being second in command of the Minute company.

Ashburnham[2] heard in the afternoon, when Captain Jonathan Gates left with thirty-eight men. The men living on the outskirts rallied on the Common and thirty-three more in the gray of the morning started under Captain Deliverance Davis.

The alarm was carried by Edward Weatherbee[1] as far as Simon Tuttle's on the road to Littleton.[1] From this town Lieutenant Aquilla Jewett, four officers, and forty-two Militia-men responded, besides several volunteers; fourteen pounds of powder and thirty-eight pounds of ball were dealt out before marching. Some of the company dropped out at Concord, but others, credited with twenty-six miles marching, probably reached Cambridge.

Groton[1] sent two companies of militia, Captain Josiah Sartell led forty-eight men, and Captain John Sawtell twenty-six, including a few from Pepperell. A hundred and one Minute-men turned out, divided between Captain Henry Farwell's company of fifty-five and Captain Asa Lawrence's of forty-six, including officers. Corporal Samuel Lawrence,[3] of Groton, was ploughing when warned by Colonel Prescott to rally his men. Mounting the colonel's horse, in forty minutes he had ridden his seven miles circuit, and three hours later the men were ready to start, reaching Cambridge Camp next day. At Bunker Hill Corporal Lawrence was struck by a ball in his beaver and received a grape-shot in his arm. He was two years in the army, marrying Susanna Parker, of Lincoln, and returning at once to the front, for, as his mother

---

[1] *History of Middlesex County*, I, 312, 263; II, 872, 540. Hurd.
[2] *History of Worcester County*, I, 198. Hurd.
[3] *Life of Amos A. Lawrence*, 1–2. William Lawrence.

remarked,[1] "If anything happened to Sam, Susan had better be his widow, than his forlorn damsel."

A member of Captain Farwell's company says in his journal:[2] "Wednsday morning, April 19, 1775. was Alarmed with the news of the Regulars Firin At Our men At Concoord Marched and Came thare whare Some had Bin ciled Puled on and Came to Lexington whare much hurt was Done to the houses thare by braking glas And Burning Many Houses: but thay was forsed to retret tho thay was more numerous then we And I saw many Ded Regulars by the way. went into a house [possibly Munroe's Tavern] where Blud was half over Shoes."

A little before noon Edmund Bancroft, Sr., reached Pepperell from Concord with the news, when Colonel Prescott at once ordered the local company and the Hollis company to join the Groton men as soon as possible. Edmund Bancroft,[3] of Captain Nutting's company, had just started on a journey to Maine when his father reached home. Saying, "Perhaps he is not out of hearing yet," Mr. Bancroft ran out into the field and, mounting a large boulder, called to his son, who returned to the house, changed his clothes, and started for Concord. One woman here[4] met her husband at the cross-roads with his coat and handed it to him with the words, "Make haste, for the Regulars are out!" The field is yet shown where Jeremiah Shattuck[4] leaped the wall and joined his company; another soldier, Nathaniel Parker,[4] hastened away, leaving his plough, still preserved in 1897. Jonathan Shattuck[4] ran a mill and would have started with the rest but was counselled by the old minister to stay behind as he was more wanted to keep supplies moving; so he hung up his gun and set to work. Although five miles further to the northeast, the Pepperell men had gathered and reached

---

[1] *American Monthly Magazine*, August, 1894.

[2] *Diary of Lieutenant Amos Farnsworth.* Edited by Dr. S. A. Green. Cambridge, 1898: John Wilson and Son.

[3] *History of Middlesex County*, 263. Drake.

[4] *Beside Old Hearth-Stones*, 60, 56. Brown.

Groton before the men of that village were ready to set out. Colonel Prescott's brother, Dr. Oliver Prescott,[1] chairman of the Groton selectmen, heard the music as their full ranks came in sight, and exclaimed, as he handed out ammunition, "This is a disgrace to us."

Abel Parker,[2] of Pepperell, later a judge of probate, was ploughing two or three miles distant and heard of the call to arms just after his company had started. Leaving his oxen unyoked in the field, he ran home, caught up his gun in one hand, his Sunday coat in the other, and set out on a run, not slackening his pace until, having passed the Groton companies, he at length overtook the Pepperell men with Nutting, at Groton Ridges, three miles below the town. These companies were too distant to engage, despite their utmost exertion.

Still another story belongs to Pepperell. Mrs. David Wright [3] of that town had two Tory brothers, Thomas and Samuel Cumings, and another, Benjamin, nineteen years of age, whose sympathies, like her own, lay with the Colony. Not long after the alarm, — and the death of her baby, Liberty — while paying a visit at her native town of Hollis she overheard her brother Sam plotting with a French war veteran, Captain Leonard Whiting — a descendant of an old Lincolnshire family — how they might guide a party of British to Groton. Hurrying home with the tidings (in the absence of men folks) she and Mrs. Job Shattuck, of Groton, were put in command of the neighboring women, thirty or forty in number, who collected at Jewett's bridge over the Nashua River between the two towns. Rigged out in their absent husbands' clothes and armed with muskets and pitchforks, they took their stand, determined that no foe should pass that way. Owing to a bend in the road here, a rider coming from the north scarcely sees the bridge

---

[1] *History of Groton*, 336, note. Caleb Butler. Boston, 1848.

[2] *History of Middlesex County*, III, 231. Hurd.

[3] *Prudence Wright and the Women who Guarded the Bridge.* Mary L. P. Shattuck. Pepperell, 1900.

ahead of him until it is almost under foot. As the women stood on guard, a little after nightfall, Captain Whiting suddenly came in view with Samuel Cumings at his side, riding with despatches from Canada to the British in Boston.

Mrs. Wright, whose "snapping black eyes" are still recalled, ordered the men to halt, when they were immediately surrounded. Whiting's first impulse was to use his pistol, but Cumings luckily recognized his sister's voice and stopped him, saying, "Hold, that's Prue's voice, and she would wade through blood for the rebel cause." Deeming resistance out of the question, the Tories dismounted and allowed themselves to be searched. Upon finding the suspected papers in Whiting's boot, the men were delivered to Oliver Prescott at Groton, the despatches forwarded on to the Committee of Safety at Cambridge, and the "Guard" disbanded. In acknowledgment of this exploit the town subsequently made a grant of £7 17s. 6d. Mrs. Wright's Tory brothers both died in exile. Captain Whiting, although from time to time "inimical to the Rights and Liberties of the United Colonies," lived out his days in the land and became a founder and trustee of Phillips Exeter Academy.

Deacon John Boynton,[1] one of the Committee of Observation, living in the southern part of Hollis across the New Hampshire line, was the first in town to receive the alarm, and carried it on, reaching about noon the house of the chairman, Captain Noah Worcester.[1] As the Deacon dashed up, shouting, "The regulars are coming and killing our men," Worcester, who had just finished dinner, was shaving before the glass. Not waiting to wash the lather from one side of his face, he threw himself on his horse and took the word forward. Captain Reuben Dow[1] was ploughing with his two sons, Evan and Stephen, when he heard. All three hastened to the Centre, leaving six year old Daniel to help his mother and sisters care for the oxen. The salt-pork barrel was quickly brought up from the cellar and strips

[1] *Beside Old Hearth-Stones*, 114–15, 109–10. Brown.

dealt out to the gathering Minute-men. By afternoon ninety-two were off, each carrying one pound of powder and twenty bullets. With them went Noah Worcester, Jr., a sixteen year old fifer.

Captain William Kendrick,[1] of Monson, a village near Hollis, fired off an alarm, and, among others, four Baileys [1] answered the summons. Daniel Bailey, his sons Daniel, Jr., Joel, and Andrew had all been busy at their saw-mill when called, and started instantly without waiting to shut the gate. Near them, three Nevens [1] brothers were building a wall and, at the moment, busy with a crowbar prying up a field stone. Seeing a galloping rider come toward them, they slipped in a stone wedge and made for the road to learn the news. Finding the countryside was rising, they hastened on to the Common, leaving the stone partly lifted, as it carefully remains to this day. Neither of the young men lived to return home, Phineas was killed at Bunker Hill, William, Jr., the following spring in New York State, and John, who enlisted for Canada, perished without being heard from. Salisbury, New Hampshire, had the alarm the next forenoon. Here Mehitable Pettengill [2] sent for Benjamin, a sixteen year old lad, the eldest of her six children, who was working in the fields with his father; and, making up a small bundle, started him off for Cambridge with the local company, carrying his father's old musket.

April 21st Captain Gerrish and sixteen men were on the march from Boscawen,[3] New Hampshire; Captain Chandler and thirty-six more from Concord,[3] New Hampshire; Colonel Cilley and one hundred volunteers from Nottingham.[4] McClary left his plough and hastened forward from Epsom,[3] the courier here blowing a horn; and John Stark,[5] closing his

[1] *Beside Old Hearth-Stones*, 130, 132, 130–1. Brown.

[2] *History of Salisbury, N. H.*, 698. John J. Dearborn. Manchester, N. H., 1890: Wm. E. Moore.

[3] *History of Merrimack and Belknap Counties, N. H.*, 173, 124, 457. Hurd.

[4] *The State of New Hampshire Revolutionary War Rolls*, 36. Concord, N. H., 1885.

[5] *Women of the Revolution*, I, 113. Ellet.

saw-mill gate at the head of Amoskeag Falls, was off in his shirt sleeves inside ten minutes at a round gallop for Medford, which had been named as the rendezvous.

The Rev. Jeremy Belknap,[1] D.D., of Dover, then thirty-one years of age, was at Dover Point on his way home from Portsmouth when he heard what had taken place, and wrote to his wife: "Before you receive this you will hear the awful news, by the express I met just now at the ferry, of the devastation the troops have made at Concord and the Commencement of a Civil war, which makes it absolutely necessary that I should proceed immediately to Boston, if it is not in ashes before I get there. I shall try and get a chaise at Greenland. As necessity has no law, the people must excuse my absence next Sabbath if I should not return before it."

At Somersworth,[2] by a vote of the town, passed at the meeting-house on the 21st, twenty men were instantly despatched "to meet the enemy."

Newmarket[2] received the alarm at daybreak of the 20th, and in less than three hours men had started.

At Exeter,[2] the earliest intimation of an outbreak was received during the evening of the 19th. Rumors quickly followed by way of Haverhill and fuller details by daybreak. Nathaniel Folsom, Nicholas Gilman, and Enoch Poor were away at Dover at this time, but John T. Gilman,[2] a youth of twenty-one (promoted lieutenant on the 22d), was active in getting the men under arms and by about nine o'clock, the morning of the 20th, 108 men paraded at the Court-house ready to march with drum and fife. "What road shall we take?" inquired one. "By Haverhill," was the reply. "Who shall lead us?" came next. Captain James Hackett, having been chosen by acclamation, promptly asked, "Are you ready?" and in response to the "Yes" that followed, cried "March!"

[1] "Old Dover, New Hampshire." Caroline Harwood Garland. *New England Magazine*, September, 1897.

[2] *History of Rockingham and Stafford Counties*, 681, 533, 247. Hurd.

These men had been joined by the company from Newmarket, and marched without incident to Haverhill, where they found many houses, as already noted, had been burned. Crossing the ferry here, the night of the 20th was spent at Bragg's tavern in Andover. The following noon they reached Menotomy, and reported at Cambridge at two P.M. of the 21st. The next day, Saturday, there was a rumor that the British had landed at Chelsea and Captain Hackett's company, with the men from Londonderry, were sent to meet them, but at Medford they heard the British had re-embarked.

Matthew Patten,[1] of Bedford, New Hampshire, enters in his diary: "April 20th, 1775, I received the melancholy news, in the morning, that General Gage's troops had fired on our countrymen at Concord, and had killed a large number of them. Our town was notified last night, we generally met at the meeting-house about 9 o'clock, and twenty of our men went directly off for our army, from the meeting, to assist them. And our son John came home from Pawtucket, and intending to set off for our army tomorrow morning, and our girls set up all night baking bread, and fixing things for him and John Dobbin. 21st our John and John Dobbin, and my brother Samuel's two oldest sons, set off and joined Derryfield men, and about six from Goffstown, and two or three more from this town, under the command of Captain John Moor of Derryfield—They amounted in number to forty-five in all. [The] Suncook men that joined them, marched on in about an hour after; they amounted to thirty-five. There was nine men went along after, belonging to Penacook or thereabouts."

About four miles from Goffstown [1] lived three families. The men were hauling and piling wood on a burnt-over plot when the news came, and started home for their guns. Two of the women begged their husbands to stay. "Oh," was the reply, "we must defend you at a distance, it wont

---

[1] *History of Hillsborough County, N. H.,* 268, 310. D. Hamilton Hurd. Philadelphia, 1885: J. W. Lewis Co.

do to let the British come here." Then the three loaded
their food on the only horse owned between them and left.
That evening the three wives sat together at Mrs. Campbell's — she bearing the stoutest heart. "Oh," sobbed
one, "we shall never see them again. They'll all be killed."
"Pooh!" said Mrs. Campbell to cheer them, "I would
not care what the devil became of *them*, if they had only
left us the old mare."

At New Ipswich,[1] New Hampshire, Deacon Appleton left
his plough in the furrow and alarmed Peterborough. Returning in the ranks with his comrades, under Captain Wilson, he
marched close to his own door, but passed it by without turning aside. One hundred and fifty Ipswich men, "the very
bone and muscle of the town," had already left, armed with
powder and lead from the magazine stored in the meeting-
house loft. The night of the 20th was spent in Acton; next
day, on reaching Concord, they visited the North bridge and
here some of the older men, convinced that war had come
in good earnest, went back to make provision for the struggle.
Many of them were Concord-born and those who had fallen
were of their kin.[1]

At Keene,[2] Captain Wyman sent out expresses to warn
the town. About thirty of the volunteers responding were
sent home to fetch food supplies, as it was foreseen "all
the roads will be full of men and there will be nothing to
get by the way." By sunrise they were off, starting from
the captain's own house, and the Walpole[2] men, when they
came along, praised the "noble spirit" shown there.

Captain Isaac Baldwin, born in Sudbury, 1736, had moved
to Hillsborough,[3] New Hampshire, in 1766. He was a French
war veteran, and engaged in framing a barn in Deering when
the news came. Hurrying home he led a party of volunteers by way of Hollis. Here a rumor reached them that

---

[1] *History of Hillsborough County*, 615, 615–6. Hurd.

[2] *History of Keene, N. H.*, 172–3, 173, note. S. G. Griffin. Keene, 1904.

[3] *Annals of Hillsborough*, 20. Charles James Smith. Sandbornton, N. H.,
1841.

the British were attacking Portsmouth, but at Thornton's Ferry, over the Merrimack, this report was contradicted, and their march was continued for Boston; the Sunday before their arrival was spent at Billerica, where they all attended church in a body.

It is estimated that no less than two thousand men were under way from New Hampshire upon receipt of the tidings.

Within twenty-four hours the alarm had travelled to Scarborough,[1] Maine. When it reached Bath [1] a number of men were busily hewing masts at the King's dock, under Edward Parry. The news changed all this. About thirty inhabitants under Colonel Sewall marched up and stopped the work. Parry was seized, and kept prisoner a year before being released, while the British only saved themselves from a like fate by taking to their boats at Jones' eddy, and joining Mowatt's fleet.

According to a London [2] paper, Captain Brocklebank heard of the outbreak April 23–24, and hastily put to sea from Sheepscutt, in a new ship he was building. The inhabitants could not be induced to furnish a sufficiency of supplies, and the crew were obliged to make shift on a single barrel of beef and a little bread, with what fish they caught, until, twenty days later, they made St. George's Channel.

To return to the Old Bay State. The towns of western Massachusetts and across the Connecticut border were too distant to come up with the pursuit, but stories are told of their zeal in starting and of the anxiety and suspense at home.

Marlborough [3] sent upward of 180 men; Captain Daniel Barnes had 54 men in his company; many left the 19th, others followed on after; together with Captain Cyprian Howe's company of 48, Captain William Brigham's of 49, and Captain Silas Gates' little group of 35. At Hop-

---

[1] *Maine His. Soc. Coll.*, III, 196; II, 215.
[2] *Morning Post and Daily Advertiser*, June 24, 1775.
[3] *History of Middlesex County*, III, 822. Hurd.

kinton[1] it had been agreed that any man might "train under that Captain he liketh best." Captain John Homes, of the West Company there, reported the 19th at Roxbury with 90 men. Captain Roger Dench led the East Company, and Captain John Jones the Alarm company. The Westborough[2] men arrived in camp the night of the 20th, the town sending a month's provisions after them by wagon. It was not always easy to avoid mistakes with so many teams carrying supplies, and May 2d the Essex *Gazette* advertised, "Lost out of a wagon in Westborough, two Packs and one great Coat, also a Cartridge Box and Powder Horn. The Packs contained two white Shirts, one check Shirt, two pair of Stockings, some Provisions &c., &c. Whoever shall take up the above, and send them to Captain Stedman's of Cambridge, shall be handsomely rewarded. April 24. LEMUEL POMEROY.

N. B. It is very likely the Packs was by mistake put into a wrong waggon."

Shrewsbury got word about ten o'clock, the post rider's white horse was remarked by several, steaming hot and stained by spurring. The call, "To arms! To arms! War has begun," brought the old veteran General Artemas Ward[3] to his door and next day saw him at the front bringing the hastily marshalled troops into something like order. Ensign Howe,[2] a French war veteran of Captain Job Cushing's company, was out with his oxen, and Nathan, his fourteen year old son, had been riding the horse helping his father. Slipping the traces Lieutenant Howe took the lad's mount and lost no time in rousing his company, while little Nathan cried because he was "too young to march away with the men." Northborough[2] had the news before one o'clock and in some three or four hours Captain Samuel Wood paraded fifty Minute-men in his yard. Then the Rev. Mr. Whitney having commended them to the God of Armies,

---

[1] *History of Middlesex County*, III, 788–9. Hurd.
[2] *History of Worcester County*, II, 1341; I, 797, 456. Hurd.
[3] *Beneath Old Roof Trees*, 275, 281. Brown.

they set forth. One of Captain Wood's nieces here sat up all night casting bullets, and the next day had a daughter born.[1]

Before noon the express, Israel Bissel,[2] had reached Worcester, thirty-six miles to the westward. Still the shout was, "To Arms! To Arms!" and, leaving his good white horse,[3] which dropped dead before the Meeting-house, the tireless courier, with a fresh mount, bore the message on, up among the hills. As he rode away the Meeting-house bell was ringing behind him, and the long cannons,[3] on the ridge back of the Court-house, were giving as faithful warning as in the old days when the Indians were abroad and they stood in the ancient block-house north of Adams Square. After prayer by the Rev. Mr. Thaddeus Maccarty[3] the Worcester Minute-men were quickly off under Captain Timothy Bigelow, and in an hour or so Captain Benjamin Flagg followed with the trainbands. In all about 110 men. Flagg caught up with the others at Sudbury [4] Inn and they all went on together.

Just before sunset nearly one hundred men left Grafton,[3] the Rev. Mr. Grosvenor in their ranks. As the messenger bearing the tidings passed through North Millbury he gave the news to Isaac Chase,[5] a lad of fourteen, who, with an old neighbor, was engaged in repairing the road after the winter storms, that being the easy country fashion of settling one's taxes. When he heard that blood had been shed at Lexington, the old man exclaimed, "Alas! alas! there will be war," and wept like a child. Two years later Isaac Chase enlisted, and before he was twenty had seen considerable service. Colonel Jonathan Holman,[3] of Sutton, a French war veteran, led his mounted men at full speed through the whole night to Concord.

[1] *History of Worcester County*, II, 134. Drake.

[2] *Records of Oxford*, 369. Mary De Witt Freeland. Albany, N. Y., 1894.

[3] *History of Worcester County*, II, 1582, 943, 972. Hurd.

[4] *History of Worcester*, 97–8. William Lincoln. Worcester, 1862.

[5] "Autobiographical Sketch of Prof. Irah Chase, D.D." *Baptist Memorial and Monthly Record*, March, 1850.

Four towns not far from here seem to have had an unusually large number of soldiers "refreshed" as they passed through, and received correspondingly large allowances. To the selectmen of Holliston [1] there was granted £61 9s. 0d.; to the committee of supplies at Upton,[1] £16 12s. 11d.; to the selectmen of Mendon [2] (four companies marched from here), £38 4s. 4d., and to the selectmen of Bellingham,[1] £7 3s 4d. Leicester received word at noon. Captain William Henshaw [3] writes: "I saw the express that came from the town of Lexington, informing that the enemy had killed several men in that town." At four o'clock every Minute-man was on the Common [and this in a town [4] of scattered farms over six miles square]. They were without uniforms, but they came with their Queen's arms, and with their powder-horns and shot pouches. Members of their families and other friends were assembled to render assistance and to bid them Godspeed. Seth Washburn,[5] captain of the company, had left his forge, where he was fashioning a ploughshare, and fired his signal gun. The Rev. Benjamin Conklin, a "high Liberty man," was on the Common and offered a prayer while the men rested on their muskets. "Pray for me, and I will fight for you," said the captain, and, parting from his "venerable" mother, he gave the command, "Forward." With him went forty-three men. They had not thought it advisable to delay until a store of supplies ordered from Worcester should come to hand, and set off as they were.[5] One of the men, Nathan Sargent,[5] came from Cherry Valley, and while they halted here his father ran some extra bullets from the clock weights. A second company, making the number seventy-two in all, was off before sundown. Thirty-five men went from

---

[1] *American Archives*, IV, 4th ser., 1417. Force.

[2] *American Archives*, IV, 4th ser., 1415, 1440. Force. And *Annals of Mendon*, 332–3. John G. Metcalf, M.D. Providence, R.I., 1880: E. L. Freeman and Company.

[3] *History of Worcester County*, I, 696. Hurd.

[4] *Mass. His. Soc. Pro.*, October, 1876.

[5] *Leicester in the Revolution*, 19, 20. Emery Washburn. Boston, 1849.

Paxton. Jason Livermore,[1] of this town, was ploughing at Pudding Corner with his three sons. He cried, "Boys, unyoke the cattle, and let us be off." Hurrying home, the household pewter was swiftly run into bullets, and they were ready. Mrs. Livermore, with a little twelve year old son to help her, carried on the farm in their absence, making one hundred pounds of saltpetre for the army, during the summer, in addition to the daily chores.

The selectmen of Spencer [2] procured provisions for the men from Mr. Jeremiah Whittemore, and were allowed £6 8s. 3d. in compensation. Nearly a year after the battle Samuel Gearfield [3] bethought him that he had not received any "Reward" for his time, although he marched the evening of the 19th and "Bore his own Expenses" seven days, after which, as no immediate movement was looked for from the British, he "thought it best to Return home to his Large famely." He was of the Militia, but "not made up in any Role." Despite his hopes and public spirit, the endorsement reads, "Leave to withdraw." Fifty-six men from this town went through Paxton soon after dark, and the Brookfield [4] company before morning. The farmhouses had lights [4] left burning to cheer them on. Dr. Honey-wood,[4] an Englishman, seeing the people's spirit, remarked, "They *will fight*, and what's more they *won't be beat*."

A horseman with a red flag brought word of the battle to New [5] Salem. The Militia of the neighborhood thereupon turned out and leaned on their muskets, awaiting Captain G——'s word to march. He was suspected of being a Tory, and as he delayed, murmurs began to be heard in the ranks. At length the 1st lieutenant, William Stacey, took off his hat, drew out his commission, and said, "Fellow-soldiers, I don't know exactly how it is with the rest of you, but for one, I will no longer serve a King that murders my

[1] *History of Worcester County*, I, 577, 581. Hurd.

[2] *American Archives*, IV, 4th ser., 1434. Force.

[3] *Mass. State Archives*, Vol. 180, p. 368½.

[4] *Leicester in the Revolution*, 22. Washburn.

[5] *Historical Collections* (Mass.), 264. Barber.

own countrymen;" and, tearing the paper in shreds, he took his place in the ranks. The men gave a cheer, Captain G—— could not hold them, and the company disbanded. Stacey was then made captain and led them to Cambridge. The selectmen of this town received a grant[1] of £16 6s. 11d. for food furnished.

Athol[1] had a similar amount, £16 8s. 3d. allowed, and Templeton[1] £18 9s. 3d. New Braintree,[1] which is nearer Paxton, received £23 15s. 0d.

Mrs. Elizabeth Porter,[2] of Hadley, writes in her diary the Sunday following the fight: "April 23, In the afternoon my Husband set out for Brookfield as a post, to hear what News, for last Wednesday the Troops and our men had a Battle, numbers lost on both sides, but it seems as if we were most favored. O most gracious Lord, save from the spilling of human Blood, pray save Thy people, our Eyes are unto Thee. . . . Our Fathers trusted in thee, and were not ashamed; we desire to come out of ourselves, to renounce our own strength. The Race is not to the swift nor the Battle to the Strong, Salvation is the Lord's."

At Deerfield the alarm ran: "Gage has fired upon the people! Minute-men to the rescue! Now is the time, Cambridge the place!" fifty marching in response.

Chesterfield, a mountain town west of Northampton, was a little longer in hearing what had taken place. The following extracts are from a diary[3] kept by a Deerfield Tory then visiting in Chesterfield. "April 21. . . . The rest of the forenoon I spent at home; after dinner Mr. —— came in from Northampton. He bro't a Letter from [C]ol Pomroy to C[ol] Eager in which were orders for him to Muster the Comp.s & immediately march to Head Quarters; he also bro't. another Letter directed to Patterson which was broke open by him here; which gave an Acct

---

[1] *American Archives*, IV, 4th ser., 1417. Force.

[2] *Under a Colonial Roof Tree*, 47. Arria S. Huntington. Syracuse, 1892: Wolcott and West.

[3] From a Manuscript in the possession of the Hon. George Sheldon of Deerfield.

& Reasons of ye Muster which was this: a Brigade consist'g of about 1000 marched from Boston up to Lexington in order to apprehend Jno. Hancock and others, when yy were faced by a Militia Compy upon which yy fired, killed six, wounded four; & that upon ye Peoples Mustering, yy had got into a warm Engagement & had killed Numbers on Each Side.

Eager set upon Mustering ye People here, one was sent one way & another, another; and about sunset he got the Comps together determined to have them set out this Evening." However, they could not get ready, and did not start until daylight the next morning.

April 22, three companies from the west marched by.

April 23, a fine company from East Hoosac in uniform "blue turned up with buff" led by Lieutenant Smith, staid one night.

April 24, "About 8 a.m. Williams Town Company came in. . . . At 11 the Pittsfield Comp came, Dr. Childs led them." At this time it was understood that "400 Regulars" were "missing." All through the week varying rumors went about, the Regulars were said to have broken "two 24 Pounders and Plugged up another, and destroyed 70 Barrels of flower belonging to ye People & [to] have Killed about 40 of our men." Two days later it was said "300 of ye Regulars killed & 50 of our Men, and that yy were taking ye Tories at Hardwick and confining off them."

This same April 27th two old friends of his arrived — "just at Sundown, four Men from Pittsfield came along with Elisha Jones & Moses Graves of sd. Town, who being considered as Tories were going to take ym to Nhampton Goal, Jones and Graves wanted to talk with me but I refused, consulting yr Safety." April 29, "Had a letter & a half Jo from my Dada with Orders to be Inoculated. He told me that Halderman not Piercy was killed but that Col. Leslie was."

Another rumor reached him "yt when ye Second Brigade Marched out, Captain Gardner of Roxbury drew up his men to oppose ye Troops but yy bringg up ye Artilery Gardner's Men left him & run & he could not get ym together again."

Northfield [1] heard at noon on the 20th, Elihu Lyman beat the long roll, and before night the men were gone.

To the selectmen of Ashfield [2] £3 9s. 0d. was paid for food provided. It was Sunday morning when the alarm got to Stockbridge. [3] At eight o'clock Esquire Woodbridge and Deacon Nash came along toward the Hon. Timothy Edwards' house, each with his gun. Mr. Edwards met them at the cross-roads, before the door, carrying his own musket and they fired in succession, this being the prearranged signal. Colonel William Edwards, then a child of four or five, remembered it was a rainy morning; the people collected on the piazza of his father's house; the Rev. Dr. West made a prayer and the Minute-men got away before noon.

The diary of the Rev. Stephen Williams, [4] of Longmeadow, well shows the state of mind he was thrown into, and the varying rumors that ran about. Parson Williams [5] had been taken captive at Deerfield in 1704, and served as chaplain in the French wars. He was now over eighty years of age and writes in the heaviness of his heart:

April 20 This morning as soon as it was light, the drum beat and three guns were fired as an alarm. The story is that some of the troops had marched from Boston to seize some military stores at Lexington, or Concord, and that some men had been killed, but the accounts are vague — we must wait. The Lord mercifully prepare us for the tidings we

[1] *History of Northfield.* J. H. Temple and George Sheldon, 323. Albany, 1875: Joel Munsell.

[2] *American Archives*, IV, 4th ser., 1417. Force.

[3] "An Incident of the Revolution." Fanny Edwards Rogers. *Magazine of the Daughters of the Revolution*, July, 1893.

[4] *The Longmeadow Centennial Proceedings*, note H., published 1884 by the Sec. of the Centennial Com[t]. Copyright, R. S. Storrs.

[5] "Two Centuries and a Half in Longmeadow." Julia M. Bliss. *New England Magazine*, July, 1898.

may have. The minutemen are gone to town, and men are collecting from various parts, and we have reason to fear much mischief is done.

21st. This morning at 4 o'clock another message is come advising that there has been a sharp engagement at Concord between the regulars and our people, and many killed, but we have but an uncertain account. 'Tis said houses are burnt, and women and children killed — sad work, indeed — more men are collected and going forth. I prayed with a company. The Lord be pleased to go with them and prosper them; keep them in thy fear. This day [Friday] we met together for prayer in the Meeting House and I offered some remarks from the 3rd chapter of Jonah.

22nd, This morning the post, Mr Adams, came along, and we got his account of matters; they are very indistinct, but we learn that there has been a battle between the King's troops and our people, and that on both sides it was supported with great spirit; thus a war is begun. In the evening our people except the minutemen came home and bring an account that the King's troops are gone back to Boston; the account of the battle is yet very uncertain. It is said that General Haldiman is killed.

23rd, By the Post from Hartford, tis said that a number of men at Hartford went to the Post office and took away a packet of letters to General Gage. This is a very unadvised, imprudent measure, in my opinion, and doubtless we shall be looked upon as in a state of daring rebellion.

24th. Various reports; accounts of mens' gathering together from all parts of the Country, and tis said that a number of men from Rhode Island went to Marshfield and killed and took a considerable number of the King's troops, and laid many houses in ashes of such people as took part with the King's forces.

25th. Reports still various; some things reported yesterday, contradicted this day. In the p.m. we met for prayer. Jonathan Stebbins and Deacon Coulton prayed.

I read a sermon of Dr. Doddridge's from Deut. 23.9, and we concluded with singing.

26th. The story of Marshfield being laid in ashes is contradicted, and whether any persons have been killed there is yet uncertain; the most probable account is that they are contriving to collect an army to be raised by the New England Provinces and Colonies. Messengers are sent to Hartford, where the Connecticut Assembly is now sitting. The Lord give wisdom, prudence, discretion and moderation. I learn the people are very ready to misrepresent my words, and even in prayer. The Lord be pleased to direct and assist me and keep me from doing anything displeasing to His Majesty.

27th. I perceive the people are out of humor with me for things that I have said and done. My own conscience don't upbraid me for what they pretend to be uneasy at. I desire to refer myself to the Lord and cast my care upon Him, praying that I may be kept from sinning against God and that my usefulness may not be obstructed.

28th. George Cooley, who went with a wagon and provisions, is returned. He says that our men, who went from home, are stopped at Waltham at present. I wish that they may behave as becoming their Christian profession: reports are so various that we know not what is to be depended on.

May 5th, Various reports indicating the disquietness of the times.

6th, Our country is in tumult by reason of the late measures taken by the King's troops; blood is shed and people are in a great uproar and distress, especially in Boston: where the inhabitants are shut up as prisoners and people are got to be jealous of one another, because they have different opinions as to the times and measures taken. The accounts from home [*i.e.* England] are very different; some are for violent measures with the Colonies and Provinces, some for lenient and moderate measures. The Lord be pleased to help, pity, and reform.

11th, A public fast.   Mr Trotter of Stafford came hither to preach for me; his forenoon text from Job 36. 18; p.m. from Luke 18. 1–8.   He appears a bold and daring man, was very popular, and doubtless greatly pleased our warm people.   Some of his notions I could not join in with; but I hope his calls to repent, reform, and engage God's presence may be well attended to.   I myself shamefully fell on sleep in the time of his forenoon sermon.   The Lord be pleased to humble me.

In contrast with this diary is the following where one reads:[1] "I would not be without a gun if it cost me five guineas, as I shall be called a Tory or something worse if I am without one.   Pray don't fail of sending me a gun! a gun! a gun and bayonet; by all means a gun! a gun!"

With the New Haven soldiers marched two men, Earl[2] and Doolittle,[2] who are remembered by Four Views of the battle, drawn by the one and engraved by the other, which were offered for sale the same year at six shillings plain and eight shillings colored.   The series has just been re-engraved[3] at forty dollars plain and fifty-five colored, and is already increased in value.

[1] *Historic Mansions*, 370.   Drake.
[2] *American Monthly Magazine*, October, 1895.
[3] By Charles E. Goodspeed, Park Street, Boston.

CHAPTER VIII

THE day of the battle a messenger set out from Watertown to the town clerk of Worcester; a duplicate account sent on thence thirty-eight miles to Daniel Tyler, Jr., of Brooklyn, Connecticut,[1] was received at eight in the morning of Thursday, the 20th. Mounted men, with beating drums at once carried the news of the uprising broadcast through Windham County. At three in the afternoon a second express reached Pomfret, addressed to Colonel Ebenezer Williams, sent via Woodstock. One account makes Israel Putnam [2] at work in a leather waistcoat, building a stone wall when the alarm came. By another [3] version he sprang on one plough horse and his man rode after him on a second. Whatever work he left, he told the gathering men on Brooklyn Green to wait to be regularly called out, and start with their officers; and then pushed on through the night himself, riding one hundred miles in eighteen hours [4] and arrived in Cambridge Camp on the 21st. He shortly wrote as follows:[1]

CONCORD, April 21.

To Col. Ebenezer Williams.

SIR, I have waited on the Committee of the Provincial Congress, and it is their Determination to have a standing Army of 22,000 men from the New England Colonies, of which, it is supposed, the Colony of Connecticut must raise 6000, and begs they would be at *Cambridge* as speedily as possible, with Conveniences; together with Provisions, and a Sufficiency of Ammunition for their own Use.

[1] *History of Windham County*, II, 144, 146. Larned.
[2] *History of the U. S.*, VII, 315. Bancroft.
[3] *Diary of the American Revolution*, 105. Moore.
[4] *Lexington Centennial*, 28.

The Battle here is much as has been represented at Pomfret, except that there is more killed and a Number more taken Prisoners. The Accounts at Present are so confused that it is impossible to ascertain the number exact, but shall inform you of the Proceedings from Time to Time, as we have new occurences; meantime

I am, Sir,

Your humble servant,

ISRAEL PUTNAM.

N. B. The Troops of Horse are not expected to come until further notice.

Killingly,[1] Connecticut, is supposed to have received the Lexington alarm even earlier than Pomfret, by a direct express from Boston to Hezekiah Cutler. Cutler had charge of the town's supply of ammunition, which was stored in the church Rising from bed, he fired his gun three times, and set off with fifteen others before sunup.

Before marching he had given orders that the remaining men were to be served with half a pound of powder apiece when they came to march, and accordingly his house was filled all day Thursday with squads of soldiers receiving their portion.

James McLane [2] of Glastonbury, Connecticut, on getting the alarm saw his shoemaker and told him that he must have a new pair of shoes ready before night; he then walked five miles to a gunsmith and had his gun repaired. The following day he set off in good order, one of the 3,600 Connecticut men starting from forty-seven towns as soon as the word was brought.

From Suffield,[3] Connecticut, Captain Elihu Kent led fifty-nine men; a provision wagon also went from there. The soldiers were under way before daybreak of the 20th and are said to have been the first citizen soldiers to pass through Springfield, occasioning "tumultuous applause."

Benedict Arnold, captain of the Governor's Guards,

[1] *History of Windham County*, II, 145. Larned.

[2] *Concord Centennial*, 143.

[3] *American Monthly Magazine*, February, 1893.

when the news reached New Haven [1] at noon Thursday, soon had forty men all ready to start, except for their quota of ammunition, which the town at first refused to place at his disposal. Arnold quickly marched his men where the selectmen were sitting, and said, if the keys were not sent to him in five minutes he would break the lock. The keys were handed over, and the men speedily set off by way of Wethersfield and Pomfret, where Putnam is said to have joined them. This company was quartered at Elmwood,[2] Mr. James Russell Lowell's home in after years. Because of its superior equipments, it is said, this company was selected to act as escort to the body of Lieutenant Hull on the 3d of May, as already noted.

Early Saturday, April 22d, Lieutenant-Colonel Storrs [3] led a party to Windham Green, where men from Coventry, Mansfield, and Windham had assembled. After prayer in the church, toward sunset they marched off for Pomfret, Colonel Parsons, of Lyme, passing them on the road. Representatives from Ashford and Canada Parish were also present; indeed, the companies were so numerous as to become embarrassing; and at five P.M. of Sunday, the 23d, a picked fifth of the whole body was sent forward to Boston, that night being passed at Moulton's tavern in Woodstock, close to the Massachusetts border.

With so many men away from home the women became nervous and fearful. Colonel Malbone, the Tory, was said to have armed his negroes and in the Killingly [3] hill settlement it was even affirmed that "Malbone's niggers were butchering and burning" right and left.

Judge Ephraim Cutler, writing in Marietta, Ohio, in 1820, tells how, as a boy, he stood sentinel on top of his grandfather Cutler's gambrel roof, but without seeing anything to occasion alarm. Only a few old men and no arms had been left in town, and the house was filled with fright-

---

[1] *Field Book of the Revolution*, I, 421-2. Lossing.

[2] *Memorial History of Boston*, III, 114.

[3] *History of Windham County*, II, 145-6. Larned.

ened women and children, who had kettles of boiling water swung on the cranes as an impromptu means of defence.[1] A story is told of Windham, illustrating the temper of the times. The parson's wife here, Mrs. Cogswell,[1] had met with the sad loss of her youngest daughter, Betsey Devotion, the previous March by a malignant fever. In the face of the prevailing feeling against the use of tea, she had been persuaded to take some for its soothing qualities. This indulgence was immediately resented by the community at large with such heat that the situation might have become intolerable but for the Lexington alarm, which turned the people's thoughts into a fresh channel.

Rachel Abbe, the wife of Captain Samuel McClellan,[1] of Woodstock, had a warm, enthusiastic nature, and exulted so in anticipation of the patriots' success she set out four memorial trees so soon as the men had marched. These sapling elms, fetched on horseback from her Windham home, were planted in front of her door on the slope of the neighboring common. Two still survived in 1880.

The story is told [2] of one Connecticut town that a drum and bell having called the villagers to the Green, thirty men were chosen to start for Boston. By noon the men who were to go had returned from their homes and were taking leave of their friends. One rich old miser was so moved by the sight he took several of the poorer soldiers aside, and to their astonishment put about thirty dollars in hard cash in their hands, saying in a low voice: "Beat the rascals! Beat them! If you come back, perhaps you will pay me; if not, God bless you!"

It is related [3] of a gentleman, travelling through Connecticut shortly after the rising, that he met an old gentlewoman, who told him that she had fitted out and sent five sons and eleven grandsons to Boston when she heard of the engage-

[1] *History of Windham County*, II, 147, 143-4, 147. Larned.

[2] *The First Book of History*, 122-3. Peter Parley. (S. G. Goodrich.) Boston, 1852.

[3] *Diary of the American Revolution*, 71. Moore.

ment between the Provincials and Regulars. The gentleman asked her if she did not shed a tear at parting with them. "No," said she, "I never parted with them with more pleasure." "But suppose," said the gentleman, "they had all been killed." "I had rather," said the noble matron, "this had been the case, than that one of them had come back a coward."

Lieutenant Thomas Burnham's [1] wife, Judith, showed a similar spirit, fitting out four sons — the youngest only fifteen — for the war, saying as they left her, "Never let me hear that one of you was shot in the back."

The whole country was filled with rumors and rallying men. A letter [2] received at Portsmouth, New Hampshire, early on the 20th, gives a little fuller picture.

NEWBURYPORT, April 19.

SIR: This town has been in a Continual alarm since mid-day, with reports of the Troops having marched out of Boston to make some attack in the country. The reports in general concur, in part, in their having been at Lexington. And it is very generally said they have been at Concord. We sent off an express this afternoon, who went as far as Simon's at Danvers, before he could get information that he thought might be depended upon. He there met two or three gentlemen who affirmed, the Regular troops and our men had been engaged the chief of the morning, and that it is supposed we had 25,000 men engaged against 4000 Regulars; that the Regulars had begun a retreat. Our men here are setting off immediately. And as the sword is now drawn, and first drawn on the side of the Troops, we scruple not you will give the readiest and fullest assistance in your power. And send this information further on. In behalf of the Committee for this Town.

Your humble servant,
JAMES HUDSON."
Chairman.

[1] *Catalogue of the Loan Exhibit*, 68, by the Daughters of the Revolution. Copley Hall, Boston, 1897.

[2] *American Archives*, II, 4th ser., 359. Force.

One force from New Hampshire [1] marched fifty-five miles in twenty hours and was at Cambridge Common by sunrise of the 21st. General Green, of Rhode Island, was also at Cambridge, and General Stark, already referred to, was at Chelsea on the 22d.

April 20th Parson Stiles, of Newport, writes: [2] "At VIII o'Clock this Morn.g an Express arrived in Town from Providence" with news of the fight for Governor Wanton, enclosing one from S. Hopkins dated "Wednesday night, 10 o'clock." One of these letters is referred to by a gentleman, writing to New York, as reporting: [3] "The King's Troops are actually engaged butchering and destroying our brethren in the most inhuman manner. The inhabitants oppose them with great zeal and courage." Stiles [2] continues, "An Express left Cambridge yesterday [20th] & came to Providence about XI[h] this forenoon, & the news reached Newport at V[h]. this Afternoon Inform.g that yesterday there were assembled 16 or seventeen Thousd. Provincials of which 7000 were at Cambridge, 4000 at Charlestn., & 4000 at Roxbury." On the 22d it was rumored that Gage having recalled the Marshfield detachment the Minute men opposed their leaving, and the town was fired.

23d, "Ldsday. I preached on Hosea XII, 6, . . . at the desire of Mr William Vernon . . . I read Ps. LXXIX and LXXX as adapted to the present melancholy Ocasion. . . . 24th, Gen.l Gage sent 2 Transports on Wesdy last to take off the Troops at Marshfield. And it is said that they embarked on friday Noon."

New York had word, by way of Rhode Island and New London, early Sunday morning, but did not credit the news until confirmed by the arrival of an express between churches.

On Monday, a New Yorker wrote: [3] "I do not doubt but the interesting news from Boston must give every good

---

[1] *Lexington Centennial*, 28-9.   [2] *Diary*, I, 535-7.
[3] *American Archives*, II, 4th ser., 362, 364. Force.

and virtuous man much concern, that from present appearances, a reconciliation between us and Great Britain is at a farther distance than we, of late, had rational grounds to hope. Surely this proceeding on the part of Gen. Gage is not the olive branch held up by Government. Yesterday this whole city was in a state of alarm; every face appeared animated with resentment. . . . Many persons of influence, who have been thought inimical to the cause, now come out boldly."

Thomas Ellison, Jr.,[1] wrote to his father as follows:

NEW YORK, April 25, 1775.

You will see in Yesterday's paper the melancholy account from Boston which is this day confirmed by the way of Waterford. I fain would hope it is not so bad as represented, yet I fear there is too much in it. If any lives are lost it will be attended with bad consequences and no doubt will raise America unanimously against the troops; for who could see their countrymen butchered and not endeavor to prevent it. Should the troops have made the attack on the people it will unite every man against them. There were two sloops at our dock loaded with flour &c. for the army at Boston which were immediately unloaded, though Sunday.

April 29, Ever since the news from Boston, the city has been in tumult and confusion, but has subsided some; and hope we shall soon be in order as people of every turn, warm as well as moderate, will join in establishing it. . . . By the latest accounts from Boston, it appears the regulars have lost, killed and taken prisoners, 332; and the loss by the Bostonians 30 or 40. There is a report in town that a cessation of arms has been agreed on which may be confirmed.

We hear that the Bostonians have sent home all their men except 18 of each company, who are kept as an army of Observation, lest the troops should make another excursion. Our City which was divided about the mode of redress, is now united, and of one way of thinking, that spirited meas-

---

[1] *Magazine of American History*, August, 1890.

ures will be most likely to bring on a reconciliation; as we can not bear the thought of being dragooned into measures we disapprove of!

When news of Lexington fight reached Philadelphia, Robert Morris,[1] a native of Lancashire, forty-two years of age, with many more, was engaged in celebrating St. George's Day (23d of April) at the city tavern. All but a few poured into the street and the gathering was broken up; from that time onward Morris's credit as a merchant, unexcelled in the community, was at the service of America.

If it stirs one to read of the calling out of the Scottish clans, it can do no less to follow the post rider southward bearing his summons. The particulars have come down to us through Christopher Marshall's diary.[2]   He writes:

Philadelphia, April 24, An Express arrived at Five o'clock this evening, by which we have the following advices:

WATERTOWN, Wednesday morning, near 10 of the clock.

To all friends of American Liberty, be it known, before break of day, a brigade consisting of about 1000 or 2000 men landed at Phipp's Farm, at Cambridge, and marched to Lexington, where they found a company of our Colony militia in arms, upon whom they fired without any provocation, and killed six men and wounded four others.   By an express from Boston, we find another brigade are now upon their march from Boston, supposed to be about 1000.   The bearer Trail[3] Bissel [Israel Bessel], is charged to alarm the country quite to Connecticut; and all persons are desired to furnish him with fresh horses as they may be needed.   I have spoken with several, who have seen the dead and wounded. Pray let the Delegates from this Colony to Connecticut see this, they know Col. Forster [of Brookfield] one of the Delegates.

J [or T.] PALMER, *one of the Committee.*

[1] *Lives of the Signers to the Declaration of Independence,* 235.   Rev. C. A. Goodrich.

[2] *Passages from the Diary of Christopher Marshall.*   Ed. Wm. Duane.   Philadelphia, 1839–1849.

[3] *American Archives,* II, 4th ser., 366–70.   Force, for variation in names.

Having reached Worcester, thirty-six miles distant, about noon, Bissel set off at once for Brooklyn, Connecticut, thirty-eight miles further. Norwich, twenty miles beyond, was reached at four P.M. and New London, thirteen miles to the southward, at seven. Passing through Lyme and striking the post-road from Boston via Providence, the next stage, Saybrook, twenty miles on, was made at four A.M. of Friday. This was Hurd's route, who may have been the new rider. After this the way skirted the Sound, through Killingworth, East Guilford, Guilford, and Branford to New Haven. At each of the above towns the papers were duly attested and soon after leaving New Haven the following note was added:

FAIRFIELD, Saturday, April 22, 8 o'clock.

Since the above was written we have received the following by a second express.

SIR, I am this moment informed by an express from Woodstock, taken from the mouth of the Express, then two of the clock, afternoon — That the contest between the first Brigade that marched to Concord was still continuing this morning at the town of Lexington, to which said Brigade had retreated, that another Brigade had, said to be the second mentioned in the letter of this morning, landed with a quantity of artillery at the place where the first did. The Provincials were determined to prevent the two Brigades from joining their strength if possible, and remain in great need of succor.

N. B. The Regulars, when in Concord, burnt the Court House, took two pieces of cannon which they rendered useless; and began to take up Concord bridge on which Captain —— (who with many on both sides were soon killed) made an attack upon the King's troops, on which they retreated to Lexington. I am,

EBENEZER WILLIAMS.

To COL. OBADIAH JOHNSON.
Canterbury.

P. S.   Mr McFarlan of Plainfield [Camfield] Merchant, has just retreated from Boston, by way of Providence, who conversed with an express from Lexington, who further informs, that 4000 of our troops had surrounded the first brigade above mentioned, who were on a hill in Lexington, that the action continued, and there were about 50 of our men killed, and 150 of the regulars, as near as they could determine, when the express came away: it will be expedient for every man to go who is fit and willing.

The above is a true copy as received per express from New Haven, and attested by the Committee of Correspondence, from town to town.

Attest: JONATHAN STURGIS
                        ANDREW ROWLAND
                        THADDEUS BURR
                        JOB BARTHAM
                            Committee.

The above was received yesterday [Sunday, April 23d] at four o'clock, by the Committee of New York, and forwarded to Philadelphia, by Isaac Low, chairman of the Committee of New York.

PHILADELPHIA, April 26, Wednesday, 12 o'clock.
By an Express just arrived, we have the following:

WALLINGFORD, Monday morning, April 24, 1775.
DEAR SIR, Col. Woodsworth [Wadsworth] was over in this place [most of] yesterday and has ordered 20 men from each company in his regiment, some of which have already set off, and others go this morning. He brings accounts which came to him authenticated as late as Thursday afternoon. The King's troops being reinforced a second time and joined, as I suppose from what I can learn, by the party who were intercepted by Col. Gardiner [Gardner], were then encamped on Winter hill, and were surrounded by 20,000 of our men who were entrenching. Col. Gardiner's ambush proved fatal to Lord Percy, and one other General Officer, who were killed on the spot by the first

fire. — To counterbalance this good news, the story is, that our first man in command (who he is I know not) is also killed. — It seems they have lost many men on both sides — Col. Woodsworth [Wadsworth] had the account in a letter from Hartford.

The Country beyond here are all gone off, and we expect it will be impossible to procure horses for our waggons, as they have or will in every place employ their horses themselves. In this place they send an horse for every sixth man and are pressing them for that purpose. I know of no way but you must send immediately a couple of able horses, who may overtake us at Hartford possibly, where we must return Mr Noy's [Noyes] and Meloy's, if they hold out so far. Remember the horses must be had at any rate.

I am in great haste,

Your entire friend and humble servant,

JAMES LOCKWOOD.

P. S. Col. Gardiner took 9 prisoners and 12 clubbed their firelocks and came over to our party. — Col. Gardiner's party consisted of 700, and the regulars of 1800 instead of 1200, as we heard before. They have sent a vessel up the Mystic river as far as Temple's Farm, which is about half a mile from Winter hill. These accounts being true, all the King's Troops, except 4 or 500, must be encamped on Winter Hill. At the instance of the gentleman of Fairfield just departed this copy is taken verbatim from the original, to be forwarded to that town.

ISAAC BEARS.

The above is copied and authenticated by the several Committees through Connecticut, New York and New Jersey.

∴ Winter Hill is about two miles from Boston.

Wallingford is fourteen miles from New Haven.

Such were the first imperfect accounts and their progress [1] may be traced far to the southward.

---

[1] *American Archives*, II, 4th ser., 366. Force.

NEW HAVEN, April 24, 1775.
half past nine o'clock, forenoon.

PIERPONT EDWARDS.

FAIRFIELD, April 24, 3 o'clock afternoon.
A true copy, as received per express.

THADDEUS BURR
ANDREW ROWLAND
ELIJAH ABEL

NORWALK, April 24, seven o'clock, afternoon.
A true copy as received per express.

JOHN CANNON ⎫
THADDEUS BETTS ⎬ *Comt*
SAMUEL GERMAN ⎭

STAMFORD, April 24, ten o'clock evening. A true copy.

JOHN HAIT, JR.
SAMUEL HUTTON
DAVID WEBB
DANIEL GRAY
JONATHAN WARRING, JR.

GREENWICH, April 25, three o'clock morning.
The above is forwarded to the Committee of Correspondence at New York.
A true copy, received in New York, 2 p.m. Tuesday, April 25, 1775.

ISAAC LOW, *Chairman, New York Comt.*

A true copy, received at Elizabethtown, 7 o'clock in the evening, Tuesday, April 25, 1775.

JONATHAN HAMPTON, *chairman of the Committee.*
GEORGE ROSS
JOHN BLANCHARD

A true copy, received at Woodbridge, 10 of the clock in the evening, Tuesday, April 25, 1775.

NATHANIEL HEARD ⎫ *Three*
SAMUEL PARKER   ⎬ *of the*
JONATHAN CLAWSON ⎭ *Committee.*

The above received at New Brunswick, the 25th April, 1775, twelve o'clock.

WILLIAM OAKE ⎫
JAMES NEILSON ⎬ *Committee*
AZ. DUNHAM ⎭

A true copy, received at Princeton, April 26, 1775, half past three in the morning.

THOMAS WIGGIN ⎫ *Members of*
JONATHAN BALDWIN ⎭ *the Committee*

The above received at Trenton on Wednesday morning about half after six o'clock and forwarded at seven o'clock.

SAMUEL TUCKER ⎫ *Three*
ISAAC SMITH ⎬ *of the*
ABRAHAM HUNT ⎭ *Committee*

PHILADELPHIA, 12 o'clock, Wednesday, received and forwarded at the same time by

LAMB. CADWALADER, ⎫ *Com.*
WILLIAM BRADFORD, ⎬ *for the*
THOMAS PRYOR, ⎬ *City of*
ISAAC MALCHER, ⎭ *Philadelphia.*

CHESTER, 4 o'clock Wednesday evening received and forwarded by

FRANCIS JOHNSTON
ISAAC EYRE
SAMUEL FAIRLAMB

NEW CASTLE, 9 o'clock Wednesday evening received and forwarded.

Z. V. LEUVENIGH
STEPHEN SPENCER

Wednesday night, Christeen Bridge, 12 o'clock forwarded to Col. Thomas Couch, Esq., who received it this moment, and he to forward it to Tobias Rudulph Esq., head of Elk, in Maryland.

Night and Day to be forwarded.

S. PATTERSON.

27 April, 1775, half past 4 o'clock morning received and forwarded to Patrick Hamilton Esq., in Charlestown by

> TOBIAS RUDULPH,
> JOSEPH GILPIN,

BALTIMORE, April 27, 1775, received 10 o'clock evening

> JOHN BOYD,
> *Clerk of the Committee.*

A true copy, received in Annapolis, Friday, April 28, 1775, half after nine o'clock morning and forwarded at ten, per express.

> MATTHEW TILGHMAN
> CHARLES CARROLL of Carrolton,
> CHARLES CARROLL,
> J. HALL.
> THOMAS JOHNSON, JR.
> SAMUEL CHASE.

Comt. of Cor. for Md.

Friday, Alexandria, 8 o'clock evening we received the enclosed from Annapolis at 6 o'clock; please forward it to Fredicksburgh.

I am for self and the Com.t of Correspondence in this place, Gentlemen,

> Your humble servant,
> WILLIAM RAMSAY.

To the Committee of Correspondence in Dumfries.

> DUMFRIES, April 30, Sunday,

Gentlemen:

The enclosed came to hand this morning about 10 o'clock. In one hour I hired the bearer to convey it to your place to the different Committees.

For self and the Committee of Correspondence in this place,

I am, gentlemen,

> Your most obedient humble servant,
> WILLIAM CARR.

FREDERICKSBURGH, Sunday evening half past 4.

Gentlemen, The enclosed arrived here about an hour ago, and is forwarded to your Committee by your very humble servants,

> JAMES MERCER.
> GEORGE THORNTON,
> MANN PAGE JR.
> HUGH MERCER.
>
> *Comt*

KING WILLIAM, May 1, 1775.

Gentlemen, The enclosed arrived here today, and is forwarded to your Committee by your most obedient servant

CARTER BRAXTON.

SURRY COUNTY, May 2, 1775.

Gentlemen, The enclosed arrived here this evening and is forwarded by your most obedient humble servant

ALLEN COCKE.

WILLIAMSBURGH, May 2, 1775.

Gentlemen, The enclosed is this moment come to hand, and I forward it to you by express, with the request of the Committee of Williamsburgh that you will be pleased to forward the papers to the southward, and disperse the material passages through all your parts.

I am very respectfully &c

RO. C. NICHOLAS,

Chairman.

SMITHFIELD, May 3, 1775, 5 o'clock in the morning.

The enclosed arrived here this morning, and is forwarded to your Committee of Correspondence by

Your humble servants,

ARTHUR SMITH

NATHANIEL BURUNE.

To the Com.t of the County of Nausemond or any of them.

An express from Boston.

NAUSEMOND, May 3, 1775.

Gentlemen, The enclosed is this moment come to hand, and we forward it to you by express, with the request of the Committee of Nausemond, and you will be pleased to forward them to the southward. We are Gentlemen Your most obedient servants,

WILLIS RIDDUH.
WILLIS CEOWPER.

To the etc. by express.

May 3, 1775. Gentlemen, The enclosed papers we have just received, and forward them by express to you, to be sent to the Southward.

We are gentlemen,

Your obe.dt servants.

The Committee of the County of Chowan,
To the etc. by express.

EDENTON, May 4, nine o'clock, 1775.

Gentlemen: The enclosed is this moment come to hand, and we forward to you by express, with the request that you will be pleased to forward the papers to the Com.t of Craven County immediately, and disperse the material passages through all your parts.

We are gentlemen etc.

JOSEPH BLOUNT, *chairman.*

THOMAS JONES.	JNO. HAMILTON.
CHARLES BONDFIELD.	ROBERT HARDY.
JNO. GREEN	ROBERT SMITH.
WILLIAM BENNET.	S. DICKINSON.

To the etc.
Beaufort County.

BEAUFORT COUNTY, May 6, 1775.

Gentlemen,

The enclosed is this moment come to hand, and we

forward to you by express, with the request that you will forward the different papers to the southward immediately.
We are Gentlemen
etc.

ROGER OSMOND.
WILLIAM BROWN.

To the com.t of Craven County.

BATH, May 6, 1775.

Dear Sir, In haste have sent to request you will peruse the enclosed papers; and that you will do, by opening the packet herewith sent the moment it comes to your house. Get three or four of your Com.t to write a line, and send the whole, enclosed, to the next southward Com.t with the utmost despatch.

We are, dear Sir, with regard,
Your most humble servants.
WILLIAM BROWN.
ROGER OSMOND.

To Abner Nash Esq., or either of the Com.t for the County of Craven.

Per express.

NEWBERN, May 6, 1775.

Gentlemen; The enclosed arrived here about an hour past, and is forwarded immediately to you; and desire you will keep a copy of James Lockwood's letter; and send them on as soon as possible to the Wilmington Committee.

We are etc.

SAMUEL SMITH.	A. NASH.
B. COGDELL,	JOSEPH LEECH.
JOHN GREEN.	JOHN FONVIELLE.
WILLIAM TISDALE.	WILLIAM STANLY.
THOMAS McLIN.	JAMES COOR.

N. B. We have enclosed our last paper, which gives an account of the first beginning of the battle, which please to send to Wilmington &c. and send all the bundle of papers forward as soon as possible you can.

To the etc.

ONSLOW, Sunday morning, 10 o'clock, May 7.

Gentlemen,

About an hour past I received the enclosed papers. Disperse them to your adjoining County. Keep a copy of James Lockwood's Letter; and pray write to us what to do.

We are for Onslow.

WILLIAM CRAY   EDWARD WARD
SETH WARD   ROBERT SNEAD
JOSEPH FRENCH

Enclosed is the last Gazette from Brunswick.

To the Wilmington and Brunswick Com.t

For Cornelius Harnet, Esq.

Col. John Ash, or any one of the

Com.t for Wilmington. (Express.)

NEW RIVER, May 7, 1775.

Received and forwarded by William Cray,

WILMINGTON, May 8, 1775, 4 o'clock afternoon.

Dear Sir, I take the liberty to forward by express the enclosed papers, which were received at 3 o'clock this afternoon. If you should be at a loss for a man and horse the bearer will proceed as far as the Boundary House. You will please direct to Mr *Marion,* or any other gentleman, to forward the packet immediately with the greatest possible despatch.

I am with esteem, dear sir, your most etc.

CORNS. HARNET.

p.s. For God's sake send the man on without the least delay; and write to Mr. Marion to forward it by night and day.

To Richard Quince, Esq.

BRUNSWICK, May 8, 1775, 9 o'clock p.m.

Sir, I take the liberty to forward by express the enclosed Papers; which I just received from Wilmington; and I must entreat you to forward them to your community at Georgetown, to be conveyed to Charlestown from yours with all speed. Enclosed is the newspaper giving an account of the beginning of the battle; and a letter of what happened after. Pray don't neglect a moment in forwarding.

I am your humble servant.

RICHARD QUINCE.

To Isaac Marion, Esq., at the Boundary.

May 8, 1775.

Dear Sir, Though I know you stand in no need of being prompted when your Country requires your service, yet I cannot avoid writing to you, to beg you to forward the papers containing such important news; and pray order the express you send to ride night and day.

I am, dear sir, in the greatest haste

yr etc.

R. HOWE.

Isaac Marion, Esq.

Boundary.

Boundary, May 9, 1775. Little River.

Gentlemen of the Committee,

I have just now received express from the Com.t of the northward Provinces, desiring I would forward the enclosed Packet to the Southern Com.ts. As yours is the nearest, I request, for the good of our Country and the welfare of our lives and liberties and fortunes you will not lose a moment's time, but despatch the same to the Com.t of Georgetown, to be forwarded to Charlestown.

In meantime etc. etc.

ISAAC MARION.

To Danness Hawkins, Josias Allson and Sam.l Dwight, Esq. and Messrs Francis and John Allston,

Gentlemen of the Com.t for Little River.

Wednesday, 1 o'clock, May 10, 1775,

Gentlemen, The enclosed papers were just now delivered to me by an express from Little River. I make not the least doubt but you will forward them with the utmost despatch to the General Court at Charlestown.

I am etc.

BENJAMIN YOUNG.

To Paul Trapier, Esq. Chairman of the Com.t at Georgetown.

half past 6, Wednesday evening,

Gentlemen, We have received your letter, — and shall be careful to execute with all the diligence in our power, whatever you have recommended. We send you by express a letter and newspaper, with momentous intelligence, this instant arrived. We are etc.

PAUL TRAPIER.   P. TRAPIER, JR.
S. WRAGG.   ANTHONY BONNEAU

To the Com.t of Intelligence in Charlestown to the care of the Hon. William Henry Drayton, Esq."

per express.

So the message ran through the land, and the response was swift, beyond New England as well as within her borders. Joab Houghton was present at the Hopewell Baptist Meeting-house when he heard of the battle. Stilling the breathless messenger, he waited until the service was over, and then, mounting the stone horse-block in front outside, he told the people what had taken place, ending, "Men of New Jersey,[1] the redcoats are murdering our brethren of New England. Who follows me to Boston?" And every man there, the story goes, fell into line and answered "I!"

On the 25th of April, William Ellery[2] wrote from Newport, Rhode Island, to the Philadelphia Committee of Correspondence an account of the battle, which was received there on May Day and forwarded to Annapolis. He enclosed a "hand bill" brought by a gentleman who "left Cambridge on Thursday last in the forenoon," and also a newspaper. At this time he writes: "A large body of men,

---

[1] *Historical Magazine*, May, 1859.
[2] *American Archives*, II, 4th ser., 382. Force.

not less than 20,000, are assembled, and form a semi-circle from Charlestown to Roxbury." His letter concludes, "We had hoped that the dispute between Great Britain and these Colonies would have been settled without bloodshed; but the Parliament and Great Britain, it seems, have determined to push their iniquitous, unconstitutional measures by dint of arms."

Ten days after the battle John Dickinson [1] wrote with considerable warmth of feeling from Fairhill to Arthur Lee, agent for Massachusetts in London. Referring to the morning encounter at Lexington, he remarks sarcastically, "This victory was gained by the Grenadiers and Light Infantry, without the assistance of any other Corps, though their numbers, it is said, did not exceed 1,000, and the Provincials amounted to at least, as it is reported, 25 or 30 men!" He had also received the erroneous report respecting Lord Percy and wrote: "The advices by several expresses are positive, that Lord Percy is killed, which gives great and general grief here, and also General Haldimand, the two first in command." Much of the letter would be but repetition; the end, however, is of general interest.

I cannot say I am conviced of the truth of all the particulars above mentioned, . . . But these facts I believe you may depend on: That this most unnatural and inexpressibly cruel war began with the butchery of the unarmed Americans at Lexington; that the Provincials, incredible as it may be at St. James' or St. Stephen's, fought bravely; that the Regulars have been defeated with considerable slaughter, though they behaved resolutely; that a Tory dare not open his mouth against the Cause of America, even at New York; . . . Why was not General Gage at least restrained from hostilities until the sense of another Congress could be collected. It was the determined resolution of some, already appointed delegates for it, to have strained every nerve at that meeting to attempt bringing

[1] *American Archives*, II, 4th ser., 443. Force.

the unhappy dispute to terms of accomodation, safe for
the Colonies, and honorable and advantageous for our
mother country, in whose prosperity and glory our hearts
take as large a share as any Minister's of State, and from as
just and generous motives, to say no more of them. . . .
Will the distinctions between the Prince and his Ministers,
between the People and their Representatives, wipe out
the stains of blood? . . . Our smiths and powder-mills
are at work night and day; our supplies from foreign parts
continually arriving. Good officers, *i.e.* well experienced
ones, we shall soon have, and the Navy of Great Britain
cannot stop our whole trade. Our towns are but brick
and stone, and mortar and wood; they perhaps, may be
destroyed; they are only the hairs of our heads; if sheared
ever so close, they will grow again. We compare them not
with our rights and liberties. We worship as our fathers
worshipped, not idols which our hands have made.

I am, dear Sir, your sincerely affectionate friend.

JOHN DICKINSON."

A Philadelphia [1] letter of April 28th shows how the public mind was affected there:

The Confusions we have had in this Country for
the last twelve months, are mere trifles to what actually
exist at this present moment, occasioned by an Express
which arrived here last Monday, from Boston, which
brought intelligence, that the Regulars and Provincials
had certainly commenced hostilities, and an engagement ensued, wherein many were slain on both sides. As
soon as the News arrived here, the whole City was in the
greatest ferment. The accounts the Express brought were
publickly read at the Coffee-House to multitudes of people,
who were animated almost to madness at what they called
joyful news; such news as I am sure must make every
humane hearer shudder with horror. An Association was
entered into at once and signed by great numbers, who are

---

[1] *Lloyds,* June 16–19, 1775.

JOHN DICKINSON

forming into Companies, and exercising every day. Most of the Counties in this Province are in the same state; in short from Nova Scotia to Georgia all are in arms, and all animated with a zeal really surprising. The Association is become so general here, that I am afraid both Mr —— and myself will be under necessity of signing it, or be marked as Tories. Notwithstanding I like this country so well, and have formed so many valuable connections in it, yet I cannot forget that England was the Country of my birth, though we have been neuter and could wish to remain so, but of that we are doubtful unless we sacrifice more than Prudence dictates.

A later Philadelphia letter of May 15th is referred to in the London *Chronicle* of June 29th–July 1st, in which a correspondent states: "Even the Quakers have their Companies. It is a strange sight to see the young ones exercising and to hear the words 'Shoulder thy firelock.'"

The *British Chronicle*, July 21–4, reports a Philadelphia letter of June 10th, brought by the *Industry*, Captain Woolcomb, arrived at Falmouth. It says:

Yesterday arrived here the *Charming Sally*, Captain McCullock; in him came passengers five officers, one of whom was Governor Skeen who was going to his government of Crown Point. Within two or three days' sail of Philadelphia they met a vessel, that informed them of the skirmish at Concord, near Boston; the Governor insisted on taking the command of the ship, and steering to Boston instead of Philadelphia; but being overpowered by the Captain and Crew, they confined them in irons, and carried them prisoners into Philadelphia, where they remained under a strong guard, and will be tried for mutiny on the high seas.

From the Western post rider [Ben.j Mumford[1]] Stiles learned that Major Skeenes, appointed governor of a new

---

[1] *Diary*, I, 554, 571.

Province, with Ticonderoga for capital and bound for Quebec, heard on the Banks that Ticonderoga was taken, and changed the course for Philadelphia. Upon reaching there, however, seventy chests of arms on board were seized. A ship-master, Captain Chester, saw Colonel Hancock of Boston "on board the ship elevated into a mere Extasy of Joy on the Occasion."

The heart of the country was roused and men had laid aside their every-day toil to make a final stand for their liberties. What was needed now was a leader, and he was on the way. Already Colonel George Washington had left home to attend the Congress at Philadelphia. A few weeks later would see him taking command of an eager, undisciplined, partially armed force of earnest men under the old elm (yet standing) in Cambridge. In view of all he was to become to the Continental Army, to these United States, and even in the later years of cordial good feeling to the people of Great Britain, it is especially interesting to read Washington's letter[1] to his old friend, George William Fairfax, then in England, dated from Philadelphia, May 31st, as follows:

DEAR SIR, Before this letter will come to hand, you must undoubtedly have received an account of the engagement in the Massachusetts Bay, between the Ministerial Troops (for we do not, nor can we yet prevail upon ourselves to call them the King's Troops) and the Provincials of that Government. But as you may not have heard how that affair began, I enclose you the several affidavits which were taken after the action.

General Gage acknowledges that the detachment under Lt. Col. Smith was sent out to destroy private property, or, in other words, to destroy a magazine, which self-preservation obliged the inhabitants to establish. And he also confesses, in effect at least, that his men made a very precipitate retreat from Concord, notwithstanding the reen-

forcement under Lord Percy; the last of which may serve to
convince Lord Sandwich, and others of the same sentiment,
that the Americans will fight for their liberties and property, however pusillanimous in his Lordship's eyes they may
appear in other respects.

From the best accounts I have been able to collect of
that affair, indeed from every one, I believe the fact, stripped
from all coloring, to be plainly this: that if the retreat had
not been as precipitate as it was, (and God knows it could
not well have been more so,) the Ministerial Troops must
have surrendered and been totally cut off; for they had not
arrived in Charlestown, under cover of their ships, half an
hour, before a powerful body of men from Marblehead and
Salem was at their heels, and must, if they had happened
to be up one hour sooner, inevitably have intercepted their
retreat to Charlestown. Unhappy it is, though, to reflect
that a brother's sword has been sheathed in a brother's
breast, and that the once happy and peaceful plains of
America are either to be drenched with blood, or inhabi-
tated by slaves. Sad alternative. But can a virtuous man
hesitate in his choice?

I am, with sincere regard and affectionate Compliments
to Mrs. Fairfax, dear Sir,

Yours &c.

As early as April 27th the Committee of Safety [1] wrote
from Cambridge to the selectmen of Boston, objecting to
the current rumor that General Gage reproached the Provincials with opening the attack. "Such a report," said
they, "occasions astonishment and resentment." And they
ended with reference to General Gage: "He is a man, we
trust, of too much honor to propagate such a false account,
and has been scandalously deceived by his officers." Wishing to set the matter in a true light, depositions, having
particular reference as to who fired first, had already been
taken under oath [2] before William Reed, Jonah Johnson,

---

[1] *American Archives*, II, 4th ser., 424. Force.
[2] *Mass. His. Soc. Pro.*, April, 1858.

Jonathan Hastings, John Cumming, William Stickney, and Duncan Ingraham, Justices of the Peace for Middlesex; their standing being certified to by Nat.[1] Gorham, Notary Public at Charlestown. The assistance of two persons was procured [1] for duly authenticating the affidavits, and Saturday, the 22d, many witnesses appeared and gave testimony at Lexington, Colonel Barrett's statement being taken at Concord. James Marr, at Concord, and John Bateman, at Lincoln, prisoners, also deposed Saturday. On Sunday Robbins' statement was taken, and on Monday the Lexington men very generally came forward, Lieutenant Gould being called upon at Medford. Wednesday, the 26th, Hannah Bradish at Worcester swore to a true account of what had befallen her *"in perpetuam rei memoriam"* before Thomas Steel and Timothy Paine, Justices of the Peace.

In this connection it is interesting to note a petition presented to "The Hon.ble Council and Hon.ble House of Representatives in General Court assembled at Watertown, March 28, 1776." from Joseph Perry [1] of Shutesbury, Hampshire County, "in the Colony of Massachusetts Bay," wherein he states that he, "being on a journey, did on the night next after the 18th Day of April, 1775, Lodge at Lexington, and being alarmed the same night did Assemble with ye Inhabitants of said Lexington and at the Request of the Militia Officers of said Town was Detained Five Days and a half in order to his being examined and making affidavit." This put him to a considerable charge for himself and horse and he prayed allowance for his loss of time. The same being endorsed by John Bridge, captain, and Jos. Simonds, lieutenant, at Lexington. Pamphlets containing the Depositions were eventually printed and ordered [2] to be distributed July 4th, 1775, by Dr. Taylor, Mr. Lothrop, and Mr. Jewett.

Previous to this, on May 2d, Mr. Gerry, President Warren, Hon. Mr. Dexter, Colonel Warren, and Colonel

---

[1] *Mass. State Archives*, Vol. 180, pp. 273, 369½.
[2] *American Archives*, II, 4th ser., 1483.   Force.

Gerrish were formed [1] into a Committee to forward to the Continental Congress authenticated copies of the Depositions, the address to the inhabitants of Great Britain, and the letter to Mr. Franklin, lately sent to England. It was perhaps from this source Colonel Washington made his copies for Fairfax.

Lest a mischance should overtake the first despatches sent over seas, another original set of papers was sent off the same 2d of May, to be forwarded by a vessel sailing from the Southern Colonies to London.

April 27th Dr. Joseph Warren [1] wrote to Arthur Lee, Esq., in London, dating from Cambridge:

. . . Lord Chatham and our friends must make up the breach immediately, or never. If anything terrible takes place, it will not do to talk of calling the Colonies to account for it; but it must be attributed to the true cause — the unheard of provocation given to this people. They will never talk of accommodation until the present Ministry are entirely removed. You may depend the Colonies will sooner suffer depopulation than come into any measures with them. . . .

p. s. The Narrative sent to Dr Franklin contains a true state of facts; but it was difficult to make the people willing that any notice should be taken of the matter by way of narrative, unless the Army or Navy were taken or driven away.

Realizing the importance of presenting the American side in a fair spirit, Richard Derby,[2] of Salem, sent his son, Captain Richard Derby, across in a swift vessel with letters, outstripping the Government despatches by eleven days. Captain Derby [3] brought home the first intelligence of how the tidings were received in London, and also enjoyed the distinction of bringing to America from France the first news of Peace. His orders ran: [2]

[1] *American Archives*, II, 4th ser., 782, 425. Force.
[2] *Siege of Boston*, 85. Frothingham.
[3] *Mass. His. Soc. Pro.*, April, 1858.

Make for Dublin, or any other good port in Ireland, and from thence cross to Scotland or England, and hasten to London. This direction is given that so you may escape all cruisers that may be in the chops of the Channel. . . . You are to keep this order a profound secret from every person on earth.

The London press refers so vaguely to the port made by Derby's ship one might almost suppose it was designedly left in question. The *Gazetteer and New Daily Advertiser,* dated London, Tuesday, May 30th, observes:

Sunday night about 9 o'clock Captain Danby of the ——, from New York, arrived express from Southampton, where he left his ship, and has brought papers, dated the 25th April last, which mention an engagement having happened on the 19th of the month.

The account which follows is amusing enough to give somewhat fully.

. . . The following is the substance of the account of the above mentioned affair which is handed about at Lloyd's and Garraway's. General Gage having heard that the insurgents were drawing some cannon a few miles from Boston, he dispatched an officer, with some troops to demand them to be delivered up, which the insurgents refused to comply with. — A second message was sent, when the officer informed them, that he must obey his orders, which were, in case of refusal that he must fire on those that surrounded them, but which he hoped they would prevent, by immediately relinquishing them. This they absolutely refused to do; on which the troops fired on them, and killed about sixty. On this the Country arose, and assisted the insurgents, to load the cannon, and they were directly fired upon by General Gage's troops, which did great execution, near an hundred being killed, and sixty wounded. The noise of the cannon alarmed General Gage, who immediately sent Lord Percy with a larger party of troops, to enquire into the matter. When his Lordship came to the place, he heard the Officer's account of the dispute, and then returned back with the troops to General Gage's intrenchments, as he did not find any authority he had to proceed further in it.

The London *Chronicle* [1] under the heading, "May 30, Portsmouth," has this reference,

This afternoon a vessel from the Isle of Wight arrived here, the Captain says that a vessel lay at the back of the above island, which came with dispatches from General Gage, which they had put on shore that morning, and that she should lie there two or three days before she came up to Spithead; for what reason was not mentioned, nor was anything to be got from the people relating to the affairs at Boston.

The same paper states,

Thursday, June 1st, Yesterday evening a messenger arrived express from Gen. Gage to the Earl of Dartmouth, at his house in Charles Street, S. James' Square; his Lordship was at his country house at Blackheath, and the express was immediately dispatched to him; on the receipt of which his Lordship went from Blackheath to His Majesty at Kew.

These despatches are rumored elsewhere in the paper to have been "brought by a ship arrived at Bristol" from the Colonies.

A later number of the *Chronicle* [1] has such an absurd version of the affair that at the risk of making tedious repetition it is given as published:

To the Printer, Sir,

A gentleman who was at Bristol when the news arrived there of the engagement in America, writes to his friend in the following manner: "A battle has been fought in

---

[1] *London Chronicle*, May 30–June 1, June 10–13.

the Massachusetts Bay, in which (dreadful prognostic to our tyrannic ministers) General Gage's forces have been worsted."

Upon the 20th of April a provincial congress was held at Concord; General Gage sent a brigade of one thousand men to interrupt the Meeting: they surrounded the Court House, and demanded the dispersion of the deputies; which, not being complied with, they pulled down the whole building. The same day a Company, consisting of seventy of the provincial militia being at exercise, a detachment of regulars demanded of them to resign their arms; and upon their not doing so, they fired on them, and killed five. The next day a party of four thousand provincials assembled, and marched against the regulars to revenge the death of their countrymen, to assert the honour of their congressional deputies, and to convince the whole World, that Britons who traverse the Atlantic, change the climate, not their hearts. Gage's troops posted themselves on an eminence, where they were immediately attacked etc. etc. . . . You may rely on every article contained in the preceding letter being an absolute fact.

RALEIGH.

From the contemporary newspapers we learn that stocks [1] fell 1½ per cent. on receipt of the bad news that the Colony was actively in revolt. *Lloyd's Evening Post* of May 31st prints the fullest account, giving the Essex *Gazette's* narrative entire; Dr. Joseph Warren's letter to the inhabitants of Great Britain and T. Palmer's letter written "near 10 of the clock" April 19th, at Watertown; besides the depositions. The account was premised, "We are desired by authority to request that the publick would suspend their judgement upon that event until they can be more authentically informed of the particulars."

To quiet rumors the following notice had already been issued from the Secretary of State's office, Whitehall, under date of May 30th:

---

[1] *London Chronicle*, May 30, 1775.

A report having been spread, and an account having been printed and published, of a skirmish between some of the detachment of His Majesty's troops, it is proper to inform the public, that no advices have as yet been received in the American Department of any such event. There is reason to believe that there are despatches from Gen. Gage on board the *Sukey*, Captain Brown, which, though she sailed four days before the vessel that brought the printed accounts, is not yet arrived.

A private correspondent acutely replies [1] to this:

If the people in power did not know the truth of the American accounts, how came they to know that the *Sukey*, Captain Brown, sailed four days before the vessel that brought the printed account. What bird of passage brought this intelligence?

Officially it met the following response [2] on the same day from Arthur Lee, agent for the House of Representatives in Massachusetts:

To the Public, Tuesday, May 30.

As a doubt of the authenticity of the account from Salem touching an engagement between the King's troops and the provincials, in the Massachusetts Bay, may arise from a paragraph in the *Gazette* of this evening, I desire to inform all those who wish to see the original affidavits which confirm that account, that they are deposited at the Mansion House, with the right hon. the Lord Mayor, for their inspection.

An original set of these memorable depositions has since been given by the younger R. H. Lee [3] to Harvard University and the University of Virginia.

May 31st the following paragraph appeared: [4] "This

---

[1] *London Chronicle and London Advertiser*, June 2, 1775.

[2] *London Chronicle*, June 1.

[3] *Readers' Handbook of the American Revolution*, 27. Justin Winsor.

[4] *Lloyd's Evening Post.*

morning the Right Hon. the Earl of Dartmouth had a levée at his house in Charles Street, St. James' Square, at which a number of American agents and merchants attended." [*i.e.* No. 1, occupied by Wm. Legge, second Earl of Dartmouth. Now the West End branch of the London and Westminster Bank.[1]] The same day [2] "His Majesty came to Town, and there was a full levée at St. James'. The ministers staid after the levée broke up, and a Cabinet Council was held, said to be on the very extraordinary and unwelcome news from America. The Spanish Ambassador and indeed every Foreign minister in town was present at the levée."

Another bit of gossip that leaked out was to the effect: [2]

As soon as the news, or rather report, of the Provincial troops investing Boston reached the Premier's ears, notwithstanding he knew there was no foundation for such a report, 'tis said he immediately sent for Governor Hutchinson to consult with him on the matter, and to know his opinion, what would be the best measure to take if such an event should happen; but the Governor proved that such a thing was almost impossible to be effected by the Provincials. Certain it is that few men are better informed of proceedings in America or know better what the Provincials are capable of doing than the Governor.

A London letter received in New York bearing date June 1st gives a vivid, contemporary account: [3]

On the arrival of the news of the defeat and retreat of the detachments under Lord Percy and Col. Smith, this great City was agitated to its centre. . . . Runners were sent to every part of the City, who were authorized to deny the authenticity of the facts; and so distressed was Government, that they officially requested a suspension of belief, until despatches were received from Gen. Gage. . . . The King,

---

[1] *History of St. James' Square*, 223. Dasent.

[2] *Morning Chronicle*, June 1, 6.

[3] *American Archives*, II, 4th ser., 870. Force.

after having heard the news read, asked what mode should be pursued to support the dignity of the Nation. . . . Lord North replied, that there were 30,000 Troops in Quebeck and Canada, ready to march to Boston for Gen. Gage's relief, that more men of war should be sent out, and that the Admiral should have positive orders to seize provision vessels. . . .

To facilitate this accursed plan, the Gen. is to assure the officers of the King's determination to promote them; and to stimulate the soldiers to acts of butchery, their pay is to be increased, to which purpose £50,000 were sent off last night to Boston. The General has positive orders to destroy the Magazines, to spike the cannon, to order the riot act to be read, and to set up the King's Standard immediately. . . . This evening some of the principal Common Councilmen meet, to revive and effectually equip the Military of London, which consists of 8,000 men, in order to co-operate with the Americans in forcing a relinquishment of the present infernal politicks, and in supporting constitutional liberty throughout the British Dominions.

Another London letter sent to Philadelphia on the 4th of June has the following: [1]

. . . friends are daily added to the American Cause. Even Hutchinson is become a convert. I hope he will live to make amends for all the harsh things he has said and wrote against America. . . . One avenue, indeed, seems to have been unguarded by Congress, through which they may attempt to break the Association with impunity, and that is by importing goods and manufactures from the Island of Guernsey, where large quantities of goods, suitable to the American consumption have been landed . . . be watchful and circumspect of all arrivals from that quarter.

A correspondent in the *Evening Post* says: [2]

Though the Ministry effects to put a negative on the

---

[1] *American Archives*, II, 4th ser., 903. Force.
[2] *Lloyd's Evening Post*, May 29–31.

advices from New England, it is evident they are not without their fears of the truth of what they call a Report only: and it is asserted, that a Noble Earl declared last week, in the Upper Assembly, that he did not doubt but the next accounts from Gen. Gage would be, of the Colonies being in actual rebellion.

Another wrote:[1]

The Friends of Government are very busy in decrying the account just published of the Skirmish between the King's Troops and the Bostonians; but the list of killed and wounded are facts that they cannot get over: to swallow this hard morsel, they tell you, that the Americans killed the King's Troops by bush fighting, and firing at them from behind the houses and bushes as they marched along. As the second General Congress was to meet in the beginning of May, at Philadelphia, the late defeat, or rather retreat of our Forces, will not fail to strengthen their Resolutions; though we hope notwithstanding things have been carried to great lengths, some favorable Circumstance will start up to prevent the further effusion of blood.

The correspondent cited above reckoned without his host in proclaiming Governor Hutchinson a "convert," as his diary and letters at this time abundantly testify. "May 29" he records:[2]

Cap.ⁿ Darby came to town last evening. . . . The Opposition here rejoice that the Americans fight, after it had been generally said they would not. The conduct of the Boston leaders is much the same as it was after the inhabitˢ were killed the 5 March 1770. They hurry away a vessel that their partial accounts may make the first impression. I think Gage's will be different. . . . I am greatly anxious for my family and friends. I carried the news to Lord Dartmouth, who was much struck with

---

[1] *Lloyd's Evening Post*, May 29–31. [2] *Diary*.

it. The first accounts were very unfavorable, it not being known that they all came from one side. The alarm abated before night, and we wait with a greater degree of calmness for the accounts from the other side. General Harvey called to inquire: Lord Gage: Sr. Sampson Gideon, &c. . . . Hancock, the Adamses, Cushing and Paine, set out for Philad. the day after the Action.

The Governor, in writing to his son, Thomas, speaks thus: [1]

LONDON, St. James's Street, 31 May, 1775.

MY DEAR SON, — Cap. Darby, in ballast, arrived at Southampton from Marblehead the 27th, and came to London the next evening. I am greatly distressed for you. Darby's own accounts confirm many material parts of the narrative from the Congress, and they that know him say he deserves credit, and that he has a good character: but I think these people would not have been at the expense of a vessel from Marblehead or Salem to England for the sake of telling the truth. I am sometimes inclined to wish myself with you, rather than to be at this distance in a state of uncertainty concerning you. Government waits impatiently for the arrival of Brown, who is said to have the despatches from the General. I have secret hopes that they will be more auspicious. I pray God to keep you in safety, and am your Affectionate Father.

On the same day, to General Gage he writes:

The arrival of Capt. Darby from Salem . . . has caused a general anxiety in the minds of all who wish the happiness of Britain and her Colonies. I have known the former interesting events have been partially represented; I therefore believe with discretion the representation now received. It is unfortunate to have the first impression made from that quarter. I am informed that this manoeuvre was conducted so privately that the ship's crew

[1] *Diary*, I, 456.

did not know they were bound to England until they were on the Newfoundland Banks. . . . Ministry is profoundly silent, and will be till they hear from you.

May 31,[1] A report in the morning that Gage's dispatches were arrived — but ill founded. Lord D. desired to see me, but had nothing particular. He read me a card from Ld. N., which says the beginning of action in America was rather inauspicious; but hopes the account in the *Mass' Gazette* was exaggerated. There appeared a degree of that apathy which I think Lord N. has a great deal of. . . . Pownall has a scheme of putting Connecticut and Rhode Island into Gage's commission. Extending that authority would not add to the power. I called upon Gen. Harvey, where I found Grant and Dalrymple. Harvey swore, and reproached them — chiefly Dalrymple, because he wanted more forces — with this expression, 'How often have I heard you American Colonels boast that with four batallions you would march through America; and now you think Gage with 3000 men and 40 pieces of cannon, mayn't venture out of Boston!' He was much heated in talking of the last advices from Boston. Grant asked if the Americans were not in rebellion, and whether notice ought not to be taken of a man sent over in a vessel on purpose to bring and publish papers giving an account of, and vindicating their rebellious doings?

June 3,[1] Went into the city to Mr Lane's Counting House. Found that Capt. Darby had not been seen since the first instant, that he had a Letter of Credit from Lane ["Lane & Fraser were for several generations the London Correspondents of the Derby [2] family] on some House in Spain. Afterwards I saw Mr Pownall at Lord D's office . . . [who] was of opinion Darby was gone to Spain to purchase ammunition, arms, &c. Vessels are arrived at

---

[1] *Diary*, I, 460–1, 463–5.
[2] "The Cruise of the Quero." Robert S. Rantoul. *Century Magazine*, September, 1899.

GOVERNOR HUTCHINSON

Bristol which met with other vessels on their passage, and received as news, that there had been a battle, but could tell no particulars. . . . It is said that Darby left his lodgings the 1st instant, and is supposed to have sailed. Mr. Pownall sent to Southampton to inquire, and the Collector knew of no such vessel there. It is supposed he left [it] in some small harbour or inlet, and came in his boat to Southampton. Many people began to complain of the publication, and wondered he had not been taken up and examined. . . . He has said to some, that he had a vessel gone or going to Spain with a cargo of fish: to others, that he was going for a load of mules. . . .

The E[ast] wind still continues and our anxiety with it. I hear Junius Americanus (Lee), who received the dispatches from the Congress, says we shall soon see Genl. Gage in England.

June 6, I called upon Mr. Fraser, but could get no further intelligence, he assuring me he had no letter by Darby. Mr. Blackburne tells me betts of 100 guineas are offered in the Coffee House, that I have letters and conceal them. . . . An airing towards Blackheath: the roads full of holiday people: Whit Tuesday.

London then had no daily papers, but several small sheets were issued bi-weekly. Such as they were they now teemed with allusions to the situation, some jesting, others aiming to be helpful.

Lloyd's Evening Post, June 5–7, gives one of the latter, as follows:

A correspondent requests me to say, that some Gentlemen, by confounding or putting together two things, totally distinct and unconnected, seem to try to invalidate the whole, throwing out at the same time the most illiberal insinuations against respectable characters, and affecting to doubt what every man of humanity to be sure wishes to disbelieve. — The printed anonymous account of the action in the Salem paper, is no way authenticated, and therefore deserves no more credit than other nameless, imperfect publications, any further than it agrees with the authenticated accounts, and the reason of things; but the Affidavits and Address from the Provincial Congress, signed by Dr. Warren, (by which is meant the Authenticated Accounts) are not to be called in question, and contain of themselves a very plain, sufficient, consistent, and apparently impartial, but woeful account, so far as they go; all which will most assuredly be found to be true. — Captain Derby, who is no stranger here, but well known to many in London, besides the house of Messrs Lane, Son & Fraser, is a cool, sensible, impartial, moderate man, as every one acknowledges who has conversed with him, of unblemished character and independent circumstances, and those who know him would as soon believe his representations as they would Gen. Gage's, or any other persons of established character.

The *Morning Chronicle* continues in the same strain:

June 9, The emissaries and tools of administration are busy in representing the news of an engagement in America as a mere fiction. In order to carry on their falsification with more efficacy, they do not stick to say, that Capt. Derby has absolutely absented himself, as if conscious of having deceived the public, when it is well known that he daily frequents the Boston or New England Coffee House behind the Exchange. But what shall we say to Mr Lee, the agent of Massachusetts Bay, who communicated the advice? He is responsible to his employers, and to the public for his Conduct. And further, what must we think of the Lord Mayor of London [Wilkes] who admitted the affidavits relating to the melancholly affair into his office, as authentic records or verifications of it? No Lord Mayor of common abilities would, without sufficient grounds, take notice of such oaths, a man of Wilkes' superior understanding cannot be supposed to become the dupe of false and forged intelligence.

Again we have an instance of Captain Derby's wariness in Lloyd's[1] next issue, June 7th–9th.

We are told that Mr. Secretary Pownall waited upon Capt. Darby, and desired him to attend Lord Dartmouth, which he refused to do without an official letter, signifying his Lordship's request, and for what purpose, assigning as a reason for this caution: That he had heard of instances, where, after having pumped every article of intelligence from persons in similar circumstances with himself, facts had been grossly misrepresented, and a very improper use made of the information: he was determined therefore to have some authority for what he did, to justify himself to his Countrymen in America, from any imputation that might be thrown on him hereafter, when the Ministry had made all the use of him they could.

The two following letters bear on this circumstance. The first is from Governor Trumbull[2] of Connecticut to General Schuyler:

LEBANON, July 24, [1775]
. . . Captain Derby, who went to England with the Provincial account of the Lexington fight, is returned. He informed he had twenty-seven days passage; tarried eight days in England, and when he came away, Gen. Gage's express, which sailed four days before him, had not arrived. Our friends published the account of the fight; Lord North was thunderstruck with the news, the people uneasy, the merchants distressed for their property in America, the stocks fell, and every thing in a ferment when he came away. The Administration published that they had not received any accounts from Boston; that they did not believe the story; were sure the New Yorkers would fall off, and thereby the Union of the Colonies be broken and the opposition be at an end.   What turn matters will take when Gen. G.'s account arrives, is uncertain.   Capt. Derby's Schooner never

---

[1] *Lloyd's Evening Post and British Chronicle.*
[2] *American Archives*, II, 4th ser., 1722.   Force.

went into port, but plied on and off while he tarried. He never appeared in publick, kept with our friends, the Lord Mayor, Dr. Lee &c. Lord Dartmouth sent for him, but our friends advised him not to put himself in their power.

The next [1] is an extract from a letter to a Philadelphia gentleman, dated:

WATERTOWN, July 20.

Captain Derby, who went to England with the account of the battle of the 19th of April, returned two days ago. He was there eight, and came away before Gen. Gage's packet arrived. He says trade and stocks were amazingly affected in that short time. Lord Dartmouth sent for him three times, but he refused to go; and when he threatened him, he decamped, got on board, and came off without clearing or entering.

After he had sailed, the *Morning Chronicle*, on "very respectable authority," affirms that Captain Derby had "no sooner unloaded his vessel than he set sail for Bilboa, in order to take in arms, ammunition, &c for the use of the Provinces." Captain Derby's ship is described in *Lloyd's* [2] as a small, schooner-rigged vessel of about sixty tons and quite light [the *Quero*, in point of fact, was sixty-two tons' burden [3] while the *Sukey* was about 200 tons, and "heavily loaded to a capital house in the Boston trade." A correspondent in the *Chronicle* [4] further suggests, it is absurd to blame Administration because Captain Brown's packet is delayed. Though he sailed before Captain Derby, bad weather during those first four days might oblige him to put into some port for repairs, and all advantage in the start be lost. On the 7th of June the Constitutional Society of London met at the King's Arms Tavern, [5] Cornhill, when a subscription of £100 was collected

---

[1] *American Archives*, II, 4th ser., 1695. Force.

[2] *Lloyd's Evening Post and British Chronicle*, June 2–5.

[3] "The Cruise of the Quero." Robert S. Rantoul. *Century Magazine*, September, 1899.

[4] *London Chronicle*, May 30–June 1.

[5] *Mass. His. Soc. Pro.*, April, 1858.

"for the widows, orphans, and aged parents of our beloved fellow subjects faithful to the character of Englishmen."[1]

This fund was ultimately paid over by Mr. Horne through Messrs. Brownes[2] and Collison to Dr. Franklin's account, and the 25th of October following, a committee was appointed[2] to make distribution and report; the members being the Hon. Mr. Whitcomb, Mr. Prescott, Mr. Holten, Mr. White, Major Hawley, Mr. Devens, Colonel Barrett, and Mr. Stone, of Lexington; the last four being added later. It is probably through this source that Mrs. Jason Russell of Menotomy received the Bible already referred to. For publishing[1] particulars relating to this popular subscription the Rev. John Horne, better known as Horne-Tooke, was indicted for seditious libel and July 4th, 1777, brought to trial before Lord Mansfield.

Many Englishmen sympathized with the colonists. It is said that the father of Rogers, the poet, sorrowfully announced what had taken place at morning prayers. He felt so keenly about it, indeed, he put on mourning, and, when asked if he had lost a friend, or relative, replied[3] sadly, "Yes, many friends, many brethren at one blow in Lexington and Concord in America."

The *Morning Chronicle* of June 10th has these lines:

> Receive, oh consecrated strand,
> The ashes of a patriot band;
> And oh record, with noble pride,
> The gen'rous claim for which they died!
>
> When stern oppression hov'ring o'er,
> Had burst in thunder on their shore;
> They dar'd to meet the Monster's force,
> And check'd its rage, and stop'd its course.
>
> On the bleak Hellespontic plain,
> Let Sparta boast her warriors slain;
> For rights invaded, native laws,
> These deaths were equal, and their cause.

[1] *Lexington Centennial*, 61.

[2] *American Archives*, II, 4th ser., 921; III, 4th ser., 1476. Force.

[3] *Union Celebration at Concord, 1850*, 106, and *Mass. His. Soc. Pro.*, January, 1869.

Mark, Goddess, mark this chosen band!
First victims to thy dread command;
And bid thy deathless laurel bloom,
To consecrate their humble tomb.

If blood must flow — behold our veins!
Joyful we pour it o'er the plains,
Nor other pray'rs shall pierce the sky,
Than when we fall like *these*, to die!

Walpole [1] thus deplored the rupture in a letter to Sir Horace Mann, dated:

STRAWBERRY HILL, June 5, 1775.

. . . You must lower your royal crest a little, for your Majesty's forces have received a check in America; but this is too sad a subject for mirth. I cannot tell you anything very positively: the ministers, nay, the orthodox *Gazette*, holds its tongue. This day se'nnight it was divulged by a London *Evening Post* extraordinary, that a ship on its way to Lisbon happened to call *at* England, and left some very wonderful accounts, nay, and affidavits, saying, to wit, that General Gage had sent nine hundred men to nail up the cannon and seize a magazine at Concord; of which the accidental captain owns, two cannon were spiked or damaged. An hundred and fifty Americans, who swear they were fired on first, disliked the proceeding, returned blows, and drove back the party. Lord Percy was dispatched to support them, but new recruits arriving, his Lordship sent for better advice, which he received, as it was, to retire, which he did. The King's troops lost an hundred and fifty, the enemy not an hundred. The captain was sent for to be examined, but refused. He says, Gage sent away a sloop four days before he sailed, which sloop, I suppose, is gone to Lisbon, for in eight days we have no news of it. The public were desired by authority to suspend their belief; but their patience is out, and they persist in believing the first account, which seems the rather probable, in that another account is come of the mob having risen at New York, between anger and triumph, and

[1] *Letters*, IX, 203–5. Ed. Toynbee.

THE HON. HORACE WALPOLE

have seized, unloaded, and destroyed the cargoes of two
ships that were going with supplies to Gage; and, by all
accounts, that whole continent is in a flame.

So here is this fatal war commenced!

> The child that is unborn shall rue
> The hunting of that day!

. . . Those gentlemen do not seem to be at all afraid of
your question, whether they could not be sent for over, and
tried. A colonel of their militia has sworn before a justice of
peace that he ordered his men to fire on the King's troops,
and has sent over a copy of his affidavit — perhaps in
hope of being knighted.

Well, we don't mind all this — we the nation. We go
on diverting ourselves, and are to have a regatta on the
Thames the end of this month.

Somewhat later he writes[1] the same friend:

I am what I always was, a zealot for liberty in
every part of the globe, and consequently I most heartily
wish success to the Americans. They have hitherto not
made *one* blunder; and the administration have made a
thousand, besides the two capital ones, of first provoking,
and then of uniting the colonies. The latter seem to have
as good heads as hearts, as we want both.

The historian Gibbon [2] makes this allusion in a letter
to his connection, Mr., afterward Lord Eliot, who had helped
him to his seat in Parliament:

DEAR SIR, I am happy to hear from various quarters
that you have at length reached Bath in good health,
spirits, and a disposition to take the amusements which the
law of Moses may prescribe to you. John, I am sure,
William, I hope, are happy and well, but I hear that Mrs.
Eliot already begins to turn her eyes toward Cornwall.
With regard to yourself I must beg the favour of a line to

---

[1] *Letters*, IX, 244. Ed. Toynbee.

[2] *Magazine of American History*, May, 1883.

inform me of your intended motions. If you do not mean to proceed further westward, I will certainly contrive to run down to Bath for a week rather than miss the opportunity; but if inclination or business leads you to the capital, my literary engagements will persuade me to defer till the autumn my arrears visit to Mrs Gibbon, and to content myself for the present with saluting my rustic cousin from a distance.

You have seen by the papers the unpleasant news from America; unpleasant, as a single drop of blood may be considered as the signal of Civil War. For otherwise it was not an engagement, much less a defeat. The King's troops were ordered to destroy a magazine at Concord. They marched, did their business and returned, but they were frequently fired at from behind stone walls, and from the windows in the villages. It was to those houses that they were obliged to set fire. Ensign Gould (of North-amptonshire) had been left with twelve men to guard a bridge, and was taken prisoner. The next day the Provincial Congress sent a vessel without her freight express to England: no letters were put on board but their own, nor did the crew know their destination till they were on the banks of Newfoundland, so that Government has not any authentic account. The master says that the day after the engagement, the country rose, and that he left Boston invested by 1500 tents with cannon, and under the command of Col. Ward, who was at the head of a Provincial Regiment in the last war; but unless Fanatacism gets the better of self-preservation, they must soon disperse, as it is the season for sowing the Indian Corn, the chief subsistance of New England. Such at least is the opinion of Governor Hutchinson, from whom I have these particulars.

I am, Dear Sir,

most sincerely yours,

E. GIBBON.

LONDON, May the 31st, 1775.

CHAPTER IX

ENGLISH PRESS COMMENTS. EXCHANGE OF PRISONERS. GAGE'S PROCLAMATION. EVE OF OPEN HOSTILITIES

SOON after the first published account one paper,[1] in utter darkness as to the character of the New Englanders, observed:

In order to soften the obduracy, and conciliate the affections of some Leaders among the Americans, we are informed that services of plate, to a considerable amount, have been some time preparing, which are to be distributed at proper opportunities.

Elsewhere one reads:[2]

The Americans certainly are not such worthless people as they have been represented to be; if they were, would G—t offer £500 a head for a number of them. No, surely; the worth of a thing is the price it brings; consequently the Americans must be a very valuable set of people etc., etc.

Another[3] doubts "the facility of reducing the Colonies by military force," and exclaims, "Heaven forbid that the bravery of such troops as the English should be so vainly, so fatally employed."

A controversy was carried on through several numbers over the part taken by Justice Gardner, of Brookline, who was killed, it will be remembered, at Watson's Corner, during the retreat. The zeal of his friends, as well as of his enemies, was so far in excess of their knowledge, the

[1] *Lloyd's Evening Post*, May 29–31.
[2] *Morning Chronicle*, June 1, 1775.
[3] *London Chronicle*, May 30–June 1.

337

dispute is still entertaining. On May 31st the *Morning Chronicle and London Advertiser* opened the fray as follows:

A Correspondent observes, that it would well become some of our *very forward* patriots to make an enquiry how far Gen. G—e's commission extended, and whether he had any orders from His M— to shed the precious blood of those whose only crime was, that of practising the art of self defense.

Ye Oliviers, ye Gilberts, beware! throw down your foils and retreat! rebels as ye are, nor dare once more to teach our young nobility the art *militare,* lest ye and they share the fate of Col. Isaac Gardner and the brave Americans.

The *Gazetteer and New Daily Advertiser* of June 1st would not suffer Mr. Gardner to pass as a martyr or hero. This was a Tory paper and "Politicus" took up the cudgels for Government, sparing none with patriot sympathies. His retort began:

If rebels attack the King's troops, the soldiers will really be so brutal as to kill them if they can.   The idiotism of the American rebels equals their madness.   They have given a list of their wounded, which will unavoidably consign them to the gallows whenever they are taken.   A very true idea may be formed of many of the New England Justices of the Peace, from the case of Mr Gardner of Brookline, who was killed fighting against his Sovereign.

"Politicus" then continues in reference to Dr. Benjamin Franklin:

That he has embarked for America is for him a fortunate circumstance, as by this time he would most probably have been lodged in Newgate. In the days of our glorious Queen Elizabeth, an early exit at Tyburn would have smothered all his execrable plots in embryo. . . . I am surprised that the moment the news arrived . . . that the other two Massachusetts agents were not immediately taken into custody. . . . If the two Adams', Hancock, Cushing, Cooper, the Boston Town Clerk, his brother, the parson, the Drs. Church and Warren and a few more of the ring-leaders were attainted, and their estates confiscated, it would have as good an effect towards extinguishing the rebellion as many victories.

The *Morning Chronicle and London Advertiser*, June 2, echoing the *Gazetteer* of the same date, "most fervently hopes, that the General Officers will immediately, on their arrival at Boston, adopt the principles of the late Duke of Cumberland, [Billy, the Butcher, victor at Culloden] which, with a few of the Prime Rebel Heads grinning over that execrable Temple of Discord and Sedition, the notorious Faneuil Hall, will have an admirable effect in again reducing those worst kind of traitors to Reason."

Another evening paper says:

There is no doubt Gen. G. has orders to seize some of the principal people of Boston, and send them here to be tried; and there is no doubt, if he does, but they will be tried by a jury of Middlesex Justices, under the auspices of Lord Mansfield. After what these juries have done, in the case of Wilkes, Almon, &c. &c. there can be no doubt they will find the Bostonians guilty.

To return to "Politicus," in the *Gazetteer* of June 9th, he falls on an objector in this wise:

The paragraph-maker in the *Ledger*, who ventured yesterday to make his remarks on the letter signed Politicus must be the most foolish, or the most impudent of mankind. . . . This paragraph-maker and bull maker seems to have but a *Potato head*, for he says also that the whole country rose in arms against the King's troops, and yet adds immediately after, that Isaac Gardner, the Justice of Peace, was killed when he was peaceably riding along the road. One of these declarations must be false. If the whole country rose, I. G. was amongst the rebels; if I. G. was riding peaceably along, then the whole country did not rise.

This poser brought a lull in the controversy until Gage's report came to hand, when Politicus enthusiastically embraced all the mistakes.

This account, he writes[1] triumphantly, "dated the 24th April says, that I. G. took nine prisoners, that twelve soldiers deserted to him, and that his ambush proved fatal to Lord Percy and another General Officer, who were killed the first fire.   Mr Potato Head must therefore be, to use one of his *own* polite epithets 'a most audacious scoundrel' to impose the *fictions* of his own sodden Head upon the Public for authentic intelligence from America.

Several other anonymous correspondents wrote for the *Gazetteer;* "The Taylor of Tottenham Court," as he styled himself, offering the following couplet:[2]

> Riots or skirmishes like these
> Must not be nick-named, massacres.

After the headline:[3]

BOSTON INVESTED BY THE PROVINCIAL REBELS.

was printed:

> "Ah! Ah! Ah!"

Another most abusive correspondent calls himself sarcastically "A Boston Saint."   In the *Gazetteer and New Daily Advertiser*, June 2d, he expresses a belief that the affidavits were made by false witnesses, and distrusts the stories of cruelties inflicted on the wounded by the Regulars, saying justly:

"The common people of England have been ever renowned for their humanity," and adds that "the French and Spaniards, our bitterest enemies, yet speak with the most grateful admiration of the humanity of our troops, . . . the compassionate behaviour of our officers and soldiers to the wounded and prisoners of the enemy,

---

[1] *The Gazetteer and New Daily Advertiser*, July 4.   [2] June 6.
[3] *Morning Chronicle*, June 5.

has tended more to render the character of the English nation respectable and revered, than even their intrepid valor in the day of battle.

He ends by casting slights upon the New England commanders.

Respecting Colonel Preble he says:

A scratch in the neck, received just thirty years ago, comprises the whole of his military experience. Indeed, old Jedidiah would be employed much more in character in the Eastern Country, in cutting down and shipping his lumber.

The valorous Col. Putnam too, it seems, is marching at the head of 6,000 Connecticut rebels to join the Saints mustered at Worcester. . . . The rarity of commanding may perhaps intoxicate him. However that may be, it would be much wiser in Israel, during the summer, to be a hay making at Pomfret.

Should the rebels really attempt to block up Boston Neck, a few 12 and 24 pounders would send some of them to the Devil, and the rest to the Woods, after a very few discharges.

The Villainy of the New England rebels does not stop merely at perjuring themselves; they have also *forced* the officer [Lt. Gould] and the few soldiers whom they overpowered, to put their names to the depositions ready drawn up for them; a species of the most infamous cruelty. This diabolical method of procuring false evidence, is a practise quite common in Massachusetts. Hundreds of the rebels have attacked single men on the highway, and by dint of blows, and every sort of barbarous treatment, obliged them to curse the King, Parliament, and Old England, and to sign papers which they were not even allowed to read. Col. [Israel] Williams, [of Hatfield] for refusing to join them, was lately shut up in a room, and almost smoked to death, till he consented to sign a paper, approving of their rebellious conduct; . . . When we have a full detail of the particulars of the late skirmish, we shall find that the rebels were soundly beaten. By information already arrived, it is certain that the engagement began at six miles from the rebels' magazine; that Col. Smith drove the rebels before him for these six miles, from Lexington to Concord, where he destroyed their magazine; that then, having executed his commission, he returned to Boston. Another fact that ought to be attended to, which is, that the rebels who began the attack were collected from a circle of forty miles round Boston; the ring leaders not being able to muster a sufficient number in any one district who would venture to fight. The rebels are in great consternation. A principal man amongst them has even absconded, and circulated an account of his own death. Captain Brown may be hourly expected, as he sailed the 24th April. . . .

A BOSTON SAINT.

The *Morning Chronicle* of this date alludes to the attack on the convoy, as headed by the Rev. Mr. Payson, "a dissenting clergyman." Upon which the *Gazeteer and New Daily Advertiser* [1] comments:

In the beginning of the last Civil War, a *Parson preached* and fought, who came from America; in this now begun, a *Parson hath preached and fought* also in America. The initial letters of both Parsons is P. — Parson [Hugh] *Peters*, [of Salem] and Parson Payson. I am not superstitious, but whenever a *priest* or a *woman* is concerned, there is always much mischief in the wind. Parson Peters lived to see the end of the rebellion, and [at the Restoration] was hanged at Tyburn with several Old England Saints; Parson Payson, it is hoped, will be speedily taken and brought over, and meet with the same deserved fate, at the beginning of the rebellion, with some of the New England Saints.

June 2d, It was reported that ships had arrived bringing "news of a more pleasing nature than was expected, on which stocks rose $\frac{1}{2}$ per cent." The same day John Staples

wrote from Stepney Green to the *Chronicle*[1] complaining
of the non-appearance of an original letter from Salem giving a different account of the rebels there from any that
had been published. "The Printer," runs his complaint,
"pretended he had lost the Letter, though I saw his Messenger put my Letter together with an Advertisement in
one and the same Pocket; and the Advertisement appeared.
This week I sent the same Paper an account" etc. etc.,
which it appeared had been likewise suppressed, all of which
made Staples feel that the paper had no title to the epi-
thet "Impartial." He concludes severely: "Yours as you
behave," and is promptly chaffed in the next *Chronicle* by
Veritas, who suggests he would be better employed on his
craft plying his trade of lighterman. "It is not at all
probable," writes another correspondent, in the *British
Chronicle*, June 5th–7th, "that the King's troops were
defeated as has been reported, and in Capitals published
in some of the papers; but it will doubtless be found that
they had thought it most prudent to retreat before night
came on, when they saw the whole country rising upon
them; and it is most likely that we shall hear the main
body, at least, retreated in tolerable good order, though
perhaps at first they or their detachments were a little
discomposed, as was very natural when they found, contrary
to the doctrine so industriously instilled into them all last
winter, that the Americans would fight, as it now pretty
fully appears they will.

"Of their veteran courage they gave a very sufficient specimen at Concord Bridge, where the principal Landholders
of the County, and some of the Clergy, boldly marched and
nobly faced the King's troops, who had taken possession
of that important pass to the great annoyance of his
Majesty's subjects; and here to the amazement of the
picked grenadiers stationed at the place, these cowards, as
they have been called, drew up in battle array within pistol
shot of the King's troops, and coolly waited their first fire,

[1] Quoted June 2–5 in *Lloyd's Evening Post.*

and then as calmly returned and continued it, till this detachment of two hundred men fled to the main body."

Another observes:[1]

If the Americans really vanquish the King's troops, they will be in as comical situation as the most sanguine Saint could wish for, viz. sheep who had not lost, but run their heads against, and killed their shepherd.

One can readily sympathize with the Hon. Mrs. Boscawen, writing to Mrs. Delany[2] at Colney Hatch from Glan Villa, June 5th:

MY GOOD MADAM, I feel so frequently a disposition of mind unlikely to amuse anybody, and especially those who so kindly wish me easy and happy, that I am (very properly) deterr'd from sitting down and giving a picture of it. Indeed, during the past week having had the favour of two letters from you, I should certainly have wrote — if my thoughts had not been at Boston, and alas! my cares also; I do not mean that I give credit to all these stories of the insurgents (and as yet we have no other), but — the sword is unsheath'd! and it cannot be but its *glare* must be painful in eyes as *sore* as mine.

FRANCES EVELYN GLANVILLE BOSCAWEN.

The 8th Hutchinson[3] writes:

[The] Wind changes today. . . . Lord Gage called, who professes to believe nothing that is unfavourable, but appears very anxious notwithstanding. . . . Campbell, who came from Newport to Liverpool, . . . examined by Mr Pownall. He sailed the 21st in the morning: heard the day before of an engagement between the troops and the inhabitants at Lexington, but knew no particulars. . . . The inhabitants of Newport were marching out to the assistance of Massachusetts.

---

[1] *Morning Chronicle*, June 9.
[2] *Life and Letters of Mary Granville* (Mrs. Delany).
[3] *Diary*, I, 465.

Conjecture had come to that stage that, as the *Morning Chronicle* of the 9th remarked, "It seems we can have no solid political satisfaction till the arrival of the desirable *Sukey* is announced."

Upon which it breaks forth in verse:

> Ye gentle gales that swell the sails,
> Where Sukey ploughs the briney main;
> Oh! bring her quick, (ere patience fails)
> To ease perplexing doubt and pain.

Lloyd's Evening Post, 9–12 June, brought relief to many by announcing that the vessel so long waited for had arrived off Portland. Later [1] she was "booked at Lloyds to have arrived at Dover," and on Saturday morning, June 10th, the despatches were brought by Lieutenant Nunn, R. N., to Lord Dartmouth's office. On their arrival there they were immediately forwarded by hand to His Majesty at Kew, and at the same time notices [2] were sent to Lord North, Lord Gower, and the Secretary of State, several of whom set off at once for Kew, where a Conference was held "on the subject of them." The publication of the *Gazette* [3] was delayed nearly to midnight that it might include Gage's report.

By the same post Mr. Saul Wentworth,[3] agent for the Government of New Hampshire, received a letter from Boston "informing him, Lord Percy was unhurt, and that he had gained great honour in the skirmish; an extract of which letter was sent to Sion House, to the great joy of the Northumberland family." A letter from Lord Percy to his father is also reported as arriving at Northumberland House, with an account which was said not to differ materially from the published narrative.

These were busy days in the Northumberland household, for on Thursday, June 8th, the Right Hon. Lord Algernon Percy, second son of his Grace the Duke of Northumber-

---

[1] *London Chronicle*, June 10–13.

[2] *Lloyd's Evening Post*, June 9–12.

[3] *Morning Chronicle and London Advertiser*, June 12.

land, had been married [1] to Miss Burrell, daughter of Peter Burrell, Esq., of Beckenham in Kent; the ceremony being performed by the Rev. Dr. Percy, Chaplain to his Grace. Great had been the rejoicings in the Market Square of Warkworth.[2] Ale and punch were drunk and the bells rung. Among the toasts were "Their worthy Member, Lord Algernon and his Lady;" "Earl Percy;" "A speedy reconciliation with the Americans;" etc., etc. When the official account, dated from Whitehall, appeared, the newspapers made merry. One paragraph reads: [3]

> "The mountain's delivered at last!
> Here's the *Gazette*, here boys, here;

containing all the right, true, and particular account of the apprehending, seizing, taking, burning, and destroying a great number of gun carriages, cart wheels, powder barrels, flower tubs &c at Concord in America, by a detachment of heroes from Gen. Gage's army; after which they retreated with all possible expedition back to Boston."

A squib ran,[3] "'Tis droll enough, says a correspondent, that the M—l Miss Sukey (for whose long expected arrival there has been such a fuss about) should at last *turn out a nun;* which proves that her lover the Premier, is popishly affected. "The *Morning Chronicle* opens June 15th with:

> Old News, Old News,
> buz, buz, Queen Ann's dead!
> Sukey! Sukey comes!

and brings an account of *what we have heard before.* The modern Zenophon's account of the late *retreat* of the regulars from Concord to Boston, is, without mincing the matter, (upon the whole) a most wretched relation. The detachment is sent to destroy the Provincial stores at Concord, in their way they are alarmed by the ringing of bells &c., and such is the panick, that two bridges are secured, to prevent any interruption; at Lexington, a few simple country

---

[1] *The Gazetteer and New Daily Advertiser,* June 13.

[2] *The London Chronicle,* June 24–27.

[3] *The Morning Chronicle and London Advertiser,* June 15, 17.

militia men exercising in a green close,[1] upon the regiment advancing (and enquiring the reason of their assembling, run off in the greatest confusion; after which, the victorious party vent their fury on the stores at Concord, whilst this service was performing, a great number of the rebels (so called) attack and drive the Light Infantry from the bridges. Now for the retreat: the troops are fired at from behind walls, ditches, trees, and other ambushes, but up comes the gallant Lord Percy quite to Lexington, with a couple of cannon, time enough, (O glorious achievement!) to run away with the former, and now again the Americans keep up a scattering fire from behind stone walls and houses, during a retreat of fifteen miles, the regulars never once facing about, as if their heroic ardor was quite exhausted on the inanimate objects of their vengeance at Concord. Lastly comes a queer kind of compliment on the Generalship of Lord Percy [*i.e.*, Gen. Gage says that "too much praise cannot be given to Lord Percy for his remarkable activity during the whole day"] a list of killed and wounded, and there's an end! ! !

"According to private letters from Boston," says one,[2] "the King's troops, had not more than three rounds of powder left, when they arrived at Gen. Gage's lines, from which it appears, that there was either a great neglect, or else they set out in a very peaceable disposition."

"Strictures" on the *Gazette's* account were published, in which occurs the following:[3] "The *Gazette* tells us that 'Gen. Gage detached in the night the Grenadiers and Light Infantry of his army to destroy some stores at Concord.' Everyone knows that this description comprehends the best and most active troops of the whole body. They have the advantage, too, of stealing a march upon the people. We might have

[1] *American Archives*, II, 4th ser., 946. Force. The account sent out from White Hall, June 10, states: the troops "found a body of the country people under arms on a green, close to the road," etc.

[2] *Lloyd's Evening Post*, June 9–12.

[3] *American Archives*, II, 4th ser., 948. Force.

expected some enterprise and exploit of moment and magnitude, equal to the preparation, the secrecy, and confidence of this expedition. But, alas, the trunnions of three old iron ordnance are the vast object of this mighty achievement. . . . We are left to conclude, from their continuing to annoy, kill, and wound the troops on their return (as it is generally termed) from Concord, that the Light Infantry were driven from their post and defeated. . . . But let us accompany the Army in its return, and we find them met by Lord Percy, at Lexington; with sixteen companies and the Marines, amounting in all to about twelve hundred men, with two pieces of cannon. We have now almost the whole army that was collected at Boston, under so active a leader as Lord Percy, with the assistance of Col. Smith and Major Pitcairn, 'doing everything' (so says the *Gazette*) 'that man could do,' and two pieces of cannon. We may now expect that not a man of the unheaded poltroon Provincials will be left alive, not quite so bad. The *Gazette* tells us dryly that 'the rebels were for awhile dispersed'. . . . If this was not a flight, and if Lord Percy's activity was not in running away, I should be glad to know," etc., etc., "yet I think, that when the military lend themselves to fight against the freedom of their fellow-subjects, they deserve to be both disgraced and defeated. . . . General Ward sent word to General Gage that his surgeons were at liberty to come into the Provincial camp and attend the wounded prisoners, if General Gage had more confidence in them than in the Provincial Surgeons.' The Public will hardly believe that so fair and generous an enemy could be guilty of barbarity and cruelty, because an unfair and ungenerous Ministry are their accusers."

To continue from Hutchinson: [1]

June 10th, A Lieutenant in the Navy arrived about noon at Ld. Dartmouth's office. Mr. Pownall gave me notice, knowing my anxiety: but though relieved from sus-

[1] *Diary*, I, 466-7.

pence, yet received but little comfort, from the accounts themselves being much the same with what Darby brought. The material difference is the declaration by Smith, who was the Commander of the first party, tho' not present at the first action,—that the inhabitants fired first: . . . I assured many gentlemen who would give no credit to Darby's account, that it would prove near the truth; and now they are more struck than if they had not been so sanguine before.

[Lord Gower, Jenkinson, and others he notes, seemed to be about ready to order a prosecution in connection with the hundred pounds collected by the Constitutional Society.]

11th, About six in the afternoon Mr. Taylor came in with my [1] letters . . . sent them to Lord Dartmouth at Blackheath.

12th, At . . . Board of Trade's Chamber. Saw the Advice of the Council of New York to the Lt. Gov. to write to Gage that if he continued his military operations, it would render vain any expectation of success to the conciliating plan which was received the day after they had the news of the skirmish in Lexington. Mr. Pownall tho't some extraordinary measures should be taken. Lord Dartmouth was for putting the most favorable construction upon it. I mentioned a Proclamation, with a general pardon to all who should return to their allegiance. Lord D. said he was for having it done long ago, but thought there should be some exceptions. Lord North has not been in town since the news. . . .

13th, . . . a letter Bliss received from Mr Putnam, from Boston, dated the 23d April [gives] a fuller account of the action than any other.

Tuesday, June 13th, Captain Lawrence of the *Earl of Dunmore* packet, arrived express from New York, leaving his ship at Portsmouth. He sailed May 8th and brought despatches for Government; and carried as passengers [2] "a

---

[1] *Diary*, I, 467. Hutchinson.
[2] *The Morning Post and Daily Advertiser*, June 16.

lady and six of her children obliged to come over on account of the confusion." One of the first of many Loyalist refugees to return to the Mother-land.

A few days later the *Chronicle* [1] has this suggestive item, "Lord North appeared at Ranelagh, with his hair about his ears, as if he had been frightened by the last American news." Frightened or otherwise, he continued stubborn and nothing was done to check the tide of events. One has but to read the letters of such men as Warren, and Dickinson, and Washington, and then turn to the contemporary London press to see that while many deplored, many jested over the course things were taking and few realized the nature of the men they were dealing with. That in effect the two countries were already parted, and the war to follow would but give outward expression to an inward fact. While the New Englanders still looked back with attachment to the land whence they had sprung; in leaving, they had passed out of the lives of the home race; and had come to be regarded by those in power as a source of revenue; and just now a vexatiously obstinate source, that must be taught reason.

On the 17th Hutchinson enters: [2] "Lord Hillsboro' . . . told me Ld. Suffolk, Ld. Rochfort, Gower, Sandwich and the Chancellor, with Lord North were all of one mind for a vigorous part: that Ld. Dartmouth was alone."

He continues:

19th, Walked after breakfast into the city to Mr. Blackburn's in Bush Lane, Cannon Street. He has been sanguine that the majority at New York would be in favor of Government, but now he says they will conform to the Congress at Philadelphia. Mr Gibbon called. He says many who were strong for the measures of Parliament, are much discouraged by the news from America, they having been made to believe there would be no action.

[1] *The Morning Chronicle and London Advertiser*, June 26.
[2] *Diary*, I, 471-2.

CONNOISSEUR

Tea Garden

I think, in general, he will be in Opposition: dropped something like Ld. Chatham's being a necessary man in such difficult cases. 22d . . . Mr Strahan,[1] stationer, and member of Parlt. an old friend of Franklin's, told me at Court, he [F.] went away in a most rancorous state of mind, declared he had rather have his health drank by the Congress than Lord High Treasurer of England.

Somewhat later Hutchinson mentions Mr. Keene's calling: "complains of Gage: says his wife has said she hoped her husband would never be the instrument of sacrificing the lives of her countrymen." Mrs. Gage, it will be remembered, was related to the New York[1] Van Courtlands.

The *Gazeteer and New Daily Advertiser* of June 21st makes one of the Cabinet Council say at their last meeting on American affairs, "I should be for withdrawing the troops, blocking up their ports, and leaving them to starve among themselves, in time, but that our merchants on this side would be losers of £2,000,000 in arrears."

The next letter of the Hon. Mrs. Boscawen to Mrs. Delany[2] begins anxiously under date of "Glan villa, June 23: O cruel *patriots* to rejoice in the blood of your countrymen, provided you can wade through it to the Treasury-bench. It is from *hence* those deluded wretches are encourag'd to ruin themselves and distress others. Heaven vouchsafe to help us!" We feel the relief with which she could close a few days later: "Wednesday — *Au reste* — I have had to-day by the post a letter from my poor dear boy at Boston; he assures me that he is in perfect health, and I thank God I shall be in perfect spirits tomorrow when I have such friends to visit me."

In her letter that follows, likewise to Mrs. Delany, allusion is made to Ensign Boscawen's description of the battle. It is much to be hoped that this may some day be found and made public.

[1] *Diary*, I, 475, 497 and note. Hutchinson.
[2] *Life and Letters of Mary Granville* (Mrs. Delany).

GLAN VILLA, July 5, '75.

As for me, I own to you, dear Madam, my mind is in a very uneasy state; I *cannot help* thinking of my poor dear only remaining boy, and I cannot think of him without *great agitation and anxiety!* Thank God we have heard from him again; I have had a letter from him, dated the 9th of May, and Mrs. Leverson one since, dated ye 13th, in which he gives her a very circumstantial account of the unfortunate skirmish, in which he lost an invaluable friend, Lieut. T. [Joseph[1]] Knight, an officer of his regi.t, who had taken a great kindness for him, and was (by all accounts) a person of extraordinary merit. My poor George laments him most pathetically; indeed his whole letter, wch freely expatiates (to his sister) upon many subjects, is a masterly performance, and nobody that read it would guess the age of the writer; yet to me the only very pleasant part is that in wch he tells her that the "climate seems to him better than that of England; one reason of which may be that he has never had an hour's illness since he has been in it." Indeed I should add that the expressions of duty and affection towards me, the care that he is under lest I should be uneasy at his situation, and the desire he expresses that his sister (whom he supposes at Plymouth) should spare me all the time she possibly can — all these are earnests of my future comfort in him, if it pleases God to spare him!

Before the campaign was over the lad's mother had a poem addressed to her by Mrs. Hannah More, entitled "Sensibility." It contains allusions to Sir Joshua Reynolds, Mrs. Barbauld, Garrick, and Dr. Johnson. Of Mrs. Boscawen she says:

> Or you, Boscawen, when you fondly melt
> In raptures none but mothers ever felt,
> And view, enamour'd in your beauteous race,
> All Leverson's sweetness, and all Beaufort's grace!
> Yet think what *dangers* each lov'd child may share,
> The youth if *valiant,* and the maid if *fair?*

It concludes with these lines:

[1] *The Evelyn Family in America.* Scull.

'Tis this, whose charms the soul resistless seize,
And gives Boscawen half her pow'r to please.
Yet, why those terrors? why that anxious care?
Since *your last hope* the dreadful war will dare?
Why dread that energy of soul which leads
To dang'rous glory by heroic deeds?
Why tremble lest this ardent soul aspire?
You *fear the son* because you *knew the sire.*
Hereditary valour you deplore,
And *dread,* yet *wish,* to find *one hero more!*

Through all this crisis the colonies found a firm friend in the city of London. At a meeting [1] of the Livery of London, in Common Hall assembled, on Saturday, the 24th of June, it was "Resolved that the Thanks of the Lord Mayor, Aldermen and Livery, in Common Hall assembled, be given to the Right Hon. the Earl of Effingham, for having, consistent with the Principles of a true Englishman, refused to draw that sword against the lives and liberties of his Fellow Subjects in America, which has hitherto been employed to the honour of his Country."

The 2d of July his acknowledgment was dated from The Holmes and addressed to William Rix, Esq., Town Clerk's Office, Guild Hall. Not content with privately voicing their approval of Lord Effingham, the Lord Mayor, Aldermen, and Livery of the city of London next proceeded to draw up a Remonstrance [2] deploring "the miserable predicament [His Majesty's Ministers] have brought this [Country] as well as America, into, by embroiling us in a Civil War;" and conclude, by beseeching His Majesty to dismiss such evil Counsellors forever from his presence. The London *Chronicle* [3] prints the Remonstrance entire and adds, "From which petition, Walter Humphries, Citizen and Fishmonger, dissented." The *Gazetteer and New Daily Advertiser,* [4] with the intention of casting a slight on the Opposition, declares that while sixty-six Common Coun-

---

[1] *Lloyd's Evening Post and British Chronicle,* June 21-4.
[2] *Morning Chronicle and London Advertiser,* June 26.
[3] July 4-6.
[4] July 11.

cilmen had been for the proposed Address to the King, no less than fifty-one had been against it.
However this may be, we find[1] on Friday, July 14th:

At noon, the Right Hon. the Lord Mayor, attended by six Aldermen, the two Sheriffs, City officers and fifty-eight of the Common Council, went in procession from Guild Hall to St. James', "to present their humble address and petition, relative to the unhappy dispute between Great Britain and her Colonies;" after its being presented and read, His Majesty was pleased to declare he would persevere in and follow the advice of his Parliament and Council. There were present the Lord Chancellor, the Dukes of Beaufort and Roxbury, the Earls of Hertford, Suffolk, Rochford, Sandwich, Dartmouth, Lords North, Townsend, Craven, the Lords in Waiting &c.

The *Gazetteer* saw fit to parody[1] this petition and an effort seems to have been made to discredit the standing of the remonstrants. The *Morning Chronicle*[2] does not stick at implying "Mr. S., a lottery office man, and Mr. W., keeper of a gin shop, wore Councillors' gowns to increase the number taking part in the demonstration, but they were detected and recognized despite of rolling by with raised" glasses in their coach windows. The *Morning Post and Daily Advertiser*[3] follows up the same line of witticism:

MR. EDITOR, Being in town on a visit, and hearing that the Lord Mayor, Aldermen &c. were to go yesterday to St. James' with an humble petition to the King, I thought I should have a good opportunity of seeing those *worthy patriots*, and therefore went to the palace for that purpose, but I happened to be too late to see his Lordship, who was just gone into the Gateway; however, the figure of a gentleman, who was then stepping out of a chariot, took my attention;

[1] *The Gazetteer and New Daily Advertiser*, July 15, 17.
[2] July 15.
[3] July 18.

from his many curled wig I supposed him to be an Alderman of great importance, but going through St. Paul's Churchyard today, I saw the very same great man with an apron before him, rolling out paste for penny puffs; well, thinks I to myself, I will buy some of this pastry, that I may say that I have had the honour of eating puffs made by a man who has abilities to dictate to the King and both Houses of Parliament, so in I goes, takes up two tarts and a cheese cake, paid my six old ha' pence for them, made him a very low bow, and retired, fully satisfied with the honour I had now acquired, and the great consequence of a London Common-Councilman.

A MAN OF KENT.

Saturday, July 15, 1775.

A week later it is hinted [1] that the next petition of this sort had best be received by the King throned on a State barge, moored opposite Billingsgate, then, let the Councillors embark at high tide from Three Crane stairs, and knock their heads off coming under the centre arch of London bridge, when perhaps a new bridge would succeed and two evils be done away with.

Raillery could not hide a perplexing side to the issue, and there appeared [1] some "Questions offered to Lord North.

How are the merchants to get remittances from the Americans?

How are the manufacturers and traders to get payment from the merchants?

How are mechanics and handicrafts to be employed by the manufacturers and traders?

How are the load of taxes to be paid?

No Orders!

No Remittances!

No Employ!

How are the troops of all sorts to be supplied?

How is the Civil War to be carried on?

[1] *The Morning Chronicle and London Advertiser*, July 21, 15.

How the dignity of the Nation to be supported?
How your proceedings to be justified?"

An extract from a Norwich letter of July 16th is given
in the *Morning Chronicle and London Advertiser*,[1] expressing
sympathy with "our distressed brethren" in America, and
lamenting the poverty brought on "this once flourishing
City." The merchants there had purposed sending in a
remonstrance to the throne, but were daunted by "the bad
success and disappointment the City of London met."

The future continued to look dark and threatening, but
a correspondent, signing himself "A friend to America,"
dating from Cheapside, July 19th, wrote to the *Morning
Chronicle and London Advertiser*,[1] stating that the American
merchants in London were packing goods for shipment upon
the close of the troubles, and that they were more likely to
know if the crisis was soon to pass than Councilmen never
out of sound of Bow bell. To his mind this was "far more
conclusive than even the patriotic Mr Saxby's asserting
that whoever advised the present measures with America,
were enemies to Great Britain; or that wise looking crea-
ture, Alderman Lee, asserting that the King's troops were
thieves and robbers, and ought to be tried for felony."

Lloyd's Evening Post and British Chronicle recommended
to the Councilmen of London for "summer reading" the
statute of the 25th of Edward III., lest they become treason-
able in their practices. The *Gazetteer*[2] proposed a plan of
utter submission by New England, five Regiments to be
quartered in perpetuity on Boston, and the ringleaders
there to be handed over.

The *Morning Chronicle and London Advertiser*[1] suggested
transportation for life to serve the East India Company as
a fit punishment for rebels.

The atmosphere was one of suspense, but no one seems
to have gauged the force of the opposition that had been
awakened, or to be warned by the Colonists' resolution.
Their grit and determination were as yet lightly esteemed,

[1] July 20, 21, 7.   [2] July 5.

and the *British Chronicle* of July 17–19, just prior to the receipt of the despatches relating to the Battle of Bunker Hill, could calmly outline the following programme:

News of a decisive action in New England is expected in the first week in August, as the army was to be ready to march out of Boston on the 24th of June. It is, however, apprehended that the Provincials will not stand a battle. The Army in such a case is to proceed into the Country slowly, establishing posts as they advance, and receiving the submission of such as shall submit and deliver up their arms.

After thus marking the manner in which the news was received in London, it is time to return and see what became of the British prisoners taken in the late action.

Perhaps the earliest allusion is found in the accompanying letter to Colonel James Barrett in Concord, now printed from the manuscript.[1]

"HEADQUARTERS, April 26.

SIR, I am informed that there are a number of Prisoners in Concord Gaol, ten of whom were conveyed thither yesterday that were taken in the late skirmish, who have since that unhappy Event, been at Newton and done some Labor; but being absent I cannot judge so well whether it is safe to trust them as you may upon the Spot: —

Therefore I refer it to you, to do with them, and any other Prisoners of the like Sort, as you shall find best, pray keep them from any infection that may arise from putting too many in one Room: — Air them when necessary: Provide everyThing needful for their comfortable Sustenance: — no doubt you have Things convenient for them in Concord: & will be at some future time satisfied for your Trouble.

I am Sir,

A. WARD.

Parson Gordon[2] met many of the prisoners confined in Concord gaol and preserved a number of their names for us:

[1] *Mass. State Archives*, Vol. 193, p. 70.
[2] *American Archives*, II, 4th ser., 628. Force.

4th Regiment, James Marr of Aberdeen, Scotland; 23d, Evan Davies, George Cooper; 38th, William McDonald; 18th, Royal Irish, Saml. Lee, 52d, John Bateman.

The old parson purposed by his interview to discover which side fired first. At this time Bateman was in an adjoining room, too ill to be disturbed, but the others had witnessed his deposition, confirmed by "the solemnity" of an oath taken on the Bible, and Lee assured him it "was the talk" among the soldiers that Pitcairn "fired his pistol, drew his sword, and ordered them to fire." Bateman subsequently died and was buried in Concord.

April 27th, the Hon. Stephen Hopkins [1] wrote from Providence: "Yesterday Mr John Brown, one of the principal merchants of this Town, being at Newport . . . to purchase provisions for the use of this and your government, was seized" by the British. On learning this, the following resolution was immediately passed by the Provincial Congress sitting at Watertown.

Whereas, a worthy friend to the liberties of America, Mr. John Brown, of Providence, hath been lately seized, and with two other persons, carried on board a British Ship of War at Newport:

Ordered, That Samuel Murray and two other officers of Gen. Gage's Army, as are now prisoners of war, and not disabled from travelling on account of their wounds, be immediately sent under a sufficient guard to Providence, and delivered to Hon. Stephen Hopkins Esq. or other friends of said Brown; to be made such use of as they shall think proper, for obtaining the liberty of the said Mr Brown.

At the same time the Massachusetts Congress wrote to Mr. Hopkins in regard to a policy of retaliation: that to seize the Crown officers as proposed might "hurl on us and our sea ports sudden destruction, before they have an opportunity of saving themselves." And adds: "We had it in contemplation to send a letter to the General, acquainting

[1] *American Archives*, II, 4th ser., 421, 432. Force.

him that we should treat the Crown officers with severity,
if Mr. Brown should be so treated by him; but we are appre-
hensive it would produce an unhappy, rather than good
effect, as he has a greater number of our friends than we
have of his.   We desire you to give us your further sentiments of the matter.

The very day this was written (the 28th) Governor
Hopkins [1] despatched a second letter by Mr. Joseph Brown
and Mr. Moses Brown — whom he endorses as "principal Merchants, and gentlemen of distinction and pro-
bity" — stating that their brother, it was since learned, had
been sent round to Boston, together with the flour.   A
fuller account is given by Parson Stiles,[2] of Newport:

This day came here Mrs. Gordon from Roxby remov.g to
Philadelphia for safety.   Mr. [Rev. William] Gordon tarry-
ing behind. . . . 26th Two vessels full of Passengers sailed
this Morn.g for Philadelphia. . . . This Afternoon the
two Providence Packets loaded with 4 or 500 Bbs. flour
here today, sailed for Providence, but were immed.y stopt
by the Man o' War [*Rose*] Capt Wallace, who seized them,
& intend to send them to Boston.   They have dismissed
all the pple., except Mr. Jno Brown of Providence, whom
they retain as a prisoner, in Revenge as is supposed for his
being concerned in Burning the Gaspee Schooner a year or
two ago. . . . 27th, This day at Noon sailed the two
Provid. packets seized yesterday, & in one of them Mr.
Jno. Brown is carried off for Boston." . . .

May 4th, "A little before Sunset Mr. Russell of Providence came to Town & informs that Mr. Jno. Brown was
dismissed & came home to Providence last night about
XI h. at night.   That he was first put on board Adm.
Graves, then brought before Gen. Gage.   Capt. Wallace's
pretence for apprehendg. him was that he was concerned
in burning the Gaspee Schooner.   Applica. was made to

[1] *American Archives*, II, 4th ser., 430.   Force.
[2] *Diary*, I, 540.

Judge Oliver of the Commissioners . . . he testified that no Accusation was exhibited against Mr. Brown, upon which Gen. Gage dismissed him, paid him for his flour, order'd the Packets to be returned to Providence and to be paid Demorage, & has sent off a Reprimand to Capt. W. of the Rose Man o' War here. A humbling stroke to the Tories! The General & Admiral treated Mr. Brown politely & dismissed him with Honor. An Army of 30 Thous.d speaks Terror."

Returning to Murray, — from a General Order [1] dated Cambridge, June 15th, we learn further: That Samuel Murray "be removed from the jail in Worcester to his father's homestead Farm, in Rutland, the limits of which he is not to pass until further orders. And all persons are hereby strictly forbidden to offer any violence to said Murray so long as he continues in the peace of God within those limits. [Signed] Joseph Ward, Secretary.

P. S. The above mentioned homestead Farm bounds Northwardly on the County Road; Westwardly on Mr. Buckminster's homestead; Southwardly, on Dr. John Frink's homestead; Eastwardly, partly on land of Mr. Clarke, and partly on land of Mr. Blake.

Published by order of the Com.t, William Young, per order."

Finally a petition is on file: [2] "That Samuel Murray taken prisoner April 19, 1775, and Confined since to his father's farm, Rutland, may be freed on parole, in return for same liberty to Captain John Johnson of Col. Knox's Artillery, lately taken at Long Island." Before passing on to the other prisoners the following reference to the elder Murray, taken from the *Morning Chronicle and London Advertiser*, June 29th, is of interest, but, like other statements in the London papers of the day, must be taken with a grain of salt:

A gentleman from New York informs us that John M—y one of the new fangled Council at Boston, went

---

[1] *American Archives*, II, 4th ser., 1003. Force.
[2] *Mass. State Archives*, Vol. 182, p. 298. A.D. 1777.

to that Country from the North of Ireland, about the year 1730, and was there a common peddlar, carrying a pack about the country for eight or ten years before he was able to buy a horse; but he was diligent and saving in his business and no fault found with his honesty; and having originally been a butcher; — Gen. S—y, when advanced to the command of the army, after Braddock's overthrow, employed him to supply part of the troops at Lake George with fresh provisions, by which he got money, and sat down on a new plantation in one of the out towns, where Sh—y made him an officer of the Militia, and P—l who succeeded Sh—y in the Government advanced him to be a Lt. Col., B—d entered into a close friendship with the said M—y, who had judgement enough to find out the Governor's weakness, [*i.e.* Sir Francis Bernard, appointed Governor 1760, as the successor of Thomas Pownall and William Shirley] and on account of the use he made of this discovery, had other favours conferred on him, to the astonishment of all the respectable people in the province; and on Lord D—th's applying to Gov. B—d last year for a list of proper persons to compose the new Council on the dissolution of the Boston Charter, among others B—d recommended this M—y, who is now by Mandamus, a Counsellor at Boston, and where, if he had been allowed to take his seat, he must have made his mark to any business he subscribed, for gentlemen from New England aver he never was taught to write! It was the son of this same M—y who undertook to pilot the troops to Concord, where it is said he lost his life for his officiousness; such unaccountable appointments have gone as far as anything to sour and disgust the Americans against the administration of this Country.

Another prisoner, Lt. Edward Thoroton Gould,[1] as already noted, had an income of £1900 and is said to have offered £200 ransom. He was the son of Edward Gould, Esq., of Mansfield Woodhouse, Notts., his mother being

[1] *Evelyn Family in America.* Scull.

daughter of Robert Thoroton, of Screveton Hall. Ensign of the 4th Foot in 1767, he was promoted Lieutenant in 1771; "little" Gould subsequently sold out in January, 1776. Later in 1808 he volunteered for service in the Peninsular and finally died in Paris, 1830. Lieutenant Gould's marriage to Lady Barbara Yelverton, — heiress of Henry, third Earl of Sussex, — with whom he eloped, took place [1] October 27th, 1775. In reference to this, the Hon. Mrs. Boscawen wrote to Mrs. Delany [1] in November:

Have you not pitied poor Lady Sussex, my dear Madam? She has been often at this village (Colney Hatch), with her sister (Mrs. Durrell), of whom I have enquired after her health, and have had a very bad account, her agonies having been very great.   My Lord has made a Will, which cuts off this ungrateful child with one shilling, but it is to be hoped he will live to cancel it and forgive her; but it must be a very bad child, I should fear, that can plant a dagger in her parents' breasts, in return for all their care and tenderness: *Such a child too!*   The boldness amazes me.   She was sixteen last June.   Lt. Gould, her husband, is the same young man who was wounded and taken prisoner in ye first action with the Americans; he came over after ye second (being exchanged), and came to me at my son's desire, to bring his letters and assure me of his safety, he and my boy being in the same regiment.   Gould is not a soldier of fortune, but has a small estate in Nottinghampshire in possession, his father being lately dead.   One of his sisters is married to Lady Sussex's brother, from whence I suppose this unhappy connection arose.

To return once more to the prisoners. May 4th, Lieutenant Barker,[2] of the 4th Regiment, wrote:

They wont give up any of their Prisoners, but I hear they treat 'em pretty well.   I wonder the G—l will allow any of their people to quit the Town 'till they return the Prisoners; one wou'd think he might get 'em if he'd try.

[1] *Life and Letters of Mary Granville* (Mrs. Delany).
[2] *Atlantic Monthly*, May, 1877.

Again on the 13th he wrote:

The Com.r in Chief having received advice that three soldiers of the Royal Welsh Fusileers and 12 marines are Prisoners in the Gaol at Worcester, and have manly despised the offers, and defied the threats of the Rebels who have tried to seduce them to take Arms against their King, and fight against their Brother soldiers; it is the Gen.ls Orders that money be given by 3d Corps to Majr of Brigade, Moncrieff, who has an opportunity of conveying it to the above Men, to prevent such brave spirited Soldiers from suffering.

The *Morning Chronicle and London Advertiser*, July 5th, reports: "Account is brought ten of the soldiers supposed to be killed were in Worcester prison. . . . Gen. Gage immediately set about getting some communication to them in their confined state, and with some difficulty got a guinea a man conveyed to them in prison."

A further glimpse is given in the *Pennsylvania Journal*[1] of May 24th:

May 10th, the Commanding officer at Cambridge has given leave to the Regulars who were taken Prisoners, either to go to Boston and join their respective Regiments, or have leave to work in the Country for those who will employ them. In consequence of which, those who were confined in Worcester, Massachusetts, fifteen in number, heartily requested to be employed by the people, not choosing to return to fight against their American brethren, though some of them expressed their willingness to spill their blood in defence of their King in a righteous cause. They all set out yesterday for different towns.

It is probable that a Revolutionary petition on file[2] has reference to one of these very marines. It is as follows:

---

[1] *Diary of the American Revolution*, 76–7. Moore.
[2] *Mass. State Archives*, Vol. 182, p. 324.

To the Hon. Council and House of Representatives, Now Setting in Boston

The Petition of your Petitioners Humbly Sheweth, that whereas John Maddin, a Marine, was made a prisoner on the 19th of April, 1775, at Menotomy and has resided in the Town of Gageborough almost ever Since, and supported himself untill the 1st of September, 1776 — and since has been in such a Low State of Health that has Rendered him uncapable of Supporting himself — and upon application made to the Selectmen of the Town of Gageborough, and upon Examination found said Prisoner in a Suffering Condition. Ordered said prisoner Billetted out, unto the date hereof. And we desire your Honors to Refund so much Monies from the Publick Treasury of this State as is Allowed for the Relief of Prisoners in Distress and pay the same to Benjamin Mills of Chesterfield. And your Petitioner as in Duty bound shall ever pray   Dated in Gageborough this 3d day of April, 1777.

JOHN BROWN	*Selectmen of*
WILLIAM CLARK	*Gageborough*
JOSIAH SAFFORD	[*now Windsor, Berkshire County.*]

So far as known the following petition [1] is also published for the first time.

State of Massachusetts Bay in New England.

To the Hon.ble Council & Hon.ble House of Representatives assembled at Boston, November 18, 1776.

The Inhabitants of the Town of Lexington, Petitioners, on behalf of John Tingle of the 3d Division of Marines in the British Service, taken prisoner on the 19th of April, 1775, And in November following Cheerfully and Voluntarily entered the Continental Service in Captain Abijah Child's Company, in the Regiment commanded by the late Col. William Bond, and endured all the Fatigues and Hardships of the Campaign in Canada which so impaired his Health that the Hon. Gen. Gates gave him his Dis-

[1] *Mass. State Archives*, Vol. 211, p. 243.

charge at Ticonderoga, September 18, from which place after Many Difficulties he arrived at this Town, and is now in a poor State of Health, without Comfortable Clothing; but still hearty in the American Cause, intending when his Health is restored to engage again in the Continental Army, all which circumstances your Petitioners Pray that your Honours would take into your Wise Consideration and afford him such relief as to you shall seem meet.

By order of the Selectmen,

JOSEPH MASON, *Town Clerk.*

Lexington, November 18, 1776.

Endorsed on the back:

In House of Representatives, Nov. 28th, 1776, Resolved that the Selectmen of the Town of Lexington afford to John Tingle named in their Petition all necessary Relief under his Present Circumstances, and lay their Accompts Before the General Court of this State for allowance.

Sent up for Concurrence.

SAMUEL FREEMAN, *Speaker.*

In Council November 28th, 1776.

Read & Concurred.

The sequel is told on the service catalogue at the State House. John Tingle, credited to town of Lexington, Colonel Thomas Marshall's regiment, Captain Philip Thomas's company. Reported as deserted July 26, 1778. He drew clothes 1777–78.

Although Lieutenant Barker felt there was slackness in effecting an exchange of prisoners; even before he had written, on the 2d of May at Watertown, it had been "Ordered[1] that Mr. Freeman, Dr. Taylor, Mr. Lewis, Col. Dwight, and Squire Gardner, be a Committee to consider what measures are proper to be taken for liberating those persons who were taken prisoners by the Troops under the Command of Gen. Gage, on the 19th of April."

The following afternoon the Committee reported[1] the

---

[1] *American Archives*, II, 4th ser., 781–2, 784. Force.

following Resolution,[1] which was accepted, viz.: "That it is the opinion of this Congress, that an application be sent to Gen. Gage, signed by the wives or nearest relations of such prisoners, and the Selectmen of the Towns to which they respectively belong, desiring that he would discharge their friends from their said imprisonment; and they are empowered hereby to offer to send in to the General an equal number of his Troops, now in the hands of this People, who were taken prisoners on the aforesaid 19th of April, upon his liberating their friends as aforesaid." They likewise deemed it "highly expedient to take such measures in assistance to the friends of these unhappy captives as, in their wisdom, they may think proper.

April 29th, four days prior to this, it had been voted:

That Colonel Gerrish be desired to send Major Dunbar, now a prisoner at Head Quarters, to Woburn, under a strong guard, and order him to be there kept in safe Custody, till farther orders from this Committee. Voted that Captain Hill, and Company be furnished with Provisions at any tavern they see fit to call at, in conveying Major Dunbar to a place of Safety, at the expense of the Government.

A Committee, appointed subsequently "to enquire into the Conduct of the several Towns relative to the prisoners of war," reported[2] May 4th that they had "attended to that Service." There seems to have been occasion for their labors since they found "at the town of Woburn one Regular officer and his waiter belonging to Gen. Gage's Troops, and one from Canada with his waiter. Who are Guarded by a Captain and 44 soldiers." Moreover, said they, "one of these officers is supposed to write Letters and Ride about the Town with a Guard of one person only. All the Guard upon wages and Draw Billeting out of the Colony Stores.

JONAS DIX, pr order.

The Com.t beg lieve to sit again."

---

[1] *American Archives*, II, 4th ser., 748.
[2] *Mass. State Archives*, Vol. 138, p. 29.

The Provincial Congress on the 5th of May [1] saw fit through Mr. Wyman to apply to the Committee of Safety and see what measures could be devised to "remove the necessity of keeping so large a guard," attest Samuel Freeman, Sec'y.

The charge of the prisoners was becoming burdensome, and the exchange which took place June 6th at Charlestown was hence doubly welcome. The Essex *Gazette* relates the particulars in its issue of the 8th:

Tuesday last, being the Day agreed on for the exchange of Prisoners between 12 and 1 o'clock, Dr. Warren and Brig. Gen. Putnam, in a Phaeton, together with Major Dunbar, and Lt. Hamilton of the 64th Regiment on Horseback; Lt. Potter of the Marines in a chaise; John Hilton of the 47th; Alexander Campbell of the 4th; John Tyne, Samuel Marcy, Thomas Parry and Thomas Sharp of the Marines, wounded men in two carts; the whole escorted by the Wethersfield Company, under the command of Captain Chester, entered the Town of Charlestown, and marching slowly through it, halted at the Ferry, where, upon a signal being given, Major Moncrieff landed from the *Lively*, in order to receive the Prisoners, and see his old Friend, Gen. Putnam: — Their meeting was truly cordial and affecting. The Wounded Privates were soon sent on board the *Lively;* but Major Moncrieff and the other officers, returned with Gen. Putnam and Dr. Warren, to the House of Dr. Foster, where an Entertainment was provided for them. About 3 o'clock a signal was made by the *Lively*, that they were ready to deliver up our Prisoners; upon which Gen. Putnam and Major Moncrieff went to the Ferry, where they received Messrs. John Peck, James Hews, James Brewer, and Daniel Preston of Boston; Messrs. Samuel Frost and Seth Russell of Cambridge; Mr. Joseph Bell of Danvers, Mr. Elijah Seaver of Roxbury; and Caesar Augustus, a negro servant to Mr. Tileston of Dorchester;

[1] *Mass. State Archives*, Vol. 138, pp. 29, 32.

who were conducted to the House of Captain Foster, and there refreshed; after which the Gen. and Major returned to their Company, and spent an Hour or two in a very agreeable Manner.

We may form a little notion of the magnificence of Cæsar Augustus's attire from contemporary advertisements: for instance, a castor hat, black wig, green coat faced with red, scarlet ratteen waistcoat, and blue breeches, no less! The sailors, as we learn from descriptions of deserters, wore sometimes Dutch caps, heavy outside jackets, inner light-colored jackets trimmed with black tape and black buttons, and long trousers.

Between 5 and 6 o'clock Major Moncrieff,[1] with the officers that had been delivered to him, were conducted to the Ferry, where the *Lively's* Barge received them; after which Gen. Putnam, with the Prisoners who had been delivered to him, &c., returned to Cambridge, escorted in the same manner as before. The whole was conducted with the utmost Decency and good Humor, and the Wethersfield Company did Honour to themselves, their Officers and their Country. The Regular Officers expressed themselves as highly pleased; those who had been Prisoners politely acknowledged the genteel, kind Treatment they had received from their Captors; the Privates, who were all wounded men, expressed in the strongest Terms their grateful sense of the Tenderness which had been shewn them in their miserable Situation; some of them could do it only by their Tears. It would have been to the Honour of the British Arms, if the Prisoners taken from us, could with Justice have made the same Acknowledgement.

Daniel Green,[2] another Regular, wounded and taken prisoner in the Lexington fight, must have been severely hurt, for as late as July 9th he is mentioned, on the records, as being in Watertown, and apparently only just then

---

[1] *Essex Gazette*, June 8, 1775.

[2] *American Archives*, II, 4th ser., pp. 1503–5. Force.

able to be taken into custody and conveyed to Mr. Jones, prison-keeper at Concord.

Not long after the exchange of prisoners had taken place the following document was issued:

By His Excellency the Hon. Thomas Gage, Esq. Governor and Commander-in-Chief, in and over His Majesty's Province of Massachusetts Bay and Vice Admiral of the same:

A Proclamation.[1]

Whereas, the infatuated multitude, who have long suffered themselves to be conducted by certain well known incendiaries and traitors, in a fatal progression of crimes against the constituted authority of the State, have at length proceded to avowed Rebellion; and the good effects which were expected to arise from the patience and lenity of the King's Government have been often frustrated, and are now rendered hopeless, by the influence of the same evil counsels; it only remains for those who are invested with supreme rule, as well for the punishment of the guilty, as the protection of the well-effected, to prove they do not bear the sword in vain.

After denouncing the Patriot leaders and the Press of the country as the source of every evil, General Gage takes exception to the Yankees firing on the 19th from "behind walls and lurking holes;" objects to the New Englanders "effecting to hold the Army besieged by a preposterous parade of military arrangement;" and proceeds loftily:

In this exigency of Complicated Calamities, I avail myself of the last effort within the bounds of my duty, to spare the effusion of blood; to offer, and I do hereby, in His Majesty's Name, offer and promise his most gracious pardon to all persons who shall forthwith lay down their arms, and return to their duties of peaceable subjects, excepting only from the benefit of such pardon, *Samuel Adams* and

[1] *American Archives*, II, 4th ser., 967-970. Force.

John Hancock, whose offences are of too flagitious a nature to admit of any other consideration than condign punishment.

And to the end that no person within the limits of this offered mercy may plead ignorance of the consequences of refusing it, I, by these presents, proclaim not only the persons above named and excepted, but also all their adherents, associates, and abettors, (meaning to comprehend in those terms, all and every person and persons, of what class, denomination or description so ever,) who have appeared in arms against the King's government, and shall not lay down the same as aforementioned; and likewise all such as shall so take arms after the date hereof, or who shall in any wise protect or conceal such offenders, or assist them with money, provisions, cattle, arms, ammunition, carriages, or any other Necessary for Subsistence or offence; or shall hold secret correspondence with them by letter, message, single or otherwise, to be Rebels and Traitors, and as such to be treated.

Martial law is then proclaimed, and protection assured to the loyal, whom he requests to "stand distinct and separate from the parricides of the Constitution, till God in his mercy shall restore to his creatures in this distracted land that system of happiness from which they have been seduced — the religion of peace, and liberty founded upon law."

The proclamation then closes,

Given at Boston, this 12th day of June in the fifteenth year of the reign of His Majesty King George III. by the Grace of God, of Great Britain, France, and Ireland, King, Defender of the Faith &c.

Annoque Domini, 1775,

THOMAS GAGE.

By His Excellency's Commands:

THOMAS FLUCKER, *Secretary.*

GOD SAVE THE KING.

JOHN HANCOCK

Captain Harris,[1] whose letters have already been quoted, gives us the best insight of how Boston then appeared from an army standpoint. The 5th of May he wrote home: "At present it should seem we have the worst of the fight, for, however we block up this port, the rebels certainly block up our town, and have cut off our good beef and mutton, very much to the discomfiture of our mess. But, while I get sufficient to sustain life, though of the coarsest food, with two nights out of three in bed, I shall not repine, but rejoice that fortune has given me a constitution to endure fatigue."

He describes the fortifications going up, in which he has taken hand, besides planning and directing, for he would "set them [his men] a good example in not being afraid of work." He continues: "when you tell my mother this, mark if an approving tear does not steal down her ancient cheek. She often said 'George; make the men love you, but do your duty.'" He ends:

I have now before me one of the finest prospects your warm imagination can picture. My tent-door, about twenty yards from a piece of water, nearly a mile broad, with the country beyond most beautifully tumbled about in hills and valleys, rocks and woods, interspersed with straggling villages, with here and there a spire peeping over the trees, and the country of the most charming green that delighted eye ever gazed on. Pity, these infatuated people cannot be content to enjoy such a country in peace. But, alas! this moment their advanced sentinels are in sight and tell me they have struck the fatal blow. Where it will end, but in their destruction, I cannot see.

On the very day Gage's Proclamation appeared, Captain Harris again wrote:

Affairs at present wear a serious aspect. I wish the Americans may be brought to a sense of their duty. One

[1] *Life of General Lord Harris.* Lushington.

good drubbing, which I long to give them, by way of retaliation, might have a good effect towards it. At present they are so elated by the petty advantage they gained the 19th of April, that they despise the power of Great Britain, who seems determined to exert herself in the conflict. Troops every day coming in, and such as will soon enable us, I hope, to take the field on the other side the Demel, alias the Neck. At present we are completely blockaded, and subsisting almost on salt provisions, except such as the Americans (so strong is the old leaven of smuggling in them, about which these troubles arose) bring in to us.

He speaks with wonder of his promising garden, cucumbers, beans, and peas, making great headway within six weeks from the first turning of the soil. He finds it "really surprising" and feels "quite Uncle Toby;" but concludes hastily: "My house will be struck over my head, if I do not quit it, as a change of ground is to take place immediately. I only wish the movement was towards the Americans, that we might sooner bring this unpleasant business to an issue, and get home to our friends. . . . Holmes says we shall be last, so adieu."

This fine young officer met with a severe wound in less than a week's time in the Battle of Bunker Hill, and his letters in reference to it are well worth the reading.

On June 19th, realizing the struggle before them, the Committee of Safety[1] suggested to the Massachusetts Congress, "that the Selectmen of each Town in the Colony should enter on their Town books and transmit to Congress the names of such as were killed or wounded 'during the present unnatural contest, in order to transmit to future generations the names of such who have gloriously suffered in the cause of liberty and their country." Notice was also taken[1] of the confusion and plundering incident to the late battles, and the town officials of Massachusetts and the neighboring Colonies were "earnestly requested"

[1] *American Archives*, II, 4th ser., 1028, 1371. Force.

to seek out and return such unappropriated household furniture as came to their knowledge, Mr. Joseph Peirce Palmer, Quartermaster-General, being prepared to receive such on behalf of the rightful proprietors.

A committee was formed to consider selectmen's petitions in regard to provisions[1] furnished on occasion of the alarm, the Innholders' accounts being required by December 20th. A committee was likewise appointed to receive petitions for allowance[1] from those who had been wounded or met with losses. To avoid "occasions for fraud and impositions," on February 12th, 1776, it was ordered[1] that no petitions respecting losses on the 19th of April and 17th of June would be considered after the second Tuesday of the Court's next sitting, and the Watertown and Cambridge papers were asked to print said order "three weeks successively." A petition of Jacob Bacon is referred to under date of January 29th;[1] and on December 19th[3] an account of Ely Lewis[1] and others, belonging to Captain Styles' Company, Colonel Sargent's Regiment. Detailed reports do not appear to have been preserved in all instances at the State Archives, the above names being cases in point. January 20th Jonathan Hastings[1] (doubtless of Cambridge) represents that he had previously sent in a petition asking compensation for his "time and trouble for the accommodation of officers and others." This petition was laid on the table. Charles White,[1] praying compensation for a horse carried away April 19th, had equally cold comfort; viz., leave to withdraw.

As we have seen, reinforcements were continually arriving; the mother country evidently wishing to stamp out the kindling flames of rebellion before they had time to spread. April 25th word reached Newport[1] through a gentleman arrived "this afternoon" from Providence "that two Men of War had arrived at Boston, and brought the three Generals that have been expected; and that

[1] *American Archives*, IV, 4th ser., 1314; 1239, 1437, 1300; 1425, 1346; 1404, 1388; II, 4th ser., 382. Force.

6000 Troops had embarked for that place when these Men of War left England." The 28th a Cambridge [1] letter, dated three P.M., runs:

This minute arrived from Boston Mr. Henderson Inches he further brings advice by the last vessel from England, that when the Regiment of Light Horse were going to embark, the populace rose and prevented their embarkation; and the General Officers that came away, were obliged to go on board incognito; but he further says the Government have ordered 10,000 Troops more to be sent, but they will not be here till the last of May.

We get an interesting glimpse of the voyage of one of these later transports from *Lloyd's*, June 21–23, as follows:

By a letter from Mr. Jenkins of the 49th Regiment, on board the *Diana*, dated On the Atlantic Ocean, May 15th, lat. 47° 17′ We learn that the transports from Cork were then well, excepting the *Laurel*, which lost her fore top-gallant mast in a gale of wind, and that the troops did not expect to be in Boston in less than a month from that date. This letter came by a ship, which was met by the transports on her way to Portsmouth.

Finally we read, in a letter from an officer of rank to a gentleman [1] in London, dated Boston, June 18th, that he left Cork early in April, and "after a very tedious and disagreeable passage of seven weeks," arrived in Boston on the 16th of June. He adds the regiment to which he belonged was not ordered out in the Bunker Hill battle of the 17th, concluding with this postscript, "Since I wrote the above, I fell into conversation with a gentleman who was present in both actions, and who told me that the King's Troops must have been totally destroyed in each, had the Provincials known their own strength, particularly on the former's return from Lexington to Boston on the 19th of April.

[1] *American Archives*, II, 4th ser., 429; 1021. Force.

The battle of the 17th, just alluded to, and the events of the siege which terminated with the fortifying of Dorchester Heights and the British evacuation, March 17th, 1776, do not properly belong to this account.

In closing this story of the first shots interchanged in the Revolutionary War it is well to realize the spirit and temper with which our fathers engaged. Here on the eve of the conflict, reading their own words, we find them still full of warmth and life; clear, forcible, free of bitterness — a motherly word from the mother country would have sufficed to hold their allegiance.

And first let us read the appeal [1] made to the Indians of the Six Nations, lest there should be risings and distress from that source. It is addressed to the Mohawks, Oneidas, Tuscaroras, Onondagas, Cayugas, Senecas, from sixty-five delegates assembled at Philadelphia.

After explaining the past relation which the Colonies had borne to the home island — "Whenever they were struck, we instantly felt as though the blow had been given to us — their enemies were our enemies:" it goes on to tell of the change in all this:

They now tell us they will slip their hand into our pocket without asking, as though it were their own; . . . That our vessels may go to *this* island in the sea, but to *this* or *that* particular island we shall not trade any more.

To bring the case clearly home to their hearers, they finally put their plea in the form of an allegory:

Brothers, thus stands the matter betwixt Old England and America. You Indians know how things are proportioned in a family, between the father and the son, the child carries a little pack — England we regard as the father; this island may be compared to the son. The father has a numerous family, both at home and upon this island; he appoints a great number of Servants to assist him in the

[1] *Journal of the Proceedings of the Congress held at Philadelphia, May 10, 1775,* 154–161. July 13, 1775.

government of his family: in process of time, some of his servants grow proud and ill-natured — they were displeased to see the boy so alert, and walk on so nimbly with his pack; they tell the father, and advise him to enlarge the child's pack — they prevail; the pack is increased — the child takes it up again; as he thought it might be the father's pleasure, speaks but few words, those very small, for he was loth to offend the father. Those proud and wicked servants finding they had prevailed, laughed to see the boy sweat and stagger under his increased load. By and by they apply to the father to double the boy's pack, because they heard him complain; and without any reason said they, he is a cross child, correct him if he complains any more. The boy intreats the father, addresses the great servants in a decent manner, that the pack might be lightened; he could not go any further; humbly asks, if the old fathers, in any of their records, had described such a pack for the child: after all the tears and intreaties of the child, the pack is redoubled; the child stands a little, while staggering under the weight, ready to fall every moment: however he entreats the father once more, though so faint he could only lisp out his last humble supplication — waits a while — no voice returns. The child concludes the father could not hear — those proud servants had intercepted his supplications, or stopped the ears of the father. He therefore gives one struggle and throws off the pack, and says he cannot take it up again, such a weight will crush him down and kill him, and he can but die if he refuses.

Upon this, those servants are very wroth, and tell the father many false stories respecting the child; they bring a great cudgel to the father, asking him to take it in his hand and strike the child.

Then dropping the allegory they continue:

. . . Brothers! we are now necessitated to *rise*, and *forced* to fight, . . . We think our cause is just; therefore hope God will be on our side. We do not take up the hatchet and struggle for honour or conquest; but to maintain our civil constitution and religious privileges, the very same for which our forefathers left their native land and came to this country. . . .

This is a family quarrel between us and Old England. You Indians are not concerned in it. We don't wish you to take up the hatchet against the King's troops. We desire you to remain at home and not join either side; but keep the hatchet buried deep.

Meanwhile much had been written to England. April 26th, Joseph Warren,[1] as President pro tem., signed a letter to Dr. Franklin, already alluded to, in which he trusted such publicity would be given to the Depositions that "all who are not determined to be in everlasting blindness" might be convinced. Ending: "It is the united efforts of both Englands that can save either. Whatever price our brethren in the one may be pleased to put on their constitutional Liberties, we are authorized to assure you, that the inhabitants of the other, with the greatest unanimity, are inflexibly resolved to sell their's only at the price of their lives."

The same day Dr. Warren, in behalf of the Provincial Congress, addressed the inhabitants of Great Britain assuring[1] them that, despite the late occurrences, our people were not "yet detached from our Royal Sovereign." "We profess to be," he writes, "his loyal and dutiful subjects, and so hardly dealt with as we have been, are still ready, with our lives and fortunes, to defend his person, family, crown, and dignity. Nevertheless, to the Persecution and Tyranny of his cruel Ministry we will not tamely submit. . . .

"We cannot think that the honor, wisdom, and valour of Britons will suffer them to be long inactive spectators of measures, in which they themselves are so deeply interested. . . . Measures, which if successful, must end in the ruin and slavery of Britain, as well as the persecuted American Colonies.

[1] *Journal of the Proceedings of the Congress held at Philadelphia, May, 1775,* 19–20; 40–1.

"We sincerely hope, that the Great Sovereign of the Universe, who hath so often appeared for the English Nation, will support you in every rational and manly exertion with these Colonies, for saving it from ruin, and that in a Constitutional connection with the Mother Country, we shall soon be altogether a free and happy people."

June 12th a fast [1] was appointed, that, throughout the English Colonies, supplications might be made "to the all-wise, omnipotent, and merciful disposer of all events," . . . praying, among other things, "that all America may soon behold a gracious interposition of Heaven for the redress of her many grievances, the restoration of her invaded rights, a reconciliation with the parent state, on terms constitutional and honourable to both: and that her civil and religious privileges may be secured to the latest posterity."

Preparing for the worst, while loath to give up all hopes of reunion, June 15th Colonel George Washington [1] was unanimously chosen Commander-in-Chief of the Patriot forces.

Once more an appeal was made, this time to the King; [1] its wording is such you would suppose no ruler would go on and force a breach with Colonies that were so readily disposed to add strength to the kingdom and only desired the continuance of their chartered rights. It runs in part:

"We beg leave farther to assure your Majesty, that notwithstanding the sufferings of your loyal Colonists, during the course of this present controversy, our breasts retain too tender a regard for the kingdom from which we derive our origin, to request such a reconciliation as might in any manner be inconsistent with her dignity or her welfare. These, related as we are to her, honour and duty, as well as inclination, induce us to support and advance; and the apprehensions, that now oppress our hearts with unspeakable grief, being once removed, your Majesty will find your faithful subjects on this continent ready and willing at all times, as they have ever been, with their lives and

[1] *Journal of the Proceedings of the Congress held at Philadelphia, May, 1775*, 74–6, 79; 130–147. July 8, 1775.

fortunes, to assert and maintain the rights and interests of your Majesty, and of our Mother Country. . . .

"Remembrance of former friendships, pride in the glorious achievements of our common ancestors and affection for the heirs of their virtues, have hitherto preserved our mutual connection; but when that friendship is violated by the grossest injuries; when the pride of ancestry becomes our reproach, and we are not otherwise allied than as tyrants and slaves; when reduced to the melancholy alternative of renouncing your favor, or our Freedom; can we hesitate about the choice? Let the spirit of Britons determine."

In a word, in respect of their treatment, Congress felt as its members put on record in their Declaration [1] of Grievances:

What terms more rigid and humiliating could have been dictated by remorseless victors to conquered enemies? In our circumstances, to accept them, would be to deserve them. . . .

We are reduced to the alternative of chusing an unconditional submission to the tyranny of irritated ministers, or resistance by force. — The latter is our choice. — We have counted the cost of this contest, and find nothing so dreadful as voluntary slavery. — Honor, justice, and humanity forbid us tamely to surrender that freedom which our innocent posterity have a right to receive from us.

Well did they redeem the pledge that follows:

In our own native land, in defence of the freedom that is our birth-right, and which we ever enjoyed till the late violation of it — for the protection of our property, acquired solely by the honest industry of our forefathers and ourselves, against violence actually offered, we have taken up arms. We shall lay them down when hostilities shall cease on the part of the aggressors, and all danger of their being renewed shall be removed, and not before.

[1] *Journal of the Proceedings of the Congress held at Philadelphia, May, 1775,* 125, 127, 129. July 6, 1775.

INDEX

Abercrombie, General, attacks Ticonderoga, I, 8.
Lieutenant-Colonel, letter, III, 242.
Acadians, expulsion of, I, 7.
Acton, Massachusetts, men in fight
from Concord, III, 43.
Adams, Abigail, letter, II, 39, 41, 48,
66, 118; III, 244.
Mrs. Hannah, British rack house, III,
122.
John, I, 29, 104, 170, 229, 336; II,
52, 293.
quotation, I, 12, 14, 15, 50, 55, 64,
70, 72, 132, 136, 237, 238, 262, 331,
358, 380; II, 2, 4, 40, 44, 45.
drafts Quincy resolutions, I, 28.
declines office, I, 110.
counsel for Hancock, I, 115.
committee on Royal Address, I, 121.
defends *Pitt* sailors, I, 124, 125.
counsel for Captain Preston, I, 242,
243, 258, 259, 260, 261.
delegate to Congress, I, 369; II, 14.
Samuel, I, 43, 71, 83, 91, 98, 104, 114,
116, 126, 133, 149, 235, 236, 237,
238, 263, 264, 331, 335, 357, 368,
369, 377; II, 11, 46, 273, 293, 340,
347; III, 82.
early life, I, 23.
drafts petition to King, I, 117.
intimates strife, I, 121.
committee on Royal Address, I, 121.
speech, I, 249.
plans Committee on Correspondence,
I, 275.
a member, I, 283.
tea importation, I, 295, 296, 304, 316.
appeal to Colonies, I, 360.
delegate to Congress, I, 369; II, 11,
14.
resides at Lexington, II, 315.

Agnus, Mr., stamp collector, I, 52.
Aix-la-Chapelle, Peace of, ends War of
Austrian Succession, I, 5.
Albany, New York, Congress of, I, 6.
Allen, Joseph, Boston Massacre, I, 231.
William, of Philadelphia, I, 42.
Amherst, Sir Jeffrey, captures Louisburg, I, 8.
declines to command in America, II,
198.
Andrews, John, quotation, I, 303, 309,
314, 315, 316, 334, 362, 365, 366,
367; II, 1, 8, 9, 11, 13, 14, 15, 17,
18, 23, 24, 25, 26, 27, 28, 39, 43,
48, 50, 54, 55, 59, 60, 63, 67, 70,
113, 114, 115, 116, 117, 118, 121,
122, 123, 124, 125, 128, 130, 132,
133, 137, 142, 144, 147, 148, 154,
156, 158, 161, 163, 164, 166, 168,
169, 170, 278, 279, 308, 311; III,
189.
John, of Ipswich, tried by Star
Chamber judges, I, 2.
Andros, Sir Edmund, arrives as Governor of Massachusetts, I, 2.
recalled, I, 3.
Appleton, John, of Ipswich, tried by
Star Chamber judges, I, 2.
Nathaniel, I, 189, 190.
Boston committee, I, 296.
Archbald boys, I, 181, 182, 183.
Arlington, Massachusetts, flight from
Concord, III, 146.
Army, American, Massachusetts re-
solves to form, II, 293.
enlistment roll, II, 293.
Arnold, Benedict, goes to attack on
Boston, III, 294.
Ashe, Speaker John, I, 42, 43.
Assessment, Andros levies in Massa-
chusetts, I, 2.

381